San Francisco

Building The Dream City

Mission St. Francis de Asis (Mission Dolores): Dedicated on October 8, 1776.

San Francisco
Building The Dream City

James Beach Alexander & James Lee Heig

SCOTTWALL ASSOCIATES
San Francisco ～ 2002

"There it lay, a constellation of lights, a golden radiance! San Francisco, the impossible city of miracles! Of it and its people many stories have been told, and many shall be, but a thousand tales shall not exhaust its treasury of romance. Earthquake and fire shall not change it. Terror and suffering shall not break its glad, mad spirit. Time alone can tame the town, rob it of its nameless charm, subdue it to the commonplace. May time be merciful — may it delay its fatal duty until we have learned that to love, to forgive, to enjoy, is but to understand."

—From *Heartline*, by Gelett Burgess, 1907

Scottwall Associates, Publishers
95 Scott Street
San Francisco, CA 94117
Telephone (415) 861-1956
E-mail: Scotwall@pacbell.net
www.Scottwallpub.com

Book and cover design: Lawrence Reed Peterson
Editor: James Lee Heig, Scottwall Associates
Photograph on dustjacket of Beach Alexander: Christopher Irion
Printed in Singapore by Imago

First Edition: 5 4 3 2 1

Library of Congress Cataloging in Publication Data:
Library of Congress Control Number: 2001119149
Main entry under title:
San Francisco: Building the Dream City
Includes index
James Beach Alexander and James Lee Heig
1. San Francisco history — Spanish & Mexican California — Missions — Gold Rush — Architecture — Willis Polk — 19th & 20th Century architects.
2, Architecture — San Francisco — 19th & 20th Century architects — Willis Polk — Missions — Rincon Hill — Nob Hill — Van Ness Avenue — Western Addition — Pacific Heights.

ISBN: 0-942087-13-5

Contents

PART VII:
THE TOWN GOD SPANKED ~ 1906-1950

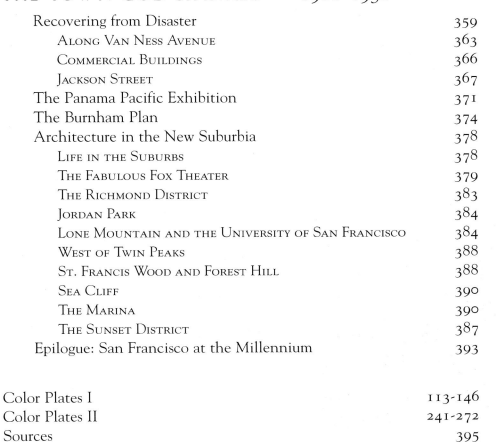

ACKNOWLEDGEMENTS

I have spent some sixty years haunting second-hand bookstores, libraries and historical societies, looking for pictures, books, postcards, and other historical treasures. The pleasure of discovering new materials was equalled by the delight of coming to know many highly knowledgeable people, many of whom, unfortunately, are no longer with us.

At the California Historical Society, librarians James Abajian and Mrs. M.K. Swingle spent hours digging through files for me. Dr. Elliot Evans and Mrs. Helen Giffin at the Society of California Pioneers not only found documentary materials but also kindly arranged interviews with members of old San Francisco families, including Mary Greenleaf and Mrs. Hugh Brown, granddaughter of Captain Martin Roberts. Mrs. Jenny Henderson, sister of Templeton Crocker, and her cousin, Mrs. Helen Potter Russell, granddaughter of Charles Crocker, provided rich first-hand accounts of the notable Crocker clan. Mrs. Phillip Landis, a descendant of Mayor Thomas Selby and of William Ralston, generously shared a wealth of family materials with me.

Mrs. William Hilbert, granddaughter of Eli Sheppard, gave me valuable information about Russian Hill. Mrs. Hilbert had worked with Bruce Porter on the murals at the Swedenborgian Church. My friends Tony Hail and Charles Posey told me about their house at 1055 Green Street, dating to the 1860s.

My dear friend, Helen Holdredge, biographer of Mammy Pleasant, offered unflagging encouragement, and introduced me to Allan Ottley and Carolyn Wenzel, custodians of the historical materials at the California State Library. My father's best friend, Hugo Herz, manager of the old Orpheum Theater, told me countless stories as did the great actress Maude Adams, who created the role of Peter Pan. The late George Cabaniss had a file of 3 x 5 cards outlining the lives of early-day socialites; I was amazed at how much of a lifetime can be entered on a 3 x 5 file card.

Donald Biggs, then the young director of the California Historical Society, introduced me to the California Heritage Council, a pioneer organization dedicated to the preservation of historic landmarks. I worked side by side with architect John Campbell, attorney Augustin Keane and his son Carter, architect Ted Moulton, and Frank Fenton, president of San Francisco State College; from these gentlemen I learned not only facts but patience in dealing with historical matters.

My thanks go to Susan Little for editing. I am deeply grateful to Charles Fracchia and Patrick McGrew, who read the manuscript in its early stages and offered valuable advice. The late Dr. Albert Shumate, a distinguished historian, very generously helped me sort out the names and addresses of pioneer denizens of Rincon Hill and South Park. I am also indebted to George Livermore and to Jake and Nancy McNear, who gave me information about the Ralston and McNear clans, as well as years of enthusiastic support.

James Heig and I are especially grateful to Pat Akre and her staff at the History Room of the San Francisco Public Library. The photo collection there is excellent, and it is growing rapidly. Recent acquisition of the photographic archives of James Scott have substantially enriched the collection; several of his photographs appear in this book, with his kind permission.

My good friend Alex Brammer, who knows more about Nob Hill's glittering history than anyone, made countless contributions of information and photographs, and boosted my morale when I needed it most.

— *James Beach Alexander*

INTRODUCTION

This book is a blending of my two chief interests: San Francisco history and architectural history. It is not intended to be a comprehensive history of the city, which would require an even larger book than this one, but rather a personal history, a collection of pictures, data, and anecdotes collected over sixty years, relating to San Francisco's brief but colorful past.

My love affair with San Francisco began when I was twelve years old, and went to a kiddy matinee at the El Rey Theater on Ocean Avenue. I sat, open-mouthed, and watched the MGM production of *San Francisco*, starring Clark Gable and Jeannette McDonald, set in 1906. Never could I have imagined a place so filled with wickedness and hair-raising drama as was the city depicted in that film.

That same year, at Newbegin's Bookstore, I bought a beautiful old book called *Artistic Homes of California*, published in 1887, and began my career as a junior historian, asking friends and relatives for stories about the city. Many of the stories seemed amusing to me, but one woman exclaimed, "It's not funny!" Then she told me about the fire of 1906, when she and her mother looked down a street that was a tunnel of flame; her father remembered seeing a man explode from the intense heat of burning buildings on Second Street.

As I grew up I kept collecting pictures, brochures, flyers, books — anything I could get my hands on that had to do with old San Francisco. I developed a fervent longing to experience at least one day in the fantastic vanished city. I have continued collecting to this day. My collection has formed the core of this book, which is intended not to satisfy, but only to stimulate the appetite for information about the city's architecture.

The explosive growth of San Francisco during and after the Gold Rush resulted in a city that was unlike any other on earth, and it has carefully preserved a reputation for eccentricity down to the present. It has always had a mystique. Isolated from the rest of America, three thousand miles from New York and Boston, San Francisco was destined to conduct itself differently from other cities. H.L. Mencken, who came here in the 1920s, said, "What fetched me instantly (and thousands of other newcomers with me) was the subtle but unmistakable sense of escape from the United States." Millions of visitors since have had the same feeling.

An eccentric city is likely to have an eccentric architecture. The highly decorated 19th-century houses in San Francisco are called exuberant by admirers and excessive by critics. But, like them or not, they contribute much to the city's unique character. Redwood was plentiful, cheap, and easily milled or carved into any shape one could dream up. The gold and silver that poured into the city from the mines meant that there was always a demand for competent workers. Skilled carpenters and stonemasons were arriving daily from Ireland, Germany, England, Italy and Scandinavia, eager to realize their dream of owning a little cottage or a great mansion, or something in between. After the invention of the cable car in 1873, the hills were no longer obstacles to developers. The pace of building in the city was astonishing. Cottages, row houses, flats, duplexes, villas and mansions sprang up to replace goat pastures and vegetable gardens. The amazing thing is, thousands of these structures still exist. Exuberant or excessive, they are what was built here — the dwellings, commercial buildings, and houses of worship that reflect the beguiling spirit of the people.

As I walk or drive around the city I find its history to be enormously enriching. Of the Native Americans' ten-thousand-year residence here there is no visible reminder except for a few artifacts unearthed during excavation for new buildings. Beautiful Mission Dolores, completed in 1791 by Native American laborers, and carefully maintained as the single remaining adobe structure in the city, is the starting place for anyone who wants to get some understanding of San Francisco and its reason for being here. Wandering through the streets of the Mission District, I see the names of the Mexican citizens who came here to realize their dream of a prosperous, agrarian society in a gentle climate: Valencia, Guerrero, Sanchez, Noe, Castro. Potrero Hill (originally Potrero Nuevo, the New Pasture) was granted to the 18-year-old twins, Ramon and Francisco De Haro, who dreamed of building a rancho until they were shot down by Kit Carson in 1846. Strolling through the lobby of the Palace Hotel, originally the dream of William Ralston, one thinks of all the splendid and tragic events that are connected with it. A little wooden church, Old St. Patrick's, which once stood on the site, was moved to make room for the hotel; ironically, the church, out of the fire zone on Eddy Street, has survived, but the original Palace Hotel was destroyed in 1906 and replaced with today's far more modest structure.

The early Yankee settlers, too, have left their names behind: Folsom, Howard, Spear, Beale, Leidesdorff, Larkin, Van Ness, Montgomery, Stockton. Place names — Portsmouth Plaza, Union Square, Russian Hill, Telegraph Hill, Sutro Forest — have meaning only if one knows something of the city's history. The past is with us, every day, if we are informed enough to recognize it.

The people of San Francisco were really no better than anyone else, and the architecture which reflected their lifestyle wasn't always first-rate, but reading about both can be a very entertaining pastime. A city which has burnt down seven times in its short life, and has as its official emblem a golden phoenix arising from its ashes, can offer only a partial record of its colorful beginnings.

San Francisco never produced a style of architecture distinctly its own. The slanted bay windows of the Italianate style, the square bays of the Stick Style, and the curved bow windows of Queen Anne houses were all dreamed up by English designers. Basements built above ground were peculiarly San Franciscan, simply because the sandy soil was not conducive to a dug cellar. Our genius has been adapting imported styles to our own particular environment, like a lady upon whom almost anything looks good. Most Victorian houses were built to house two or three generations — parents, children, in-laws, maiden aunts, bachelor uncles, all shared the same board. The family dinner in the dining room was a ritual no family member could miss.

Visitors to San Francisco are struck by the history of the place; having heard about the rowdy Gold Rush city, the cable cars, the 1906 disaster, Fisherman's Wharf and the Golden Gate Bridge, they are eager to learn more. Surprised at the number of 19th century houses that survive, they wave from the tour bus at homeowners tending their little front gardens, and are delighted when the homeowners wave back. The intimacy of the city charms them, and the fact that people walk everywhere, and talk to each other without having been introduced. Every first-time visitor runs the risk of falling in love with the city and deciding to stay here, in spite of a zero vacancy rate and the high cost of housing. Like Mary Ann Singleton in *Tales of the City*, they call home and ask their parents to send on their belongings. "I was afraid it would be this pretty," said author Gail Sheehy upon arrival.

What is the special quality that draws so many visitors? San Francisco has for years been the top destination for American vacationers, and ranks near the top for Europeans. Of course it is the views, the food, the hills, the French bread, the bridges. But it is also the history of the town and its people, the beautiful Spanish names (including San Francisco), and the enduring spirit of the city, which is palpable, and which anyone can feel, sitting at a sidewalk cafe, or walking along California Street, or riding the splendid old streetcars which now carry people from Castro & Market to Fisherman's Wharf. People may come for the food, but they leave with the sense of having been in a place unlike any other on earth.

Residents love the city too, and can't imagine living anywhere else. They like the fog and the cold summer winds, the deluges of rain in the winter, and the sunny days in January when the clouds have cleared away. They complain about the Municipal Railway, but they are secretly proud of it, and boast of it to strangers. Many of them spend years of their lives and a major portion of their incomes in restoring and maintaining old houses. They join historical societies and tenacious neighborhood preservation groups, and they march on City Hall when it is necessary to save an old building, sometimes to no avail. Their dream is to preserve what is left of old San Francisco for future generations.

Restoring an old house makes extraordinary demands on the temperament, patience, and purse. Such a house is not just a shelter; it acquires a life of its own. It makes demands, it insists, it intrudes itself, it makes you realize that it will be there when you are gone. It will have another life after the one you have lived in it. It takes a part of your life and keeps it for its own, and you can never get it back. But as a result of your labor you become a part of the city's history, and that is ample reward.

The course in San Francisco history is the second most popular class offered at San Francisco State University (the first is Human Sexuality). This indicates that younger people too are interested in the city's past. And the city is full of young people — students, white-collar workers, dot.com wizards, hippies. It is not uncommon to enter a restaurant in the Haight or the Castro district or south of Market and find that everyone in the crowd is under thirty. These youngsters are the future of San Francisco, and the reason they love it, and are willing to pay an exorbitant rent to share a small apartment or flat, is that they can be happy here, in a way that no other location can match. They feel comfortable in a worn, lived-in place, a city that is not sleek, not all stainless steel and glass; in short, a place that has a past, and a sense of continuity between generations. For our children and grandchildren, we must preserve the traditions, the history, and the buildings that make San Francisco what it is.

It has been said that in order to understand the people of a past era one must examine the buildings they left behind. The archival photographs in this book show many houses, both interiors and exteriors, that were destroyed in 1906. They are included in the hope that they may convey some sense of what life was like in old San Francisco, in the days of gaslights and horse-drawn streetcars and matched teams of horses pulling fine carriages. They show some of what was lost, and remind us of how fragile is our hold on the tip of the peninsula.

All the newcomers to San Francisco have arrived with a dream of one kind or another: to establish missions and convert the natives, to build a hacienda on a huge land grant, to make a fortune in gold, to build or buy a house and raise a family, to get a job with a future, to escape the constrictions of life in Ireland, Italy, Germany, Sweden, or midwestern America; to live in a place where one can be oneself, day and night, and in any company. Many of them found that place, and changed it in one way or another, for better or worse, and realized their dream. To the tourist standing on a hillside in Marin County and looking at the city through the cables of the Golden Gate Bridge, San Francisco truly looks like a dream city, floating above the cloud of fog hugging the water, a place too beautiful to be real. Fortunately for us, the dream and reality coincide.

— *James Beach Alexander*

The Louis Glass house, on Jones Street between Washington and Jackson, on the north slope of Nob Hill, looks fresh and sparkling in the morning sunlight, with lace curtains at all the windows, a gaslight beside the gate, and a neatly clipped lawn, a rarity in San Francisco. The rectilinear lower windows contrast with the arched upper ones; unusual single window caps give the design unity. (Courtesy Alex Brammer)

EDITOR'S NOTE

In ten years of working with Beach Alexander, editing and revising the text and choosing pictures for this book, I have learned a great deal about San Francisco, especially about life in the city before 1906. Beach's large collection of photographs, drawings and documents was both an inspiration and a barrier to our progress. We once spent a whole week making hard choices from his 150 photographs of Rincon Hill, narrowing them down to the fifty pictures included in that section.

Ten years is a long time for a book to incubate. Our work was of necessity intermittent; other, less complex publishing projects, with more urgent deadlines, took time away from this one. At one point it seemed that the book might never be finished, and our spirits flagged; then Lawrence Peterson's continued interest in the project offered a new page design for the book, and we returned to the task with new enthusiasm. Lawrence's experience and skill as a book designer saved us from defeat, and we are very grateful.

One benefit of the long preparation was the advent of new technology for improving scanned photographs. Some of the black and white prints were in bad condition, or were so faded and indistinct that they seemed unusable. Again, Lawrence came to our rescue, by improving the contrast, sharpening the focus, and otherwise bringing the pictures to the point where they would be legible to the reader, but without altering their historical accuracy. These improvements were especially important for the pictures of South Park, including the very rare interior shots, taken around 1860, which were very indistinct in the original.

The color photographs, with one or two exceptions, are by Stephen Fridge, who took them between 1992 and 1994. Some of the buildings shown have changed since the photographs were made: a new color scheme, street trees grown to obscure a façade, bougainvillea covering a porch. Stephen was often welcomed by homeowners, who have probably given up hope of ever seeing their houses in print.

Since it was impossible to include every bit of San Francisco history that came to hand, some choices had to be made. The Bay Bridge and the Golden Gate Bridge, completed in 1937, are already the subject of numerous books; their design and construction are far too complex to be considered within the scope of this book. Obviously they had enormous impact on San Francisco, but not really on its architecture. Fortunately the Ferry Building was not demolished when the original ferries stopped running. It will very likely see throngs of commuters in the coming years.

As anyone can tell, this book is a labor of love — love for the distant past, which is largely intangible, and for the more recent past, as represented by the buildings that have survived from the 19TH and early 20TH century. Some readers may object to our choices, and may dislike our personal attitudes and tastes. To such critics we can only say that the field is wide open for others to write their own account of San Francisco's endlessly fascinating and turbulent past, with the hope that they will have at least ten years to complete it.

— James Heig

Captain Charles Adams built this fine Italianate house in the 1860s, at 300 Pennsylvania Street, on the northeast slope of Potrero Hill, with a superb view of the Bay. In the 1950s the house was sold, with its original furniture and family portraits and possessions, to the Iaconi family, who spent many years carefully restoring it. In 1992 the curved front steps were rebuilt by Skeeter Jones, an expert restoration carpenter.

San Francisco
Building The Dream City

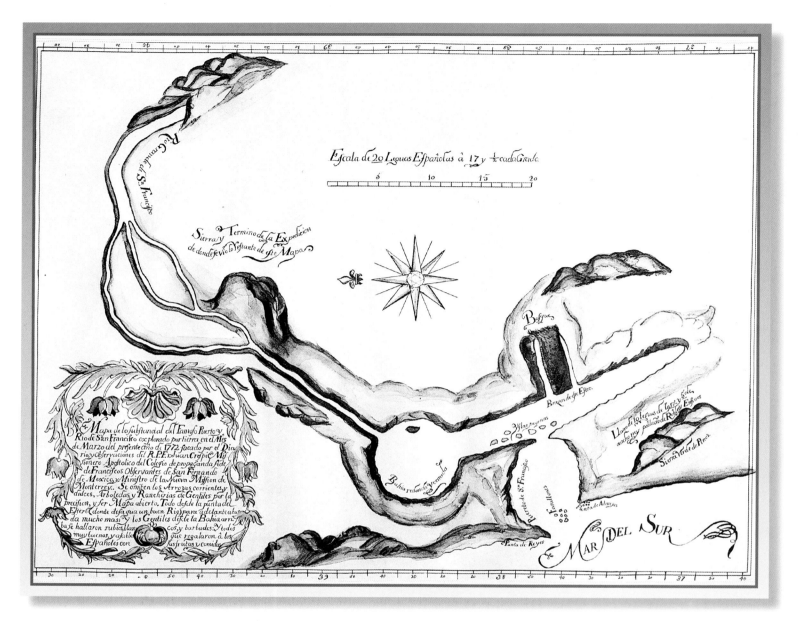

This first map of San Francisco Bay was made by Juan Crespi in 1772, just four years before Lt. Moraga brought the first settlers to San Francisco. It was based on observations made during a land expedition, which may explain its curious distortions. Point Reyes and "Punta de Almejas" (Shellfish Point, today's San Pedro Point, in Pacifica) hold the seven Farallones in a tight embrace. Inside the entrance to the real San Francisco Bay is a row of seven islands, with "Bahia redondo y cerrada" (round and hilly bay) to the north, today's San Pablo Bay. "Rio Grande de San Francisco" (the Sacramento River) flows down from the northeast. Two esteros frame a forest (Bosque), today's Alameda. On the peninsula is a plain ten leagues long and five broad, with many oak trees, and Sierra Verde de Pinos (mountains green with pines). (Courtesy Lowell High School Library)

THE WILDERNESS OUTPOST

1776 - 1821

THE SPANISH SETTLEMENT:

IN A SHELTER OF BOUGHS which Lieutenant Jose Joaquin Moraga ordered to be built on the bank of Laguna Dolores, Fra Francisco Palou celebrated the first Christian mass in what was to become San Francisco, on June 29, 1776, a date the city now observes as its birthday. This crude shelter was the first structure built in San Francisco by European settlers. Camp Street, a short street leading east from Guerrero between 16th and 17th, marks the site of that first encampment of fourteen *soldados de cuera* (leather-jacketed soldiers) of Spain, their wives and children, all of whom would soon become the first garrison of the San Francisco Presidio.

With them were seven families of settlers, plus some muleteers, servant boys and *vaqueros*, who had driven 200 head of cattle up from Monterey in the hope of establishing a settlement at the Presidio. Fra Palou and his confrere, Fra Pedro Cambon, accompanied by two servants and three native converts, had brought the supplies and tools they would need for founding the new mission, along with 86 head of cattle for the mission herd.

The northern tip of the San Francisco peninsula was perhaps the least hospitable of all the sites chosen for the 21 California missions. The lands near Laguna Dolores (today's Mission District and Noe Valley) were reasonably sheltered, as they are today, from the cold wind and fog coming in from the Pacific, but they could hardly have been called verdant. Live oaks and laurels lined the creeks flowing down from Twin Peaks and Lone Mountain. Willows crowded the edge of the lagoon, which provided an ample supply of fresh water. Three months earlier, explorer Juan Bautista de Anza had named it *Laguna de los Dolores de Nuestra Senora*, for the sorrows of Our Lady, because he had discovered it on Good Friday. The lagoon, the seasonal creeks

This drawing by Louis Choris records the celebration at Mission Dolores of Saint Francis Day, 1816, some forty years after the founding of the mission. The artist was mainly interested in portraying the natives, who are dancing in today's Dolores Street, and in the powerful juxtaposition of the exotic dancers and the Christian cross. The picture suggests that life for the neophytes at the mission was not all hardship. The padres, at left, have allowed the natives to use their own costumes and rituals in the observance of a Christian ceremony. Choris took liberties in drawing the buildings, giving the Mission façade fanciful spiral columns and providing a most improbable scalloped wall. To the right of the mission is the *convento*, or priests' quarters; behind the cross is the *guardia* (barracks). At far right is the majordomo's house.

Choris, a Frenchman, arrived aboard the Russian frigate *Rurik* on October 2, 1816. His pictures were later published in France, as part of a descriptive account entitled *Voyage Pittoresque Autour du Monde* [1822], one of the most important sources of information about California in the early 19th Century.

This picture, printed in France, differs considerably from the original watercolor which Choris made in California. The figures to the left of the lead dancer—two padres and nine natives, including five children—do not appear in the original, which is at the Bancroft Library. They were apparently added by the engraver, perhaps for clarity.
(Author's collection)

A fair-sized village. The mission church is large and is connected with the house of the missionaries, which is plain and reasonably clean and well kept. The mission always has a guard of three or four soldiers from the presidio. The village is inhabited by fifteen hundred Indians; there they are given protection, clothing, and an abundance of food. In return, they cultivate the land for the community . . . A general cooking of food takes place, at a given hour each day, in the large square in the middle of the village; each family comes there for its ration, which is apportioned with regard to the number of its members. They are also given a certain quantity of raw provisions.
— *Louis Choris, 1816*

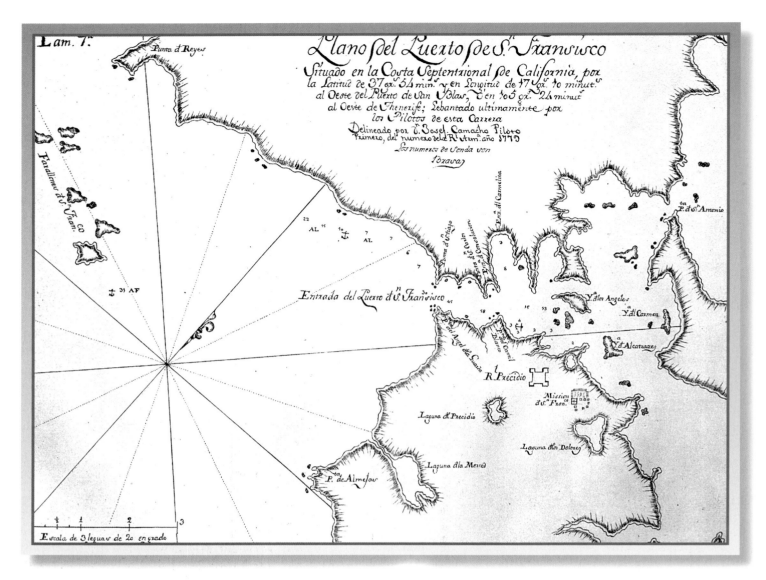

This map, entitled "Plano del Puerto de Sn. Francisco," was made by Josef Camacho y Brenes in 1779. It is the first map to show the Mission and the Presidio. Three lakes are shown: Dolores, Merced, and "Presidio" (Mountain Lake), as well as Angel Island and "Alcatraze," the original name for Yerba Buena Island. The name was later attached to today's Alcatraz. (Courtesy Lowell High School Library)

flowing into it, and the grassy valleys above it made it the only possible site for the founding of the mission.

To the east were marshes and salt flats, with grassy hills (Rincon Hill, Potrero Hill and Bernal Heights) rising abruptly from the water's edge. To the north were sand hills, cupped around Yerba Buena Cove, and a long, rocky east-west ridge dropping down to the bay on the north. Black Point, named for the dark color of the laurel trees growing there, was the only forested area; the rest was covered with chaparral and sparse grasses, struggling to stay rooted in the blowing sand.

The spot de Anza had chosen as the site for the Presidio was a tableland with a commanding view of the entrance to the bay, but without even one tree to break the wind from the ocean. A small lake (today called Mountain Lake) supplied fresh water, the only amenity. To the west was the barren, broken terrain of Point Lobos, and south of that an enormous wasteland of shifting sand dunes, stretching from the beach up to Twin Peaks. Below the dunes to the south was little *Laguna de Nuestra Senora de la Merced*, (today shortened to Lake Merced) surrounded by willows.

Crowning the peninsula were Twin Peaks, which the Spaniards called *Los Pechos de la Choca*, the Breasts of the Indian Maiden (curiously translated by Captain Frederick Beechey on his 1826 map as "Paps"), and the isolated fingertip projection of Lone Mountain, probably called *El Cerrito de Plata* by the Spaniards, and translated as "Silver Hummock" by Captain Beechey. It was an important landmark for navigators searching for the entrance to the bay.

The plan of the Spanish government for California was to build an empire on the foundation of a native population converted to Christ and industry, under the overlordship of Castilian officers and priests. The success of any mission was measured by the number of its converts, the size of its herds, the richness of the soil, and the abundance of fresh water. On all of these counts, Mission San Francisco de Asis faced a bleak future. Not only was the terrain less than promising, the native population was sparse. Wind-swept sand dunes and a cold, foggy climate made a poor environment for naked Indians. The absence of forests meant a dearth of big game, and cool summers were not conducive to the ripening of wild fruits and seeds. Oak trees were scattered, so that acorns, a staple of the natives' diet, were far from plentiful. Since the bay provided an abundance of fish, shrimp, clams and mussels, the native villages were clustered around waterways and tidal flats along the eastern shore of the peninsula.

The two Franciscans, Fra Palou and Fra Cambon, assigned to establish the mission, described the natives as being of fair stature; the men, while bearded, were completely bald, and had plucked off their eyebrows. The men wore capes made of pelican feathers, and nothing else. The women wore short aprons of animal skins. On cool days the natives smeared themselves with mud for insulation, and if the day warmed they jumped in the bay to wash off.

The padres considered it fortunate that these people had no religious beliefs which might interfere with their Christian teachings. In this matter they were, of course, quite mistaken, for the natives had strong beliefs concerning their origins and the hereafter, as well as many legends to account for the world as they saw it. The Pacific Ocean they called the "Sundown Sea," and the shore was the edge of the world. The Farallon Islands, visible on clear days, were where the spirits of the dead went. They recounted a story of a great earthquake which had cleaved the opening from the ocean to the bay. The earth and all plants and animals were imbued with a living spirit, worthy of respect and veneration.

This then, is a brief sketch of what the Spaniards found at the tip of the long peninsula. Here, in this desolate and remote wilderness, the natives, the Franciscans, and the soldiers were to pass their remaining years. Few if any of them would live long enough to hear about the Declaration of Independence, which, in a distant, unheard-of place called Philadelphia, was

signed just six days after that first mass was said on the banks of Laguna Dolores.

CHANGE — often at a breakneck pace — has been constant in the building of San Francisco. Laguna Dolores has long since been drained, filled and covered with the houses and factories of the Mission District. The crest of Lone Mountain became the site of a Catholic college for women. Near the site of the original Presidio the Americans built the massive brick Fort Point, later overshadowed by the anchorage for the longest and most beautiful suspension bridge in the world. The sand dunes have vanished under countless blocks of streets and houses. The tule huts of the native villages were replaced by adobe houses, then miner's tents, then wooden, brick, stone, concrete buildings, freeways, great skyscrapers sheathed in gleaming glass.

But here and there are fragments of what came before. In an excavation for a huge modern building on Market Street, human bones and the remains of a shell mound were discovered, deep in the earth. Mission San Francisco de Asis, by some miracle, has survived earthquake, fire, and urban development, and stands today as the radiant heart of San Francisco's history and culture. Twin Peaks are still bare, and still are thought to resemble breasts, though they are now encircled by paved roads and vista points packed with tour buses. Lake Merced, tamed and manicured, still marks the spot where the San Andreas Fault comes inland from the sea, to remind us of our precarious hold on this tip of land. And the rolling waves of the Sundown Sea still spend themselves, sighing and whispering, on the sandy shore.

If the reader is expecting to find here a picture of a great Spanish colonial civilization which was vanquished by the arrival on these shores of the hated gringo, he will have to turn to the writers of fiction. No period in American history has been so obscured by the mists of romantic myth and polite surmise as has the Spanish conquest and settlement of California. We all know how human it is to fill in the lack of factual information with wishful invention, and that is precisely what generations of well-meaning myth-makers have managed to do to our Spanish and Mexican legacies.

Somewhere in the moldering archives of Mexico City and Madrid there are detailed reports of the daily activities of California's Spanish presidios and missions, for the Spanish crown, through its vice-regal representatives, kept a close check on all that transpired in California, the most remote and isolated province in the world's largest empire. The little first-hand evidence we do have suggests a bureaucratic stranglehold by the military governors, who regarded any show of personal initiative among California's earliest settlers as a punishable offense.

Unable to defend her most remote holdings, and fearful of covetous foreign powers, Spain saw to it that there was little in California for anyone to covet. Spain regarded California as strictly a missionary enterprise; there was no plan for trade, nor even for export of any agricultural products to the mother country. The missions, supported by contributions from the Church Pious Fund, were intended by the Spanish government to convey the marvels of Spanish civilization to the natives. Once the padres had converted the natives into good Christian farmers and artisans, the missions were to be dissolved.

It was further understood that all of the missions were to be under the protection of a presidio. California had four such military outposts, whose garrisons of some thirty or forty soldiers, with their wives and often enormous broods of children, comprised the only nonclerical settlers. The soldiers were responsible for maintaining order at the missions in their district, for capturing and punishing runaway Indians, and for challenging any foreign intruders.

The soldiers' first duty after settling in was to round up quantities of natives for the padres to convert. This they did presumably through enticement or persuasion; there is no record of forcible kidnapping. About 81,000 natives (out of an estimated total population of 300,000) were baptized at the 21 missions in California; one can only wonder whether all of them willingly left their villages and families. At any one mission the native converts, called "neophytes," might come from a dozen or more different tribes, depending on their docility or their bad luck. Once the mission padres had persuaded them to worship Christ, the neophytes were taught to work as farmers, herdsmen, or craftsmen, in return for which they were clothed, housed and fed. The soldiers saw to it that they obeyed orders. Escapees, if caught, were publicly flogged and imprisoned.

Throughout the decades of Spanish rule, only three official pueblos, Los Angeles, Santa Cruz, and San Jose, were established. These were nothing more than a collection of adobe hovels clustered together for protection from the howling wilderness. Their occupants, mostly *invalidos* (retired soldiers and their families), were granted a few acres on which to raise crops for themselves and the nearby military garrisons. Any real commerce, which we today think of as the life-blood and sustaining force of a community, was non-existent.

The Spanish Crown strictly forbade commercial exchange with any foreign vessel which might happen to enter any of California's desolate ports. But then the residents of these wretched little settlements had little or nothing to exchange.

As to the legendary Spanish land grants, these were few in number, limited in size, and made with so many restrictive contingencies (one being that a grant was good only for the lifetime of the grantee) as to be hardly worth the asking. The Spanish grants in California were "haciendas," that is, farms, not ranchos. If any of their products were ever exported, that trade was cut off when in 1814 the Mexican revolution for independence prevented any Spanish cargo ship from entering California waters. In the eight-year interval before Mexican independence was finally achieved, not a single government transport came to the presidios with supplies, and not a penny was paid to the soldiers. The burden of feeding the garrisons fell upon the grudging charity of the mission fathers.

DURING THIS PERIOD, when California had been cut adrift from Spanish control but was more or less ignored by Mexico, several European governments, as well as the United States, sent expeditions to California to spy out the land. From the published reports of the English and American captains, today's historians have gained most of their information. While some of these reports are strongly biased, they all agree that the active and prosperous missions stood out in dramatic contrast to the lethargy and poverty of the four presidios and three pueblos. The reports show clearly that California was a mission enterprise, not a commercial one.

All reports praise the energy of the Spanish-born friars, who, supported by the military guards (usually seven or more guards from the nearest presidio were stationed at each mission) hoped to convert the natives into Christian farmers and artisans, working for the glory of Spain. Each mission complex had a series of workshops where the women were taught to weave blankets and clothing, and where the men learned such skills as carpentry, the tanning of hides, and the making of shoes and saddles. In the later stages of development of the missions, natives learned how to operate kilns to make the tiles for floors and roofs. Many neophytes were taught to till the fields and tend the vines and orchards; others worked as vaqueros (cowboys), watching over herds and flocks of biblical dimension. Even the children had tasks to perform.

It had always been officially understood that each mission was to continue only until the mission fathers had converted and trained the natives, at which time all mission lands were to be divided up among the converts. Originally it was thought that the training period was to last just ten years. One can only imagine the difficulties faced by two missionary teachers with a thousand pupils speaking a dozen different native languages or dialects. Meanwhile, epidemics of white men's diseases, to which the natives had no resistance, often wiped out whole segments of a mission's population.

Today the missions are among California's chief tourist attractions, yet it is doubtful that many visitors are given a true understanding of what courage, patience and ingenuity went into their construction. Confronted with today's luxuriantly planted mission courtyards and sparkling fountains, a visitor is apt to overlook the fact that the heavy walls and tile roofing were created not merely to shelter the faithful, but also as a defense against Indian uprisings, stampeding cattle, and wild animals.

Visitors seldom hear about the pit saw, an eight-foot-long device which operated vertically, requiring one man to pull it up and another, standing at the bottom of a deep pit, to pull it down. This painfully exhausting system took months just to fashion beams to hold up a heavy tile roof. Indeed, the saw was used as a form of punishment for miscreants. The saw and the primitive adze, used to smooth out the rougher bumps on the beams and other woodwork, were practically the only metal tools the missionaries had brought with them. In some instances skilled artisans were sent from the Mexican capitol to serve as molders and carvers or to fashion a bit of ornamental ironwork. The iron, of course, had to be imported.

THE NINE MISSIONS of Father Serra's day were simple wooden structures with dirt floors and thatched roofs. During the administration of Fra Fermin Lasuen, Fr. Serra's replacement (1785 - 1803), the plain wooden churches were replaced by adobe-walled structures, still with thatched roofs. But when an angry Indian at Mission San Luis Obispo sent a flaming arrow into the thatch, the entire mission quadrangle was destroyed in a matter of minutes. After that, roofing tiles became a requirement at every mission. Using crude kilns with no temperature controls, workers took ten years to make enough tiles to cover the church and the dependencies of one mission. Square floor tiles were the crowning refinement, added only in the final years of construction. At some of the missions, only the churches themselves were built with an eye to esthetic charm or permanence. Other structures

The pit saw, shown here in a modern drawing, was the only method available during the Spanish period for cutting logs into beams and planks. Miscreants and runaways were sometimes punished by being forced to work in the pit. (Courtesy San Mateo County Historical Association)

surrounding the open courtyard were often of far simpler construction. For this reason, at most of the missions only the church itself remains standing.

Since all but one of the twenty-one California missions followed the pattern of a compound enclosing an open court, one may only surmise that the design was pre-ordained by the church hierarchy in Mexico City. Of course, as in Europe during the Middle Ages, the courtyard was a place of refuge in times of attack. Certainly in California, where few missions escaped attack, this was a very practical arrangement.

Every mission padre was trained to have some knowledge of architecture. It is said that every one of the small libraries at the missions had its copy of Vitruvius's *Ten Books on Architecture*. Marcus Pollio Vitruvius, a first-century Roman architect, had painstakingly set down a complete encyclopedia explaining all the mysteries of Roman engineering. architectural design and planning. These works, which thirteen hundred years later were found preserved in the great monastery at St. Gore, Switzerland, were the only written account of the building techniques of the long-lost Roman Empire. The works of Vitruvius were greeted by the architects of the Renaissance as the answer to a prayer. Here were the engineering techniques for building arches, barrel

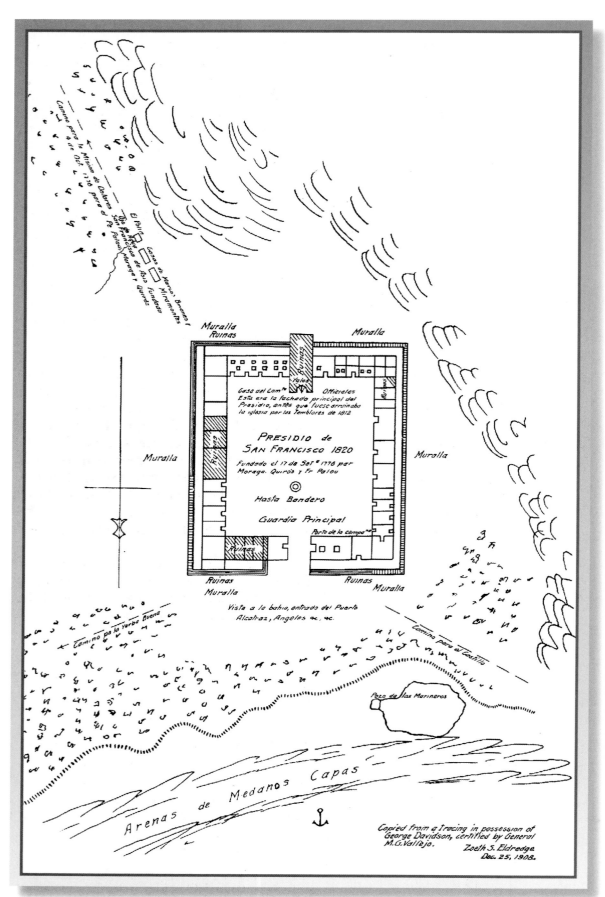

Map of the Presidio,
1820. The legend inside
the compound explains,
"This was the principal
façade of the Presidio,
until it was ruined in the
earthquake of 1812."
The chapel (Ygles), some
of the walls (Muralla)
and other buildings are
in ruins. At left a trail
leads to Yerba Buena
Cove. At lower right is
the path to the Castillo,
or fortress, on the bluff
where Fort Point was
later built. At top left is
the trail to the mission,
passing the houses of
Marcos Briones y
Miramontes, and El
Polín, the spring whose
waters had magical
powers. At bottom is the
Pozo de los Marineros,
apparently a pond
frequented by sailors.
From *The Beginnings of
San Francisco*, by Zoeth
Eldredge [1912].

vaults and domes, bridges, sewers and aqueducts. Also included were instructions for the decorative application of the Greek Orders, Corinthian, Ionic and Doric. He was called "Vitruvius Arbiter," and no work of Renaissance architecture was adjudged correct unless the architect had turned to the *Ten Books* for guidance. Vitruvius even included a chapter on the making of adobe bricks.

The Renaissance period not only heralded the rebirth of classical learning; it was also the age of great exploration and the Spanish settlement of the New World. To the mission fathers setting out to carve their establishments in the American wilderness, the works of Vitruvius were indispensable. The classical Vitruvian influence is found in the arches, barrel-vaulted ceilings, and the church façades (as at the San Francisco and Santa Barbara Missions) with pedimented fronts and engaged columns.

A Moorish influence is also evident in the architecture of the missions, chiefly in the use of adobe as a building material, a practice adopted by the Spanish during the eight hundred years that the Moors occupied southern Spain. The Moorish word *atob*, meaning sun-dried brick, became the Spanish *adobe*.

In the Americas the first *conquistadores* were no doubt astonished to discover, in Mexico and in our own Southwest, ancient mud-walled cities which reminded them of home. Thick earthen walls, a structural necessity, provided not only insulation in the hot desert climate, but also protection against a subjugated, often hostile people.

California natives built their shelters of mud-daubed branches, twigs, and tules, so the first Spanish settlers had to adapt themselves to a very similar kind of construction until the natives could be taught to make adobe blocks. That process took years. So the missions were expected to pass through three stages of development. The first missions had walls of *palizada* construction: poles stuck upright in the ground and held in place with rawhide; the roofs were thatched with tules (bulrushes). Second was the adobe stage, gradually refined by the addition of tiled roofs and floors. In the third stage the adobe was to be replaced with stone; the mission churches at Carmel and San Juan Capistrano were California's only two stone structures. The great earthquake of 1812, which was felt throughout the entire length of California, completely destroyed the ambitiously conceived domed church at San Juan, and thus apparently discouraged any further efforts to build with stone.

Because the tiled, adobe-walled missions were literally created out of the soil, they have often mistakenly been described as an indigenous architecture, in which the Franciscan builders "drew their inspiration directly from the land." Such an idea overlooks the fact that, despite the lack of proper tools and the use of primitive, unskilled labor, the mission fathers were attempting to reproduce the great stone churches they had known in Spain and Mexico. This intention extends to every detail of the mission churches, right down to their painted interior decorations: the faux marble and crudely imitated classical perspectives executed in vegetable dyes illustrate the brave spirit of the builders, who were struggling to create something of the grandeur of the churches they had known in their homeland.

And despite the efforts of latter-day Spanish Colonial Revivalists to prove otherwise, the architecture of the missions had no effect whatsoever upon the secular buildings of presidio, pueblo, or rancho.

THE PRESIDIO:
DEDICATED SEPTEMBER 17, 1776

MOST SAN FRANCISCANS have some understanding of the city's Gold Rush history, but of its actual beginnings many people know very little. The descendants of the American pioneers may take deserved pride in the exploits of their Yankee ancestors, but too often they are ignorant or scornful of those early Spanish settlers who also marched through the wilderness to find a promised land. From those earliest pioneer days, there remains only the little adobe church, Mission San Francisco de Asis, known today as Mission Dolores.

At the Presidio, a small adobe remnant of the former Spanish Comandante's house survives as a part of the officers' club. In a little valley nearby is an ancient well, known simply as "El Polin," whose waters once guaranteed fertility to any woman who partook of them. These, then, along with Mission Dolores, are the only physical reminders of San Francisco's Spanish beginnings.

To be sure, San Francisco still abounds in old Spanish place names which set it apart from other American cities. Imagine our city with a name like "Montgomery" or "Stockton," and you will better understand the poetry of our Spanish heritage. Such place names as "Potrero," which once designated a pasture near the old mission, and "Embarcadero," the name still used for San Francisco's port, add color to the city, but many people never think of their original meanings. Indeed, the very name "Presidio" (derived from the ancient Roman *Praesidium*, an entrenched fort) has no meaning to most Easterners, while many San Franciscans think of it as a modern army base with an odd name.

The 1600-acre San Francisco Presidio was established in 1776 by Colonel Juan Bautista de Anza, who blazed California's first overland trail, from the frontier outpost of Tubac, near what is now Tucson, Arizona, to San Francisco Bay. Before this, Franciscan missionaries and Spain's leather-jacketed frontier soldiers had come to California by ship only. After his exploratory trip and return to Tubac in 1775, de Anza recruited 240 men, women and children to follow him overland to California. Leaving behind forever all that was dear and familiar, these courageous people braved the dangers and hardships of an unknown wilderness, perhaps in the hope for a better existence, if not for themselves, then at least for their children.

The hardy settlers from the Spanish and Mexican eras would have vanished and been forgotten were not several San Francisco streets named for them: Valencia, Guerrero, Sanchez, Noe, Castro, de Haro, Pacheco, Moraga, Arguello. Bernal Heights and Bernal Park recall Jose Cornelio Bernal, whose cattle once grazed in Visitacion Valley. Those first colonists were simple frontier soldiers and farmers, often mixed-blood *mestizos,* not the blue-blooded grandees so beloved of the California mythmakers. De Anza himself described his departure from the colonists:

> On taking my leave of these good people whom I have led from their fatherland, to which I am returning, I remember the good and bad treatment which they have experienced at my hands, [and] I am filled with compassion. They showered me with embraces, best wishes, and praises which I do not merit . . . Up to now I have not seen a single sign of desertion in any one of those whom I have brought to this exile. I may record this praise of a people who, as time goes on, will be very useful to the monarchy in whose service they have voluntarily left their relatives and their fatherland, which is all they have to lose.

THE SAN FRANCISCO PRESIDIO, guarding the entrance to the Bay, and the San Francisco mission, on a sheltered inland cove four miles away, were sixteen years old in 1792, when Sir George Vancouver, the first foreign visitor, came on the British flagship *Discovery* to spy out the land. As he sailed into the Port of San Francisco, Vancouver observed a group of low adobe and thatch structures clustered around an open plaza, which he took to be "a pound for cattle." This turned out to be the Presidio compound. So much for the grandeur of this remote Spanish colony.

At the south side of the quadrangle, the comandante's house, where Vancouver and his men were received graciously, consisted of two long, low rooms with an overhead loft. The rooms were in perpetual gloom, for their only light came from a few small, unglazed windows fitted with rough shutters and wooden bars. The Comandante's wife and well-mannered children, all neatly dressed, were seated on mat-covered wooden platforms raised a few inches above the earthen floor. The few other furnishings in the room were equally primitive.

Following Captain Vancouver's first visit to San Francisco Bay in November 1792, (he was to pay a second visit in October 1794) work began on the construction of the Castillo de San Joaquin. Perhaps it was the visit of this first foreign representative at the port of San Francisco which stirred the Spanish officials toward a better defense of their long-neglected and most remote claim in the New World.

Erected on a promontory overlooking the entrance to the Bay (the site of Fort Point today), this modest pile of adobe faced with kilned bricks could hardly be regarded as much of a threat to any foreign invaders. Shaped like a horseshoe, it measured only about one hundred by one hundred twenty feet. According to legend, the castillo greeted the arrival of any vessel with a booming salute from its eight antique cannons, whenever powder was available. (Some of these cannons, still to be seen at the Presidio and at Fort Point, date to Spain's conquest of Peru in the 16th century.) The reverberations of a salute sometimes caused large sections of the old castillo to collapse, but portions of the building remained intact for many decades. When preparations were being made in the 1850s for the construction of the massive brick Fort Point, the entire promontory and whatever remained of the old castillo were blasted away.

Most of our information about the fifty years of Spanish occupation of the San Francisco peninsula comes from the journals and drawings of foreign visitors who put in at the port of San Francisco for water and supplies. These carefully detailed reports were intended for the eyes of government officials in Paris, London or St. Petersburg, who were highly curious about California.

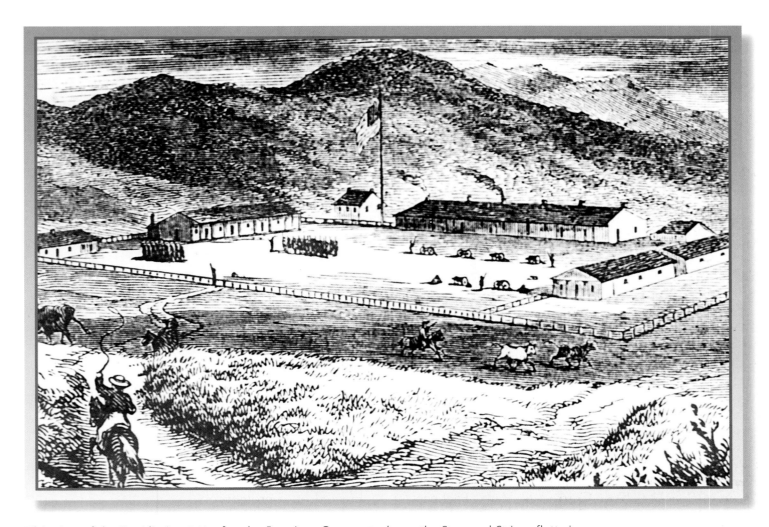

This view of the Presidio in 1846, after the American Conquest, shows the Stars and Stripes fluttering from the flagpole, while vaqueros chase cows outside the walls. Inside the compound are six cannon, probably the ancient bronze guns which Fremont claimed to have disabled; they are still to be seen today on the parade ground in front of the Officers' Club. (Courtesy California Historical Society)

One of the earliest visitors after Vancouver was Count Nicolai Rezanov, the Czar's chamberlain, who sailed from Sitka, Alaska, in 1806, with the sole intent of finding supplies for starving Russian colonists there. Rezanov's visit is best recalled not for his narrative descriptions of the Bay Area, but rather for his proposal of marriage to Comandante Arguello's daughter, Concepcion. Although Rezanov's motives for this proposal are open to question, the love affair between the worldly explorer, formerly a chamberlain in the court of Czar Alexander I, and the fifteen-year-old Concepcion Arguello has become a part of San Francisco legend.

After much deliberation, the local mission padres and the girl's parents allowed the couple to announce their engagement despite their different religious backgrounds. Rezanov, after delivering the supplies to his beleaguered colonists in Alaska, set out for St. Petersburg to obtain permission to marry from the Russian Orthodox officials. If nothing else, this legend illustrates the isolation of the Californians, for it was not until eleven years later, in 1817 (some sources say 1841!) that Concepcion learned of her lover's death in Siberia in 1807, while he was enroute to the Russian capital.

Perhaps as a result of this prolonged engagement, Concepcion eventually took the veil to become the first native-born Californian nun. In the early 1850s she became a teacher at the Dominican Convent in Benicia. Despite the tragic story of her girlhood, she was remembered as a plump and jolly old lady. After her death in 1857, she was buried in the Dominican cemetery at Benicia.

As to the appearance of the Presidio at the time of Rezanov's visit, one need only consult Comandante Arguello's report to his governor about a strong earthquake which rocked the San Francisco Peninsula in 1808. He noted that, despite the violence of the quake, the Presidio had sustained little damage because there was not much there to damage. Governor Arrillaga's response was a note of sympathy and a box of figs.

Astonishingly, in all those years of Spanish control, the Presidio could claim no mode of water transport other than the balsa craft fashioned by local natives. In an attempt to improve this circumstance, Comandante Arguello sent a crew north to build a large raft of timbers from the Mendocino coast. He planned to use these timbers to rebuild the crude huts and crumbling defenses of the Presidio compound. But the clumsy raft ran into the coastal rocks and was completely destroyed. When word of this mishap reached the ears of the military governor in Monterey, he sent a letter chastising Arguello for having the temerity to undertake such a feat without first requesting official sanction.

In the absence of available documentation, we can only speculate about the influence of Russian traders and settlers on California's history. Rezanov's visit to the Port of San Francisco (officially titled *Puerto de San Francisco*) was just one facet of an incursion which included the Russian establishment of Fort Ross in 1812, with a farming center and trading post at Bodega Bay, just fifty miles up the coast from San Francisco. These settlements illustrate the ineffectual defenses of Spanish and later of Mexican California, for they were not withdrawn until 1841, by which time the Russians had completely obliterated the sea otter population of the Pacific coast. Despite the establishment of Mission San Rafael in 1817 and Mission San Francisco Solano in Sonoma in 1823, and the later removal of the Presidio garrison from San Francisco to Sonoma by General Vallejo in 1835, nothing discouraged the Russian interlopers in their settlement of the territory nearby. By the end of 1835, the San Francisco Presidio stood abandoned, with just one soldier, Juan Prado Mesa, to guard what was rapidly becoming a deserted, crumbling ruin.

As word about California's inadequate defenses spread, the number of foreign ships arriving in the province's desolate ports increased. England, France, and Russia were seeking to extend their holdings in the New World, and the United States hoped to expand westward. All these countries cast speculative glances upon Alta California and the territory which lay to the north.

CALIFORNIA HAD BEEN a possession of the newly independent Mexican Republic for five years when, in November 1826, the sixteen-gun British sloop *Blossom* entered San Francisco Bay. Bypassing the landing place below the Presidio, the ship sailed on and dropped anchor at Yerba Buena Cove, the same spot chosen by Captain Vancouver

some thirty-three years before. In his *Narrative of A Voyage to the Pacific and the Bering Strait in the Years 1825-1828*, published in London in 1831, Captain Frederick Beechey of the Blossom described the same dismally undeveloped countryside that Vancouver had left some three decades earlier.

Here was the same magnificent harbor surrounded by windswept hills, with no signs of human habitation except for the Mexican fort on the southern promontory at the entrance. Those aboard the *Blossom* heard a voice projected by a speaking trumpet from the little Castillo, but nobody aboard the British ship could understand what it was saying. Captain Beechey noted that the Presidio did not dispatch a boat to make inquiries. There was no boat at the Presidio to send.

The structures in the little Presidio compound must have been arranged much as they had been in Vancouver's time—storehouses and living quarters set three or four yards inside a heavy, crumbling wall of timber and earth. The space between the houses and the wall seems to have been used for planting kitchen gardens and for chicken pens. One corner of the outer wall had collapsed and, as the area was filled with refuse, coyotes and other wild animals prowled the site. On the southeastern side of the quadrangle was a white-washed adobe church, flanked on the right by the officers' quarters and on the left by the comandante's one-story dwelling. Unlike the other buildings in the compound, these three structures were not thatched with tules, but were covered by kilned tiles. (The present-day Officers' Club, although totally rebuilt except for a tiny segment of adobe wall, occupies the site of those original three structures — the Commandancia, the chapel and the officers' quarters.) The tile roofing and white-washed chapel walls probably dated from the few futile efforts at improvement made by Comandante Jose Arguello after the earthquake in 1808.

G.W. Hendry and J.N. Bowman, in one of the few definitive studies of the Presidio's architectural beginnings, state that there were at least three successive Presidio compounds. The first, dedicated by Mission Fathers Palou and Cambon in September 1776, was a collection of *palizada* structures: a *comandancia*, warehouses, a church and soldiers' quarters. The second was probably built on a different site, with an adobe *comandancia* and an encircling *palizada* wall. This compound was completely destroyed in heavy rainstorms of January and February 1779. The third, begun in 1780, was constantly being renewed and rebuilt, and finally attained the appearance described by Vancouver on his first visit in 1792. By this time there was an enclosing wall five feet thick and about fourteen feet high. Vancouver described it as being of

The Presidio buildings in the 1870s: the low wing in the foreground was the original commandancia; the projecting section at center was the original chapel, a portion of which remains today as part of the Officers' Club. The Victorian house at the rear, with dormer windows, was once the home of General Pershing; while he was serving in Mexico in 1916, the house burned, and Pershing's wife and children were lost in the fire. (Courtesy California Historical Society)

"earth clods, reinforced by heavy timbers." By then the thatched roof of the adobe had been replaced by kilned tiles. Since the soil of the compound area is very sandy, the clay for the adobe bricks must have been brought from some distance. Vancouver's report states that the entire walled compound was some 330 feet square, and that it was entered by a single gate in the center of the north wall.

Captain Frederick Beechey's description of the Presidio in 1826 indicates few improvements from the time of Arguello's command. It had probably changed very little by 1835, when Comandante Mariano Vallejo was ordered to remove his troops to the northern frontier at Sonoma.

In June 1846 a group of disgruntled American settlers, many of them threatened with expulsion from California for not becoming naturalized Mexicans, staged a "Texas-style" raid on the town of Sonoma. They arrested General Vallejo, sending him to Sutter's Fort as a prisoner of war. Replacing the regimental Mexican flag with one of their own, which depicted a grizzly bear and a lone star, they declared California a republic, independent of Mexican rule. The California legislature adopted the Bear Flag as the state emblem in 1896 to celebrate the 50th anniversary of this rather over-rated event.

This uprising, now referred to as "The Bear Flag Rebellion," brought Captain John C. Fremont to the forefront of California history. The Captain gathered together a little army and announced that he had "captured" the city of Sonoma. He then traveled southward, naming the "Golden Gate" along the way to the long-abandoned San Francisco Presidio, where, according to his memoirs, he "spiked the guns." He does not mention that the guns he spiked were only a few antique cannons which lay moldering in the ruins of the Presidial defenses.

Unfortunately for Fremont, all of his bluster was wasted effort. Even before he sent his report, the United States had declared war on Mexico and, as part of its immediate action, had sent Commodore Sloat of the Navy to raise the American flag over the Monterey capital on July 7th. Two days later, Captain John B. Montgomery arrived to run up another American flag in Yerba Buena's plaza, which would henceforth bear the name of Montgomery's ship, the *Portsmouth*.

FOLLOWING CAPTAIN FREMONT's debacle, the military history of the Presidio is rather anti-climactic. No invading force has ever passed through the Golden Gate, with the possible exception of two boatloads of New York Volunteers who left the East in 1846 under the command of Captain Jonathon Stevenson. They held the optimistic notion that they were going to invade California, but by the time they reached the Pacific shore in March, 1847, the flag of the United States was already waving over the Presidio.

Until the mid-1880s, the Presidio remained the wind-blown collection of sandhills it had always been. Then a major effort was made to beautify this barren,

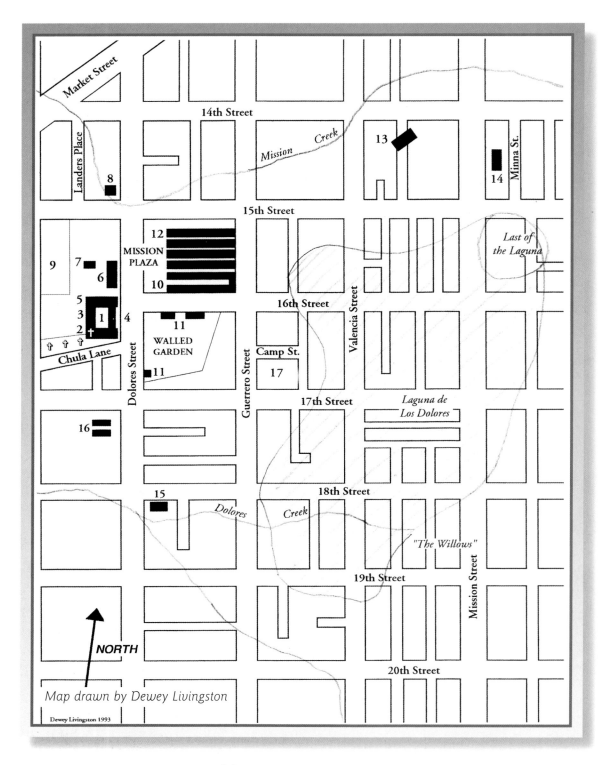

MAP OF THE MISSION:

1. Mission courtyard
2. Mission church (today's Mission Dolores)
3. Monjerio and workrooms
4. Convento: four-room Padres' house
5. Granary
6. Guardhouse
7. Jusgado (jail)
8. Molino (flour mill)
9. Corral
10. Majordomo's quarters
11. Quarters for native families
12. Quarters for native families
13. Site of the first chapel, built in 1776
14. Site of the second chapel
15. Unknown
16. Undocumented: possibly the infirmary
17. Original camp site of the de Anza settlers

windswept spot. Thousands of San Francisco school children planted forests of eucalyptus and pines which today make a park-like paradise of what was the largest urban military base in the United States. And, despite all the changes of the twentieth century, de Anza's original boundaries are still honored today.

The history of the San Francisco Presidio only begins with the Spanish occupation of California. In 1848, the adobe Comandancia with its adjoining chapel and officers' quarters were incorporated into an American officer's club, which stands today. Two of the original Spanish cannons, cast in 1673, now guard the entrance to the club. The touchhole of one still contains fragments of the file thrust in by Captain John C. Fremont in 1846. Two other cannons from the Castillo are located elsewhere on the grounds: one, cast in 1628, stands before the Presidio Army Museum, and the other, cast in 1684, is at Fort Point. Another pair flank the Lyon Street entrance to the Presidio, while two more flank the flagpole just 400 feet from the entrance of the Officers' Club. A marker, placed by the Daughters of the American Revolution, presumably identifies the northwest corner of the original Spanish quadrangle.

The later military history of the San Francisco Presidio is in itself a topic for a book, with a section devoted to its interesting and varied architecture. Of special interest is the Presidio Army Museum, at Funston and Lincoln Boulevard, which occupies the old post hospital, built in 1857. The museum, established in 1973, not only contains artifacts from the Presidio's military past, but also portrays such historic San Francisco events as the 1906 earthquake and fire. Directly behind the museum are two of the shelters built for refugees of that disaster. Of the five thousand cottages put up for disaster relief in 1906, only a handful survive.

Fort Winfield Scott, now called Fort Point, flanks a southern stanchion of the Golden Gate Bridge. Begun in 1853, the fort is a masterpiece of brick masonry, patterned after Fort Sumter in Charleston's harbor. By 1861 it was ready to guard the Golden Gate against the intrusion of Confederate gunboats, which never came. Indeed, Fort Point has never had to defend the bay from any invader. Handsomely restored, it is now open to the public as a museum.

The United States government has de-commissioned the Presidio as an army base, and the entire 1660 acres is now a National Park. Its scores of historic structures will be preserved and converted for new uses. The benefits to San Francisco and to the nation are immeasurable.

MISSION SAN FRANCISCO DE ASIS
DEDICATED OCTOBER 9, 1776

If Saint Francis wants a mission to bear his name, let him cause his port to be discovered, and he shall have his mission there.

—Visitadore Jose Galvez to Father Serra at La Paz, 1769.

SIR GEORGE VANCOUVER's description of the mission in 1792, a compound of adobe buildings facing a small body of fresh water known as Dolores Lagoon, suggests that he was far more favorably impressed than he had been with the Presidio. The church he described, with its handsome façade and heavy tiled roof, is the same structure we see today. If beauty and permanence are qualities which best define the true meaning of architecture, the church and its adjoining priests' house must be considered the only architecturally worthy structures within the mission's large complex. The rest of the compound and the scattered workshops and storehouses were little more than rustic shelters.

It may be surprising to learn that the old mission church we see today was the third in a succession of churches built for the Mission San Francisco. The crew of the *San Carlos*, aided by the Presidio guard, erected the first in the *palizada* construction style, similar to the design used in the building of North American palisaded forts. The floors were of trammeled earth, and the roofs were thatched with tule reeds. For important structures, such as a mission church, the walls were white-washed inside and out with a mixture of pulverized shells and water.

The first *palizada* structures at the Mission San Francisco were completely destroyed by heavy winds and rains in the winter of 1779. These structures

The Mission was in its prime when this drawing, by Capt. W. Smyth, who came with the Beechey expedition, was made in 1826. The lean-to appendage on the left side of the church is thought to have been the baptistry, later replaced by one at the back of the church. Beyond the church and convento is the storehouse, and beyond those the *guardia*. The long, low structures across from the Mission plaza were living quarters for the Indian families. After secularization some of these adobes were converted for use by residents of the Dolores Pueblo. (Courtesy San Francisco Public Library)

included a church with a wing for Padres Palou and Cambon, and a storehouse for supplies. After the storm, the padres replaced the buildings with structures built in exactly the same way. These first and second mission churches probably stood at the northeastern corner of the Dolores Lagoon, near today's 14th and Mission Streets.

Mission San Francisco was the sixth of nine missions which Father Serra lived to see established in Alta California. With perhaps the exception of the older church at San Juan Capistrano, Mission San Francisco was the only adobe church begun in Father Serra's time. Father Serra's lesser-known successor, Fra. Lasuen, replaced the wood-and-thatch churches of Father Serra's nine original missions with adobe and

tile structures, and added ten more missions to the "Golden Chain."

By the 1780s, the population of Christianized natives had swelled to over 1,100, and, with farming and cattle-raising, Mission San Francisco de Asis was now well enough established to begin replacing the *palizadas* of the quadrangle with more permanent structures of adobe and kilned tile. On April 15th, 1782, the Franciscans laid the first foundation stone for the future adobe church at San Francisco. The actual dates of completion and dedication of the new adobe church are unknown; the building records from 1785 to 1793 are reported lost. It is known, however, that the remains of Lieutenant Jose Joaquin Moraga, who had been buried before the altar of the second

The interior of Mission San Francisco de Asis (Mission Dolores) in a photograph taken before Willis Polk's careful restoration in 1916. Completed in 1791, this is the only California mission interior remaining intact. The paintings, statues and artifacts date from the earliest days of the Spanish colonial period. The altar was brought from Mexico around 1806. After a thorough restoration completed in 1995, the interior is virtually unchanged today. The mission and its beautiful cemetery, both open daily, are the essential first stop for any visitor to the city who wants to understand San Francisco's past, or indeed for any city dweller who wants to refresh himself within the cool, peaceful adobe walls. (Author's collection)

church, were removed for burial under the floor of the new adobe church in 1791.

Throughout the construction, scores of Indians worked at making the adobe bricks and the roof and floor tiles, a process which took years to complete. In the mountains to the south, native lumberers and Presidio soldiers felled sturdy redwoods, which were then dragged by oxen to the nearest creek and floated down to the bay, and thence to the inlet below the mission.

Vancouver and those who followed him have given no detailed descriptions of the church, other than to note its striking contrast with the other buildings. As at all of the California missions, the church was the sole object of beauty and permanence, the only mission structure built to last. Vancouver's description shows

that Mission San Francisco's buildings conformed to patterns established long before by mission authorities at the College of San Fernando in Mexico City. The church, with its sacristy at the rear, occupied one side of a large open quadrangle. Adjoining one side of the church was the *convento*, the adobe house of the padres. At Mission San Francisco, the *convento* contained a row of four large rooms, two for the two mission fathers and two for guests. Serving as corridors, and at the same time protecting the adobe walls from the rains, were long galleries both in front and in back of the priests' house. Behind the *convento* was the enclosure or courtyard.

On the third side of the enclosure, directly across from the church, was the *troja* or granary. It was separated from the padres' house by a narrow passageway

Mission Dolores had deteriorated by 1850; to the Gold Rush crowd it was little more than a curiosity, and the faithful Mexican parishioners were unable to keep it up. The priests' quarters, at center, had become a saloon, and other parts of the quadrangle were used as a hotel, in a town where decent lodgings were hard to come by. Miraculously, the sturdy mission church survived earthquake, storms and neglect, thanks to its thick adobe walls and beams secured with rawhide thongs. Today, after a careful restoration completed in 1995, it is one of the most authentically original and carefully maintained of all the 21 missions, a major historical, architectural and spiritual treasure of California. (Courtesy San Francisco Public Library)

guarded by a stockaded gate. At most of the missions, this was the only entry to the cloister-like courtyard, designed as a protection against native uprisings, and also as protection for the Indian maidens, whose quarters, called the *monjerio*, opened only into the courtyard. At night, the court's single gate required just one sentry.

Adjoining the girls' living quarters, at the back of the court, were workshops where the Indians were trained. These included a carpentry shop, an adjoining cabinet shop, and a blacksmith shop. Shoes and saddles were made in a leather shop, and, next to that, a large room held some twenty looms where Indian girls were kept busy making blankets of coarse wool from the mission flocks. Directly behind the granary was the large kitchen. The kitchens at most missions were simply set up in the courtyard under shelters of wood and thatch called *enremadas*.

The center of all mission activities, the mission courtyard was busy as a beehive. The Indian neophytes, at a signal from the mission bell, would come from their work in the fields three times a day to receive their allotments of stew or soup, ladled from two or three huge iron pots. After the noon meal there was usually time for a siesta, followed by a compulsory church service. Services always began with a roll call.

IN THE LARGE PLAZA fronting the quadrangle the entire mission flock could gather for ceremonies and general assemblies. As the years went by and more neophytes joined the flock, more structures spread out around the central quadrangle. Just north of the compound was a *calabozo*, a jail, and adjoining it were a guardhouse and quarters for the seven or eight soldiers and their families who were sent from the Presidio to guard the mission. North of this was a *molino*, or grist mill, and behind it was a soap factory.

Across the plaza from the quadrangle was a large, U-shaped house for the majordomo, the overseer or manager of the mission fields and laborers. Surrounding it were rows of long, narrow adobe quarters for Indian families. Records show that the first of eight rows was begun in 1800, and that the rows continued to expand for the next ten or twelve years. Then epidemics of measles, syphilis and smallpox began to decimate the population dramatically. To meet these tragic emergencies an infirmary was built. Finally, in desperation, the mission fathers were forced to establish an *asistencia* in

During the 1850s the priests' quarters were replaced by a New England-style wing, complete with shutters, which then served as a school house. The symmetrically planted trees and picket fence complete the transformation. The well-proportioned façade of the mission looks much as it does today. The beautiful cemetery, at left, is a small remnant of the original one, which extended under today's Dolores Street. By 1889, when this picture was taken, most of the tombstones had Irish names. From the *Overland Monthly* magazine, 1889. (Author's collection.)

the warmer climate of the Marin peninsula. By 1817 the little *asistencia* was given mission status as Mission San Rafael, known among early settlers as "the hospital mission." From a count of 1,200 in 1800, the neophyte population at Mission San Francisco by 1827 had declined to 241 men, women and children.

Another *asistencia*, built in a fertile valley on the site of today's Pacifica, in San Mateo County, was used to grow food and crops for Mission San Francisco, where the soil was poor. A third was established on the wide plain at San Mateo Creek, today's downtown San Mateo. Meanwhile, Mission Santa Clara (1777) and Mission San Jose (1797), with their warmer climates and vast arable acreage, both outstripped Mission San Francisco in population of converts and production of crops.

Padre Jose Altimira, the last Spanish padre assigned to the San Francisco mission, planned to close down both the San Francisco and San Rafael missions and to concentrate their manpower in a new mission, "Nuevo San Francisco," to be built on Sonoma Creek. In 1822 California was annexed to the newly independent Mexican Empire, and the Franciscans, well aware of their tenuous position under the new govern-

ment, allowed Fra Altimira in 1823 to establish the new mission, named San Francisco Solano, the last in the chain beginning in San Diego. Missions San Rafael and San Francisco de Asis continued in operation. But all of the missions were to enjoy only ten more years of existence.

In 1833 the Mexican Congress enacted a law which secularized all mission properties and converted the mission villages into civil pueblos, with the missions becoming parish churches. A year later commissioners were appointed by the provincial governor to take charge of the neophytes and all mission property, which was to be distributed to the Mexican civilians and soldiers and to the native converts. The mission padres were now reduced to the status of parish priests.

The Mexican Congress was simply living up to an original Spanish contract, stating that the missions were to exist under the sufferance of the government, only until such time as the natives had become trained as farmers and artisans, and, of course, good taxpaying Christians supporting the colonial system. This was all supposed to be accomplished within ten years from the founding of the first mission in 1769.

21

By 1834 some of the missions had been operating for nearly sixty years, and the mission fathers quite rightly protested that their converts were still unprepared to grasp the wonders of Spanish civilization. Now, despite the padres' protests, the Mexican Congress decided to close the contract, and the mission era came to a complete and irrevocable end.

THERE IS LITTLE first-hand information about the actual business of secularizing Mission San Francisco de Asis. Since Comandante Mariano Vallejo had under his jurisdiction all that land north of Monterey known as *"La Frontiera Del Norte,"* it is likely that the secularization of the missions at Sonoma, San Rafael, and San Francisco were left to his disposal. In his meticulous account, *The San Francisco Mission or Mission Dolores,* Franciscan Father Zephyrin Engelhardt gives only a general picture of the secularization. Not surprisingly, Engelhardt, as an outraged Franciscan, left a rather unflattering picture of Vallejo, who was only 26 when he was given the powerful post as commissioner. He was intelligent, literate, and of pure Castilian descent. Very likely he was a proud and cocky young man, which is the way Fr. Engelhardt portrays him.

The Mexican Congress intended that mission properties were to be parceled out to Mexican citizens and to those former neophytes who were prepared to become citizens—that is, they were Spanish-speaking Christians who knew how to farm or produce goods. The California *diputacion* (legislative body) in 1839-40 sent William Hartnell, a naturalized English-born settler from Monterey, to report on the distribution of mission properties. When he reached the northern frontier he was halted, on Vallejo's orders, and forbidden to continue his investigations in that area. Very few mission lands ever passed into native hands, but rather became the property of Mexican settlers and former Presidio soldiers. It was no coincidence that Vallejo rose from relative poverty, which had been the lot of all military officers, to become one of California's richest men, owning some 88,000 acres of land and 50,000 head of cattle.

In his defense, it is said that former neophytes who received lands and cattle from the missions willingly turned their property over to Vallejo in exchange for protection from attacks by hostile Indian tribes. They also worked for him: some 2,000 natives tended his vast herds and crops, built his Casa Grande in Sonoma and his Petaluma Adobe ranch house, and carried his hides and tallow to market. As to the mission converts, they were left to fend for themselves. Perhaps the terrible smallpox epidemic which swept California in 1837, killing tens of thousands of natives, might almost be regarded as providential, for those who died were spared the misery which was to be the survivors' lot under the new regime. Some found employment, under slave labor conditions, at the ranchos, while others fled into the wilderness.

El Molino (the mill) stood just north of the Mission, near the corner of today's 16th and Dolores Streets. It was the home of Francisco Ruffino and his wife, Petrona (1816-1879). The kitchen wing at left was the original mill. The author's drawing was copied from one in the San Francisco *Examiner*, March 27, 1889.

Although the Spanish-born Franciscans were invited to leave the province after secularization, most of these aging priests were too worn or infirm to leave. They passed their remaining days serving as parish priests. At Mission San Francisco, Father José Santillan, a Mexican-born Franciscan from the College of Zacatecas, served the settlements which had sprung up on mission lands at San Francisco, San Rafael and Sonoma. In 1845 the last Franciscan priest surrendered Mission Dolores to Bishop Francisco Garcia Diego, and withdrew to the former Mission Santa Clara. When Governor Pio Pico auctioned off the lands of several former missions in 1845, Mission Dolores was no longer an entity to be auctioned. In 1850 the Jesuits started a school in the *convento*, but it failed. The Dominican Archbishop Alemany took charge of Mission Dolores in the 1850s.

By 1852 the mission had become the center of a resort area, and was described by Gerstacker as containing, in the original quadrangle, "a brewery, two taverns, a dancing room, a number of private lodgings, a saloon for drinking and gambling, as well as a small hospital." The mission church remained untouched. In the late 1850s a large portion of the *convento* was replaced by a comfortable frame building that looked as if it had come from New England, built to house a boy's school.

IN 1876, THE HUNDREDTH ANNIVERSARY of the mission's founding, a new church arose on the site of the former quadrangle. This Victorian Gothic Revival structure, built of brick, was damaged so badly in the 1906 earthquake that it had to be demolished. Fortunately the sturdy little mission church, with its five-foot-thick adobe walls, sustained little damage. Fire-fighters, during the conflagration that followed the quake, were able to save the church and all the structures on the west side of Dolores Street, while all the buildings across the street were burned. The score of other buildings which once made up the mission complex have all vanished, as have the graves of some 5,000 Indians buried near the church.

In 1916 architect Willis Polk carried out a restoration of Mission Dolores, so meticulous that today it is difficult to determine which details are original and which have been restored. Besides reinforcing the walls with steel girders, Polk may have added support for the heavy rafters, which are still held in place by their original rawhide thongs. The chevron decoration on the rafters may have been restored, but the confessional doors that line the wall to the left of the entrance are original, as are the three bronze bells which came from Mexico more than two hundred years ago.

The importance of the Mission to the American immigrants is shown in an item from California's first newspaper, *The Californian*, for October 24, 1846, describing a reception held for Commodore Robert F. Stockton, who had arrived to take over as Commander in Chief of forces in California:

> When the commander in Chief had closed his reply [to the welcoming speech], the procession moved through the principal streets, and halted in front of Capt. Leidesdorff's residence, where the Governor and Suite entered, and was presented to a number of ladies, who welcomed him to the shores of California. After which, a large portion of the procession accompanied the Governor, on horse-back, to a Mission, several miles in the country, and returned to an excellent collation, prepared by the Committee of Arrangements, at the house of Capt. Leidesdorff. After the cloth was removed the following toasts were drank.

Clearly the mission pueblo was of minor significance compared to Yerba Buena, the commercial and social center of the American settlement, which had "principal streets."

Leidesdorff's house, at California and Montgomery, was the finest in the village. He also owned a building on the plaza, which he leased to J. Brown; in the same issue of *The Californian* is a paid notice forecasting changes to come:

> PORTSMOUTH HOUSE – Yerba Buena — The undersigned has opened a Public House, under the above title, where he is prepared to entertain all those who may please to call on him. His table will be furnished with the best the market affords, and his bar with the best liquors. Yerba Buena, Oct. 16, 1846.
>
> —J. Brown

The generous private hospitality of the Californios was soon replaced by public hospitality, for which the visitor was required to pay.

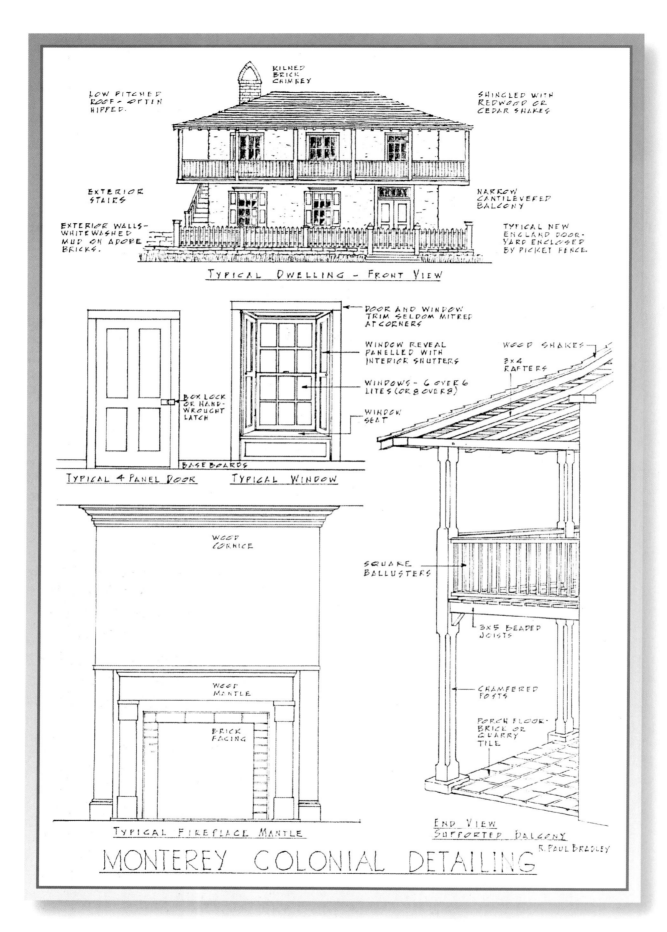

MONTEREY COLONIAL DETAILING

This drawing shows some of the details of the "Monterey Style" most of which were brought to Monterey by traders like Larkin, who employed American or English ships' carpenters to blend the comforts of New England with California's crude vernacular style.

THE MEXICAN ERA

1821 - 1846

COMMERCE BEGETS
A NEW ARCHITECTURE

O N SEPTEMBER 27, 1821, after ten years of bloody insurrection, Mexico achieved independence from Spain, annexing California as a part of the new republic. For nearly ten years California had been left to shift for herself; her people would hardly have known that a struggle was in progress, so removed were they from the tumult of battle. For ten years not a single government transport came to the presidios with supplies, and for ten years not a penny was paid to the soldiers, who went bootless, their uniforms in tatters. The burden of feeding the garrisons of California's four presidios fell upon the overworked mission fathers.

For the most part, the Californios accepted their new flag with apathy. Only the mission fathers, who were among the very few settlers who had been born in Spain, seemed to care one way or another. Perhaps they also had a premonition of the fate which was in store for the mission system. The official enactment of the Mexican Congress which placed the mission properties in secular hands and reduced the missionary fathers to the status of parish priests was not to occur for fourteen years, yet almost from the start Mexico's official acts would radically alter California's social and economic status.

The first of these acts permitted the California governors to make outright land grants to private citizens, with few of the restrictions which the Spanish crown had imposed. All the applicant for a land grant had to do was to show that he was a reliable and loyal Catholic citizen, that he would map out his claim, and that he would build fences and a house on the property to show his intention to occupy it. At first these grants were restricted in size, but eventually much larger grants were made to important citizens such as General Mariano Vallejo, Don Jose de la Guerra, and Governor Pio Pico, to name only three. So it was in the Mexican era, not the Spanish, that the great California ranchos came into being. As opposed to the few

Spanish grants, over eight hundred huge grants were made by the successive Mexican governors of California. Along with the land, the missions' huge herds of cattle were also parceled out to the grantees.

As for the old Spanish plan of holding the land in custody for the Native Americans, not more than a handful of these people were deemed worthy or capable of owning land. Following the secularization of the missions (1834-1836), those natives who had managed to survive six decades of Christian civilization either escaped into the wilderness or exchanged their bondage to the missions for bondage to the great land holders.

A second and equally important change under Mexican rule was the lifting of the old Spanish ban pro-

This superb pencil drawing, attributed to Father Prendergast, shows the Mission Pueblo in 1849. Two American flags are flying, but otherwise there is little visible evidence of the Yankee take-over. Several of the buildings east of the mission have collapsed and melted in the rains, leaving mounds of earth, left of center. The original mission quadrangle survives, but the priests' quarters are already being used as a saloon. At far right, riders on the Mission Road could hardly imagine that it will soon be planked, and riders will have to pay a toll to use it. The buildings east of the mission house some of the Mexican families, who have seen their little settlement swamped by the crowds of gold-seekers and merchants arriving daily by ship. (Courtesy California Historical Society)

hibiting trade with foreign powers. Perhaps those bans were not as foolish as at first they seemed, for once the Mexican government allowed the Americans to get a foot in the door, it was only a matter of time before they had complete possession of the land.

For years, American and British ships, bound to and from China, or on expeditions of exploration, had visited California waters. Those with merchandise aboard might exchange a few items with the mission fathers for some of the hides and tallow produced by the missions; other settlers had little to barter. Now that those formerly impoverished soldiers had become the owners of vast ranchos with thousands of cattle, the trading ships and their owners found a rich new outlet for manufac-

tured goods. And there was an endless demand in New England for the great loads of hides and tallow from California. Tallow (beef fat) was used in making candles and soap. The hides were tanned and used for saddles and harness, or for leather shoes and boots, much in demand thanks to the recent invention of left- and right-foot design, replacing the earlier shoes made to fit either foot. In the burgeoning eastern states, even ordinary workmen and farmers who had worn shoes made of wood, cloth, or carpet now demanded the comfortable new leather shoes and boots.

Realizing the potential of the lucrative hide and tallow trade, the Mexican government permitted the building of a customs house at the provincial capital of

Monterey. There, foreign vessels, after paying duty on the goods they had to trade, were free to enter any port up and down the coast.

If in the past there had been little incentive to raise cattle, there was a strong one now. Little money was exchanged in the transactions, but for every cowhide a rancher could get two dollars' worth of merchandise. The Boston traders, their holds fitted out with shelves to display their merchandise, soon enjoyed a brisk and profitable trade as long lines of Indians marched from rancho to loading dock, each bearing a bundled cowhide on his head. And the traders provided necessities and even luxuries that most Californios had never dreamed of.

Besides badly needed farm implements and carpenters' tools, the ships brought bolts of calico and cotton stuffs, housewares of copper, brass and pewter, and sets of Victorian walnut furniture upholstered in horsehair. (No California ranch house, Hollywood mythmakers notwithstanding, was ever furnished with objects from Spain.) From China the traders brought pieces of Canton ware, shaving bowls, even entire dinner services in the blue and white willow pattern. There were handsomely embroidered silk shawls, some in the old rose color so admired by the California ladies, and from the Philippines came tall tortoise-shell combs. There were even sets of Chinese furniture made in the European style expressly for export. And despite the long tradition of wine-making at the California missions, many Californians wanted European wines imported via Boston.

Along with this brisk new commerce came a new kind of "missionary," of English or American stock, known as the "factor." Acting as representative for one of the big export concerns, he would establish a trading post, either in a pueblo or in a former mission village, or, as in the case of San Francisco, on a plot of land granted by one of California's Mexican governors. In time, these trading posts expanded into thriving commercial centers which would eventually become California cities. Los Angeles got its start as a commercial center mainly through the efforts of New Englander Abel Stearns. In San Diego it was Captain Fitch, while in Santa Barbara Captains John Wilson, Daniel Hill, and Alpheus Thompson acted as go-between in trade. In Monterey, Thomas Larkin and his half-brother John B. Rogers Cooper were both leading merchants from Boston. The English Captain William Richardson and Ohioan Jacob Primer Leese were the founders of the trading post which would become the metropolis of San Francisco. These were but a few of the better-known Anglo merchants.

These shrewd traders established a new commercial enterprise in California, and prospered mightily in doing so. All but Larkin, who married a proper Boston lady, married into California's leading families and adopted the Roman Catholic faith required to become naturalized Mexican citizens. All, without exception, soon became some of the biggest land and cattle owners in California. Unlike the heedless young forty-niners who later proclaimed themselves pioneers, these canny gentlemen adopted the lifestyle of their host country, speaking Spanish and becoming at least outwardly devout. Their influence in commercializing California not only brought the province into the modern world, but also profoundly changed the lives of the Californios, a change which many chroniclers of the period have overlooked. They created an architecture to match the prosperity their commerce had built.

WHAT WE NOW CALL Monterey style architecture resulted not from a conscious effort on the part of its Yankee purveyors to create a new style, but simply from a natural attempt to introduce the comforts and graces of New England houses as an improvement to the cheerless adobe buildings that were the legacy of Spanish colonial times. In 1835 Thomas Larkin began the first combined dwelling and place of business in Monterey, a building which was to revolutionize the domestic architecture of Mexican California.

Fortunately, the Larkin adobe, now a museum run by the California Department of Parks and Recreation, has suffered few of the alterations which came to so many of the adobes surviving from this period. It stands today as the first and most eloquent statement of the new style. With its twelve-over-twelve window panes, four-paneled doors, interior shutters, and delicately detailed interior woodwork, it clearly proclaims its New England influences.

The Larkin house also contrasts with the poverty of its California predecessors, for it was the first dwelling with an interior fireplace (the Spaniards did their cooking out of doors, and used pans of hot coals for warming rooms). Until the Larkin house was built there was not a single two-story dwelling in California except for those built by the Russians at Fort Ross. One or two of the missions probably had planked floors, but the Larkin house was the first dwelling not to have floors of trammeled earth. Larkin introduced upright corner posts to support his second story and to allow wider window openings (this feature was later found to be unnecessary).

The lives of Californios living near the mission were changed radically in 1849, when entrepreneurs built the first planked road out from Yerba Buena Cove, allowing citizens to ride or drive out to the mission in relative comfort, for a modest fee. The road followed approximately the path of today's Mission Street, parallel to Market Street, which existed only on Jasper O'Farrell's map of the town. The builders of the Mission Road ran into great difficulty and expense when they had to span an underground lake near today's Seventh Street. (Author's collection)

Adobe as a building material for California had two major drawbacks: it was vulnerable to both earthquakes and rain. In the old days, to prevent erosion, adobe walls were first given a coating of mud, inside and out, and over this a coating of lime whitewash, made of burned and pulverized shells mixed with water. This process demanded frequent re-applications, and was generally regarded as part of the women's housewifely chores. In later years it was discovered that a mixture of tar or *brea*, when added to the usual mixture of mud, straw and water, would help prevent erosion. Since a standard method of mixing the ingredients was to drive cattle round and round a watered clay pit, we can assume that there is probably another, more pungent additive in many adobe walls.

A second system for protecting walls from erosion was to shield them with wide, overhanging eaves or porches. This custom, dating from Spanish times, was carried over into the Mexican period, so that even the two-storied adobes like Larkin's by necessity were surrounded by two-story galleries. Some of these, with tall piers reaching from the ground to the roof, recalled those graceful porches found on houses of the antebellum South. But most were fronted with a double gallery with doors and windows of the second floor opening out to a covered deck. The cantilevered balcony, found on only a few two-story adobes of the Mexican period, has rightfully been accepted as a signature of the Monterey Colonial style, but historically it is rather rare. Whatever the style, all these porches were rather shallow, extending only five or six feet out from the façade.

Another innovation in the Larkin house was the hipped roof, that is, a roof with four sloping sides. Larkin's was the first roof in California to be covered with wooden shakes. Despite the popular belief that all California buildings were roofed with tiles, closer investigation shows that a thatch of tules was typical, covered with *brea* (tar) where it was available. Only at the missions, where native labor could be impressed, were tiles used. Of course, after secularization many house builders were able to scavenge tiles from the ruined mission buildings.

A pit saw at Mission Santa Cruz produced planks and beams for Larkin's house; these were sent to Monterey by ship. John Cooper established California's first steam-powered sawmill near the Russian River in 1834. John Reed's water-powered sawmill in Mill Valley followed two years later. Isaac Graham's sawmill at Santa Cruz may also have supplied Larkin with lumber.

Whether or not Larkin imported his window glass and frames from the East is a matter for conjecture, but it is known that by 1835 there were some twenty former ships' carpenters living in the vicinity of Monterey. Without question, these men, well trained in New England building skills, brought to the Larkin house those innovative features which would inspire California's early Anglo and Hispanic homebuilders of the Mexican era. Ironically, the houses that have come to be regarded as the embodiment of California's Spanish Colonial architecture bear the earmarks of New England craftsmanship and design.

The Dolores Pueblo

By 1835, one year after the Mexican Congress' secularization of mission property, five of Northern California's missions had been reduced to parish church status; Mission San Francisco was one of the unlucky number. Its once all-powerful fathers now served as parish priests for a civilian village or pueblo which was emerging on the shore of the shrinking Dolores Lagoon.

Originally it was thought that the Presidio, not the Mission, would become the nucleus for a pueblo, but of course nobody cared to settle on that treeless, windswept wasteland by the entry to the bay. Former garrison members and other settlers almost unanimously elected to move to the Dolores Pueblo and its beautiful, sheltered valley.

In 1835, Francisco de Haro became the pueblo's *alcalde*, or mayor, and moved his family into what had been the old mission barracks. Two years later, he acquired the former majordomo's large adobe house, where he raised his nine children. De Haro is best known as the father of twin sons who were gunned down in San Rafael by Kit Carson, Fremont's wilderness scout, during the Bear Flag incident in 1846; de Haro never recovered from the calamity and died of grief one year later. One of de Haro's daughters married Francisco Guerrero, who had occupied an abandoned mission building near the majordomo's house, at today's 15th and Guerrero Streets, on a small grant called *Las Camaritas*.

Another son-in-law of de Haro's, Charles Brown, was one of the American sailors sheltered by Juana Briones. For years, he and his wife lived in an adobe which still stands in Woodside, California. Then, at the death of his father-in-law, they moved to the mission pueblo. Brown wrote a fascinating description of his life in the pueblo, which is in the collection of the

Bancroft Library in Berkeley. From 1848 until his death in 1883, Brown and his wife occupied the old majordomo's mansion.

This house, which fronted the mission plaza, today the northeast corner of 16th and Dolores Streets, was a large U-shaped building (Number 10 on the map, p. 16). Before the mission was secularized, the majordomo was José Bernal, who lived in the house from 1828 until 1843, when he moved to his recently granted rancho.

Another interesting occupant of the Dolores Pueblo was Francisco Guerrero. His adobe (number 11 on the map, p. 16) was another remodeled out-building of the Mission. Originally from Tepic, Mexico, Guerrero was one of the members of the Hijar-Padres expedition of 1834. This group, led by José Hijar and José Padres, was a collection of 250 civilian colonists, ranging from professionals and artisans to hair-dressers and jewelers, all the way down to the sweepings of Mexico's jails. Rather like participants in a lottery, they were promised a share of the spoils from the secularized missions.

Governor Figueroa and such early colonists as Commandante Mariano Vallejo, however, regarded the expedition as a threat to their own power. They saw to the immediate disbanding of the company, whose members they scattered up and down the coast from San Diego to Sonoma. The two leaders, Hijar and Padres, were accused of sedition, clapped in irons and sent back to Mexico City. Nevertheless, while a fiasco, the expedition was successful in bringing a more accomplished class of settlers, such as Guerrero, to California.

Indeed, Guerrero, trained as a lawyer, left a distinguished record as a civic leader in San Francisco. He held such positions as customs collector, *juez del campo* (justice of the peace) and *alcalde* (mayor) in Yerba Buena. He also was the grantee of several town lots and ranchos, one of which was near the Presidio. He was

A pencil drawing, made by an unknown artist in 1885, shows the sad condition of the Mission buildings almost forty years after the American conquest. The adobe walls have been weakened by rain and earthquake, and many of the roof tiles and beams have been taken away to be used in newer buildings. (Author's collection)

murdered in 1851, and his widow continued to live on their mission holding into the 1880s.

All in all, some forty adobes were located near the mission. For a brief time it was thought that the mission pueblo would outdistance its Yerba Buena neighbor. Efforts to incorporate the Dolores Pueblo failed, however, and it was annexed by San Francisco in 1850.

Although they were eventually united, there were distinct early differences between Yerba Buena and the Dolores Pueblo. Yerba Buena was essentially an Anglo town, given over entirely to commerce, while the Dolores Pueblo was predominantly an Hispanic social center. With the old mission church as its nucleus, the pueblo attracted ranchers from all over Northern California. They came to attend baptisms and weddings, or to enjoy the family gatherings.

Although California's Spanish settlers were exposed to all the rigors of hardship and isolation, they knew how to make the best of things. Living out of doors in the healthful California sunshine, they were a handsome, athletic people. Tall and lithe, the young men moved with the easy grace of the athlete, while the young women were a match for their brothers and husbands in riding and swimming. Blissfully unaware of the Yankee idea that "time is money," they whiled away their days, riding across their land, horse-racing, attending bull-and-bear fights, or dancing. Bancroft's *California Pastoral* gives us a wonderfully active picture of the sort of fiesta which might have been held at the Dolores Pueblo. This picture certainly differs from Hollywood's notions of what a Spanish *baile* (ball) was like.

BANCROFT RECOUNTS how a group of young people could be summoned with little notice to attend a ball which might begin in the early afternoon and last well into the following morning. In preparation for the *baile*, a large space in front of a house was cleared for the erection of an arbor, roofed with boughs, with three sides covered with white cotton cloth and decorated with ribbons and flowers. The fourth side was left open, and there a group of horsemen would jockey for a favored position along the fence, which was used to prevent the intrusion of horses. Around the three enclosed sides were seats for the women. The musicians, consisting of a violinist, a guitarist, and two or three singers, stationed themselves in a corner, out of the way.

The master of ceremonies, *El Bastoñero*, organized everything for the ball. It was his duty to lead each of the women out when they danced alone. Clapping his hands, he would take steps to the music in front of the lady whom he chose to call out. Rising, she would move to the center of the enclosure and, with both hands extending her skirts to either side, she would execute a heel and toe shuffle known as a *jarabe*. This movement demands that the body be held in a rigidly upright position, and it always surprised the Anglo visitors, who had expected something more flamboyant. After taking a turn or two in the center of the room, the woman would retire, her place being taken by another young lady.

During couples' dances, the horseman who wished to take part dismounted, removed his spurs and hung them on his saddle horn. Then, with hat in hand, he would step into the enclosure to select a partner. When the piece ended, he would guide the lady back to her place and return to his saddle.

Californios called these balls *fandangos*, and though all were much alike, there were countless variations on the theme. In some, the couples danced facing one another until the music suddenly halted, at which time the man was expected to recite a couplet extolling his lady's charms. Then the dance would continue as before. At other times, a couple would be joined by additional dancers. Holding hands, the group would extend into two circles, the men on the outside and the women within. When the music stopped, the man would dance with the partner facing him.

With the coming of later, more worldly colonists, the waltz was adopted by the Californios, despite threats of excommunication made by the scandalized padres. Don Juan Bandini, son of a migrant from Andalusia, Spain, introduced the waltz to the people of San Diego, and from there it swept the province. One charming custom was the *Cascarone* ball, in which eggshells filled with perfumed confetti would be broken over the head of an unsuspecting dance partner. In such merrymaking the people of Dolores Pueblo passed their leisure hours. Many of the Anglos who first settled in California discarded their own puritanical notions to join in the fun.

Over time the neighboring trading post of Yerba Buena grew into the City of San Francisco, and the Dolores Pueblo was absorbed into its larger, more commercially-oriented neighbor. The notion that the Dolores Pueblo was once intended to be its own incorporated town was soon forgotten. A perfect symbol of this decline is the story of the adobe dwelling of Candelario Valencia, one of the Dolores Pueblo's earliest residents.

For several decades, the members of the diminishing Valencia clan clung stubbornly to their decaying relic of a house, which stood on the south side of Sixteenth Street, between Dolores and Guerrero. Then, in the winter storm of 1878, the rambling old pile completely collapsed. To neighbors who had long regarded the adobe as an eyesore, the fall of the house of Valencia was a matter for rejoicing. Digging through the ruins, they found an old man who had holed up in one of the less damaged rooms. Saying that he was a surviving member of the Valencia family, the old man told them that the glory that had once been associated with the Valencias had vanished long ago and was just as well forgotten. Then he slowly walked away and was never seen in the neighborhood again.

THE WORLD OF JUANA BRIONES

ONE OF THE MOST fascinating figures in San Francisco's early history is the Widow Briones. Because a few documents concerning her life were rescued from the ruined Hall of Records in 1906, and because her little adobe ranch house has become one of the oldest landmarks in Los Altos, some 45 miles south of San Francisco, she is better known than most of her contemporaries. Born in 1796, she lived to be almost one hundred years old. But she is perhaps most noteworthy as the first householder in San Francisco's North Beach, and also as California's first divorcee.

Juana Briones was born at the mission at Carmel in 1796. Her parents died young, and she and her twin sister, Luz, were sent to the San Francisco mission to be reared. At the age of twenty, rather an advanced age for that day, she married Apolinario Miranda, a soldier at the San Francisco Presidio. It wasn't until 1833 that the couple, now with five children, could move from their crowded two-room quarters in the old Presidio compound to a small plot of land outside the Presidio walls. Today the intersection of Lyon and Green Streets marks the site of their small adobe. Nearby was a well, known as *Ojo de Agua de Figueroa*, which gave the little two-acre rancho its name.

When the Presidio *comandante*, Lt. Mariano Vallejo, was ordered to transfer his command to Sonoma in the mid-1830s, the Mirandas detached themselves completely from Presidial duties and moved across the sandy wasteland to the western foot of Telegraph Hill. Here, near today's intersection of Powell and Filbert Streets and the playground of Saints Peter and Paul Church, the couple built a one-and-a-half-story adobe, the first private house built between the Presidio and the mission. Perhaps it was also at this time that Juana adopted three more children, orphans taken off a ship bound for Australia.

With eight children to care for, the growing family certainly needed a much larger house for its future. In the meantime, however, Juana decided that her crowded adobe could do with one less occupant — namely her sparring-partner husband. Today, old documents tell us what the family's Presidio neighbors must have known all along: this couple was not "living in perfect harmony." Official papers from the *Alcalde*'s office

There are no known pictures of Juana Briones; this artist's conception, drawn by Robert Gebing, is based on a description and a picture of a niece. From *Los Altos Hills*, by Florence Fava [1976]. (Courtesy Gilbert Richards)

ordered that the couple be separated at a distance of not less than fifty miles "to avoid the impertinences of Señora Briones' husband." (It is interesting to note that Apolinario Miranda is referred to as "Señora Briones' husband"; nowhere is she referred to as Señora Miranda.) The Señora received custody of the house and the children, becoming California's first divorcee. Shortly after the separation, Miranda died and was buried in the mission cemetery, but even before her husband's demise, Juana was known as "The Widow Briones."

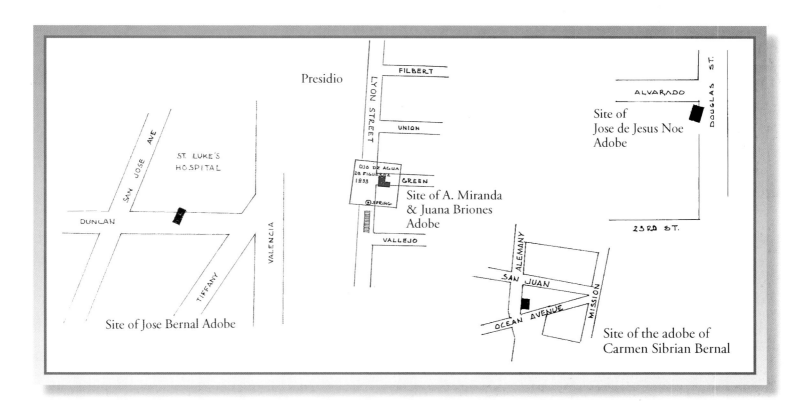

These diagrams show the location of four adobe houses from the Mexican period.

This view of North Beach, painted in 1849 by an artist named Tobin, shows the shallow cove extending far inland, with North Point and Black Point (today's Fort Mason) ranged behind it. The small buildings on the beach were probably put up during the year since the discovery of gold. But the more substantial buildings further inland, at left, were probably older. Juana Briones' house, with one story plus an attic and a veranda, stood in today's Washington Square, which would be precisely the area at the left of this picture. (Courtesy Society of California Pioneers)

Besides her busy life as a nurse and midwife at both the Presidio and the Mission, the Widow Briones found time to raise some cows and to tend a vegetable garden in the area of today's Washington Square. Aside from these occupations, this enterprising woman also rented horses to sailors on shore leave. Most interestingly of all, she offered her attic as sanctuary to more than one sea-weary tar who jumped ship at Yerba Buena Cove. There she would keep the escapee hidden until her brother, Felipe, could remove him to a safer spot down the peninsula.

The Widow Briones lived in remote circumstances, at least until the Yerba Buena settlement was established nearby. Her fame as a healer and her generosity made her a legend even in her own time, when today's North Beach was called "La Playa de Juana Briones." According to one legend, she was caring for a sick Indian girl from the Mission one night, preparing a broth to cure the child, when the wind blew out her fire. Fearing that the girl would die without this warm brew, she saddled a horse and rode several miles in the dark to reach the Presidio, where she picked up a flaming brand and returned to North Beach. This legend has no finale, but we must assume that she re-lit her fire, heated the curative broth and restored the Indian girl to health.

Juana Briones's ability to meet any emergency with dispatch was recalled by a young American sailor, who described a visit to this good woman. When he asked her for some milk for his shipmates, then living on a ship anchored in the bay, Juana handed him a well-scrubbed chamber pot filled to the brim with milk, with the instruction that the vessel be returned *muy pronto.* "If half the men in California were as enterprising as this good lady, California would be in a far more prosperous state," he said.

About 1845 Juana bought *Rancho La Purisima Concepcion,* the site of today's Los Altos and Los Altos Hills, where she lived for more than fifty years, raising livestock and farming, caring for her children and grandchildren, and dispensing remedies and hospitality to all who needed help. Charles Lyman, a surveyor, stopped at Juana's rancho in 1848:

> We find our quarters at Madam Briones quite comfortable. The family is composed of the Widow Briones, three daughters (two grown), two or three boys, half a dozen Indians, two little pet pigs in the cook house and fifteen or twenty dogs . . there are two sick persons in the house, an Indian girl, of fever, and a man, a sailor, apparently a Portuguese, who has a very bad cough.

Described by her grandchildren, Juana Briones was tall and handsome, with a light complexion. She wore her hair in two long, dark braids, and across her shoulders she draped a lavender shawl. So she passes from recollection, one remarkable figure from San Francisco's earliest days.

RANCHOS IN SAN FRANCISCO

GIVEN SAN FRANCISCO'S NARROW geographical limitations, it might be surprising to find that, aside from the lands occupied by the Presidio, the Dolores Pueblo, and Yerba Buena, there was still room for twelve private land grants inside today's city limits. These ranged in size from the 1.77-acre grant next to the Presidio, made to Apolinario Miranda, Juana Briones's abusive husband, to the grant of 14,639 acres made to José Antonio Sanchez, a famous Indian fighter and former *comandante* of the Presidio. These grants, made by California's Mexican governors, followed on the heels of mission secularization in 1834.

The mission was still in operation in 1827, when José Sanchez received tentative approval for his *Rancho Buri Buri*, which stretched from the southeastern edge of today's city limits southward, to include present-day Colma, South San Francisco, San Bruno, Millbrae and north Burlingame. The mission's claim to all lands south of the mission village held up actual confirmation of the grant until 1835, after secularization. As late as 1841, the twin sons of Francisco de Haro petitioned Governor Micheltorena for permission to run their cattle on the land known as *Potrero Nuevo* (New Pasture); the governor did give permission for the boys to use the unoccupied half league of land, but he made it clear that this property rightfully still belonged to the mission neophytes and could not be sold. The grant was eventually approved, thanks to powerful men like Mariano Vallejo and his cousin, Governor Juan Alvarado. De Haro Street today crosses Potrero Hill, commemorating the de Haro family.

In 1839 *Alcalde* Francisco Sanchez, son of Jose, was granted the *Rancho San Pedro*, the large, well-developed *asistencia* to Mission Dolores on the site of today's Pacifica. The 8,926-acre rancho, dating to the 1780s, included an adobe quadrangle with a small church, storehouses, and extensive living quarters; their sites are identified by historic markers today. At one time the *asistencia* was home to more than 800 native converts. It was then known as *La Cañada de las Almejas* (Valley of the Clams), in memory of the feast of shellfish held in that canyon by the starving members of Captain Portola's expedition in 1769. This site is listed as State Registered Landmark #393.

Only a few yards west of the *asistencia* site is the handsome two-story adobe ranch house built by Don Francisco Sanchez. Completely restored and furnished with the correct period furniture, this Monterey Colonial style house (State Landmark #391, one mile from the coastal highway south of Pacifica) is the only surviving Mexican era adobe house located in what was once San Francisco County. The era of the rancho was rapidly becoming history when, in 1856, the southern portion of San Francisco County became the newly established San Mateo County. The new county line, besides ceding Rancho San Pedro and Rancho Buri Buri to San Mateo, ran across the boundaries of three other ranchos in the southern portion of San Francisco County: *Rancho Visitacion*, Bernal's *Rancho Potrero Viejo*, and Francisco de Haro's *Rancho Laguna de la Merced*.

In 1841, the *Rancho Visitacion* (full name: *Rancho Cañada de Guadalupe de la Visitacion y Rodeo Viejo*, which included today's Visitation Valley) consisting of some 8,900 acres, was granted to a wheeler-dealer from Ohio, Jacob Leese, a co-founder of Yerba Buena. Since Leese had recently married General Vallejo's sister Rosalia, he apparently felt it prudent to locate himself closer to his brother-in-law's seat of power; he immediately swapped his San Francisco rancho for the Rancho Huichica, a four-league tract between the Sonoma and Napa Valleys. This feat of Yankee ranch-swapping, unique in the rancho period, made Robert Ridley the owner of Rancho Visitacion. Bancroft describes Ridley as a handsome Cockney saloonkeeper who married one of Juana Briones's daughters. The ranch house, probably built by Ridley, since Leese's tenure was so short, stood near what is now Alvarado Street in Brisbane, west of Visitacion Avenue. Duboce Street in San Francisco was once named for Ridley.

In 1839 José Cornelio Bernal (pronounced bear-*nahl*) was the grantee of *Rancho El Rincon De Las Salinas y Potrero Viejo*, loosely "The Salt Flats and the Old Pasture," 6,780 acres south and east of the mission, whose old pasture gave the rancho its name, and down past the present city limit. The Bernals' modest adobe ranch house stood at the southern edge of today's St. Luke's Hospital. After Bernal's death in 1852, his widow, Carmen Sibrian (sometimes spelled Cebrian or Cibrian) built a house for herself at the present corner of Alemany Boulevard and Ocean Avenue. Later maps, dating to the early 1850s, show the Bernal rancho belonging to Robert Ridley.

IN 1845, José de Jesus Noe, a justice of the peace and resident of the Dolores pueblo since 1834, requested from Governor Pio Pico a grant of one square league (4,340 acres), known as *Rancho San Miguel*. Bordering

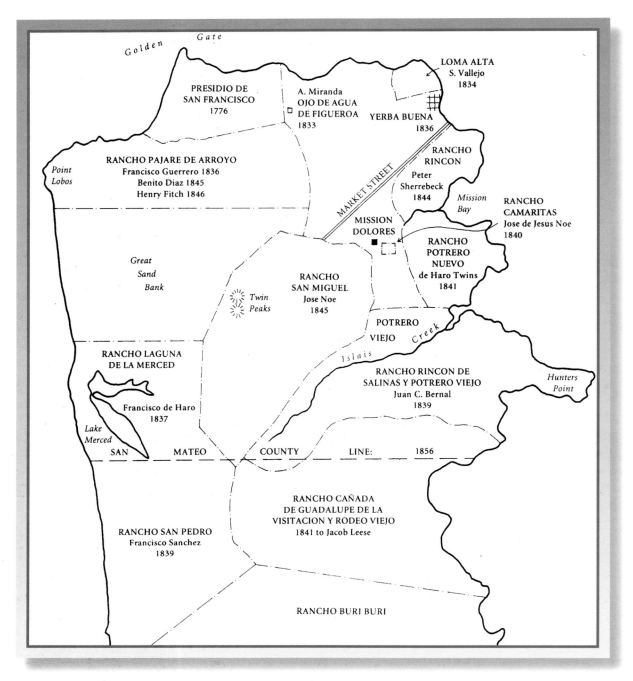

This map of the land grants within the boundaries of San Francisco can only be approximate, because no two sources agree exactly on the borders of the grants. Two or three of the grants changed hands during the Mexican period, which led to confusion when the claimants appeared before the U.S. Land Commission beginning is 1851.

the great sand bank on the west, it covered the western slopes of Twin Peaks, extending north to today's Golden Gate Park, adjoining Bernal's ranch on the south and the Dolores pueblo on the east. Noe's "mansion" was a one-story adobe facing today's Douglass Street near Alvarado. In the land commission hearings this house was described as being worth $30,000, an enormous sum even in the 1850s, when carpenters were getting $16 per day.

Noe, like Guerrero, was a member of the Hijar-Padres Metropolitan Company which brought a number of professional people from Mexico. Obviously Noe had some education, for he was immediately appointed *Jues de Campo* (Justice of the Peace), served as assistant *alcalde*, and after the American conquest, as treasurer under Lt. Bartlett's administration as *alcalde*. In 1840 Noe was the owner of the small Rancho Camaritos, on the northwest corner of 16th and Mission Streets. This holding was taken over in 1846 by Francisco Guerrero. Both Guerrero and Noe passed their later years at the Dolores pueblo.

Rancho Laguna de la Merced (named for Our Lady of Mercy), a half-league tract which included Lake Merced, was granted in 1835 to José Galindo, a corporal in the San Francisco militia. Two years later he traded the entire 2,180 acres to Lt. Francisco de Haro for 100 cows and $25 in goods; one wonders where he pastured his cows, having traded his land for them.

In that same year, 1837, de Haro was elected *alcalde*, and in the following year he had to order the imprisonment of his old friend Galindo, who had done somebody in. This created something of a dilemma for de Haro, as there was no secure jail in the pueblo. After keeping Galindo under guard for some time, de Haro finally sent him to jail in San Jose, which had a sturdy *calabozo*. With so few families living in the pueblo, such happenings must have been awkward. De Haro, incidentally, was married to a daughter of his neighbor, José Sanchez. It was certainly a tight little world for the residents of the pueblo, with so many of the families intermarried.

Francisco de Haro's twin sons, Ramon and Francisco, were gunned down by "The Great Pathfinder," Kit Carson in 1846, under the order of General John C. Fremont, who told Carson not to bother with taking prisoners. The two boys and the aging José Berryessa were on their way to Sonoma to see how Berryessa's cousin, Sonoma's *alcalde*, had fared during the Bear Flag uprising. Just as their raft reached the *embarcadero* of Mission San Rafael, the three unarmed men were shot by Carson and his men. In later years, when Fremont was running for President of the U.S., his political foes did not hesitate to bring up the ghosts of a defenseless old man and two martyred boys. Fremont lost the election.

Rancho Pajare de Arroyo (Place of the Ravine), granted in 1836 to Francisco Guerrero and in 1844 to Benito Diaz, covered a half-league to the south of the Presidio and extending west to Pt. Lobos. Diaz was in charge of the customs house in Yerba Buena. Guerrero, a man of outstanding position and character, was best known for the strawberry fiestas he held annually near Pt. Lobos. Since the earliest times this area had been known for the succulent wild strawberries flourishing in the sandy soil. Each spring when the berries ripened Guerrero would invite all his friends and neighbors to a huge barbecue and feast, with music for dancing. The custom seems to have continued well into the 1850s.

In 1846 a portion of the area south of the Presidio was granted to Henry Delano Fitch, a son-in-law of General Vallejo. The U.S. Land Commission, sitting in the 1850s, heard conflicting claims from Fitch, Guerrero and Diaz, and denied all of them. Only the Widow Briones was able to get a patent on her claim for the tiny 1.77-acre *Ojo de Agua de Figueroa* (*Ojo de Agua* was a spring, literally an "eye of water"), but it took her twenty years to get approval.

Another of the claims denied by the Land Commission in the 1850s was that of Jacob Leese and Salvador Vallejo, younger brother of Mariano Vallejo, for a tract of land called *Punta de Loma Alta* (Point of the High Hill). This tract, including Telegraph Hill and the land surrounding it, was supposed to have been given to Leese and Vallejo in 1839.

Peter Sherrebeck, a native of Denmark, came to Yerba Buena as a trader in 1840. Four years later he was granted the *Rancho Rincon* (the Corner Ranch), a modest-sized but valuable hill separating Yerba Buena Cove from Mission Bay. Sherrebeck held the office of Port Collector in 1846, and was a member of the town council in 1847.

During the 25 years of Mexican rule, California saw the development of seven trading centers and over a thousand large ranchos. The settlers, once freed of Spain's bureaucratic controls, were able to govern their affairs fairly well. Happily isolated from the constant wars and upheavals perpetrated by the ruling families struggling for control of the Mexican empire, Californios were left pretty much on their own. When the government sent dictatorial governors to California, the Californios would often send them back to Mexico City. Trade with the Yankees gave the Californios financial independence and enabled them to create a pleasant and stable society, despite their rustic isolation. Ironically, the aggressive Yankee commercialism which made their pleasant life possible eventually spelt its doom.

One incident illustrates the changing face of life in the San Francisco area after the American military takeover of California in 1846. Four years went by before California was granted statehood in 1850. During that period, the military governors wisely allowed people to continue the same form of local government they had established under Mexican rule, with some changes in personnel. Lt. Washington Bartlett, U.S.N., was given the post of *alcalde* of Yerba Buena. (In 1847 he changed the name to San Francisco.) Military custom has always been to maintain troops by foraging off the land and requisitioning supplies from the citizens of the occupied territory. The *rancheros* of California did not take kindly to this practice.

In December 1846 Bartlett led an armed scouting party to Rancho San Pedro, where he planned to requi-

The last surviving adobe residence in the city stood near the corner of 20th and de Haro Streets on Potrero Hill. It was still there when a row of Edwardian houses was built along de Haro Street, at the right of the adobe, and it survived until the 1930s. (Courtesy California Historical Society)

sition supplies, horses and cattle. Francisco Sanchez and several other angry *rancheros* and their *vaqueros* captured the party and took them to a camp in a marshy area near Mission San Jose. The *rancheros* planned to use the captives as hostages, and to demand that the seizure of private property should stop. A contingent of American troops set off down the peninsula with a cannon, ready to do battle for the prisoners. When they reached the camp a skirmish took place. Amid the popping of muskets came three mighty reports from the cannon. There were no casualties, although several Californios were said to have been scared to death. The cannon became stuck in the mud and had to be left there. On January 3, after a cease-fire, the two sides sat down to talk, and a few days later they agreed on a treaty stipulating no more raids on the ranchos. Thus ended the "Battle of the Tules," as it was later called.

PRESIDENT JOHN F. KENNEDY once raised the ire of a lot of Texans when he said that "the Mexican War was not our shining hour." With guns and troops, we backed up the squatters who had settled in California and refused to become Mexican citizens. We acquired California and all of our southwestern states under the slogan of "Manifest Destiny." If the tactics used to grab those territories cause us some embarrassment, our legal treatment of the Hispanic settlers in those territories should indeed make us blush.

With the signing of the Treaty of Guadalupe Hidalgo in 1848, it was understood that all former citizens in the occupied territories would be entitled to claim their lands and property under the new government. The ink on this treaty was hardly dry when California was inundated by thousands of Yankee migrants who, under the banner of Manifest Destiny, began helping themselves to the choicest pieces of land. Squatters arrived and settled on land that looked empty; boundaries of Mexican land grants were approximate at best. Many Mexican citizens were illiterate, and could not read even the papers which substantiated their claims; virtually none of them spoke English, which was the language in which the U.S. Land Commission—usually called the Claims Court—conducted its hearings. It was a great day for lawyers and money lenders. Typically a lawyer would offer to represent the claimant for a substantial fee, or for a large portion of the land being claimed. The claimant either had to borrow money to pay the lawyer, who saw to it that the case dragged on for months or even years, or surrender a part of his property. Or the lawyer, sometimes in collusion with the judge, would arrange to buy the claim for a few cents per acre. Many claims were not settled for years, even decades; a number of cases went to the Supreme Court. Disputes over title still turn up in cases today.

The biggest, most important building in San Francisco, the Montgomery Block (1854) was tenanted almost entirely by lawyers. Over a thousand claims were brought before the Claims Court; fewer than 600 were confirmed for the claimants.

In 1820, Don Luis Peralta of San Jose received the earliest land grant made in the San Francisco Bay Area. His huge grant contained some 43,000 acres, encompassing the present East Bay cities of San Leandro, Oakland, Alameda, Emeryville, Piedmont, and Berkeley. Although the land might technically be deemed a Spanish grant, Peralta's land came in the last hours of Spanish claim to California, at a time when contact with the revolution-torn capital in Mexico City, much less with the mother country, would have been nearly impossible. This grant therefore must be attributed to Governor Sola, California's last Spanish and first Mexican governor, who ruled from August 1815 to November 1822.

After the Yankee conquest squatters began fencing off portions of the Peralta rancho. During the 1850s thousands of Peralta's cattle were rustled and transported by night to the slaughter houses in South San Francisco. San Leandro, Oakland and Berkeley had all been established on their land before the Peraltas received any satisfaction from their claims. One of the Peralta brothers was able to save his own house only by leasing it to the French consul; it stood a better chance of protection under a foreign flag.

It is true that the land grant boundaries were very roughly established, by maps called *diseños* (designs), which were not drawn to any scale. They were sketches showing hills, trees, streams, rocks, or other landmarks in order to establish points of ownership. Many such landmarks were subject to change. Ownership had often depended upon agreement with one's neighbors. The Claims Court could not regard such drawings as proof of exact boundaries.

The author has found four "official" maps dating from the 1840s to the 1860s, each purporting to establish the boundaries of the twelve land grants in San Francisco. No two of these maps agree; the differences often amount to hundreds of acres. Little wonder that the courts found it difficult to judge the validity of a claim.

YERBA BUENA
1836 - 1847

WHEN YERBA BUENA was chartered by Governor Figueroa on June 25, 1835, to become the trading center for the Port of San Francisco, a grumble of disapproval went up from the ranchers around the Bay. Yerba Buena's location, at the isolated tip of the San Francisco Peninsula, was far removed from the ranchos around the Bay's perimeters, which stretched as far north as Sonoma and as far south as San Jose. Transporting goods at that time required the use of groaning *carretas*, pulled by plodding teams of oxen, and thus the ranchers had hoped for a more accessible trading center. With the establishment of Yerba Buena, however, ranchers now had to transport their loads of hides and tallow to the most inaccessible spot in the entire Bay Area.

The settlement was named *"El Pajare de Yerba Buena"* (The Place of Good Herbs) for the beds of sweet-smelling mint which grew near the inner cove of the bay, sheltered from the storms which blew in from the Pacific. Since Vancouver's visit, sailors had preferred it as a docking place over the smaller cove at the foot of the Presidio. Their choice was significant, for it was now up to the Yankee merchants and skippers to determine where and when they would establish their commercial center.

In keeping with San Francisco's flavor today, the little town from which it grew was remarkably diverse. Yerba Buena's first foreign settlers, though few in number, were cosmopolitan. The majority were either English or American. There were also two Danes, a Swiss national, and a sprinkling of French in the budding metropolis.

William Antonio Richardson, a native of Kent, England, was Yerba Buena's first resident. Arriving in 1822, he began his new life by teaching boat building at the San Francisco Mission. In order to acquire acreage in what is today Marin County, he converted to Catholicism and thereby earned the Mexican citizenship required to own land in California. Shortly thereafter, he married Maria Antonia Martinez, daughter of the Presidio Comandante, Ignacio Martinez.

The Richardsons moved to Mission San Gabriel in 1829, where William worked as a builder. Then, in 1835, when General Vallejo appointed him Captain of the Port of San Francisco, he and his wife moved to an elevated spot above what would soon become

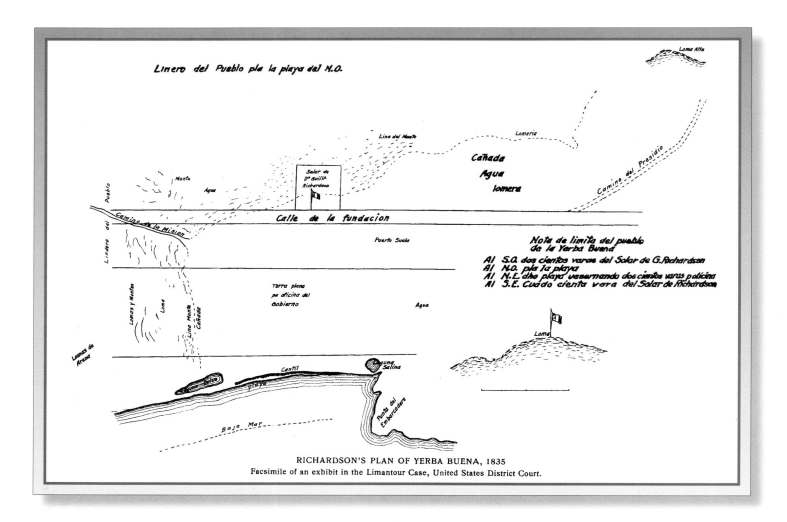

RICHARDSON'S PLAN OF YERBA BUENA, 1835
Facsimile of an exhibit in the Limantour Case, United States District Court.

William A. Richardson was asked by the Mexican Governor to lay out a plan for the Yerba Buena Pueblo in 1835, so that trading ships could anchor in the sheltered cove, rather than in the violent tides and surf near the Presidio. Richardson's plan shows the Calle de la Fundacion as the centerpiece (it would later become Dupont, then Grant Avenue). Above it he claimed a parcel of land as his own, with the Mexican flag marking it. Trails led to the Mission (left) and the Presidio (right). At bottom, the *playa* (beach) is today's Montgomery Street. The tiny Laguna Salina at right was a tidal lagoon, where the first bridge in California would be built, at the foot of Jackson Street. The Lina Monte Cañada follows the present course of Sacramento Street, and leads to a fresh-water lagoon. At right, on Telegraph Hill (Loma),flies the Mexican flag. Other hills surround the pueblo, whose borders are roughly today's' Pine Street on the left and Stockton Street at the top. (Author's collection)

Yerba Buena in March, 1847. Leidesdorff's house, second from left, with a hip roof, is at California & Montgomery Streets, with his hide-and-tallow warehouse just below, on the beach. Along Montgomery Street, on the waterfront, are the Hudson's Bay store, Nathan Spear's store, and Hinckley's house. Sam Brannan's house is just above the Custom House, behind the flagpole in the Plaza.; Brown's Hotel, at Clay and Kearney, is apparently the largest building in town. Twin Peaks and Lone Mountain rise in the background. (Courtesy California State Library)

Portsmouth Plaza. Here he erected a shelter of redwood boards, roofed over with a canvas sail. This simple shack was the first house in what would become the actual site of San Francisco.

The following year this make-do arrangement was replaced by Richardson's imposing Monterey style adobe, "La Casa Grande," which may be discerned vaguely in views of Yerba Buena from the 1840s. Of one and a half stories, with a row of dormer windows projecting from its hipped roof, the house contained eight rooms and a *sala* large enough for dancing. The latter feature seems to have been a prerequisite; at least one old-timer recalled that "In Mexican California every house was a ballroom."

Shortly before Richardsons' canvas shelter was replaced in 1836, another foreigner, Ohio native Jacob Primer Leese, arrived in Yerba Buena from Monterey, where he had engaged in the hide and tallow trade.

The frame house he erected on the lot adjoining Richardson's was a substantial structure some twenty by sixty feet. Years later, it too would be declared San Francisco's first permanent dwelling, though at the time it was known as "Wind Whistle Lodge."

And so it is left to us to decide whether either of these houses, Richardson's or Leese's, deserves the title of "San Francisco's first," since "San Francisco" here means only the pueblo of Yerba Buena, excluding the Presidio and the Mission buildings, as well as Juana Briones's house and several other adobes. Further complicating the matter, a building in today's Chinatown, on the southwest corner of Grant Avenue and Clay Streets, bears a bronze plaque stating that it was the site of Leese's dwelling, San Francisco's first house, and that the city's "first white child" (Rosalia Vallejo Leese) was born here in 1838. One may well imagine how the descendants of our Spanish pioneers feel about that.

41

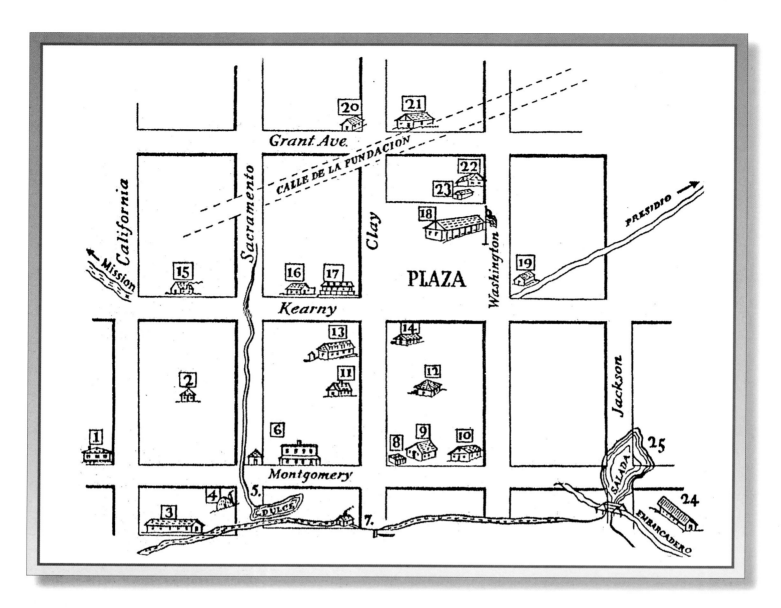

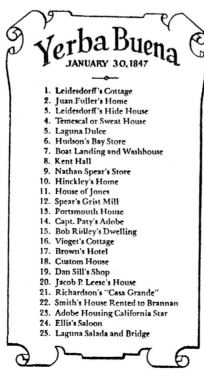

Yerba Buena
JANUARY 30, 1847

1. Leidesdorff's Cottage
2. Juan Fuller's Home
3. Leidesdorff's Hide House
4. Temescal or Sweat House
5. Laguna Dulce
6. Hudson's Bay Store
7. Boat Landing and Washhouse
8. Kent Hall
9. Nathan Spear's Store
10. Hinckley's Home
11. House of Jones
12. Spear's Grist Mill
13. Portsmouth House
14. Capt. Paty's Adobe
15. Bob Ridley's Dwelling
16. Vioget's Cottage
17. Brown's Hotel
18. Custom House
19. Dan Sill's Shop
20. Jacob P. Leese's House
21. Richardson's "Casa Grande"
22. Smith's House Rented to Brannan
23. Adobe Housing California Star
24. Ellis's Saloon
25. Laguna Salada and Bridge

This diagram, from a charming book called *An Hour's Walk through Yerba Buena*, by Douglas S. Watson [1937], shows the buildings in the little settlement just before its name was changed to San Francisco. The drawings are remarkably accurate, even showing the bridge across the saltwater lagoon at the foot of Jackson Street, and the stream running down Sacramento Street to the freshwater pond, where native Americans had built a Temescal or sweat house. Richardson's original "Calle de la Fundacion" runs beneath the two original houses (20 & 21) belonging to Leese and Richardson. (Courtesy San Francisco Public Library)

This view, painted in 1849-1850, shows William Leidesdorff's house (left), with its sheltering galleries and pyramidal roof, at the southwest corner of today's California and Montgomery Streets. In 1846 the Leidesdorff house was the most civilized dwelling in San Francisco, with a flower garden, imported furniture, and room for a reasonably large reception for Commodore Stockton. (Author's collection)

Actually the first white child was born in San Francisco on August 10, 1776, to the wife of a soldier named De Soto.

Leese's house was completed on July 4th, 1836, a perfect occasion for its shrewd Yankee occupant to throw San Francisco's first public relations party. The celebration made social history in Yerba Buena, for some sixty guests attended from the Presidio, the Mission, Sonoma, and all the ranchos around the settlement. Three vessels in the harbor, two American and one Mexican, contributed bunting for the occasion; the American and Mexican flags floated amicably above. Members of the ships' crews provided music, punctuated from time to time by a five-pounder aboard one of the ships. Dancing and feasting continued for two days and the intervening night. General Vallejo, who had brought his large family from Sonoma, gave a fine speech on the life of General Washington, and of course there were toasts that lasted well into the night. Surprisingly, only one casualty resulted from all this merriment: a sailor came down with colic from drinking too much lemon extract.

One surprising outcome of Leese's grand celebration was his marriage in 1837 to General Vallejo's sister, Rosalia. Although the General was said to have rather disapproved of this match, Leese eventually moved to Sonoma with his new bride. His adobe mansion still stands today on one side of the Sonoma Plaza. In time, like many another naturalized Mexican from the East, he became one of California's largest landowners. And like many other naturalized landowners, he lost everything after the American occupation.

Jacob Primer Leese was a first-class wheeler-dealer. He swapped his first land grant, the Visitacion Valley Rancho, to Robert Ridley for Rancho Huichica, between Sonoma and Napa. In 1849 he acquired a huge grant in the Salinas Valley—indeed, most of the Salinas Valley. He lost both of these grants to squatters and to lawyers in his legal battles before the Land Commission in the 1850s. We next find him dealing with Mexico's deposed President Benito Juarez, during the Maximilian-Carlotta debacle of the early 1860s, for the entire Baja California peninsula. When this deal fell through, his wife, Rosalia Vallejo Leese, divorced him, claiming that he had squandered her dowry. She turned their Monterey home, the former Larkin Adobe, into a boarding house to support herself and their eight children. Leese moved to Texas to try to recoup his losses. When his schemes there fell through, he returned to San Francisco a broken man. In his last years he worked as a janitor-custodian for the Society of California Pioneers, an organization which he had founded.

ON THE 4TH OF JULY IN 1836, however, Leese and his party were a complete success. One may well imagine the charming spectacle of *caballeros* in slashed pantaloons, scarlet waistbands and vests embroidered in gold thread, as they whirled to a waltz with señoritas in gowns of brilliant red and yellow satin, subdued by traditional shawls and headdresses of black lace. Then there were the more sober ruffled linen shirts and high chokers of the Yankee traders. Yankee and Californio alike danced and made merry until dawn, and then it all began again. "Our fourth ended after our

San Francisco looks substantial in 1849, just as the onslaught of immigrants was beginning. Leidesdorff's cottage (with a pyramidal roof, far left) was no longer the grandest house in town. Hotels and houses had grown up around the plaza, where the flag flies over the Customs House. Warehouses stand at the waterfront, and a few small houses are scattered on Telegraph Hill. (Author's collection)

fifth," wrote Leese. So, after the dancing, the picnics and the bull and bear fights, the Peraltas, Vallejos, Estudillos, the de Haros and Bernals, and the other great land owners began their long trek back to their ranchos on the far-flung hills.

Despite this dazzling beginning, it wasn't until 1844 that Mexican officials regarded Yerba Buena as worthy of having its own Custom House. This structure, which stood in the northwest corner of Portsmouth Plaza, later became witness to all the frantic activity of the Gold Rush. Characteristically for that time, the young 49ers referred to it as "The Old Custom House" when it was only four years old. Since Yerba Buena was created to be a commercial center, the Custom House was the pueblo's most important building. Made of adobes manufactured by native labor and roofed with tiles swiped from the deserted Presidio buildings, it nevertheless cost some $2,800, a substantial sum for that day.

With Portsmouth Plaza as the center of activity, Yerba Buena slowly grew to become a community of twenty houses by 1841. In 1837 Jean Jacques Vioget, a Swiss immigrant, drafted the second town plan,using Richardson's *Calle De Fundacion* as the starting point. This first street in San Francisco followed roughly the path of Grant Avenue from Pine to Jackson Street. In 1843 a warehouse for the British Hudson's Bay Company was built on the beach (Montgomery Street). By 1846, Yerba Buena could boast a population of some two hundred souls.

An interesting resident of Yerba Buena at this time was William Leidesdorff, a man of color who lived a remarkable life until he was cut down by pneumonia at the age of 38. Born in the Virgin Islands in 1810, of a black mother and a Danish father, Leidesdorff sailed into San Francisco Bay from New Orleans in 1841 in his own 106-ton schooner. For four years he skippered

trading voyages between San Francisco and Hawaii. As an agent for the Russian-American Fur Company, he collected payments of wheat from Captain Johann Sutter for his purchase of Fort Ross. In 1841 Governor Micheltorena granted Leidesdorff the 35,000-acre Rancho de los Americanos, on the site of today's town of Folsom.

In Yerba Buena, Leidesdorff was named American Vice-Consul, despite the fact that he was not an American citizen. His industriousness was amazing. He bought a side-wheel steamboat from the Russians at Sitka, Alaska, brought it down to San Francisco, and piloted it around the bay and up to Sacramento; it was the first steamboat in California. He built Yerba Buena's first hotel, as well as a warehouse and a wharf at the foot of Pine Street. He served as the town's first treasurer, and when he died in 1848, the townspeople went into deep mourning. He was buried at the San Francisco Mission.

A well-known view of San Francisco in 1849 has in its foreground the adobe house which Leidesdorff bought from Robert Ridley in 1843 at California and Montgomery Streets. With its pyramidal roof and wrap-around porches, the cottage was a clear example of the Monterey style. Jessie Benton Fremont described the house in her recollections of San Francisco in 1849. Although it had only four rooms, the cottage had at least one fireplace, and was furnished with handsome furniture of rosewood and mahogany. There was also a fine flower garden, an almost unheard-of luxury at that time. Leidesdorff Street, just off California near the former site of this house, is the only reminder of one of San Francisco's founders and first leading citizens.

On a July morning in 1846, all 250 citizens of Yerba Buena assembled in the plaza to hear Captain John Montgomery of the battleship *Portsmouth* announce the

Mormon elder Samuel Brannan built his house on Stockton Street near Portsmouth Plaza. It was later moved closer to the plaza to become the post office of Gold Rush San Francisco. In the lean-to on the left were kept the presses for California's first newspaper, the *California Star*. (Courtesy California State Library)

Samuel Brannan

Jacob Leese

annexation of California to the United States. He raised the American flag over the plaza, which would thereafter be known as "Portsmouth Plaza," after Montgomery's ship. Music for the occasion was provided by members of the *Portsmouth's* crew.

A year later, *Alcalde* Washington Bartlett stood in the plaza to announce publicly that Yerba Buena would henceforth be known as San Francisco. Two weeks later the dynamic Mormon elder, Samuel Brannan, sailed into the port of San Francisco with 250 men, women and children, hoping to claim California as a Mormon possession. Learning that California was already a possession of the United States, he and his disappointed followers nevertheless settled down in San Francisco, thus nearly doubling the population. He built a spacious frame house called "The Brannan Mansion," which became the home of the *California Star*, the first English language newspaper in the province. By now San Francisco could claim 157 buildings crowding the perimeters of Ports-mouth Plaza and the immediate vicinity.

In all, it was a leisurely time. Mrs. William Howard, wife of one of San Francisco's early merchants, later recalled that "the city moved forward so rapidly, we had two new clotheslines and a handcart in a single month."

That peaceful state of affairs quickly became a thing of the past when, on a morning in March 1848, Sam Brannan stood up on a packing crate in the middle of Portsmouth Square and, holding aloft a bottle filled with nuggets, shouted to all passers-by that gold had been discovered at John Sutter's mill on the American River. Once again, San Francisco was swept dramatically into a new era.

The incredible speed of change is shown by a tale often repeated by veterans of the days of 1849. It seems that, in their feverish haste to replace the ruins of the Hudson's Bay Company building, which had burnt in one of the first gold-rush conflagrations, workmen unearthed a coffin. A glass window in the lid gave a clear view of a well-preserved man in his middle years. Since none of the workmen knew who he was, they placed the coffin on the boardwalk in the hope that some passerby might identify the occupant. Several days passed before one passerby recognized the deceased as William Rae, the once-prominent British chief of the Hudson's Bay Company, who had committed suicide in 1845. Only four years had passed since his death, yet it took days to find a man in San Francisco who could identify the remains of a former leading citizen of Yerba Buena.

Opposite, Bottom: Jacob Leese's house on the plaza in Yerba Buena was finished in three days, just in time for a huge Fourth of July celebration in 1836, to which Leese invited all his Mexican friends and neighbors. The two American flags outnumber the single Mexican one; this was certainly the first time the Stars and Stripes flew over San Francisco. The house was 25 x 60 feet, built of lumber shipped from Monterey. Leese later sold the house to the Hudson's Bay Company and moved to Sonoma. (Author's collection)

This view of San Francisco, published in New Orleans in 1850, is from Telegraph Hill looking southward over Yerba Buena Cove. Montgomery Street parallels the waterfront, just left of center, with Kearny and Dupont (Grant Avenue) to the right. At far right is the rugged wilderness of Nob Hill. The tents of the Forty-Niners are gradually giving way to shanties and pre-fabricated houses. (Author's collection.)

THE RAG PALACE CITY

1846 - 1854

THE WONDROUS MAKE-DO HOUSES

Oh, What was your name in the States?
Was it Johnson, Thompson or Bates?
Did you murder your wife
Or fly for your life?
Oh, what was your name in the States?

—Popular Gold Rush Ditty

"THE PEOPLE OF SAN FRANCISCO are stark raving mad!" wrote a correspondent for the *New York Evening Post* in 1849. "Looking wondrously dirty and out of elbow, these self-styled millionaires have dragged me through mud and filth, almost up to my middle, from one pine box to another which they are pleased to call mansion, bank, hotel or store, and I am told that these splendid structures bring an agglomerated rental of not less than twelve million dollars a year . . . and this with a population not exceeding twelve thousand inhabitants. New York, with its population of five hundred thousand, does not give a rental greater than this!"

Steamer Day in Portsmouth Plaza, 1849. The men line up for letters, newspapers, or any news from home. Those in line at left appear to be picking the pockets of the men ahead of them. At the Garrett House, men slept three or four to a bed, and counted themselves lucky. At right is Sam Brannan's house, which doubled as a Post Office and as the printing office for the first English language newspaper in the city. (Author's collection)

It was indeed a "rag-palace" city as gold-hungry adventurers pitched their tents around the Plaza just long enough to prepare for the trip up the Sacramento River to the gold country. Wiser men, quickly realizing that even greater wealth lay in supplying the 49ers, stayed behind to contrive something a little better than a canvas shelter in which to conduct business. One would-be tobacco merchant, who found no immediate market for his latest shipment, built a house for himself out of his cases full of tobacco. Then, when a shortage of tobacco brought about a change in the market, the house disappeared just as quickly as it had been built.

One of the many bizarre means of obtaining shelter in those frantic times was by adapting sailing ships. Deserted by gold-mad crews, scores of floating derelict ships were left to rot in the harbor. Sometimes a zealous captain or crew member guarded the remains, but most were simply abandoned. One ship, the *Euphemia*, was beached and converted into a warehouse, and later a jail. Others became hotels, the guests paying as much as a hundred dollars a night to sleep in lice-ridden blankets on a hastily improvised bunk of planks. The

Cadmus, berthed at the foot of Francisco Street, became an insane asylum for young adventurers unable to cope with the harsh realities of those times. Another converted ship, the *Niantic*, first served as a hotel, then was sunk for land fill. It is said that the first Niantic building, built on the site, included a saloon which was built into the old ship's sunken hull. That building was torn down in 1870 and replaced by another, which burned in 1906. In 1978, the third Niantic building was being replaced when the remnants of the ship's hull were discovered and taken to the National Maritime Museum.

Toward the end of the Gold Rush days, when the city began expanding on filled land beyond Montgomery Street, a number of those ships (nobody knows just how many) were sunk and used for fill. Nowadays they come to light when someone excavates for a new parking garage, or when one of the streets below Montgomery suddenly develops a large hole.

Waterfront lots, which sold for $1,500 in 1850, brought $27,000 in 1853. The pace of change in San Francisco astonished Bayard Taylor, who wrote in 1849:

The first St. Francis Hotel, the tallest building in town, was made of several pre-fabricated buildings put together. Guests were fed in a tent, with an annex to accommodate the overflow. (Author's collection)

Of all the marvelous phases of the history of the Present, the growth of San Francisco is the one which will most tax belief of the Future. Its parallel was never known, and shall never be beheld again . . . When I landed there, a little more than four months before, I found a scattering town of tents and canvas houses, with a show of frame buildings on one or two streets. Now, I saw around me an actual metropolis, displaying street after street of well-built edifices, filled with an active and enterprising people and exhibiting every mark of commercial prosperity.

Actually, the "rag-palace" phase of the town's development lasted just a little more than one year. Interestingly enough, the leaders who first pulled the town out of the mud were the owners of the saloons and gambling houses. Portsmouth Square, which Richard Henry Dana described as an empty space encircled by warehouses for hides and tallow, was now filled with huge tents in those first months of the Gold Rush. Fitted out with bars and gambling tables, these resorts were the only places a lonely and homesick 49er could find companionship and amusement. At night these tents stood out like great golden balloons amid the dark and muddy streets. One could hear the strident noises of banjos and pianos, shouts and curses, and the occasional gunshot when the entire male population came out to crowd the planked walks around the plaza's perimeter.

AND WHAT A KALEIDOSCOPE of humanity it was! Men of every nationality and from every walk of life passed by the plaza. Frontiersmen in buckskin might rub elbows with a French count, a Chinese merchant, the son of a Virginia governor, a Spanish don, a New England skipper, a Baptist preacher, a Chilean *vaquero*, or a convict from Australia.

The Australians were the biggest troublemakers of them all. Calling themselves "The Sidney Ducks," these ex-convicts hung out in rough joints on the waterfront, in the area which would become the notorious Barbary Coast. When not beating and robbing the inhabitants of the Latin Quarter, whom the 49ers unanimously called "Chileños," they had an equally odious

San Francisco's first public schoolhouse, built in October 1847. Thomas Douglas, a Yale graduate, was the first teacher. In 1848 he locked the door and went to "the diggings," along with everyone else in town. The schoolhouse also served as a town hall, and later as a jail. (Both pictures courtesy California State Library)

The First Presbyterian Church, organized in 1848, met in this tent until a proper church building could be shipped in pieces around the Horn. The Rev. T. Dwight Hunt led the flock.

The Apollo Warehouse, made from a ship tied up at the foot of Sacramento Street, offered storage for trunks, chests, lumber, and trade goods. It was connected by strong bridges to the Central Wharf. Lighters bringing ships' cargo could approach at "nearly all tides." (Courtesy California Historical Society)

habit of setting fires. Naturally, when a property mysteriously went up in flames, everyone in town rushed to the scene to help put the fire out, leaving a clear field for the Sidney Ducks to rob and loot those buildings which had been left unguarded. These desperados reportedly caused six successive conflagrations within three years, including the devastating fire of 1851.

When the citizenry finally realized the cause of these fires, they quickly formed San Francisco's first Vigilance Committee. Finding the local politicians untrustworthy, a group of the leading citizens of the young town took matters into their own hands. The Vigilantes of 1851 and their 1856 successors, though rather romanticized now, were probably responsible for sending many an innocent man to his doom. In any event, they put a stop to the incendiary raids of the Sidney Ducks.

The next civic effort was to form fire brigades. Membership in one of the volunteer fire fighting companies was regarded as a badge of honor, and the companies became social institutions. The rivalry between these brigades, and the frequent fires they fought, helped keep things lively in San Francisco for the next decade.

Following each of the six conflagrations, the town took on a successively more stable appearance. The most prosperous elements of the business community, the saloons and gambling halls, led in the reconstruction. These establishments graduated from flimsy tents to large, pre-fabricated buildings sent around the Horn from eastern sawmills. But in succeeding fires, these burned almost as readily as had their flimsy canvas predecessors. Gradually the commercial center of town became as substantial as the gambling quarter, with

The north side of Portsmouth Square, today's Washington Street, looks sparkling and neat in this early photograph. Trees had been newly planted, and a handsome new fence, with gaslights at the gate, surrounds the plaza. This picture is apparently two or three years earlier than the one just below, in which the trees have grown considerably. (Author's collection)

The northeast corner of Portsmouth Plaza, at Kearny and Washington Streets, had begun to look quite civilized in the early 1850s. The Bella Union Theater, the Verandah Drug Store, the El Dorado gambling house, and the beautiful Jenny Lind Theater all lent weight to this side of the plaza. Telegraph Hill is in the background. (Author's collection)

The magnificent Montgomery Block, built in 1853 on Montgomery at Washington Street, stood for more than 100 years before being demolished for a parking lot. (Author's collection)

The Federal Customs House, begun in 1851 at Battery and Washington Streets, was designed by Boston architect Gridley Bryant in classic Greek Revival style. Its massive base of granite blocks rested on piles driven into the marshy site. Five years and more than a half million dollars went into its construction. The contrast with the tents of 1849 and the simple adobe houses of 1847 and earlier is staggering. (Courtesy California Historical Society).

buildings of brick or stone, fitted out with iron shutters and metal roofs.

The El Dorado gambling casino was a perfect example. Located at the northeast corner fronting Portsmouth Plaza, at Washington and Kearny, it began its existence as a large tent. When that was swept away in the second conflagration, it was replaced by a prefabricated structure. The locals had little time to admire its opulent interior before it too went up in smoke. The owners built a third El Dorado, only to have it meet the same fate. Then, in 1851, Tom Maguire, its proprietor, hired French-trained architect Prosper Huerne, one of the many young architects lured to San Francisco by the Gold Rush, to design a completely fire-resistant building. This new building, with its thick brick walls, iron shutters, and terne plate roof, was one of San Francisco's first fireproof structures.

In that same year, Maguire commissioned Huerne to design the Jenny Lind Theater, adjoining his El Dorado. Three stories high, it stood as a skyscraper in

This early view, taken from the wild northern slope of Nob Hill about 1852, looking toward Alcatraz, shows the houses creeping westward from Portsmouth Square toward Russian Hill. Sand hills and chaparral are slowly being changed to streets and houses. The narrow swath leading northward, with houses on both sides, is Mason Street.
(Author's collection)

the little town. Also of heavy brick construction, faced with white sandstone brought from Australia, it remained for at least two years San Francisco's handsomest building. No, Jenny Lind never sang there, and, frontier legend to the contrary, she never sang in San Francisco or in California. But "The Swedish Nightingale" was the most popular name in show business, thanks to the genius of her press agent, P.T. Barnum. For a time, the performers who were imported at great cost to entertain San Franciscans played to packed houses in the Jenny Lind. Then, when Maguire's business dropped off sharply, he sold the theater to the city for $200,000, for use as the city hall. Fireproof buildings were hard to find.

Banks and mercantile establishments were quick to follow in building fireproof structures of brick and stone. One of the most spectacular of these was the granite building commissioned by banker John Parrott. The granite for the Parrott Block, which rose at the northwest corner of California and Montgomery Streets, was quarried and shaped in China, where the architect, Gordon Cummings, arranged to have each finished block marked with a Chinese character. In this way, the Chinese workmen who were imported along with the granite could systematically unload the blocks from the ship tied up just across Montgomery Street and place them in their designated positions in the slowly rising building. Curious townspeople gathered each day to watch the Chinese in their wide coolie hats and cloth slippers, silently removing the granite blocks

from the ship, carrying them to the building site, and fitting them together.

Despite an explosion in the 1870s which wiped out several members of the Pacific Union Club, then housed in the Parrott Block's second floor, the structure remained stable enough to survive for another half century. Gutted by the flames of the 1906 holocaust, it was repaired and stood until 1926, when it was replaced by the undistinguished successor which occupies the site today.

San Francisco's growing business community rapidly replaced the make-do shanties of Gold-Rush times with more permanent stores and warehouses of brick and granite. Fitted out with cast iron shutters, they possessed a simple dignity which appeals more to present-day tastes than it did to the builders of the later nineteenth century. Several of these handsome buildings still stand on Montgomery Street, between Washington and Jackson Streets. The late Melvin Belli's beautifully restored brick building is one of them.

Then, in 1853, the Montgomery Block, a structure of hallowed memory and the engineering marvel of its time, became the first major structure erected on the marshy sand bordering the east side of Montgomery Street at Washington. Rising four stories above a deep basement, this block-square building boasted two inner courts, masonry walls more than two feet thick, and heavy iron shutters at every window. The entire building was floated on a redwood log raft sunk into the sand.

Former New Yorker Gordon Cummings, architect of the Parrott and Montgomery Blocks, borrowed the engineering skills of his patron, Henry Wager Halleck, one of San Francisco's leading attorneys. (Halleck had studied military engineering at West Point; he was to gain renown during the Civil War as Chief of Staff of Lincoln's armies.) Halleck's courage in investing the staggering sum of $3 million stands out as an example of the bravado which built the western metropolis, for what man in his right mind would float a $3-million investment on a raft? Idwall Jones, in his history of the Montgomery Block, *Ark of Empire*, described the building as "a manifestation of faith, a dream more durable than iron or stone."

The names of the occupants and of those associated with "The Monkey Block," as it came to be called, read like a Who's Who of California history. It sheltered such famed attorneys as Hall McAllister, George Peachey and Frederick Billings, as well as Halleck himself. These men were chiefly engaged in settling the nearly unresolvable disputes before the land claims court.

In later years the Montgomery Block provided office space for the newly affluent "Silver Kings" of the Comstock Lode. Then, in its gentle decline, it became the headquarters for the *San Francisco Argonaut*, the haunt of such famous journalists as Robert Louis Stevenson, Ambrose Bierce, Bret Harte, Mark Twain and Frank Pixley, the *Argonaut's* editor.

By the turn of the century, the building had become a haven for painters and sculptors. In one of the Montgomery Block's rooms, architect Willis Polk and artist Bruce Porter designed the memorial to Robert Louis Stevenson which stands today in Portsmouth Square. They first sketched the plan on a tablecloth during lunch at the Palace Hotel, and then took the tablecloth with them to Porter's studio to finish the concept.

In the bohemian restaurant run by Poppa Coppa in the basement of the Montgomery Block, these young men and a score of other local artists met to toast the great city which all believed would soon arise from the ruins left by the 1906 disaster. Many of these same men, led by Percy Stidger, the Block's manager, had helped to save the Montgomery Block from the dynamiters, and to protect those historic structures lining Jackson and Pacific Streets, many of which were later restored to become today's Jackson Square.

In the light of today's preservation movement it seems hardly possible that in 1959, as the Montgomery Block was attaining its 106TH year, it was demolished to make way for a parking lot. To avoid public outcry, the wreckers planned to make quick work of the demolition, but the building's iron framework and massive brick walls stubbornly resisted, and the carnage dragged on for months, producing a mountain of historic used brick. A dream more durable than stone? The Transamerica Pyramid now occupies the site. *Sic transit gloria.*

HOTELS AND GENTEEL BOARDING HOUSES

DESPITE THE APPEARANCE of sturdy structures in the gambling and commercial centers, Gold Rush San Francisco's domestic architecture as a whole was a shambles. Change in this matter began in the early 1850s with the advent of the "good woman" on the scene. Among the first arrivals were the wives of army and naval officers stationed in San Francisco. A few were of the simple, homespun class who crossed the plains by covered wagon. These were soon followed by the families of leading merchants, lawyers, and political figures. Having experienced the danger and misery of a voyage around Cape Horn or of the Panama crossing, these ladies were neither timid nor slow to impress on this frontier community their notions of civilized living.

Though the good women of San Francisco were a tiny minority, their influence was quick to be felt. Not only did the forces of law and order become more evident, but here and there a church spire could be seen rising above the jumble of wood frame buildings. By 1850 there were charitable organizations, such as the Ladies Protection and Relief Society, formed to aid women and children stranded here when their male relatives failed to meet them. (This organization still exists.) Church groups and asylums were formed to help the unfortunate. As early as 1851 there was even an ice-cream parlor in the burgeoning town.

In the early days of San Francisco, when it was considered too risky for families to live alone in isolated dwellings, the custom of hotel living established itself as a respectable alternative. The custom prevailed well into this century, and city directories from the 1850s through the 1890s continued to print the calling days, when ladies were officially "At Home" at each of the

Stockton Street was graded and planked by 1855, when George Fardon took this picture looking north toward Alcatraz and Angel Island. The owners of older houses had to add stairs to get down to the sidewalk after the street was graded. One of the large houses at far left was Dr. Woozencroft's boarding house, owned by Mrs. Howard. Note the carefully braced street trees along the sidewalk (Author's collection)

better hostelries. A spirit of great camaraderie grew up among the well-bred occupants of the better hotels and boarding houses, as they suffered the crowded conditions and shortages of Gold Rush San Francisco. That egalitarian spirit, born of remembered hardships, continued to pervade San Francisco society long after deprivation had become a thing of the past.

By 1852 enough of the land disputes had been settled for the city to extend south of Pine Street. Near the intersection of Bush and Battery Streets, then on the edge of the Bay, the Oriental Hotel arose. There were a number of other hotels—the first Saint Francis Hotel, established on the site of Jacob Leese's former dwelling; the Occidental, the Lick House, and a score of lesser establishments—but, for a time, the Oriental was favored above all the others. Its walls and ceilings were made of muslin tacked over wooden studs; despite the hotel's fancy reputation, guests could lie in bed and see the imprint of rats scurrying across the cloth ceilings. Nearby on Market Street, where the handsome bronze Mechanics' monument stands today, was the Donahue Iron Works. The constant din from that direction

could not have added to the attractions of the Oriental. But the Oriental had a ballroom, and that factor more than any other gave it an edge over San Francisco's other hostelries in the eyes of its hardy young clientele.

When the Donahue brothers installed San Francisco's first gas lights in 1854, the public rooms and the street in front of the Oriental were the first to enjoy this modern convenience. The owners held a grand banquet in the hotel's ballroom to celebrate the occasion. At the banquet, Mayor Garrison arose to address the distinguished assemblage, basking in the glittering light of gaslit chandeliers. Just as he opened his mouth to speak the entire building was plunged into stygian darkness. When the ensuing pandemonium quieted down, the crowd learned that some pranksters had waited until just that moment to shut off the gas.

There were few privately owned carriages in Gold Rush San Francisco, for the majority of streets were too sandy or muddy for such traffic. At great expense, one could hire one of the two or three hacks available, but distances within San Francisco's confines were not great. Ladies who chose not to travel on horseback

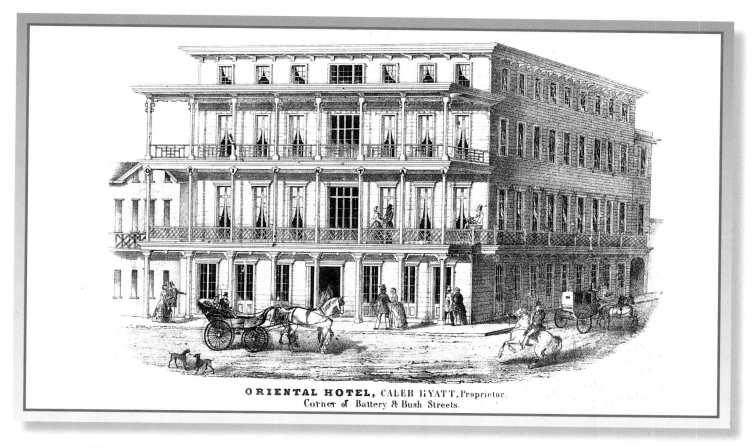

ORIENTAL HOTEL, CALEB HYATT, Proprietor.
Corner of Battery & Bush Streets.

The Oriental Hotel, built on piers at the waterfront, was the most genteel accommodation in San Francisco, and indeed the one most suitable for proper ladies. Despite its elegant galleries and draped windows, it was hardly a palace. The smell of tidal refuse beneath often obliged guests to go out for a promenade on warm afternoons. (Courtesy California State Library)

This 1851 daguerreotype, one panel of a panorama, shows the waterfront near First and Howard Streets. Sitting in the doorway of her new cabin is a woman, evidently a laundress; clothes hang on the line and decorate the chapparal at right. One man in a wide-brimmed hat is leaving her cabin; two young sailors wait at her right, and another man dangles his legs over the sand dune, where trailing roots protrude from the raw cut. She must have been a very good laundress indeed. (Courtesy California Historical Society)

A second panel from the same panorama shows a few of the many pre-fabricated houses in Happy Valley, just south of Market Street. These are of the simplest design, with board-and-batten siding and no dormers or other "frills." In the background houses are beginning to creep up the sandy slopes of Nob Hill. (Courtesy California Historical Society)

This drawing shows the building that would eventually become the Montgomery Block. Apparently made by an architect, the drawing was published before the name was changed. It suggests an elegance that the building itself may never have achieved. (Courtesy California State Library)

An engraving from Harper's Weekly shows the terrible conflagration of June 3, 1851, when the central waterfront between California and Washington Streets burned. The people in the foreground, on the long wharf extending out into the bay, are rushing to save their goods from the fire, while the hapless residents of the waterfront buildings throw their belongings out of second-story windows. The accompanying article described the fire, saying that the estimate of damage at $3 million "was no doubt greatly exaggerated." (Courtesy James Heig)

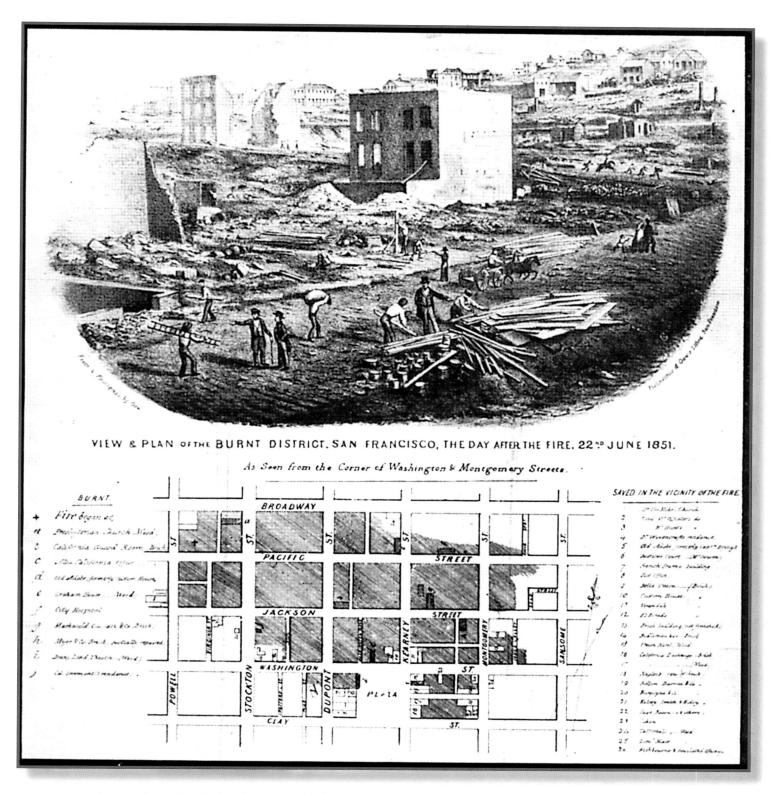

Just 19 days after the fire shown on the facing page, on June 22, 1851, another fire erupted, burning the area from Broadway to Washington Streets and from Powell to Montgomery and beyond. Whether these fires were set by the Sydney Ducks is anybody's guess, but such events provoked the formation of the first Vigilance Committee, a group of citizens determined to end the violence and arson so common in the town. (Author's collection)

could walk instead. Just across the sand wastes that would one day become Market Street was a little cluster of 25 houses in the area known as Happy Valley. These pre-fabricated "Boston houses," which may be seen in rare early photographs, sat at the foot of Rincon Hill, later to become the most fashionable part of the city. When the ladies of the Oriental chose to make their social calls, usually these modest dwellings were their destination. The ladies generally stopped at midpoint, at a lone tree on a sand dune, to empty sand out of their slippers, never dreaming that the magnificent Palace Hotel would one day replace the tree.

A FEW OF THE LARGER dwellings that escaped the frequent fires of the 1850s became rooming houses, crowded with families whose homes had been burnt. Among the more select boarding houses were Mrs. Petit's and Mrs. Leland's on California Street, and Dr. Woozencroft's on Stockton. One boarding house, which catered to young Southerners employed as government clerks was jok-

ingly known as "The Virginia Poorhouse." Of all the houses, Dr. Woozencroft's was the most favored, not because its accommodations were superior, but because its clientele included some of San Francisco's most distinguished citizens.

Actually, the owner of the house was the wife of a leading merchant, Mrs. W.D.M. Howard, who was fearful of being left alone while her husband was away. She asked Dr. Woozencroft to manage her house, which soon sheltered such luminaries as U.S. Senator William Gwin, his wife and two daughters, General David Douglas, Senator John B. Weller, and General Alden Greenough. (General Greenough's wife, Florence, later became a famous spy for the Confederacy.)

Also living in these confined quarters were Major Charles McPhail Hitchcock, his wife Martha, and their young daughter, Lillie. Naughty little Lillie, who as Lillie Coit would one day leave a memorial to San Francisco's pioneer fire fighters, drove her mother to distraction in these days by constantly running after the handcarts of San Francisco's volunteer firemen.

PRE-FABRICATED HOUSES

DURING THE EARLY YEARS of the Gold Rush, anyone who wanted to move from a tent or a shack into a proper house for his family or himself had few choices. The few sawmills in California could produce only the roughest redwood or fir planks or beams, at very high cost. There were no planing mills to produce finished siding, moldings, or trim. Such refinements had to be brought by ship around the Horn, and no lumber dealer could afford to bring in extra stock. The sensible method, then, was to import complete houses, usually shipped in sections from eastern mills.

During the late 1840s and 1850s speculation in pre-fabricated buildings was phenomenal. Even hotels were imported, thrown up in one location, disassembled and moved to another site as the need arose. Benjamin R. Buckelew, a brash New Yorker who had arrived in San Francisco in 1846, bought a shipload of unclaimed pre-fab buildings in 1852 and set up a town across from San Quentin, in Marin County, complete with hotel, saloon, houses, and a dock. He named the place California City, and then sat back to wait for customers who never came.

In 1849, Captain Joseph Folsom, an Army quartermaster who had managed to acquire the large holdings of the deceased Captain Leidesdorff, entered into a business venture with the capitalist W.D.M. Howard.

Together, they purchased 25 prefabricated houses, or "portables" as they were then called, from Captain Cole, commander of the ship *Oxnard* out of Boston. Howard moved his wife into one of these houses; Captain Folsom, a tall, handsome bachelor, lived in another, in great style, constantly entertaining his friends. Today, Howard Street is a rough indication of the locale of the Howard cottage, just as Folsom Street marks the site of Captain Folsom's house. Brannan Street also takes its name from an occupant of one of those pre-fabricated pioneer houses.

George W. Beaver, for whom Beaver Street is named, lived with his family in one of those 25 houses in Happy Valley. (Oddly enough, their neighbors on Second Street were named Badger.) A few years later, he bought a noteworthy house, which may also have been pre-fabricated, on the south side of today's Market Street, between 5th and 6th Streets. This house had been the home of James King of William (the "of William" was added to distinguish its owner from other, more ordinary men named James King), editor of the *Bulletin*. He was gunned down in 1856 by the notorious James Casey in revenge for printing some fearless articles exposing Casey's criminal activities. Casey was hanged by the Vigilantes, and the King house was sold to a General Williams, a lover of gardens, who imported rare plants

A. Page Brown

From Corrugated Iron to Solid Stone

Trinity Episcopal Church was organized in 1849 in a pre-fabricated corrugated iron building (top left) on Stockton Street. By 1852 the congregation, needing larger quarters, imported a new pre-fab iron church and set it up on Pine and Kearny Streets (middle left). In 1867 a truly grand church (top middle) was built at Post and Powell Streets, on the north side of Union Square. In 1892 the congregation built a splendid stone church at Gough and Bush Streets, where it stands today, largely unaltered (left, in a photograph taken around 1900). A. Page Brown, the architect, drawing inspiration from the great Durham Cathedral in England, created a magnificent Gothic fortress-church, with authentic gargoyles and crenelated towers, as well as one of the finest acoustic spaces in the city. (Photographs courtesy Trinity Episcopal Church)

from Europe, and who was probably the first to import and employ foreign gardeners.

Beaver bought the property from Williams. In 1935, Anna Beaver, a descendant, wrote a wonderful description of the house. When the Beavers moved in, Market Street was still a dirt road leading through a waste of sand hills. Sidewalks consisted of planks laid lengthwise along the south side of the road. Yet here, in this isolated, primitive setting, was the charming home of a cultivated family.

A unique feature of this house was a large glassed-in conservatory, entered through tall French doors from the dining room at the back. Family and guests would gather here in the evening, while the men smoked and the children played on the floor. At the center of this room was a Mound of Dew plant, surmounted by a fountain playing in a basin of white marble. Ornate metal stands holding potted ferns, cineraria, cyclamen, and other sweet, old-fashioned flowers stood around the sides of the conservatory. A fragrant wisteria with long purple festoons of blossom ran up one side to cover the ceiling. The scent of heliotrope, star jasmine, and datura, whose heavy white blossoms were a foot long, permeated the air. Because of the winds which swept across the almost treeless San Francisco peninsula, the rear garden was surrounded by high board fences. These were also used to separate the proper garden, with its Cloth-of-Damask and Lamarque roses and its borders of malva, used since mission days in California, from the grass plot, which was never referred to in those days as a lawn. Another area, enclosed by high fences, was the stable yard with horses, cows, and chickens. At one time there was a fawn, which was sent to Woodward's Gardens when it started to develop antlers. In 1868 the house was moved to another site, and the grounds were taken over by small business establishments. The Beavers then became early settlers on Nob Hill, in a house on the northeast corner of Sacramento and Mason Streets.

I N T H E B R I E F P E R I O D from 1848 to 1854, when California was in the grip of the Gold Rush, portable houses, or "Boston Houses," as they were called, became a solution to San Francisco's acute housing shortage. At first they were little more than pine boxes designed to be disassembled for shipping, requiring no more than one or two capable men to reassemble them. (After all, no one came to Gold Rush California to become a carpenter.) Fitted out with a front door and with a window at each side, pre-fabs could be purchased for as little as two thousand dollars.

In a short time, more luxurious models became available. Story-and-a-half houses contained a boxed-in stairwell, leading to a loft lit by a window at either gable end. If one chose to pay more, he could purchase little half-windows tucked under the eaves. Still fancier models offered half-dormers to extend these little windows higher into the roof. The only limit was the desire, and the wallet, of the homebuyer. The cottages purchased by Folsom and Howard, for example, were deluxe models in the latest Gothic Revival style, offering dormers and a tall front gable trimmed with wooden icicles. These additions, featured in A.J. Downing's pattern books, brought more light and space into the loft-like bedrooms. Jessie Benton Fremont in 1849 described one house "belonging to a young New Yorker, who had shipped it from home, house and furniture complete—a double two-story frame house, which, when in place, was said to have cost $90,000."

By the mid-1850s there was a veritable flotilla of Gothic Revival pre-fabs in Howard's and Folsom's neighborhood. Just below Captain Folsom's cottage stood the Howard Street Presbyterian Church, a prefabricated building in the Greek Revival style. In 1852, the Howard Street Methodist Church was built near Second Street. Another noteworthy pre-fab was the small St. Patrick's Church. Built in 1854, with an adjoining orphanage, this Catholic church stood on Market Street at the corner of Third. The little church remained at this spot for twenty years, until William Ralston bought the property to build his mighty Palace Hotel. Ralston had St. Patrick's moved, and it finally ended up at Eddy Street near Divisadero, where it stands today as one of the city's oldest structures. San Francisco's Catholics built a second St. Patrick's Church near Third and Mission to serve what eventually became the largest Irish parish in the United States. Although severely damaged in 1906, the building's sturdy brick walls still stand to serve today's congregation, and the interior is a Gothic marvel.

The Roman Catholics also met in a prefabricated church on Vallejo Street. Established in 1849, it was San Francisco's oldest Catholic church after the Mission Dolores. The Episcopalians began with a small cast-iron Gothic church on Stockton Street.

At the corner of Stockton and Sutter Streets, near today's 450 Sutter Building, Judge Burritt erected a prefabricated Gothic mansion replete with porches, dormers, gables at each point of the compass, a three-sided bay window and, above it, a fancy lancet window. This greatly admired "bit of old New England," is known to have had at least two exact duplicates. One was erected by General Vallejo for his Sonoma estate, Lachryma

Captain Joseph Folsom's stately Gothic pre-fabricated house, (at left, above) on Second Street near Folsom, was one of the first fine houses on Rincon Hill. John Wieland later bought the house and built his brewery beside it (above center), where visitors could sit in the garden and sample Wieland's beer. The brewery was one of many industries which gradually encroached on the elegant residential quarter on Rincon Hill. (Author's collection)

Montis. The other was built by his son-in-law, General Frisbie, in the little city of Benicia, then the state capital. After a series of ownership changes, the Burritt house in San Francisco was remodeled into a popular resort known as the Vienna Gardens. Both the Sonoma and Benicia houses are still standing, but the Burritt house vanished in the 1890s.

A majority of these houses were manufactured by New England mills for shipment to California. Other portable houses arrived from Belgium, France, China, and particularly from England. A number of the English and Belgian portables were of corrugated iron, for the British speculators who created them thought that such shelters were the perfect solution for an incendiary Gold-Rush town. They were wrong. During the fire of May 1850, the owner of one of the buildings took refuge with some friends in his iron warehouse. The poor, doomed souls discovered that the increasing

heat had stuck the iron doors together, and the "fireproof" building melted like chocolate around them.

In his Gold Rush journal, *Mountains and Molehills*, Frank Marryat had a good deal to say about iron pre-fabs, none of it complimentary. Aside from being miserably cold in winter, and like an oven in warm weather, these houses, he noted, also gave off an offensive odor. And finally, they were not really fireproof.

Although these first all-iron houses were a dismal failure in nearly every way, they did lead to the English and American manufacture of cast-iron architectural details, such as columns and pediments, and even entire three- and four-story façades. Most of San Francisco's cast-iron façades melted in 1906, but elaborate ones survive on commercial buildings in Petaluma.

Possibly San Francisco's most noteworthy cast-iron façade was that of the main office of the American

Trust Company, which later merged with Wells Fargo Bank, at the corner of California and Montgomery Streets. Unfortunately, it was removed in the 1950s when the building was remodeled into the undistinguished cube it is today. On the sidewalk at the California Street corner, until very recently, was a wonderful cast-iron receptacle, designed to hold feed for the horses that were once tied to hitching posts in that vicinity.

The number of pre-fabricated houses brought to Gold Rush San Francisco will never be known, for most of them furnished the fuel for the six conflagrations which swept through the town in the years between 1848 and 1852.

San Francisco's Oldest Surviving House

ON OAK STREET, west of Divisadero, set well back from the street behind a formal garden, is a beautifully restored Gothic Revival house (San Francisco Landmark #32), declared to be the oldest unaltered dwelling in San Francisco. Erected for the Phelps family in 1852 by John Middleton, it originally stood on a 160-acre farm bordered by today's Divisadero Street and the Panhandle of Golden Gate Park.

Colonel Abner Phelps, its first occupant, was a native of New Hampshire and a West Point graduate who earned his rank in the Mexican War. After his military career he became the mayor of Lafayette, Louisiana. In 1851, after the death of his first wife, he married Charlotte August Roussell, of New Orleans, whom he brought to California in 1852.

According to Phelps family tradition the house was pre-fabricated in New Orleans and shipped around the Horn. It strongly resembles typical Louisiana houses, whose main floor is often raised one story to escape flooding, and whose rooms are arranged four to a floor, flanking a wide central hallway running from front to back. The Phelps house also features tall French windows—then found only in houses of Creole origin—opening onto a deep gallery lined with slim Tuscan columns. Such features would surely have assuaged the homesickness of its young Southern mistress.

The house originally stood near the northwest corner of today's Page and Divisadero Streets, at the edge of the newly extended city limits. Divisadero was only a sandy trail linking the Mission with the Presidio. Phelps rode horseback through the chaparral to his office in the new Montgomery Block. His farm was so remote that he had to retain an armed guard to patrol the acreage against squatters.

In an 1870 census, Abner Phelps and his wife are listed with six young children, a servant, and a 35-year-old son, Edwin, apparently the child of Phelps's previous marriage. Two old watercolors signed "C. Rogers" depict the house at its original location, surrounded by a three-acre flower garden.

Abner Phelps died in 1893, at age 69, and his widow died only a few years later. Shortly after her death, regrading at the corner of Divisadero and Page Streets forced the children to move the house to a lower elevation, at 313 Divisadero Street, where it stood for only a few years behind its picket fence, shown in the photograph opposite. In 1904 it was moved to the back of the lot to make room for construction of a large meeting hall, which stands at 313 Divisadero today. For a time after the 1906 earthquake, this meeting hall was one of the few surviving structures large enough to house civic gatherings.

Gradually all the lands around the "Phelps Mansion," as it was then known, were subdivided and built on, so that the only access to the house was via a stairway leading through the meeting hall, and then down a fire escape to the front yard. The house was invisible from any street. Nevertheless the four surviving Phelps children continued to live in the house until their deaths in the 1930s. For years afterward the new owners used the Phelps house, along with the grand Mish house just behind it, as rental property.

In 1975 the San Francisco Preservation Group purchased and began restoration of the Phelps house. Three years later, they cleared a wide frontage on Oak Street, and turned the house 90 degrees to face north. For the third time the old house received a new address, 1111 Oak Street, where it stands today. In 1980 attorneys W. Urie Walsh and John J. Cullen remodeled the completely gutted interior for law offices, and commissioned the present landscaping scheme, which later won a City Beautiful award.

As owners of old San Francisco houses well know, the tracing of property history is a formidable task. Only a few records were rescued from the collapsed City Hall in 1906. Researchers must depend on fragments of

The Abner Phelps house, still standing on Oak Street between Divisadero and Broderick, and dating from around 1850, may well be the oldest surviving dwelling in San Francisco. Originally a farm house, it has recently been restored, and is a designated city landmark. This house is typical of many pre-fabricated houses sent to San Francisco; it has survived because it was far west of the fire zone in 1906. (Author's Collection)

evidence and on popular tradition, which is not always reliable. In 1981 the Mock San Francisco Court of Historical Reviews and Appeals set out to track down the origins of the Phelps house, with the help of the Historical American Buildings Survey. Their findings, on file with the Library of Congress, are generally regarded as the final word. They found that samples of the building's materials included redwood and indigenous pine, thus refuting the Phelps family tradition that the house had been pre-fabricated in New Orleans.

Those who refuse to let go of the legend might point out that a fragile frame structure of such advanced age, particularly one that had been moved three times, must have required replacement of various sections and parts, which would naturally have been made of indigenous materials. But no matter what its origin, the great historical value of this old house, with its galleries, gables, dormers and fretwork, is that it is the sole remaining example of the Gothic Revival frame houses common to San Francisco before the Civil War.

Gothic houses like the Phelps house owe their origin in this country to one Andrew Jackson Downing, a promising young landscape designer from the Hudson River area in upstate New York. Adapting the British-inspired Gothic Revival style to farmhouses and cottages, Downing collaborated with the architect Andrew Jackson Davis in the publication of several pattern books which became all the rage in America during the 1850s and '60s. In the inventive spirit of the times, America's builders expanded upon Downing's gabled cottages, adding gingerbread fretwork under the eaves, brackets, finials, and fancy chimneys, all of which, they chose to believe, were in the "pure Gothic style." The fact that these houses were usually of board and batten instead of stone troubled them not at all.

Early in the 1850s Stephan Wright commissioned architect Peter Portois to build the most magnificent banking house in the West, the Miners' Exchange Bank, on Montgomery at Washington Street. With four stories plus a hexagonal penthouse surmounted by a graceful lantern, the building puts is neighbors to shame. Its success as a bank was short-lived, for in the crash of 1854 Wright was ruined. The building soon became known as "Wright's Folly." Only its heavy masonry first floor survived the 1906 disaster. This view shows a collection of early dwellings on Telegraph Hill, in the background. (Author's collection)

The Merchants' Exchange Building, at the northeast corner of Battery and Washington Streets, is a study in neo-classical sobriety, with stately columns, a formal portico with a goddess on top, eagles cresting the two piers, and an elegant domed enclosure on the roof which appears to be purely decorative. This picture, dating from 1858, shows a construction shack in the foreground, and evidence of ongoing work on the streets. Just few years earlier this was a water lot, two blocks out from the shoreline. (Author's collection)

FIREFIGHTING IN SAN FRANCISCO

THE STORY OF FIREFIGHTING in any progressive American community is always a subject for entertaining reading. That of San Francisco's dashing firefighters certainly belongs among the most colorful. The city always has been, and unfortunately still is, a potential tinderbox, and out of necessity has developed one of the world's finest fire protection services. After all, a city which has burned seven times and has the phoenix rising from its ashes on the official city seal must respect its glorious firefighting tradition.

The Christmas Eve fire of 1849, causing a million-dollar loss, prompted Mayor Geary to hold a public meeting to discuss a means of preventing another such disaster. At that point San Francisco had only two pieces of fire-fighting equipment. One of these, a fire cart belonging to a local importing business, had broken down at its first fire and was deemed unworthy of repair. The other had originally belonged to President Martin Van Buren; its original function was to water the gardens of Van Buren's New York estate.

In response to Geary's meeting, firefighters who had gained experience in other cities volunteered their services, and various rich men donated to the cause. Among the more generous donors was Sam Brannan, who established the first fire brigade under his own name. A little later another local capitalist, W.D.M. Howard, personally traveled to Philadelphia to pick out the finest steam pumper that money could buy.

To show their appreciation of this glorious new conveyance, certain members of the Brannan Brigade changed the name to the Howard Company No. 3. This so enraged the other members of the company that they hauled off the glorious new engine and dumped it into the Bay. The Howard contingent promptly raised it from its muddy grave, cleaned it off and returned it to the company. This incident was but a prelude to the antics of rival fire companies, which by June 1850 had become six in number.

Historians have sometimes compared San Francisco's Gold Rush population to that of the participants in a war, for the population was made up primarily of young men in their twenties. Young men had the physical stamina to risk the hazardous trip west, and after that ordeal a devil-may-care bravado ruled the sentiments of most of them. There were plenty of young men strong enough of wind and limb to haul the heavy pumpers and hook and ladder wagons up and down San Francisco's steep hills. The city passed a law which exacted a fine from any able-bodied man at the scene of a fire who did not pitch in to help.

The ordinance hardly seems to have been necessary, for when the fire bell in the city hall sounded, practically the whole town turned out to aid the firefighters. Property owners and merchants were eager to prevent the flames from spreading to their own part of town. There were no living quarters in the various firehouses, so the volunteers had to run from their quarters or places of business, with representatives from every company competing with one another to arrive first at the scene. The rivalry between competing fire companies was fearsome to behold. The trophy of a foxtail was awarded to the engine company which arrived first with the most men. This often led to knock-down drag-out fisticuffs between rival companies.

Nor was this award the only cause for rivalry. From the outset, membership in these quasi-fraternal fire brigades became a matter of social *ton*. The little firehouses, usually measuring about 20 x 40 feet, could easily be converted into meeting halls, ballrooms, or banqueting halls. Each was built to rival the others as a community adornment. Monumental Co. No. 8, located on Jackson Street between Davis and Front, boasted a pedimented faux marble façade with fluted columns topped by life-sized statues of firemen in full uniform. One engine company even called itself "The Social Company"; its members stocked their engine with cases of champagne to bolster the crew's endurance during the blaze. Adding panache to the drama of fires at night, the fire companies hired local street urchins to run ahead of the engines, bearing aloft lighted torches to make the darkened streets more passable.

On one occasion the fire companies banded together and refused to answer the fire bell until the deep chuck holes in the streets were repaired. The mayor and the city council hastily met and impressed a chain gang from the Broadway jail to do the job. While everything was done to facilitate the fire volunteers' efforts, the frail little pumpers and hook and ladder were a poor match for the hair-raising conflagrations which swept the town repeatedly in the years between 1849 and 1852. One of the biggest problems was to find a water supply for the hand-operated pumpers. When a burning property was too far from the waters of the Bay, privately owned wells often proved to be too shallow. One alternative was to apply a heavy coating of mud — always in ample supply — to the walls of the burning structures and their neighbors. If this failed to quench the flames, dynamite was used. An ordinance required the owners of every structure to keep on hand at all times at least six buckets filled with water. These

Engine Company No. 11 (Courtesy California Historical Society)

buckets were usually fashioned of buffalo hide or cowhide, so that they would be less likely to burn the hands that grabbed them during a fire. The firemen's helmets were also made of leather, with high crowns and spreading brims at the back, to protect firemen from flying sparks. The helmets used by firemen today are of the same design.

Much to the relief of the local populace, the various engine companies eventually agreed to put an end to the fisticuffs and other such boyish activities, although the social competition between companies continued to flourish. In the face of major losses caused by the serial conflagrations, the fire companies, like the community they were serving, began to show signs of maturity. In 1863 the continued threat of total disaster prompted San Francisco's business community to organize the Firemens' Fund Insurance Company. Firefighters would now be rewarded for the merchandise and furnishings they rescued from the flames. This naturally resulted in a greater concentration on salvage, along with the extinguishing of fires. Actual steps toward fire prevention began when local construction changed from the frame and canvas structures of

the Gold Rush years to brick buildings with metal turn-plate roofing and heavy iron shutters, at least for commercial buildings; wood frame construction for residential buildings continues to this day.

In 1866 the volunteer fire companies were transformed into a civic fire department. At about the same time, the hand-pulled wagons were replaced by horse-drawn engines, and the manually operated pumpers were replaced by steam-operated Amoskeag engines. The old leather hoses were replaced by canvas hoses fitted out with brass nozzles. Fire hydrants were placed at strategic spots in the city. New firehouses contained second-story dormitories where salaried firemen resided during their duty hours. The classic brass firepoles were installed for hurried exits, and a tower was added for the purpose of hanging up the hoses to dry. These last two features are to be found in firehouses to this day. By 1867 the city numbered fourteen engines, three hook-and-ladder and five hose companies.

In the last years of the nineteenth century, the old firehouse on Brenham Place, on the west flank of Portsmouth Plaza, was fitted out as an alarm station. A series of wet cells set in glass jars were employed to signal

Knickerbocker Fire Company #5, on Sacramento Street near Leidesdorff, had a handsome Gothic facade sandwiched between two "fireproof" buildings with strong iron shutters over windows and doors. Lillie Coit was the mascot of this company from 1854 until her death in 1927. (Author's collection)

the forty fire stations which now dotted the city. The Chicago fire of 1871 had so alarmed city officials that the fire chief was permitted to place covered cisterns filled with salt water under the crossings of many city streets. In older parts of San Francisco the large circular rings, outlined with cobblestones or bricks, may still be seen in the intersections of several streets.

In the years preceding the 1906 holocaust, Fire Chief Dennis Sullivan, a veteran of some 26 years of service, had been badgering the city fathers to re-activate the old cisterns and to add many more. Finding the indifference of city leaders impossible to overcome, he quietly added a score of reservoirs without burdening the city council. In 1906 Chief Sullivan was killed early on the morning of April 18 by a falling chimney; he was

the only person in the city who knew where these desperately needed cisterns were concealed. This story may only be one of the countless myths bandied about by survivors of that catastrophe; there is no way to prove the truth of the tale, repeated to me by many an old-time San Franciscan.

The story of San Francisco's early-day fire companies would be incomplete without mention of the legendary Lillie Hitchcock Coit, who as a child was adopted as a mascot by the brave members of Knickerbocker Engine #5. The boys first encountered little Lillie when she was a schoolgirl. Straining to pull their engine up the perilously steep slopes of Telegraph Hill, they were beginning to flag when Lillie threw down her schoolbooks and grabbed one of the pulling ropes, urging the boys to pull harder and faster. Whenever the Knickerbocker Company was called upon, there, more often than not, would be little Lillie, cheering them on. Her mother, the wife of an Army surgeon, who considered herself an arbiter of San Francisco society, was horrified at the child's hoydenish behavior. But somehow Lillie managed to slip away from her parents whenever the fire bell rang. Once she raced after the engine while wearing a bridesmaid's gown. When a firefighting gang of competitors jeered the boys from Number Five for having a girl mascot, her own boys turned the hose on her to show that she was no sissy.

In later years, at a masked ball at Napoleon III's Tuilleries in Paris, Lillie arrived wearing the helmet of a San Francisco fireman. As long as she lived she had the insignia of Number Five embroidered on her handkerchiefs, shirtwaists and fans. After an absence of some forty years she returned to spend her last days in San Francisco. When she died in 1927 she left money for a statue in Washington Square, dedicated to San Francisco's firefighters, as well as a considerable sum to be used for a memorial to be erected on Telegraph Hill. This last bequest was used to build Coit Tower.

The story of those days of derring-do has become an ingrained part of San Francisco's most revered traditions. Today San Francisco boasts 44 active fire houses, more than 1600 personnel and 373 signal stations, as well as a fleet of fireboats (established in 1909) which stretches from the eastern waterfront to Mile Rock. Fire buffs may want to visit the Firehouse Museum on Presidio Avenue between Pine and California Streets, or the Oakland Museum, or the Petaluma Museum, where one can see magnificent antique fire engines with all their glittering hardware intact, seeming to express a defiant optimism in the face of the flames. Today's army of firefighters guard the city with the same bravery and dedication as did those first San Francisco firemen so long ago.

Originally built for the prominent Bowie family, this handsome brick house on Pike Street (now Waverly Place) later became the home and business place of madame Belle Cora, whose husband Charles was hanged by the Vigilante Committee. The house later became a Chinese Joss House. (Author's collection)

A
BOSTON
OF THE
PACIFIC

1854 - 1869

WHAT THE BISHOP SAW

Children of the next generation, to you we bequeath the contest. Living over our dust and inheriting the fruit of our labors, we pray you worthily to wage this warfare 'til you resign your weapons and join us in the land of spirits.

— William I. Kip, First Episcopal Bishop of California

CULTURALLY, SAN FRANCISCO could hardly have been called a "Boston of the Pacific," as some claimed her to be, but in her commercial endeavors and outward appearance, the city of the 1850s would not have looked out of place among the towns of the Eastern seaboard. San Francisco certainly struck Bishop William Kip, the first Episcopal Bishop of California, as an interesting, cosmopolitan city when he arrived in 1853.

This was not the rough and ready Gold Rush town he expected to find, but rather a solid, stable-looking community. Blocks of sturdy warehouses and imposing business establishments had mushroomed up on the land-filled blocks east of Montgomery Street. Above these brick and granite buildings

Episcopal Bishop William L. Kip

were frame cottages, pre-fabricated houses, and mansions packed "cheek to jowl" along the lower slopes of Nob, Russian and Telegraph Hills.

If the residential areas were not so prepossessing as the business districts, they were at least as interesting. "On one side," the Bishop wrote, "I encountered a small chateau imported from France, while in the same block were a German house of iron and heavy timbers, and next to it a Chinese house of bamboo with roll-up bamboo blinds. . . The Pine Street house assigned to me was, like its neighbors, so flimsily constructed, with its interior walls and ceilings of muslin, that I dared not trust my valuable books and papers in it. And this at a rental of six hundred dollars a month."

On the steep hillsides, frame houses on lots with small frontages prevailed. There were also iron houses from England, Belgium and France. Some were ugly, corrugated iron structures, while others had walls comprised of smooth iron panels. These pre-cut houses, generally pieced together by their owners, reflected the efforts of amateurs. Designed to sit on flat ground, most were a nuisance to assemble on San Francisco's steep hillsides. An iron cottage from Holland had to be placed on stilts to meet the steep slope of its lot on Green Street. It remained at that address only until heavy rains in 1850 deposited it onto its neighbors lower down the slope.

A number of families, willing to risk the dangers of living in more isolated areas, built themselves country villas and farm houses out on the sandy wastes to the west of town, or southward in the warmer climate of the Mission District. For a time, these houses dotted even the steep upper slopes of Nob, Telegraph and Russian Hills. Old photographs show their fences marching across the slopes in crazy patterns.

On California Street at Grant Avenue stands Old St. Mary's Cathedral, dedicated on Christmas morning in 1854. Its sturdy walls are of brick brought as ships' ballast around the Horn, while its granite foundation and trim came from China. In the ninety-foot steeple are two clocks which have served as the community's timepieces for generations. Beneath the front dial are gold letters originally intended to be a warning to those long-gone roisterers on Dupont Street: "Son, Observe the Time and Fly from Evil."

The church, which began as the cathedral for a small city, shortly became surrounded by the largest Chinese community in America. As early as 1850, the Chinese migrants to California were settling around Portsmouth Plaza's northern side. A decade later they had completely inundated the area above the Plaza, extending from Kearny Street up the slopes of Nob Hill to Stockton Street, and south from Broadway to Bush. By the mid-1870s, the area had a Chinese population of some thirty thousand residents.

Photographs of Old Chinatown reveal, behind the lantern-hung balconies and garish oriental signboards, the sober brick and frame structures of New England merchants, forgotten reminders of a time when San Francisco was described as "A Boston of the Pacific."

Pike Street was one of the early residential streets which became a part of Chinatown. One house on Pike Street was the domicile of Belle Cora, one of the most notorious madames of Gold Rush San Francisco. Her house, formerly the home of one of the town's respectable families, may be the one described in 1849 by Bayard Taylor, "A house that was not a home:"

See yonder house, its curtains are of the purest embroidered lace, and crimson damask. Go in. All its furnishings are in keeping, most expensive, most voluptuous, most gorgeous. . . . It is a soiree night. The "lady" of the house has sent the most polite invitations, got up on the most expensive, most beautifully embossed paper, to all the principal gentlemen of the city, including the Collector of the Port, the Mayor, aldermen, judges of the county and members of the legislature. A splendid band of music is in attendance. Away over the Turkish carpet whirls the politician with some sparkling beauty, as fair as frail; and the judge joins in and enjoys the dance in the company of the beautiful but lost beings, whom tomorrow he may send to the house of correction. Not an unbecoming word is said, not an objectionable action seen. The girls are on their good behavior and are proud once more to move and act as ladies. You would not suspect that you were in one of those dreadful places so vividly described by Solomon.

Life was seldom so pleasant for San Francisco's prostitutes. Mistress Belle, for example, made the fatal step of becoming involved with a hot-tempered gambler named Charles Cora. After a shooting affray, in which he killed one of the town's leading citizens, Cora was captured and jailed, and the Vigilance Committee demanded immediate punishment. Just before Cora stepped out to be hanged on the scaffolding erected in front of "Fort Gunnybags," the Vigilante headquarters, he and Belle were married. After this bittersweet event, Belle closed down her house and retired there to spend the remainder of her days in mourning. The brothel was later converted into a Chinese Joss House. In more genteel times, the name of wicked Pike Street was changed to Waverly Place.

Resorts and Houses Along the Mission Road

I N 1849 A GROUP of speculators began to plan the construction of a planked toll road, forty feet wide, in order to connect the commercial center of the town with the old settlement surrounding Mission Dolores. The path of Market Street, grandly laid out by Jasper O'Farrell two years earlier, proved impractical because immense sand hills blocked the way. A parallel line below Market Street, today's Mission Street, was chosen for the new road, and the ambitious project was begun. Two years later, after almost insurmountable difficulties in bridging a deep marsh at today's Seventh Street, and the expenditure of $96,000—about $30,000 per mile—the plank road was finally opened, with tolls of 25¢ for a man on horseback, 75¢ for a team and carriage, and $1 for a four-horse team and wagon.

Russ's Gardens, near Sixth and Harrison Streets, was the site of countless celebrations staged by many different nationalities, but was especially appealing to German immigrants, who enjoyed picnics and beer in this warm setting not far from Mission Bay. (Courtesy San Francisco Public Library.)

Francois Pioche's Hermitage, a very early pre-fabricated Gothic house, sat on low ground along the Mission Road. The house had fine gardens, an artificial lake, and a conservatory large enough to house Pioche's Lucullan banquets. It was flooded in the winter of 1862. (Author's collection)

As the mission founders had long known, the area around the mission had the finest climate and the best soil on the upper peninsula. Farmers began raising vegetables, fruit and flowers for the San Francisco market. In those days a bouquet of geraniums might fetch as much as $50; on one historic occasion Miss Bessie Thornton, a daughter of Judge Thornton, received from a young admirer a bouquet costing more than $100. Undoubtedly the Mission Road was heavily traveled, both by pleasure seekers and by wagons bringing produce to the thousands of hungry city dwellers. Whether the speculators ever recovered their enormous investment is not known, but the road must have been profitable, for a second toll road was built just three years later, in 1854, along today's Folsom Street.

A rare photograph has come to light depicting a pre-fabricated Gothic Revival mansion which stood beside the Mission Road, not far from Mission Dolores. The original owners were an Australian couple named Hart. Their widowed daughter, Mrs. Carnegie, married Colonel Stevenson, the officer who had brought the New York Volunteers to California in 1847. In 1857, the Harts sold what was already regarded as a showplace to a French banker, Francois Pioche, who added more luxurious touches. He installed lawns and flower gardens, and added an enormous flower-hung conservatory which, on grand occasions, he used as a banquet hall, seating as many as sixty guests.

Because of its remoteness, Pioche named his place "The Hermitage," and he wrote a little poem about it:

"Away from the din of the city,
The busy mart and the street,
Stands the old church of the Mission
With my Hermitage at its feet."

Pioche's contributions, both culturally and financially, were many, but what is best recalled of this remarkable man was the fact that he imported forty Parisian chefs to San Francisco so that his city would be assured a future as a center for epicures. He is also credited with founding the famed Poodle Dog restaurant. In a city which came to pride itself on the number of its *bon vivants*, he was a true pioneer. Unfortunately, in the winter of 1862, the waters of a nearby lake overflowed and inundated his lovely house and gardens. Shortly thereafter he built a fine mansarded mansion on Stockton Street. The small lake which he left behind was long known as Pioche's Pond.

ANOTHER VICTIM OF that fateful winter storm was a charming little resort called The Willows, established in 1849 near today's Eighteenth Street. A lake, Laguna de los Dolores, served as the resort's focal point. Tables and a platform for dancing were placed under the willows fringing the water. The tavern, fronting the Mission Road, provided beverages of all sorts to those who flocked there for Sunday outings, or to attend the races at two tracks further down Mission Road. There were facilities for such large celebrations as the Fourth of July, Bastille Day or Fasching.

The Willows, the first resort in the Mission area, stood on dangerously low ground on the southern border of Laguna Dolores, on today's 19th Street between Guerrero and Dolores. (Author's collection)

All of this came to an abrupt end, however, with the floods in the winter of 1862, when the lake overflowed and much of the resort floated away.

The Mansion House, famed for its milk punch, got its name from the mission padres' *convento*, which had occupied a wing adjoining the Mission Dolores. On weekends and holidays the hitching rack in front was lined with the horses and carriages of those who wanted to get away from the crowded streets around Portsmouth Square.

Early in the 1850s Christian Russ, the town's leading jeweler, moved his family from the abandoned ship's cabin they had occupied at Bush and Montgomery Streets to a fine house out in the wilds, near today's Sixth and Harrison Streets. On the site of the former ship's cabin Russ then built a fine hotel, the Russ House, where the Russ Building stands today.

On May Day, 1853, Russ invited all of San Francisco's German colony to celebrate at his country place. In a great festive parade, some eighteen hundred people marched down the Mission Road to spend the entire day dancing and drinking beer in Russ's gardens. His guests clamored for him to open the place to the public, and Russ eventually obliged, charging only a small admission fee. Russ's Gardens became a popular San Francisco resort for two decades. German settlers enjoyed enormous Sunday picnics, while in the evening guests danced and drank beer or wine in the lantern-hung gardens and trellised pavilions. Russ's Gardens were also ideal for

the French to celebrate Bastille Day and the Irish to enjoy St. Patrick's Day.

Travelers along the Mission Road had no need to go thirsty. Still another resort, City Gardens, was established at 12th and Folsom Streets in the spring of 1867. To attract the fashionable Rincon Hill crowd to its grand opening, the resort illuminated its flower gardens and winding paths with Chinese lanterns at night. There were also pretty, trellised arbors, and a dance platform where a band played nightly. Other resorts in the neighborhood were the Grizzly Bear, the Nightingale, and Witzeleben's Brewery, near the old Mission. Farther south, beyond Mission Dolores and the two race tracks, The Red House and Chris Lilley's were frequented by duelists who met there to avenge insults at dawn. "Pistols for two and coffee for one" was said to be a standing order for breakfast at Lilley's.

Perhaps the best remembered Mission District resort, and certainly the most popular, was Woodward's Gardens. Robert Woodward, the owner, made his fortune as proprietor of the What Cheer House, a hotel dating from Gold Rush days, on Leidesdorff Street. The What Cheer House offered clean and comfortable, though modest, rooms to its strictly male clientele. Opening on July 4, 1852, it became an instant success. By 1865, the What Cheer House had expanded to over a thousand rooms, and its dining room accommodated hundreds of people daily. It even had a library and a museum of curios available to hotel patrons.

The entrance to Woodward's Gardens, near 14th and Mission Streets. For thirty years the gardens were the leading resort for the people of San Francisco. At right is what appears to be an enormous bust of George Washington. (Courtesy San Francisco Public Library)

A man who appreciated the good things in life, Woodward purchased a four-acre plot in 1857 near today's Fourteenth and Mission Streets. He set out to create a handsome country house surrounded by beautiful gardens. In 1861 Woodward took his family on the Grand Tour of Europe, where they remained for a year and a half on a buying trip. The Woodwards not only picked up paintings, sculptures and exotic plants, but also brought back a number of animals for a little zoo in their gardens.

Shortly after their return, Woodward commissioned Virgil Williams, a young San Francisco painter who was studying abroad, to make exact copies of old masters' paintings then enjoying popularity on the Continent. Williams sent him eight or ten excellent copies, as well as a number of his own paintings. Woodward's taste in the arts might have been naive, but it differed little from that of other rich Americans combing Europe for "old masters." At least Woodward knew that his copies were just that; many American travelers returned with what they believed to be genuine Titians or Van Dykes. Upon his return, Woodward displayed some of his collection at the What Cheer House, but kept his favorite paintings at his Mission District estate.

With his growing collection of plants and paintings, Woodward was soon besieged by visitors. He had always been generous in letting visitors wander through his house and gardens, but the sight of multitudes of San Franciscans trying to get a glimpse of his house through the high fence led Woodward to open the gates to the public. In May 1866 he opened his estate to visitors for a small admission charge and moved with his family to a splendid estate he owned in the Napa Valley.

WOODWARD GRADUALLY BECAME quite a showman, with a genius for pleasing the public. The visitor, passing through the high-walled entrance decorated with a pair of large statues of Indian maidens and two huge, crouching bears holding flag poles, moved into a garden of delights which could be compared best to a miniature Tivoli. There were fountains, waterfalls, grottoes and an artificial lake stocked with ducks and swans. Tame animals, including ostriches, deer and small barnyard animals, roamed the grounds, to the delight of the

Woodward's Gardens, interior art gallery. The children, dressed in their Sunday best, are busily absorbing the culture Woodward had imported from Europe. (Courtesy San Francisco Public Library)

The menagerie at Woodward's Gardens apparently mixed wild and domestic animals, if this engraved advertising poster is to be believed: the Peacable Kingdom in San Francisco. (Courtesy James Heig)

visitors. There was even a tame bear who would perform for a bag of peanuts.

Among the caged attractions at Woodward's Gardens were California grizzlies, Oregon and Mexican panthers, South American jaguars, Bengal tigers, wolves, foxes, raccoons, weasels, camels and monkeys. Woodward's estate also featured the first salt-water aquarium in America. Huge glass tanks lined both sides of a forty-foot hallway made of stone, in imitation of undersea grottoes.

There were camel rides and little carriages pulled by goats for children, as well as a circular pond in which a "rotary boat" whirled laughing and screaming children around the pool's perimeter. The former Woodward house was converted into the Museum of Natural Wonders and filled with an array of curiosities which, it was hoped, would be of educational merit. In the best San Francisco tradition, there was a wonderful bandstand with flying pennants and hanging baskets of flowers. Here one could listen to band concerts every afternoon and evening, and join in the dancing. For almost thirty years, San Francisco found Woodward's Gardens with its ever-increasing number of attractions to be a favorite place of amusement. With the establishment of Golden Gate Park in the mid-seventies, however, the popularity of Woodward's Gardens began to wane. It finally closed in 1894; its collections were dispersed or auctioned off, and its hills were levelled to meet the onslaught of new housing in the area.

In the 1850s and 1860s the area south of Market Street boasted Rincon Hill and South Park as elegant residential quarters of the city, and the Mission Road was dotted with fine country places, interspersed with more modest farmsteads and lively resorts and taverns. By the mid-1860s the south of Market was filling with thousands of immigrants who came to work in the factories growing up around Rincon Point and Mission Bay, and in the slaughterhouses to the south on Bryant Street. Most of this section went up in flames in 1906, but in the areas south of 19TH Street, where the fire was stopped, the narrow side streets are still lined with workmen's cottages, while broader streets are dotted with comfortable family homes and even the occasional grand mansion. South of Market, with its sunny valleys sheltered from the wind and fog blowing in from the Pacific, appealed to people in all walks of life.

STOCKTON STREET

In the early 1850s, those first families with enough optimism to build houses in reckless, incendiary San Francisco chose to locate on Stockton Street and along the lower slopes of Nob and Russian Hills. At that time, the struggle over Mexican land titles was in full swing, so it was impossible for the town to expand south of Pine Street. In the few old views available, Stockton Street hardly appears very impressive, but it was the first street to feature planked sidewalks, and quickly became the premier locale for the fashionable afternoon promenade, as well as the most logical place for the town's more elegant shops, dwellings and boarding houses.

The city's custom of afternoon promenades grew out of grim necessity. At four o'clock in the afternoon the gentlemen would quit their places of business to join the ladies at the fashionable Oriental Hotel for an afternoon stroll along Stockton Street. This was mainly because the tides of San Francisco Bay swept refuse under the pilings of their hotel, and the smell drove them out. From the Oriental the promenaders marched up to the corner of Stockton, and walked north to Pacific Avenue. For some now-forgotten reason, this was the usual turning point; a worn hollow in the wood-planked sidewalk at Pacific marked the spot where the walkers turned. Of course, San Francisco in Gold Rush times was no place for an unescorted lady to walk. These afternoon jaunts, then, were the only opportunity for the ladies at the Oriental and the other hotels to escape their purdah-like existence and get some exercise.

The *Alta* relates the story of a herd of cattle being sent down Montgomery Street in these early days. One of the steers broke loose and headed up the hill and out Stockton Street. It paused in its flight only long enough to invade a millinery shop, where a chic straw hat in the window had caught its eye. While the shrieking proprietress took refuge at the back of the shop, the errant steer made a quick snack of the straw bonnet and then continued its escapade.

Some of San Francisco's first dwellings stood on Stockton Street. Sam Brannan's frame "mansion" stood at the southeast corner of Washington and Stockton; later it was moved to the middle of the block, west of Spofford Alley, where it served as a post office. Another wooden building on the northwest corner of Washington and Stockton belonged to Henry Meiggs when he was still known as "Honest Harry."

One of the earliest of the fine houses on Stockton Street stood on the northwest corner at Washington. A pre-fabricated Greek Revival style mansion, this was the home of one of San Francisco's most outstanding pioneers, Captain Martin Rickard Roberts. Some years ago, a grand-daughter of the Captain, Mrs. Hugh Brown, was kind enough to describe to the author some high points of this man's distinguished career.

Born in England, Roberts came to this country when he was still in his teens to enter a rowing competition. He designed his own skiff to race, but when he won the contest, the other contestants complained that the craft had given him an unfair advantage. The officials declared the race invalid and scheduled a rematch. This time Roberts used an American craft, and won once again.

By the time he was 21, Roberts had a ship of his own, picking up passengers and freight at all the Atlantic ports. His life at sea was so busy that he never had time to think about matrimony. Then, on one of his trips, he noticed a sprightly young thing among the passengers from Mobile. His interest in the young woman might have gone no further if not for the intervention of one of those terrific storms common on the Eastern Seaboard. As the wind began to rise and all the terrified passengers had been ordered below, the Captain was approached by this strange Southern belle, who announced that she had never experienced a storm on the high seas and would like to be tied to a mast. The Captain, too astonished to protest, did as she requested. When the storm ended and the girl pronounced it the thrill of her lifetime, the Captain was not only bowled over, he was smitten; the young couple were soon married.

Shortly after their first child was born, the Captain was asked to head the newly established Pacific Mail Steamship Line, and he had to sail to California at once. His wife agreed to follow him. With her new baby still nursing, Mrs. Roberts sailed down the East Coast, as had thousands of others heading for California before her. She took a river boat at Chagres, through malarial swamps and steaming jungles, to cross the Isthmus of Panama. In later years, a train made this crossing much easier, but at this time the passengers had to travel on mules. Mrs. Roberts carried with her a little three-legged stool which she sat on while nursing her infant in sheltered spots along the way to California. The stool still is a treasured family heirloom.

After arriving in San Francisco, Captain Roberts and his young family lived for a year aboard his ship, which was tied up at the foot of Broadway. Then they moved

This view, from 1865, shows the south side of California Street near Stockton, looking toward Rincon Hill in the background. The houses, built before the street was graded, needed steep stairways to provide access after grading was complete. (Courtesy California Historical Society)

The Roberts house at Washington and Stockton Streets, built in 1850, escaped five major fires that leveled most of the town. At top left is the iron Methodist Episcopal church, built on Powell Street in 1850. At right is the home of Captain Macondray, who moved to fashionable Rincon Hill in the 1860s. At the rear is the summit of Russian Hill. (Author's collection.)

Senator William Gwin built this crenelated fortress house on Pacific, west of Stockton Street. When the Gwins left San Francisco on the eve of the Civil War they sold the house to Dr. Toland, of the Toland Medical School. In later years it became a Chinese laundry. (Author's drawing, from an old newspaper of the time)

into one of the pre-fabricated houses that abounded in San Francisco. Mrs. Brown laughed, recalling life in her grandparents' house. Most houses of this type, she said, had been knocked together by their owners with the help of a carpenter or two, and the floors of the various rooms were seldom level with one another. "You had to remember this," she noted, "otherwise you could break your neck."

Captain Roberts was no man to trifle with. During the Civil War, while attending a costume ball at the Tuilleries in Paris, he was mistaken for Garibaldi. His Italian military costume was so convincing that someone in the crowd asked him to undertake a dangerous mission to Italy, impersonating Garibaldi. Mrs. Roberts was aghast at the suggestion, but the Captain took the assignment, traveled to Italy, and returned to Paris unscathed. To Mrs. Roberts, this daring feat brought back all the dangers of the early days in San Francisco, when the Vigilante bell would ring, calling out the men to deal with some unruly element of the incendiary town.

Mrs. Brown was also quick to point out that, with people of her grandparent's generation, there were no gray areas. Black was black and white was white. Captain Roberts disowned her uncle, Theodore Roberts, after discovering that he had become an actor. A photograph of the Stockton Street house, after it was "modernized" in the 1860s, reveals a "spite fence," put up by the Captain after he had some dispute with his next-door neighbor.

Adjoining the house of Captain Roberts is the one-story frame house which originally belonged to Captain Macondray. Macondray later moved to Rincon Hill, presumably before the "spite fence" incident took place. His name was later given to a lane on Russian Hill, one of San Francisco's "secret" places until it was made famous in Armistead Maupin's *Tales of the City*.

One of the most striking houses on Stockton Street was the large French town house built by Francois Pioche in 1863, after the destruction of his lovely Hermitage on Mission Road. Boasting what was probably the first mansard roof in San Francisco, it would have looked at home on one of the grand boulevards in Paris. The new "French roof" design was actually some 200 years old, and was named for the 17th-century architect, Francois Mansart. Its almost vertical slope allowed more headroom and more light in the attic. The Mansardic, or Second Empire style, was to sweep America in the post-Civil War period. Pioche, with his close connections with his homeland, was just the man to introduce this new fashion to San Francisco. A critic of Victorian architecture has called the mansard roof "the crowning indignity."

Poor Monsieur Pioche was to enjoy his fine house for only a decade. Then, for no explainable reason, he shot himself one morning in the luxurious bed chamber, with its fine view of the city. Shortly thereafter, his house, like Belle Cora's, was converted into a Chinese Joss House.

On the east side of Stockton, at Clay Street, was the former house of Jacob Leese, which Leese traded with Thomas Larkin for the aforementioned Larkin Adobe in Monterey. Larkin, a shrewd man, was one of the few Yankees in Mexican California to retain his wealth after the United States annexed the territory. In 1860 Larkin built a four-story brick mansion at 286 Stockton Street.

ON JACKSON STREET, just above Stockton, California's first United States Senator, William McKendree Gwin, built a crenelated Gothic Revival house in 1855. A strange mixture of Gothic and Italianate detailing, with a crenelated parapet, the Gwin mansion was the end result of several additions and alterations. It was also a political center in San Francisco, where elegant balls and collations which often numbered fourteen courses were an almost nightly occurrence. Mrs. Gwin's New Year's eggnog parties were famous, and the food laid out for these affairs made the Gwin house a choice destination for the hordes of young men who dutifully made their rounds of calls on New Year's Day.

Amelia Ransom Neville, in her fascinating picture of San Francisco of that day, *The Fantastic City*, wrote that a young man at this time was expected to leave his calling card at the home of each prospective hostess on New Year's Day if he hoped to be received during the rest of the year. If the lady was not at home, there was sure to be a basket for calling cards hung on the knocker of the front door.

Senator Gwin, a southerner, was the son of one of Andrew Jackson's cabinet members; as a youth he studied for the bar in Jackson's office. In later years, Senator Gwin had a mane of white hair that strongly reminded people of "Old Hickory." As a young man, however, Gwin had political aspirations of his own. He won a high political office in Mississippi, where he had established a large plantation near Vicksburg. Despite this early success, the lure of an active political life in

Francois Pioche built this house in 1862 at 806 Stockton Street, after he was flooded out of the Hermitage on Mission Road. It was probably the first in the city to boast a mansard roof. After Pioche committed suicide here in 1871, the building became a Chinese Joss House. (Author's collection)

California, which was just then struggling for statehood, proved stronger than the call of his plantation. The young aristocrat chose to forego the position he enjoyed in Mississippi for a chance at a new life in the unsettled West. After the constitutional convention in Monterey, he and John C. Fremont were elected California's first United States Senators.

While in Washington, Gwin sponsored a number of bills which were invaluable to the development and prosperity of the new state, including a bill which paved the way for the railway that would connect the East and the West. Mrs. Gwin made her own mark as one of Washington's most brilliant hostesses.

When Gwin's position as a "long term" Senator came to an end on the eve of the Civil War, the couple returned to a city plunged into turmoil. In the hysteria of the moment, many San Franciscans accused Gwin, who owned plantations and slaves in Mississippi, of trying to lead California into the secessionist camp. Though such accusations seem to have had no foundation in fact, the Senator sent his wife

The beautiful stone Grace Episcopal Church stood at the crest of Stockton Street; its altar today serves Grace Cathedral, on Nob Hill. Behind the church, leading up from Pine Street, was Sophie Terrace. At right is the finely proportioned mansion of Joseph Barron, a partner of Thomas Bell, Mammy Pleasant's consort. The iceman had many steps to climb. This picture was taken around 1860, from the Jonathon Stevenson house on the east side of Stockton. (Courtesy California Historical Society)

and children to Paris when war broke out. They were joined there by a number of other San Franciscans with Southern sympathies. Unluckily, the Senator himself delayed his departure and was arrested on a Pacific Mail steamer. For two years he languished in a Union prison for Confederate sympathizers.

After his release, Gwin joined his family in Paris as a guest of Napoleon III at the Tuilleries Palace. The Civil War was by then nearing its end, and the Senator worked with the Duc de Monthalon on a plan to establish disenfranchised Southern officers and their families in Mexico. This scheme appeared plausible during the short and tragic reign of the Emperor Maximilian and Empress Carlotta, who were installed on the Mexican throne after Napoleon III had annexed Mexico as part of the French Empire. France hoped that dispossessed Southerners, joined by some of California's gold miners, would migrate to Mexico and exploit its rich, untouched resources. With the deposition of Maximilian, however, the plan fell through, and Gwin abandoned his Mexican scheme. Nevertheless, after Senator Gwin was allowed to return to California, the local press dubbed him "The Duke of Mazatlan."

At the end of the war, the resilient Senator was able to reclaim his devastated plantations in Mississippi as

Three adjoining houses are classic examples of pre-Civil War dwellings in San Francisco's first fashionable neighborhood. The Carpenter Gothic Bonnestel house at 512 Stockton, center, is identical to several other pre-fabricated Bay Area houses, including the Mariano Vallejo house in Sonoma and the Captain Walsh house in Benicia. The little boy on the front stoop is Chesley Bonnestel, who became a well-known artist. His last effort, a series of paintings of California missions, was published in 1978. (Author's collection)

well as a very productive California gold mine. These operations allowed the Gwins to live in great style in a mansion on Rincon Hill. By this time, the Stockton Street house had become the home of Dr. Toland, founder of a medical school in San Francisco. In later years it became a Chinese laundry.

Another hospitable Stockton Street mansion belonged to the McAllisters. Members of a prominent Savannah family, the brothers Ward, Hall, and Cutler McAllister came to California during the Gold Rush but soon found that practicing as lawyers was far more lucrative than working with a pick and shovel. Ward, the oldest son, soon abandoned the

crudities of life in Gold Rush San Francisco for a position as the social arbiter of Newport and New York. With Mrs. John Jacob Astor, this gentleman established the list of four hundred people who defined New York society.

Remaining in San Francisco, Cutler and Hall McAllister found the practice of law to be so remunerative that they sent for their father, old Judge McAllister, to come join them. The Judge, perfectly happy in Savannah, saw no reason to give up his comfortable position. Then he received a birthday gift of an enormous bank draft from his sons. In no time, the Judge sold his Savannah properties and headed west to

One of the fine houses on Stockton Street, on a steep lot just north of California, was the home of Colonel John Stevenson, who had brought the New York Volunteer Regiment to San Francisco by ship in 1846, with some idea of conquest, only to discover that the American flag was already flying in Portsmouth Square. The house boasts a double stairway leading up from the street, with an elegant veranda and balcony. (Courtesy California Historical Society)

join the rest of his family. "Those boys were so careless about money," said the Judge, "that I felt it was my duty to come west in order to keep them in hand." The old Judge found his trip west to be personally rewarding, too, for he became circuit judge for the entire Bay Area.

Perhaps their father was right about needing to keep an eye on his extravagant sons; we learn from Mrs. Ransom Neville that Hall McAllister, an inveterate gambler, lost his new South Park house to "the dashing Captain Harry Lyons" in a poker game. When Stockton Street was no longer considered fashionable, the McAllisters all moved to Rincon Hill.

IN THOSE DAYS, before the so-called "Chinese invasion," Stockton Street and its environs were crowded with the homes of distinguished San Franciscans, but today many of their names are forgotten. Besides Gwin, Pioche, and the McAllisters, Captain Macondray, U.S. Senator Milton Latham, banker Alfred Borel, William Lane, Colonel John Stevenson, and Lieutenant Governor John B. Welles lived on or near Stockton Street. Several residents were judges: Arrington, Thornton, Crittenden, Hoge, Clements. Of such men, Gertrude Atherton wrote, "They trod the earth like giants and the earth shook at their tread. Now, alas, they lie forgotten in San Francisco's Lone Mountain cemetery." Mrs. Atherton and others of similar sentiment must have been truly shaken when, years later, the city sold Lone Mountain Cemetery to developers. Many of the old marble tombstones were used as fill during the extension San Francisco's Marina into the Bay. On a calm day, one can actually read the inscriptions on some of the headstones dumped into the water along the shoreline.

One name that California historians of this era do remember is that of Edward Vischer, Consul of Bavaria. In the 1860s, Vischer and his talented wife, Sophie, collaborated on a large album entitled "Pictorial California." This publication, the first of its kind, included large photographic views of the California Missions and of such scenic marvels as Yosemite and the redwoods. Not surprisingly, the Vischers' own abode, in the block between California

Author's sketch of Sophie Terrace, the Edward Vischer cottages on Pine and Stockton Streets, site of today's Ritz Carlton Hotel

and Pine Street just below Stockton, was a place of truly unique charm.

Named for Mrs. Vischer, "Sophie Terrace" was not a single structure but actually four separate Gothic Revival cottages, arranged along the uppermost of three terraced gardens. One of the cottages contained parlors and a dining room; a second held the kitchen. Cottage number three served as the Vischers' studio, and the fourth contained the bedrooms.

Guests of the hospitable Vischers might be invited to enjoy tea beneath a flowering apple tree. While breathing in the wonderful scents from the surrounding garden, they could enjoy an unobstructed view of the waterfront, where ships with their folded sails looked like sleeping birds. In those days, most San Franciscans had to buy drinking water from Sausalito by the bucketful, but the Vischers had their own artesian well, whose waters they shared with their neighbors. They passed the remaining years of their lives on Sophie Terrace, graciously entertaining their friends. Sophie died in 1871, and Edward in 1878.

Just above Sophie Terrace lived Joseph Barron, whose wealth from the New Almaden Quicksilver mine near San Jose enabled him build a handsome mansion on Stockton Street. He and his wife held a ball there in 1863 which surpassed anything previously seen in San Francisco. It left the newspapers carolling its praises for days. Said the society scribe for the *Argonaut*: "Those who had invitations were happy; those who had not were miserable." Guests mounted a stairway carpeted in white canvas, "lest the fairy-like Cinderella slippers of the ladies might be contaminated by contact with the vile earth . . . All was enchantment, the gowns from Paris, the glittering chandeliers and the sweet sounds of music." The scribe went on to list every inch of lace, tulle, ribbon and feathers, and of course all the diamonds worn by San Francisco's select.

Adjoining the Barron mansion, overlooking the corner of California and Stockton Streets, was the handsome new Grace Church, its communicants having left their former church on Pine Street in the '60s. When flames destroyed that entire block in 1906, nothing remained except the stone altar frontal of Grace Church. On it were inscribed the strangely prophetic words, "First an Earthquake, then a fire, then a still, small voice." This cherished remnant of the former church was later rescued and mounted on the front of one of the altars at the new Grace Cathedral on Nob Hill. Today, the colonnaded Metropolitan Life Insurance Company building, now remodeled as the Ritz-Carlton Hotel, occupies the site of Sophie Terrace, the church and the Barron house.

TELEGRAPH HILL AND NORTH BEACH

O Telygraft Hill, she sits proud as a queen,
And the docks stand below in the glare,
While the bay runs beyant her all purple and green
Wid a gingerbread island out there,
And th' ferryboats toot at owld Telygraft Hill,
And the Hill it don't care if they do,
While the Bradys and Caseys av Telygraft Hill
Joost sit there and enjoy the view.
For the Irish they live on the top av it,
And the Dagoes they live at the base av it,
And the goats and the chicks
And the brickbats and schticks
Is jumbled all over the face av it,
Av Telygraft Hill,
Crazy owld, daisy owld Telygraft Hill!

– Wallace Irwin

DESPITE ITS ELEVATED REMOTENESS, Telegraph Hill has always vibrated with the warmth and abiding magic of San Francisco. Rising north of the shore of Yerba Buena Cove, the hill was known as Loma Alta (High Hill) during the Spanish and Mexican periods. In 1839 the windswept hill and its immediate environs were granted by Governor Alvarado to General Vallejo's brother, Captain Salvador Vallejo, but, as with his other possessions, the conquering Americans relieved him of it. During the Gold Rush it was known briefly as Prospect Hill, and later as Billygoat Hill.

As San Francisco developed from sleepy Mexican settlement to frantic American boom town, the arrival of a ship became the most important event in civic life. Impatient for news of incoming ships, Joseph MacGregor, a Scottish dealer in nautical instruments, erected a two-story lookout with an observation platform on its roof. A pole passing through the roof of this tiny structure secured it to the ground. For a few months MacGregor operated his signal station, flashing the news when a ship was sighted by means of a heliographic code. From then on it has been known as Telegraph Hill.

In January 1850, George Sweeny and Theodore Baugh, proprietors of the Merchants' Exchange, bought the lot and MacGregor's station. On top of the lookout platform, they installed a semaphore tower whose black arms could be clearly discerned from the city below. Another signal station at Point Lobos, visible from the hill, relayed information. Now a ship that was still miles at sea could be spotted, and news of its place of origin, type, size, and content was on its way. A lookout on the hill would unfurl a signal flag, and the indicator on the station roof would stretch forth its ungainly wooden arms, reminiscent of a windmill's. At the signal, merchants, bartenders, gamblers, lawyers, just about anyone who could walk would rush down to the docks for mail and merchandise, or just to get the latest news from "back in the States."

Everyone knew the meaning of the complicated signals from Telegraph Hill. A familiar story tells of an actor in a melodrama at the American Theater on Portsmouth Square, who, in a tense and dramatic moment, flung up both arms, crying, "What does this mean?" From the balcony came the shout, "Side-wheel steamer!" An appreciative audience gave the quipster a rousing ovation.

In September 1850, the semaphore heralded the approach of the mail steamer *Oregon*, bearing the news that California had been admitted to the Union. That night the ship's arrival was heralded by a huge bonfire blazing on the very summit of Telegraph Hill. The time came, however, when the arrival of a ship no longer brought crowds to the wharf to celebrate. In 1855 the semaphore was abandoned. In 1871 the old signal station blew down in a windstorm, and the town took a moment to mourn its passing. The old wooden walls, where hundreds of people had carved their initials, wound up as firewood.

Originally the dome-shaped hill rose up steeply from the water's edge, and was a landmark for ships heading for Yerba Buena Cove. For all the roles that Telegraph Hill has played, and continues to play, in the life of the

The steep north slope of Telegraph Hill, looking across to Alcatraz and Angel Island, in the 1850s. The posts in the water denote boundaries of water lots. The house at center is another typical pre-fabricated Carpenter Gothic. (Author's Collection)

city at its feet, there has always been a feeling of remoteness hovering around its lofty summit. This could hardly be said of its lower reaches, three sides of which have been dynamited away over the years—first to provide ballast for departing ships, and then for fill for the flat areas on the east and north sides of the hill.

By 1850 THE TENTS of the 49ers had given way to rows and clusters of tiny cottages, clinging to the rocky slopes of Telegraph Hill. The cottages were reached by Jacob's ladders on the eastern slope, or by winding, seemingly endless flights of steps leading up from Broadway. On the lower, western slopes, the streets of the Chileño quarter attempted to follow the regular grid pattern of the city below. Halfway up, the attempt was abandoned, so that the rather isolated clusters of cottages near the top were reached by paths originally trodden by goats.

Today those narrow streets and alleyways, which often dead end at a steep drop, are paved; yet even the incursion of modern apartment buildings has done little

to alter the curious byways that make parking or driving a feat of bravery. That is part of the charm of the hill; residents feel secluded, tucked away in a secret place which only the insiders know. Some of San Francisco's oldest houses, like the Cooney house at 291 Union Street, are in the four or five hilltop blocks that escaped destruction in 1906. Several cottages with high-peaked Gothic Revival roofs and gingerbread fretwork under the eaves show their 1850s origins. Others have been remodeled and modernized during their 140 years of occupancy, but the careful observer can still identify them by their shape and their proximity to other old houses.

Much of Telegraph Hill's early community life centered around Broadway, the wide street running along the hill's southern slope, from Battery to Stockton Street. Broadway was the site of the city's first jail. Further up, it was the southernmost boundary of the Chileño Quarter. Still further up, near the present entrance to the Broadway tunnel, was a cluster of Mexican cottages, complete with a bull ring where

Beginning in 1849 this signal station on Telegraph Hill brought news of approaching ships to news-hungry, homesick residents of the little town. First flags, then semaphores were used to relay information from another lookout near the Golden Gate. (Courtesy California State Library)

bull-and-bear baitings were staged. Gradually, this cluster expanded eastward up the lower slopes, and the western side of Telegraph Hill became identified as San Francisco's Latin Quarter.

Photographs taken in the 1850s show the south sides of Telegraph Hill dotted with a fair sprinkling of peak-roofed cottages and, here and there, more impressive houses with two-story galleries. These larger houses were said to be the homes of "the river kings," men who controlled transportation on the vital inland waterways leading to the gold country. One river king's residence still stands at 31 Alta Street, at the crest of the hill, and has altered little from its original appearance. Built in 1852 for a Captain Andrews, it contained a kitchen and dining room in the brick ground floor section, with bedrooms and a parlor above, and a room for servants fitted under the steep gabled roof.

Another interesting survivor from the 1850s, at the northwest corner of Union and Montgomery Streets, is a thick-walled, flat-roofed, heavily stuccoed house with windows in deep-set reveals and a long balcony, suggesting it is made of adobe. It has long been called "the old Spanish house." An old photograph in the archives of the California Society of Pioneers shows the building to have been a handsome red brick edifice with a thoroughly American front porch. On the southeast corner was once a large

windmill, erected in 1850 by a man named Hudson, who used it to grind spices.

Despite the inroads of fashionable modern dwellings and apartment houses, Telegraph Hill still has much to attract those who seek the old and picturesque. Throughout its network of alleys and narrow streets are frame cottages, of Gothic and Italianate persuasion, which have attracted generations of artists and bohemians. The Compound, just below Julius' Castle; the Filbert Street steps clinging to the side of the hill; Napier Lane, with its cottages dating to the 1850s: all offer ample reward for those hearty enough to scramble up and down the crazy, precipitous hillsides of "Auld Telygraft Hill."

Henry Meiggs, one of San Francisco's first planners, worked out a scheme for a series of terraced streets, to make a kind of ziggurat out of the hill. The scheme never came to fruition, for "Honest Henry," burdened with debts, had to make a sudden departure from town. A similar scheme offered by Daniel Burnham in 1905 also failed, so the access to the crest of Telegraph Hill today is roughly the same as it was in the 1850s. The curved Telegraph Boulevard leading to Coit Tower is the only concession to the Burnham plan.

Beginning in 1849, the domed shape of the hill began to change, when the northern and eastern flanks were dynamited in order to create landing places for

This engraving shows the Metropolitan Theatre, on the occasion of Mrs. C. N. Sinclair's benefit, June 7, 1854. It is astonishing to see such an elaborate playhouse, with three balcony levels, a proscenium and an orchestra pit, at such an early date. One can't help wondering whether the artist embellished the design. (Courtesy California State Library)

cargo vessels which were arriving by the hundreds. The dislodged rock was used for ballast, or as foundations for buildings in the growing city. Destruction did not end with the Gold Rush. As late as the turn of the century, city fathers allowed Harry and George Gray to operate a quarry on the hill's eastern flank.

On an August evening in 1906, only four months after the earthquake, a mighty blast shook the hill's eastern side, lifting many of the hilltop houses from their foundations. It seems that the greedy Grays, in an effort to produce more gravel on their own property above the Embarcadero, had set off a dynamite explosion which carried away parts of several neighboring lots. Irate homeowners, accompanied by hysterical wives and children, were unable to sway corrupt city officials to stop the destruction of the entire hill. Even the shooting of one of Gray's employees had no effect. The blasting continued, on a smaller scale.

Eight years later, another shooting took place. This time it was a disgruntled employee who shot and killed George Gray. At last, the surviving brother, Harry Gray, swamped with lawsuits and injunctions, gave up his attempt to blast away the entire hill, and embarked on a less hazardous and more profitable career as an undertaker. By this time most of the Irish residents had fled to the Mission District. The ravaging effects of the Gray brothers' blasts are still clearly visible on the northern and eastern exposures of the hill. In the rainy spring of 1992, the steep cliff on the northeast exposure of the hill began to crumble, at first slowly, then faster, until a large apartment building was undermined and had to be evacuated and demolished.

The hill never lost its special color and charm, for on its western side, away from the blasts of the Gray brothers, lived the Italians. Escaping the strife that resulted from Garibaldi's campaign to unify Italy, the immigrants began settling in San Francisco in the 1860s, and before long the Spanish and South American residents of the Latin Quarter found themselves surrounded by Italians, who hung their fishnets on the back fence and made wine in wooden vats in their cellars. With their view of the bay's sparkling waters, dotted by the lateen sails of the Italian fishing boats, North Beach and the lower slopes of Telegraph Hill took on the enchanting and romantic look of Naples. Italian restaurants, pasta factories, groceries, bakeries and salami shops lined upper Grant Avenue and its cross streets, which were (and still are) redolent of garlic, tomato sauce, fresh bread and stout red wine. It has become a well-recorded part of San Francisco legend that some Italians saved their flats and cottages during the great fire of 1906 by beating out the flames with towels and blankets soaked in the wine vats in their cellars.

Ladies and gentlemen enjoy the garden of a Telegraph Hill house in the late 1850s. The men sport high silk hats and morning coats; the women wear the hoop skirts popular in pre-Civil War times. (Courtesy California Historical Society)

RARELY HAS ANY CITY been so delightfully and indelibly imprinted by the national character of an immigrant population. To many visitors, San Francisco seems to be primarily an Italian city with Chinatown as an exotic pocket in its midst. Hearty Italian food and wine, along with espresso coffee shops, attracted writers, artists, bohemians, and eventually beatniks and hippies. Among the writers who have lived on the hill are Mark Twain, Joaquin Miller, Richard Halliburton, and Frank Norris. That handsome poet, philosopher, journalist and all-around cynic, Ambrose Bierce, also called the hill his home. Bret Harte complained that the goats ate the geraniums in his second story window boxes and tramped over his roof at night "like heavy hailstones."

The great thespians Junius Brutus Booth and his sons, Junius Jr. and Edwin, shared a cottage that once stood at what is now 5 Calhoun Terrace, during the decade before Lincoln's assassination at the hands of Junius' oldest son, John Wilkes Booth. In the 1930s, a group of history buffs, planning to hang a commemorative tablet on the front of the former Booth house, arrived at the Calhoun Terrace address to find that the house had long since tumbled into the ravine below.

For those with a taste for the romantic, Telegraph Hill might be called a hill of castles. Pfeiffer's Castle, just above Stockton Street on a northern slope of the hill, was originally a large dwelling, but was converted in the 1880s into an asylum for inebriates. Pfeiffer Street and the following quatrain by Bret Harte are all that remain of it:

Lo! where the castle of bold Pfeiffer throws
Its sullen shadow on the rolling tide –
No more the home where joy and wealth repose,
But now where wassailers in cells abide.

Standing today at the end of Montgomery Street, Julius' Castle, a restaurant with a tower and a soaring façade, has been offering epicurean delights to San Franciscans and visiting firemen since 1921. Originally there was a wooden turntable in front to help customers who, even then, could find no parking place; one had only to blow the horn and a parking valet appeared to spin the car around and tuck it into a secret spot.

Frederick Layman, builder of the castle on Greenwich Street, at the top of this photograph, hoped it would rival the Cliff House as a tourist attraction, even laying a cable car line up the steep hill to make access easier. But neither Layman nor several succeeding owners could make a success of the castle, which went through astonishing changes before it burnt in 1903. (Courtesy California State Library)

But the most spectacular castle of them all was a rambling wooden pile complete with battlements, towers and a crenelated roof. The builder, Frederick Layman, intended it to rival the fashionable Cliff House on the city's western shore. Often called "Layman's Folly," the castle contained a restaurant, an auditorium and private dining rooms when it opened in 1882, but these attractions were not enough to make it a success. At first, people complained that the building was too remote, so Layman organized the Telegraph Hill Cable Railroad Company and laid a set of tracks from Powell Street up Greenwich to the Castle's front door. But even this attraction failed to draw customers. When financial difficulties forced Layman out of business, Adolph Sutro took over the castle, but he too failed to make the resort a success. Instead, the bad luck

Several small houses on the east side of Telegraph Hill survived the fire of 1906, and still cling precariously to the slope in the 1920s, when this view was taken. The houses in the foreground still line the Filbert Street steps. The turret of Julius's Castle, marking the north end of Montgomery Street, looks down on a passenger liner on the busy waterfront. (Courtesy California State Library)

continued. Legend has it that one day a loaded cable car went out of control, tore down the hill and crashed, killing several passengers.

Yet another owner, Duncan Ross, augmented the castle's medieval qualities with exhibitions of jousting and knightly battles. Every Sunday, he and a Captain Jensen, astride plow horses, would startle the Sunday picnickers as they slashed and bashed each other with swinging broadswords. For all his theatrics, however, Ross couldn't make a success of the castle either.

In quick succession, the resort became an athletic club, a vaudeville theater, an artist's studio and finally a cheap boarding house. For a time it was a bunkhouse for the Gray brothers' employees. Then, in 1903, the Castle once again opened as a resort, this time under the management of Mrs. A. Vincent. Just three months later flames broke out on the castle's roof, and the entire ruinous structure was a roaring inferno by the time the single horse-drawn fire engine could reach the summit. One part of the dilapidated structure plunged down the cliff, creating a sensational fire fall. After decades of failure, the final destruction of the ill-fated castle was spectacular.

Probably the only truly castle-like structure on the hill was the adobe fortress which Commander John B. Montgomery ordered built in 1846, shortly after he had raised the American flag in Portsmouth Square. His intention was to defend the harbor from any possible foreign aggressors. The fortress, at the site of Battery and Green Streets, was built of adobe blocks made on the banks of the Dolores Lagoon and brought to the hill by boat. Cannons were brought from the Presidio and lined up smartly, giving Battery Street its name. But no aggressors came. Eventually the cannons were returned, and the old fort melted into the ground where it stood.

Following the 1906 earthquake and fire, there was an explosion of civic consciousness, and with it a growing desire to commemorate some aspects of the city's colorful beginnings. San Franciscans, even when the city was relatively young, have always looked back nostalgically to an earlier, presumably happier day in their town's past. So it seemed a fine idea to build some sort of memorial to the little signal station of Gold Rush times. Daniel Burnham's plan had included a heroic classical monument at the top of the hill. The city's Greek population proposed to erect a copy of the Parthenon. This grand idea eventually was reduced to a simple pavement surrounded by a balustrade ornamented with huge urns. Once these were built, the public protested that the great urns blocked the wonderful hilltop view. The chastened city fathers eventually removed the entire mess.

Left: Lillie Coit (Courtesy San Francisco Public Library). Center: Coit Tower, 1996. Right: One of the oddest structures on Telegraph Hill is this tall, domed house with one room on each floor, built by Pasquale Gogna in 1930. (Courtesy California State Library)

In 1924, Lillie Hitchcock Coit, who as a child had been adopted as mascot of Volunteer Engine Company Number Five, left $100,000 to the city for general beautification, and $50,000 for a memorial to her beloved firemen. Part of her donation was spent for a large bronze statue, which stands today in Washington Square. The rest went into the erection of Coit Tower, designed by Arthur Brown, Jr., leading architect of the magnificent Civic Center. He drew what he apparently perceived to be an elegant, classically fluted column in the new Art Deco style, with a row of openings at the top to permit a sweeping view of the city. Once it was built, many people thought it was intended to look like the nozzle of a fire hose.

Indeed, there was considerable public disapproval of the completed tower. (In the 1930s we were not yet inured to architectural eccentricities, such as an office tower that comes to a point at the top, a cathedral in the shape of a washing-machine dasher, or hotels that look like a typewriter or a juke box.) San Franciscans often referred to Coit Tower as "our silo." One woman resident of Telegraph Hill was taken to court for firing a revolver at the tower; her attorney chastised her severely before the bench, saying she should have used a howitzer. Yet within a few years Coit Tower became a signature feature of the

city's skyline, shown in thousands of paintings and photographs.

Just as Telegraph Hill represents a unique geographic entity of San Francisco, so do its building patterns set it apart from the rest of the city. In the city's beginning, Gothic Revival cottages, with their fancy bargeboard fretwork, and false-fronted Italianate houses were typical of the town's modest Gold Rush dwellings. Here and there (such as at the cottage at Napier Lane), one still encounters a Yankee "saltbox" house, the model of which became a nearly universal symbol of Gold Rush times and the Yankee invasion of California. The fact that so many of these examples have survived on Telegraph Hill makes them unique in San Francisco.

Newcomers to the district are often surprised to see the "Romeo" flats or apartment houses which line many streets on the lower slopes of the hill. Dating from the post-quake reconstruction period, just after 1906, these structures got their name from the balconies which terminate each flight of outside stairs on the fronts of the buildings. These buildings appear to be unique, not just to California, but to Telegraph Hill in particular, although a few examples exist in other parts of the city. In San Francisco's mild climate, the inside hallway was dispensed with, and the stairway left open to the weather, with each balcony providing an excellent place for the formidable Italian landlady to keep an eye on goings-on in the street below.

With both front and rear stairs exposed, a Romeo flat makes an ideal multi-unit dwelling. Its building costs are low and the flats provide great privacy, as each unit has its own street entrance. Those long, dark hallways found in most apartment houses, with their attendant smells of cooking, are eliminated. In some of these North Beach and Telegraph Hill buildings today, a fancy façade curtains the formerly open stairs from the street. These façades are generally in the Renaissance Revival style, with arcaded entrances, decorative pilasters, and large oval lunettes above.

One classic example of this style is the three-story apartment house at 2055 Powell Street, designed by Suigi Mastropasqua, the architect of Julius' Castle. Its great oval windows feed light into the stairwell. Louis Traverso, A.G. Spargo, and John Porprato were other Italian-American architects who created these gifts to the slopes of Telegraph Hill and North Beach. The fact that the houses are built right to the sidewalks of the narrow thoroughfares makes one think of the crowded old walled cities of Italy.

When in the late 1920s the Art Deco craze swept San Francisco, Telegraph Hill seemed to be an epicenter. Along Montgomery Street, at the top of the hill, three or four rows of one-story cottages were swept away when the street was regraded in 1933, and in their place are three large Art Deco apartment buildings. Most notable is the block-buster at 1360 Montgomery, with a huge two-story etched-glass window in the style of Lalique, and two enormous *sgraffito* wall panels. (*Sgraffito* is created by scratching patterns through several layers of concrete.) This structure could have been a refreshing departure in another area of the city, near other large apartment houses. Here, among its diminutive neighbors, it looks like an elephant among Shetland ponies. Its huge front window has led to its nickname of "The Goldfish Tank."

In a neighborhood that expects the unexpected, the four-story tower crowned with a concrete hemisphere, at the end of Dunne's Alley off the first block of Kearny Street, seems to defy all logic. The pink, curiously phallic structure was built in 1930 by a local baker, Pasquale Gogna, and is known as "Pasquale's Tower." It consists of four rooms, placed directly one above the other, reached by an interior stairway running along the west side of the building. Kitchens and baths are set into alcoves in the corner of each square room. While the plan creates a few inconveniences, the spectacular views more than compensate. The top-floor studio is not for the faint of heart.

Telegraph Hill has been been many things to many people: a watchtower to the outside world with a signal on its crest, a goat and cow pasture, a picnic spot full of wild mustard and California poppies, a shelter first for sailing vessels with sails furled, then for side-wheel steamboats, and later still for sparkling white liners loading gaily-dressed passengers bound for Hawaii or exotic Asian ports. In wartime, crowds gathered on the hill to watch the fleets of grey battleships, destroyers, and aircraft carriers steam out on their way to battles in the Pacific. Once the bailiwick of Irish, Spanish, and Italians, it has welcomed immigrants, artists, eccentrics, playboys, gangsters, roues and their mistresses, beatniks, hippies, millionaire lawyers, art collectors, students and drag queens. Of the city's 42 hills, none offers a more stunning view of the changing colors of the bay, or of ships sweeping through the Golden Gate. In a world governed by change, a few things remain constant.

FORT MASON

SAN FRANCISCO HOUSES dating to the early 1850s are rarities to be particularly cherished. Six major conflagrations during the Gold Rush years, plus the earthquake and fire of 1906, have left precious few architectural reminders from those early years of settlement. Even today, the exact count is not known. But one spot where early houses are generally overlooked is Fort Mason, called by the Spaniards "Batteria de San Jose" because they had installed some bronze cannon on the highest point. The Americans called the place "Black Point" because of its dense growth of California bay laurel. The forested point was once separated from the land to the southwest by an enormous sand bank, sweeping from today's Gashouse Cove southeastward toward the slopes of Russian Hill.

In the days of the Gold Rush, Black Point was not a military reservation, but was simply a rather remote and inaccessible chunk of land covered with trees (a rarity in San Francisco) and commanding a splendid view of the Bay. People who liked privacy built houses there as early as 1850, and because of the peculiar location the houses escaped the fires that swept the city from time to time. The rocky underpinnings of Black Point also made the houses fairly stable in earthquakes, further improving their chances of long term survival.

Black Point (now Fort Mason) in 1860, with the Fremont house at far right and the Woollen Mill, now part of Ghirardelli Square, at left. The beach and the hillside above it are now the site of Aquatic Park, the Maritime Museum and Ghirardelli Square. (Courtesy California Historical Society)

Standing on a bluff overlooking today's Aquatic Park is a row of four such houses (there were once five) in a park-like setting of magnificent trees and greenery. Their windows take in a sweeping vista of the city, the Bay, and the hills of the North and East Bay. These frame houses, during 150 years of constant occupancy, have all been altered to suit their tenants' needs and to reflect changing styles of architecture. Originally they were little more than cottages, but with the passing years all have been substantially enlarged. An early view of Black Point shows these houses, three of which had low-pitched pyramidal rooflines extending over encircling verandas, much like some of their counterparts above Montgomery Street. With their simple, square columns around the porches, they reflected the then fashionable Greek Revival style. Since the early fires which wiped out infant San Francisco also destroyed almost every evidence of the city's Greek Revival architecture, these houses, until subsequent alterations, were rare survivors of a style which for domestic architecture had become passé by the end of the Civil War.

AMONG THE MORE NOTABLE RESIDENTS of Black Point were the famous adventurer and pathfinder, John C. Fremont, and his equally adventurous wife, Jessie Benton Fremont. In the 1850s they bought a charming, galleried one-story cottage on the very tip of the point. Here the Fremonts enjoyed a brief respite from their amazingly eventful lives, entertaining all the celebrated artists and military people who visited San Francisco. The location of the house was not ideal, however. Mrs. Fremont asked to be informed before the cannons on Alcatraz were fired for gunnery practice, so that she could open all the windows of her house to prevent their being shattered by shock waves.

Early in 1861, Fremont, by this time a general, was offered temporary command of the entire western department of the army. This meant they would have to move to St. Louis, and they packed up and left with the full intention of returning in a couple of years. The outbreak of the Civil War changed all that. In 1863 all of these houses and the lands of Fort Mason, according to an order from the Army headquarters in Benicia, were reclaimed by the Federal government, to make way for gun emplacements to "guard the Bay from Confederate aggression."

The owners of these properties challenged the usurpation, and the case was eventually carried to the Supreme Court. The claimants lost on the basis of an order, made in 1851 by President Millard Fillmore, which set aside 130 acres facing Alcatraz Island as a military reserve. The row of five houses and the land on which they stood were merely reclaimed in 1862, the high court ruled. Army engineers, sent to build gun emplacements on the Point, were moved into the row of houses, which had been declared "squatters' houses."

The federal government's takeover was probably based, ironically enough, on a report made by Fremont in 1846, when he discovered that in 1796 the Spanish had placed a cannon on Black Point, not far from the spot where Fremont would later occupy his charming cottage. The Fremont house and even the land it stood on were blasted away to create a battery of three 15-inch and six 10-inch cannons and six 24-pound guns.

Next-door neighbor to the Fremonts was the prominent Joseph Palmer, former president of Palmer, Cooke and Company, a bank which failed in the depression of 1854, when the gold mines ran out. He, too, was displaced by the army, and his comfortable house was converted to officers' quarters. It is the northernmost of the four surviving houses in the row.

Also forced to move out was attorney Leonidas Haskell, whose one-story house stands just south of the Palmers'. The Haskell house has a particularly interesting history. It undoubtedly pre-dates the others, for in their book *Men and Memories of the Spring of '50*, published by H. H. Bancroft in 1873, A.T. Barry and B.A. Patten recalled the pleasure it afforded them to come upon the hospitable Haskell house, which stood as a lone oasis on the hot and dusty trail to the Presidio. Passersby were always welcomed by the Haskells, who provided a cool milk punch and a comfortable chair on the porch.

On a blazing September afternoon in 1859 the dying U.S. Senator David Broderick was carried to the Haskell house following the most famous duel in California history. An historic marker on the shore of Lake Merced identifies the site of this duel between Broderick and a hot-tempered Southerner, David Terry, a lawyer who had got himself elected Chief Justice of the California Supreme Court. The issue involved the rights of blacks in California, which, despite the state's official stand against slavery, still remained a matter for considerable debate. Haskell, who had served as Broderick's second in the duel, carried the mortally wounded senator over the bumpy trail to his house at Black Point. Shortly after Broderick's death there, three days later, Mrs. Haskell gave birth to a son whom she named Broderick Haskell, in honor of her slain friend. Since then it has been a tradition in the Haskell family to name each first son Broderick.

According to some of the latter-day tenants, the house is often visited by the spirit of the slain man, who appears in a long, dark overcoat and a tall silk hat. What Senator Broderick was doing in a long overcoat on a hot September day remains a mystery. Although the house has undergone considerable

Jessie Benton Fremont is just visible, looking over the railing of her front porch at Black Point. The house was destroyed to make room for a cannon battery after the Fremonts had been displaced. (Author's collection)

remodeling, changing from a galleried one-story house to a two-story-with-mansard, the original front door with its modified pediment and glass sidelights is undoubtedly the door through which the dying senator was carried.

The 1860 photograph (p. 97) shows the Fremont, Palmer, and Haskell houses as one-story Greek Revival cottages with low-pitched hipped roofs and wraparound porches, and a larger, story-and-a-half house with a pair of shuttered windows in its high-pitched end gable. Built in 1855, this was originally the home of James Brook, editor of the pioneer newspaper *The Golden Eagle*. Brook sold it to Charles Cooke, probably the partner of Joseph Palmer of Palmer & Cooke Company. He in turn sold the house to Emile Grisar, who along with his neighbors was evicted by the army in 1863. The house became the residence of General Henry Halleck, General George Thomas, and General George Canby, who was later killed in the Modoc War.

Canby was followed by General Irvin McDowell, Fort Mason's commanding general, who ordered a drastic reconstruction. In 1877, he had the main part of the house removed some 300 yards to the north, leaving only the kitchen and an ell which were then incorporated into the Italianate residence known today as McDowell Hall. Rather confusingly, it is also referred to as Brook House Number One; the original Brook house, moved to the north, is known as Brook House Number Two.

Amelia Ransome Neville, in *The Fantastic City*, desrcibed the McDowells' entertainment:

> The McDowells were indefatigable hosts. Van Ness Avenue was not yet cut through, so that visitors at Fort Mason were transported by army and navy tugboats which pulled in below Fort Mason's hanging gardens. A grove of black laurels which gave the Point its name set off the gardens with their flower-bordered lawns terraced down to the waters of the Golden Gate. When it was *en fete*, with striped marquees, groups of guests in uniform and light gowns, and many parasols against the background of hills and bay, the scene was altogether worthy of the greatest enthusiasm.

The occasion described by Mrs. Neville was a reception held in 1870 for the Duc de Penthievre, a cousin of France's Emperor Napoleon III. It might have been used to describe a score or more such garden fetes held by the McDowells for such visiting luminaries as Generals Ulysses S. Grant and William Tecumseh Sherman, Major Generals Philip Sheridan, James Ord, and Arthur MacArthur, father of General Douglas MacArthur. Since 1943 McDowell Hall has served as an officers' club.

By 1873 the army had created a full garrison post with infantry companies, a squadron of cavalry, and a small artillery unit. Many buildings were constructed during this period when the post, now a port of embarkation, was named "Fort Mason," in honor of Colonel Richard B. Mason, military governor of California during the years following American annexation (1847-1850).

In later years it became a major Pacific supply base for such incidents as the Philippine Insurrection, the Boxer Rebellion, the fall of the Hawaiian monarchy, and the Klondike Gold Rush, as well as the port of embarkation for troops during the Spanish American War. In 1906 Fort Mason provided shelter for thousands of homeless refugees, as well as serving as headquarters for all organized relief efforts. In 1914 a tunnel was dug under Black Point to extend the Belt Line Railroad to the supply depot and loading docks west of the point.

The Fort Mason port facility underwent a major expansion in the late 1930s. Additional warehouses, massive reinforced concrete barracks, and the cavernous pier buildings were built—and just in time. During the 45 months of World War II, Fort Mason was "San Francisco's Port of Embarkation," where hundreds of thousands of troops left for the Pacific. Many thousands of them never returned. Among those who did come back to Fort Mason were prisoners released from Japanese camps, and survivors of the Bataan Death March.

Fort Mason was the port of departure for troops and supplies bound for Korea in the 1950s and for Viet Nam in the 1960s, although by this time air transport was replacing ships. Finally, following the Army's announcement that Fort Mason was "surplus property," the city began inviting developers to make proposals for luxury apartment complexes and shopping centers on the prime acreage of Black Point. The Friends of Fort Mason, with the help of other concerned groups, set out to make sure that the military base be converted to public use. Their efforts bore fruit when in 1972 Fort Mason became a part of the Golden Gate National Recreation Area. The great piers and barracks of the western portion are now privately managed by the Fort Mason Foundation, and have been converted for use by a score of non-profit organizations, including theaters, arts and cultural groups. Almost incidentally, the Fort Mason preservation effort resulted in the survival of some of San Francisco's earliest and most historic houses.

NOB HILL AND RUSSIAN HILL

IN THE 1860s

IN THE DAYS OF SAN FRANCISCO'S earliest development some citizens, eager to escape the fevered pace of the city, were willing to climb the steep slopes of Russian Hill and Nob Hill to build themselves country places. By the mid-1850s Nob Hill could boast the handsome Tillinghast house, with its wide galleries and spreading gardens, on the southwest corner of Pine and Mason Streets. Just above it, on Powell and California, the actress Julia Dean built a romantic eyrie which she later lost to banker Erwin Davis. Unfortunately, when Powell Street was further graded, the Davis's retaining wall collapsed, and the house was moved to Pine Street, to be replaced by the next owner, railroad builder Leland Stanford, whose million-dollar granite wall wouldn't have dared collapse; today it supports the Stanford Court and Mark Hopkins Hotels.

On Jones Street, at the very crest of Nob Hill between Clay and Washington, pioneer merchant

The William Ebbets mansion, a very early house on Jones Street between Clay and Washington, at the crest of Nob Hill, has a later addition at the left rear. Ebbets sold silk hats. (Author's collection)

William Ebbetts built his large frame house with lumber hauled up by teams of horses from a yard on Front Street. Not much is known about Ebbetts except that in one year in the 1850s he made $50,000 selling silk hats. His splendid house stood until 1906, a monument to his ability to build in such an inaccessible location.

Directly below the Ebbetts mansion, along Taylor Street northward to Jackson, were several large houses built by members of the Southern set, an "elevated" extension of the colony of aristocratic Southerners who lived below on Stockton Street. Long before the advent of cable cars on the Clay Street slope, the route to the dizzying heights of Taylor and Clay must indeed have been a circuitous one. In those days when Sacramento Street was an impassable gully of mud, Clay was the only street north of Pine giving access to Nob Hill. Before the streets were graded, there were no flattened intersections, as there are now, where the horses could rest on the way up.

On the southwest corner of Taylor and Washington, financier Maurice Dore built a fine house in the Italianate style, which would have looked at home on a shady street in an ante-bellum Southern town. Late in the 1850s the house was sold to merchant William Walton, who later sold it to William T. Coleman, who moved his family from a hotel to this hilltop mansion. Coleman, a native of Virginia, got his start in Sacramento, selling pies to miners at $10 each. A

commission merchant, he was elected head of the Vigilante Committee of 1856; his account of the committees' actions is one of the chief historical sources on the Vigilantes. Coleman later became a real estate speculator, building a number of fine houses in San Rafael and constructing Lagunitas Dam to supply them with water.

Across Washington Street from the Coleman house was a three-story brick mansion built by E. W. Gross, who in 1865 sold it to "fiery old Judge McHenry," as the local press called him. The Judge had been involved in a scheme to establish a Southern-style plantation in Sonoma, using Indians instead of blacks as slaves.

Just across Taylor Street, on the southeast corner of Jackson, Lloyd Tevis, a native of Kentucky, dry-goods merchant, miner, and real estate financier, built a handsome frame house which, like the Coleman house, suggested a Southern style with Italianate overtones. Amelia Ransom Neville recalled a ball given at the Tevis mansion when guests stood on the balconies and terraces to watch a fireworks display set off on the waterfront just for their entertainment. In 1906 the Tevises gave a grand dinner party for Mesdames Sembrich and Eames, stars of the Metropolitan Opera Company, which was performing in San Francisco with Enrico Caruso in the cast. The next morning, April 18, the guests were treated to another kind of pyrotechnics, which brought doom to the fine houses on Nob Hill.

In the early 1860s this awkward-looking tower was built by a man named Jobson, who planned to make his fortune by charging admission for the view. His hopes were dashed when people who had struggled up the hill refused to climb any further. The tower stood near the Vallejo Street peak of Russian Hill, on the site of the old Russian cemetery. One of the city's five octagon houses is barely visible on Taylor Street, to the left of the tower. (California Historical Society)

Shortly after the Tevises had moved into their Nob Hill house in 1859, they acquired new neighbors, the family of attorney William Thomas, at the corner of Sacramento and Taylor Streets. The rambling two-story Thomas house, described as being in the Spanish style, was later purchased by A. E. Head, whose daughter founded the exclusive Miss Anna Head's School for young ladies, in Berkeley. Both the Head and Tevis houses were noted for their fine libraries. The William Bourns, owners of the Empire Mine in Nevada City, were the next occupants. In later years, the great philanthropist Phoebe Apperson Hearst, widow of Senator George Hearst, moved from her house on Leavenworth and Chestnut Streets into the Head mansion, where her son William Randolph used to put on amateur theatricals in the carriage house at the back.

In 1872, capitalist James Ben Ali Haggin moved from South Park to build the first of Nob Hill's really showy mansions. This house, with its magnificent stables, occupied the entire block on the east side of Taylor between Clay and Washington Streets. Mrs. Haggin was a sister of Mrs. Tevis, and both families were from Kentucky, a factor which bridges the otherwise unbridgeable social gap between the Old Southern Set and the silver and railroad kings who would soon build their spectacular showplaces along California Street.

Actress Julia Dean built this charming little house in the late 1850s at the corner of California and Powell Streets. It was undermined when Powell Street was graded. The property was sold first to banker Erwin Davis, and later to Leland Stanford, who built his splendid mansion on the lot. Today it is the site of the Stanford Court Hotel. (Courtesy California Historical Society)

Maurice Dore's house at the corner of Taylor and Washington eventually was owned by William T. Coleman, who headed the Vigilantes in 1856. (Author's Collection)

It took a certain amount of courage to build on the steep slope bordering California Street near Jones, where Dr. Taylor kept his horses and carriage in a stable below the house. The bay window was a relatively new feature, complementing the elevated porch. (Author's collection)

James Ben Ali Haggin built the first "millionaire's mansion" on Nob Hill, complete with mansard roof and crested tower, at Taylor and Washington Streets. The stables for Haggin's riding horses and matched teams extended a whole block along Clay street. This view shows Telegraph Hill at right and the slope of Russian Hill at left. Wide planked sidewalks line Taylor Street. (Courtesy Alex Brammer)

The Gothic Revival cottage (center) at 313 Second Street, belonged to Charles A. Hawley. Cyrus Palmer built the octagonal house at 329 Second, the first of five octagon houses in San Francisco. Palmer, following Orson Fowler's directions, constructed the walls of sand and gravel, as the smooth surface shows. (Courtesy California Historical Society)

OCTAGON HOUSES

ON PAGE 81 OF Charles Lockwood's book *Suddenly San Francisco* (1978), is a rare photograph showing the Taylor Street link between Nob Hill and Russian Hill, taken from Telegraph Hill in 1865, when there were no cross streets on Taylor from Pacific to Union Street. In the picture one can discern one of San Francisco's octagon houses, near the dead end of Broadway, on the east slope of Russian Hill. Nothing is known about it except that its owner was H.S. Fitch. The picture does, however, firmly establish the fact that originally San Francisco could claim five octagon houses.

These five were but a small part of the rash of octagonal houses which sprang up all over the United States in the 1850s and 1860s. Octagonal structures had been known ever since the ancient Greeks built their Temple of the Winds. In America Thomas Jefferson had built himself such a house, a Bedford County, Virginia, retreat called Poplar Forest, recently restored. But the real craze for the style followed the 1854 publication of a small book entitled *The Octagon Mode of Building*. Its author, Orson Squire Fowler, was one of those spell-binding crackpots, like P. T. Barnum, who occasionally appeared on the American scene in the mid-19th century.

Fowler, a native of New York, had studied for the ministry with the famous evangelist, Henry Ward Beecher, brother of Harriet Beecher Stowe. Dissatisfied with the evangelical calling, Fowler took up the practice of phrenology, the art of reading bumps on people's skulls. He also published a book on male sexual vigor and female passion, the tenets of which he apparently followed, for he was married three times and was still fathering children in his late seventies. While experimenting with various materials and methods of construction, he built for himself and his large family a huge, three-story octagonal house on the Hudson River. So pleased was he with the result that he sat down and wrote his opus, *The Octagonal Mode of Building, or, The Sand and Gravel Wall: New, Cheap, Convenient, Superior and Adapted to Rich and Poor.*

Following the pattern-book style of the day, he included various plans and elevations as well as a tract on the healthful, economic and functional superiority of the octagonal over the conventional square house. In an era which knew only frame, brick, or stone construction, he pointed out the superiority of the "sand and gravel" or concrete wall. Perhaps the greatest appeal such houses had for San Franciscans, who always loved novelty, was the fact that the eight outside walls let in more sunshine. In an often fog-bound city like San Francisco, which would later make the slanted bay window its architectural trademark, the idea of such a house had great appeal.

The "Inkwell House" is here shown on its original site, on Gough Street above Union, in 1906, with its sand and gravel walls damaged by the quake. When it was moved across the street the restoration architect replaced the walls and radically altered the floor plan to suit the Society of Colonial Dames. The house is open to the public one day each week. (Author's Collection)

The Feusier octagon house at 1067 Green Street, built in 1858, was enlarged by the addition of a stylish Mansard roof sometime after 1870; even the cupola received the Mansard treatment. Now beautifully restored, the house is one of the most elegant in the city. The streamlined car in this 1930s photo has its own antique quality. (Author's Collection)

The John P. Bull octagon house at 1000 Green Street, far left, shows an unusual feature: dormer windows in the attic floor. It also had an octagonal carriage house, visible just behind it. Union Street, at the center of the photo, has been cut through the hill at upper left. The octagon house was replaced in 1902. (Author's collection)

High up on Russian Hill, on Green Street between Leavenworth and Jones, were two octagonal houses across the street from each other. One of these, on the north side, even had an octagonal carriage house in the back yard. In 1902, the McGraw family, who had bought this house from John P. Bull, sold it to O. D. Baldwin, who replaced it with a large Tudor style mansion; this house survived the 1906 fire, only to be replaced by the 1000 Green apartment house in the 1960s.

Across the street at 1067 Green, a pioneer named Kenny built a second octagon in 1858. He sold it in 1870 to a French family, the Feusiers, who occupied the house for so many generations that it came to be known as the Feusier Octagon. Mme. Feusier enjoyed recounting to later generations the story of her trip from France, when her young husband, who had already settled in San Francisco, asked her how she would like to live in an eight-sided house. She was understandably astonished when she actually saw it. In later years, while she was paying a visit to France, her husband, as a surprise, added the octagonal mansard roof to give the family more room,

making the house quite a departure from the usual octagon style.

Mme. Feusier also recalled the disheartening view from the rear windows in 1906, the barren landscape of a fire-blackened city, but noted that the city had looked just as barren when she had come to it as a bride. The Feusier Octagon was one of a group of houses at the top of Russian Hill which survived the 1906 disaster, but it was threatened in the 1970s, when the owner wanted to replace it with a high-rise apartment tower. It is now a city landmark.

A fourth octagonal house was built by Wales Palmer on the Second Street slope of Rincon Hill. This house was later occupied by a Mrs. Wyman, sister of Bret Harte. It vanished in the flames of 1906.

The fifth octagonal house still stands, at the southwest corner of Gough and Union Streets. Called by the local school children "the inkwell house," it stood on the east side of Gough until 1952, when it was purchased by the National Society of Colonial Dames and moved across the street to a lot donated by the Allyne sisters, whose own splendid Victorian stood on the adjoining property. (Their own house was left to the city by the Allyne sisters, but immediately following their death the Parks and Recreation Department had the house demolished; the garden became a small park.)

The Colonial Dames rebuilt the octagon as their western headquarters and museum, this time leaving out the sand and gravel walls as insurance against earthquakes. The little spiral stair which once led from the center of the house to an observation tower on the roof has been moved to one side to allow more space for an exhibit of colonial antiques. While remodeling the old house, workmen found a metal canister in a wall, left there by the original owner, William C. McElroy, when the house was being built. Inside was a four-page letter which McElroy wrote with an eye to having it discovered by some member of a future generation.

Dated July 14, 1861, the letter gives a fascinating account of San Francisco just after the beginning of the Civil War. Being a Virginian, McElroy refers to President Lincoln as "Old Abe." He says that the population of San Francisco had increased since his arrival in 1849 from 3,000 to 90,000. The mails, having always come by the slow route of the Pacific Mail steamers, were now being sent overland by way of Salt Lake City via the fast new Pony Express. There was talk of building a transcontinental railroad, but he doubts that this will ever occur in his lifetime.

McElroy recalled those inflationary early years when a San Francisco laborer could earn as much as $10 a day, and reported happily that the average daily wage for all kinds of mechanics was now $4. He inveighed against cheap Chinese labor, and thought the day would come when we would make war with the Chinese and "make their pigtails hop." He closed his letter with several bits of advice to young people, one of which is "to read your Bible and be charitable with your neighbors." Apparently he saw no irony in this.

The Russian cemetery which gave the hill its name was located on the very crest, where Vallejo Street dead-ends on Jones. People have always wondered why the Russian fur hunters chose this promontory to bury their dead. By 1860 the graveyard markers were gone, and on its site Captain David Jobson built a tall observation tower, thinking to improve on the 360-degree view already available from the hill, and to make his fortune by charging visitors two bits each to climb to the top. His expectations were crushed, for no one who climbed the steep hill felt inclined to climb more stairs to get a view already at hand. In time the tower was removed for a house which would one day become part of the most enchanting compounds in San Francisco.

RUSSIAN HILL

IN 1853, A CONTRACTOR, Joseph Atkinson, built an ell-shaped house near the site of the observation tower, on the eastern slope of Broadway. With its low-pitched roof, wide overhanging eaves, and bay windows, it was the perfect embodiment of the new Italian Villa style. Over the front door he placed a lintel bearing the date of construction, 1853. It is still there.

In 1893 the house suffered considerable damage from a fire. Atkinson's daughter, Katherine, commissioned the young architect Willis Polk to rebuild the house in a style in keeping with the spirit of the mellow old place. No more suitable architect for such a project could have been found anywhere. Polk, who lived just a stone's throw away, was the perfect choice. He left the exterior largely untouched, but redesigned the interior to add a feeling of spaciousness without detracting from its many warm historic associations. Here, in one of San Francisco's oldest dwellings, Polk managed to impart the rustic charm of the "countrified" city house, a style which he established in San Francisco. (Polk's career in San Francisco is considered in a later chapter.) Bruce Porter, another talented young designer, did the landscaping, which remains to complement the old house.

In 1852 Charles Homer, a builder, was supervising the construction of the huge Marine Hospital on Rincon Point. He bought the entire block bounded by Broadway, Taylor, Vallejo and Jones Streets from William Squire Clark for $5,000. Homer subdivided the block, keeping for himself the corner of Broadway and Taylor, where he built a Gothic Revival house for himself. He sold the lot just above his own on Taylor Street to his partner, William Ranlett, who built the "House of Many Corners," a curiosity in the Russian Hill neighborhood. It had three setbacks with corner windows arranged to allow extra light and provide a spectacular view of the city. In the 1890s, later owners, in the throes of a divorce, cut the house in half, and the wife took her half out to the Mission District.

On the east side of Taylor Street, directly below this compound, stands a large frame house whose original owners are unknown, but which in the 1880s became the home of Eli Sheppard, whose life could fill a fascinating volume. Sheppard bought the property after years of service as an American emissary to China, where he was one of the few Caucasians whom the old Dowager Empress condescended to receive at her court. The Sheppards enjoyed the old house with its fine view until the 1890s, when they added a complete two-story house onto the front of their property.

Originally they planned to live in the new addition, but finding it too small, they moved back into the rear house and rented the front one to E.A. Dakin, a Civil War veteran who had a fine collection of historic battle flags. Early on Wednesday morning, April 18, 1906, the Sheppard family filled tubs with water in preparation for the fire storm going on at what was first thought to be a fairly safe distance. By Thursday morning, however, the flames had come so close that the militia arrived to force the family to evacuate. Dakin remained behind, and when the heat of the flames began making the wooden trim smoke, he took the finest flag from his collection, ran it up the flagpole, and dipped it three times.

Fresh members of the 20TH Infantry happened to spot this little ceremony, and they determined not to let the gesture go unrewarded. Rushing up the hill, they crashed in the front door, and with water from the filled tubs, siphon bottles, and wet sand from the Hanford house, under construction across the street, they were able to hold fast until the fire had passed. The house has become a part of San Francisco legend as "The House of the Flag." In recent years, the developer who planned to tear it down was called to a hearing at City Hall, where he and his lawyer were confronted by Mrs. William Hilbert, Sheppard's granddaughter. Despite the lawyer's denials, she was able to prove that the story of the flag was factual, not a trumped-up legend, as the opposition claimed. The House of the Flag was spared.

Chestnut Street on the north side of Russian Hill, has remained a place of particular interest because, by happy circumstance, three historic houses of great charm escaped the 1906 conflagration. At 944 Chestnut is a Georgian style house built in 1863 by a French photographer, Alexander Edouart. In 1865 it was sold to a realtor, Francis Spring. Coincidentally, a spring flowing through the gardens saved the place in 1906; since then it has been known as "Spring Gardens." It remains a fine example of the pre-Civil War Victorian style, built at a time when classical rules of restraint and good proportion were still heeded. The fine garden, created by one-time owner Bruce Porter, adds considerable charm to this property.

The John P. Bull octagon house at 1000 Green Street was replaced in 1902 by the Tudor style mansion of O.D. Baldwin which survived the 1906 fire, but was in turn demolished to make room for today's 1000 Green apartments. (Author's collection)

On the adjoining property, at 930 Chestnut, stands another Victorian charmer with three-sided bay windows and a Corinthian porch. Built in 1861, it was "modernized" in the 1870s to typify what has come to be identified as the classic San Francisco Victorian Italianate style. At one time, this was the home of actress Ina Claire Wallace, one of the American theater's leading ladies.

At the corner of Hyde and Chestnut Streets there stood, until recent years, a landmark house known to San Franciscans alternately as the William Squire Clark house or as "Humphries' Castle." Clark came from Independence, Missouri, in 1846. Despite his land-locked mid-western origins, he constructed San Francisco's first wharf at Clark's Point, at the foot of Broadway. Either because the builder of his house was a ship's carpenter or because Clark liked a nautical touch (he adopted the courtesy title of "Captain"), his house on Russian Hill had a strong nautical cut to its appearance.

Built of oak shipped round the Horn, Clark's house had wide, deck-like porches, low ceilinged rooms, a staircase no wider than a ship's ladder, and a lookout tower on the roof which commanded a sweeping view of the entire bay. With its symmetrical plan, it would have been at home in any New England town. It did,

Russian Hill's Green Street has the distinctive flavor that we like to think of as singularly San Franciscan. The John Brickell house, shown above in an early photograph, is one of the row in the 1000 block of Green Street that were saved from the flames in 1906. It was remodeled in 1916 by Julia Morgan, whose name and the date of remodeling are inscribed on the keystone over the front door. Today it has a very different façade. (Courtesy Tony Hail)

The large left portion of this house, built in the 1860s, was the residence of Eli Sheppard, who later added the hip-roofed house fronting Taylor Street. Both were saved as the "house of the flag" in 1906. The houses now have landmark status. (Author's Collection)

This house, built in the 1850 by William Squire Clark, who also built Yerba Buena's first wharf at Clark's Point, was called "Humphries' Castle" after William Penn Humphries purchased it in 1889. It was demolished in the 1950s, shortly after its hundredth birthday. It stood at the northeast corner of Hyde and Chestnut Streets.

The 1906 Fire was halted along the Broadway side of Russian Hill, leaving an unobstructed view of this cluster of rustic houses. From left: the two Marshall cottages, and the Livermore house with the 1853 Atkinson house just below it. Willis Polk and Mrs. Virgil Williams had apartments in the next house on the upper ridge. Right, fronting on Taylor Street, is the Verdier mansion, which was almost complete when the earthquake struck. The small Roeding house, in front of it, was dismantled in 1906. (Author's Collection)

however, make two concessions to the fashionable Gothic Revival style, for it had Gothic trim over its windows and a crenelated wooden parapet surrounding its hipped roof.

Following World War I, Frank Griffin, a founder of the San Francisco Opera Association, undertook the restoration of this house, which at that time was known as "Humphries' Castle" after an interim owner, William Penn Humphries. During Griffin's residency, Walter Heil, Director of San Francisco's De Young Museum, declared the house "a rare and precious relic of early San Francisco" and urged the Board of Supervisors to purchase it for posterity. The Board could have purchased the house for a mere $15,000, but it never appropriated the money. The picturesque old landmark was razed and replaced by a colorless modern dwelling.

There was once a fine Italianate mansion with spreading gardens at 1120 Lombard Street. The builder, Judge James McMillan Shafter, was prominent in San Francisco politics, and also served as a general in the Civil War. He lived in his turreted mansion from the 1860s until 1895, when he sold it to the family of C.C.

Rohlff, founder of the Alaska salmon packing industry. For the next sixty years, the house was occupied by Miss Ella Rohlff, who kept the place exactly as it had been when she was born there, replacing any worn piece of upholstery or drapery with an exactly matching fabric.

After Ella Rohlff's death in the 1960s, the property was left to a church, which sinfully sold it, lock, stock and barrel, to a New York developer, William Zeckendorff. The elegant furnishings of the house were sold at auction, bringing over $150,000. Shortly thereafter Zeckendorff demolished the house, proposing to build a huge apartment tower, and arguing that hundreds of people would be able to enjoy the magnificent view that had previously been seen by a single elderly lady. Russian Hill residents fought the project to a standstill, imposing strict height limits in the area.

The late Thomas Church, a leading landscape designer, purchased one of the earliest of several pre-1906 houses on the north slope of Russian Hill. This Gothic Revival cottage, at 2626 Hyde Street, dates from the 1850s. Besides creating charming front and back gardens on the postage-stamp-sized lot, Church

Captain Ruskin's house, at 825 Francisco Street, is said to date from 1849, and was built with timbers from ships abandoned in the harbor. Extensively altered over the years, it stands today as possibly the oldest residence in San Francisco. (Both photos on this page: Author's collection)

Architect Louis Mullgardt designed this house on Taylor Street for J.M. Hanford. Construction was interrupted by the 1906 disaster. Paul Verdier, owner of the City of Paris store, later bought it for his bride, who refused to live in it. It was at various times a bordello, a rooming house for students, and a hippie crash pad. The house was completely renovated in 1996.

apparently added Victorian embellishments to the exterior, making the house a spectacular, if tiny, gem.

Nearby, at 765 Bay Street, the late Nora Kenyon, well-known San Francisco decorator, rescued an 1860-vintage Victorian which seems to have lost direct access to any street except Bay Street, which lies at the foot of a precipitous slope far below the house. The house greatly resembles one described by Amelia Ransome Neville in *The Fantastic City*, a recollection of life in the 1850s and 1860s:

> On the north side of Russian Hill was a house that had come around the Horn. Cut into sections, it had made the voyage from New England in a sailing vessel, to be put together in San Francisco, and some confusion in this process had completely disorganized a proper New England domicile. It stood with a funny, rakish assumption of dignity, all out of drawing. There were curious setbacks and projections where the second story didn't fit over the first, and the front door found itself far down at one side, with a blank wall

where it should have been. Tenants became adjusted to its peculiarities, however, and lived there very comfortably, as they may still, since it survived 1906.

At 825 Francisco Street is yet another building claiming to be the oldest dwelling still standing in San Francisco. This square frame dwelling is said to have been built of oak timbers removed from ships abandoned by the 49ERS. Its original owner was Captain R.C. Ruskin, who arrived in California in 1846 and presumably built his house soon afterwards. In 1854, Captain Ruskin enlarged the house with a rear addition to the existing front rooms, using redwood and octagonal nails. Despite numerous alterations made by successive owners, the old landmark still retains something of its early appearance.

A real prize among Russian Hill's "country houses" was one referred to by journalists of the time as "Manrow's Medieval Mansion." With icicle bargeboards on gables facing each point of the compass, it was a classic expression of the Gothic Revival, or

Captain Manrow's "Medieval Mansion" stood on Larkin Street at the end of Chestnut. Behind it is the great sand bank separating Fort Mason from Washerwoman's Lagoon. The house is a Gothic cottage, possibly pre-fabricated, and obviously not made of iron, as has sometimes been claimed. It may, however, have been haunted. (Author's collection)

"Cottage Ornee." Standing on the western brow of the hill, where today Chestnut and Larkin Streets meet, the Manrow house, pre-fabricated in England, had a sweeping view of the Golden Gate and the empty sand hills sweeping westward to the old Presidio. Apparently, the view was not to be enjoyed from within, for the tiny casement windows were tricked out with diamond-shaped panes of colored glass.

The English owner of this house, John Manrow, enjoyed chasing imaginary foxes over the nearby sand-hills, shouting "Tally ho!" whenever one of his hounds scared up a rabbit. Although he was described by his peers as a "lover of other men's business, property, and wives," he was nonetheless elected Judge Advocate of the Vigilance Committee.

Manrow's involvement with the Vigilance Committee, which was responsible for sending some innocent men to their doom, led the Judge and his family to believe that the spirits of the victims of his summary justice came to haunt his castle. When Manrow called

on detective Isaiah Lees to witness this invasion of poltergeists, Lees asked, "What are poltergeists?" "They are noisy ghosts," was Manrow's rejoinder. And indeed, even distant neighbors complained about the unearthly babbling and shrieks emanating from the Manrow property. After suffering from hideous specters and the destruction of household furnishings, the Manrows locked up the house and fled to a hotel. Some San Franciscans refused to believe that victims of the Vigilance Committee were responsible, but this did not mean that they necessarily disbelieved in ghosts. After all, Manrow's house was close to the burial ground of Russian sailors said to have died from cholera in the 1830s.

In later years, the talented Klumpke sisters occupied the old Manrow house, but apparently were never bothered by any spirits. One sister became a well-known writer; another was renowned as a fine astronomer, while the third studied in Paris to become a painter. Rosa Bonheur, one of the leading painters of the Victorian Era, willed this last sister a large part of her estate.

"A Boston of the Pacific" continues on page 149.

Color Plates

~

Mission St. Francis de Asis (Mission Dolores): Named for St. Francis of Assisi, founder of the Franciscan order in 13th century Italy, this fifth in the chain of California missions was dedicated on October 8, 1776. The present day church, begun by Fra Palou and Fra Cambon in 1782, took nearly a decade to complete. The large mission complex, containing some twenty structures, fronted Laguna de los Dolores de Nuestra Senora, named by Juan Bautista de Anza on Good Friday, 1776.

Designed by the Newsome brothers, Samuel and Joseph, this house, with a later wing added to the right, stands at 827 Guerrero Street. Long used as a halfway house, it has been meticulously restored after damage by a fire, and is again a private residence. The Queen Anne style house, with exceptionally fine decoration on the façade, features a moon gate entry, a Newsome trademark.

A very unusual house at 822 South Van Ness presents a puzzle to the casual viewer. The first and second floors are lavishly adorned, in a rich version of the Italianate style. The third floor is very plain, yet the cornice at the top is clearly original. In 1921, carpenters raised the entire cornice and roof, and built the third story, with lower ceilings and very plain exterior trim. The house has long been divided into apartments.

The identical row houses above, on Capp Street, feature brackets, machine carved decorations, sunbursts, spindles, and arched windows with colored glass insets, making the most of the newly available millwork. The porches, with Corinthian columns and pilasters, are simpler than the similar porch at right, which uses turned and decorated columns.

Turned spindles (above)were an inexpensive and easy way to trim a portico. More costly were decorations like those trimming a pair of arched windows, (top), which had to be carved by hand.

The portico of 27-29 Liberty Street has Doric columns, a Roman arch, and what might be called a Scandinavian gable, with ample decorations and a spindlework balcony above. The house was in the process of renovation when this picture was taken.

In the early 1850s Toribio Tanforan, an early Mexican era settler, erected a pair of matching cottages on Dolores Street, north of 16th Street. Set on a very large lot, they served originally as farm-houses for Tanforan. They are among the oldest houses surviving in San Francisco. One of them today serves as a hospice for AIDS patients.

Below: In Noe Valley, at the corner of 25th and Noe Streets, is a well-preserved stick-style house set well above the street, with a side garden and the original carriage house behind it. The buildings form one of the most attractive complexes in the city.

This striking house in the Mission District has unusual recessed windows at the right corner, a refined and elegant portico with exceptional carving in the gable, and garlands trimming the frieze. It stands on South Van Ness.

Two pictures show the kinds of changes that overtake old houses. At 573 South Van Ness near 17th Street (above) a noble old house tries to retain its dignity in the face of encroachment by gas stations, tire shops, and ugly signage. A first-time observer is brought up short by the sight of this enormous house in the midst of glaring commercial displays.

In the middle of a tow of well-maintained houses on South Van Ness (left) a modern shingled apartment house, typical of scores of such houses in all parts of the city, proclaims its functionality in the plainest terms. The horizontal glass panels below the windows, so common on houses of this type, apparently allow small pets to look out at the street.

The house, at 1198 Fulton, as famous as any in San Francisco, was designed by German immigrant Henry Geilfuss for William Westerfeld, a confectioner, in 1882, in the popular Stick style, with Italianate elements on the façade. The 14-foot-square tower provides an astonishing view in all directions. Over the course of 120 years and several owners, the house has served as a family home, a rooming house for Russian immigrants, a famous hippie pad, and a bed and breakfast, and finally is again a single family house, carefully restored and furnished. The large picture shows the house in 1992; a new color design, in darker tones with gold leaf, was applied in the late 1990s.

The interior of the Westerfeld house shows the rare and lavish details of a mansion with 15-foot ceilings, an elaborate mantel and overmantel, magnificent doors and casings, and a mahogany display cabinet built into the second parlor. The house has been decorated and furnished by its current owner, who chose Bradbury & Bradbury wallpapers and Renaissance Revival furniture for an opulent effect.

The decorative shingles on the second story of this Queen Anne house, at the corner of Steiner and Grove Streets, (above and left) create a textured plane above the siding on the first floor. The garland and wreath design in the gables and frieze are set off with strong contrasts in an especially fine color design.

Above: At the corner of Steiner and Oak Streets, new owners rescued a sadly neglected and badly damaged Classical Revival house, with handsome fluted columns on the portico. The restorers had to solve a special problem in casing the ribs below the rounded bay window (here shown exposed, top left) with a curved convex covering. The house, painted plain white with gold leaf trim, is a study in good proportion and tasteful design, with Palladian windows on the attic level.

This set of flats, at 1347 McAllister Street, with an Art Nouveau–Baroque façade and Oeil de Boeuf windows on the top floor, is by James Dunn, who designed some of the most unusual houses in the city in the early 1900s: 1250 Pine Street (1919); 1201 Leavenworth Street (1908-09); the Chambord Apartments, 1290 Sacramento Street (1921); an apartment house at 2411 Webster Street (1915); the Moorish style Alhambra at 850 Geary (1914); French style flats at 2415 Franklin (1915) and 1677 Haight Street (1905); and the amazing building at 91 Central Avenue (1904). Dunn knew how to make a statement. Every one of these buildings is worth a special visit; no two are alike.

At 1057 Steiner Street is the most elaborately restored house in San Francisco, with 17 paint colors, three roofing colors, and $6,000 worth of gold leaf. Architect William Armitage designed it for lumber baron Daniel B. Jackson in 1890. For many years it was a school for Yiddish drama and music; it later became a new-age commune. After meticulous restoration it is now a bed and breakfast inn called Chateau Tivoli.

A row of Stick Style houses (top and right), with similar floor plans but very different façades, lines Laguna Street between Bush and Pine. Varying roof treatments and vibrant color designs set these houses apart from one another.

Two houses, both built in 1891 on Scott Street at Waller, show a sharp variation within the Queen Anne style. On the left, a single-family house with a round turret and balcony, an arched recessed balcony at the attic level, and unusually fine stained glass in its front windows, abuts a two-family house on an extra wide lot, with an octagonal turret. The 24 original stained-glass panels surviving in this second house reveal a careful attention to color harmonies. The living room (below) preserves original colors in the cornice molding.

The Western Addition is sprinkled with oddities, like this formal French style house, (below) with mansard roof, on Pierce between Haight and Page. The stout columns framing the door and first-floor windows and the handsome pediment over the door give the house a strong, horizontal look, contrasting with the vertical Italianate house next door. The flats at the corner of Haight and Octavia Streets (left and left below) sport a corner bay with a jaunty cap, pierced by a bull's-eye window.

The John Nightingale house, at Waller and Buchanan Streets, exemplifies the Stick Style at its most picturesque. A complex design with a tower, a spacious entrance porch, and wonderful barge boards in the gables, this house well deserves its landmark status.

This cheerful yellow house on Oak Street near Laguna is a classic Queen Anne, with a round turret, asymmetrical façade, and a sunburst in the gable, but it has one unusual feature: a second-story veranda, matching the design of the porch below it.

Above and opposite: The Queen Anne style reaches dizzying heights at the corner of Fulton and Broderick Streets. Every variation seems to be represented, with turrets, projecting gables, patterned shingled siding, balconies, sunbursts, spindles, garlands, cartouches, and turned finials; even the exterior chimneys are decorated with inset tiles. Riotous color designs add to the exuberant mood of the block. One would hardly guess that several of these houses have very similar floor plans.

This charming and unique English-style house, made of clinker brick, sits on a steep triangular lot on Upper Terrace, a short distance below Buena Vista West. The brick exterior, the tiled roof, the multi-paned windows and the trim garden unite to form a beautifully proportioned and completely unified whole. This house served as the Japanese consulate before World War II.

The de Urioste house, built on five lots at corner of Buena Vista East and Duboce, has some of the best views in the city; it looks out toward downtown, the Bay Bridge, Potrero Hill and the East Bay. At first glance it looks like two houses, but the main entrance is at right; the other leads to the kitchen. The design is hard to classify: two fat towers on the south side suggest the Queen Anne style, but the simplicity of the decoration resembles Colonial Revival. It has recently been beautifully restored.

Another James Dunn house, at 1677 Haight Street (left), shows the refined taste of this exceptional architect. This building would be a standout even in Paris.

All Saints Episcopal Church at 1350 Waller Street was designed by Willis Polk. Its parishioneers provided food and medical care to many of the young people who were stranded here in the 1960s.

St. Joseph's Hospital on Buena Vista East, was designed by Bakewell and Brown. It has been converted to a condominium complex called Park Hill, with superb views to the east.

A Roman Villa, simple and symmetrical, looks out toward St. Ignatius Church and the tips of Golden Gate Bride, on Buena Vista West.

This enormous Queen Anne house at Haight and Baker Streets stood peeling and decrepit for forty years. It was offered for sale in 1975 for $125,000, a high price at the time. After a resale it received a thorough restoration as a bed and breakfast inn in the 1980s, with lavish period furniture and fixtures. The attic floor was completely rebuilt and finished as the owners' residence. The house was sold as a private residence in 2000 for $3.5 million. The view at left, taken in 1993, shows the house with a gray-and-rose color scheme; the view below shows the house after it was repainted in the late 1990s. Which scheme is more pleasing?

Two houses on Alta Street, at the top of Telegraph Hill, have survived earthquakes, fires, explosions, and the ravages of time and traffic. They are among the oldest houses in the city.

Two houses on Filbert Street dating from the 1850s have been much altered over the years, but are still counted among the most desirable places to live in San Francisco. Their survival is little short of a miracle.

Above: A very early apartment house on Montgomery Street, Telegraph Hill, looks squarely down at the Transamerica Pyramid.

Another very early house (far left) has survived on the crest of Telegraph Hill. Julius's Castle (center), built in the 1920s, has been a favorite resort for generations of San Franciscans.

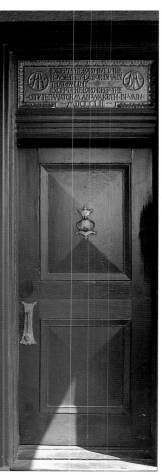

The Atkinson house, at 1032 Broadway, dating from 1853, was designed by William Ranlett. In 1893, after a fire, it was remodeled by Willis Polk, who installed the splendid fireplace mantel, among many other refinements, including the bronze plaque over the front door, with the date of the house. In the 1890s Kate Atkinson and her neighbor Gelett Burgess made the house a center of creativity and Bohemian life. Since the house was sold in 1999 its fate is uncertain

At the northwest corner of Hyde and Lombard Streets, Fanny Osborne, widow of Robert Louis Stevenson, built this fine Mediterranean villa, designed by Willis Polk. It was later enlarged and used as a convent, and is now an apartment house.

Three ages of San Francisco are shown in this Russian Hill view: the cable car, originally dating from the 1870s, a handsome apartment house built after the fire in 1906, and a 1960s high-rise apartment house in the background.

The Horace Livermore house (top) was remodeled by Willis Polk, who then built his own house (above) just behind it. Two of the four Worcester cottages (center left) complete an exclusive enclave on Vallejo Street at the top of Russian Hill, one of the most historic sites in the city.

The House of the Flag, at Broadway and Taylor Streets, is famous for the legend of its gallant rescue in the 1906 fire, and a subsequent rescue from the wrecker's ball, related on page 108. This house and an older one just below it belonged to the Eli Sheppard family. Here is history, juxtaposed against the modern city behind it.

Two houses on Russian Hill, in the very interesting 1000 block of Green Street, were saved along with their neighbors when the occupants refused to evacuate in 1906.

The Feusier octagon house (above), dating from 1858, was originally one story over a basement, but was later blessed with a second story under a mansard roof, and an observation tower.

The house at left once belonged to Clara Huntington, sculptor and daughter of Collis Huntington. Its exterior stairway makes it unique in the city.

Two of the oldest houses on Russian Hill are 925 Francisco Street (above) and at 950 Chestnut Street. The first, dating from the early 1850s, was built of timbers taken from ships abandoned in San Francisco Bay during the Gold Rush. Over the years it has been modified to suit the needs of later owners. The second (left) is Spring Hill, given that name by Bruce Porter, who lived here at the turn of the 20th century. It was built in the 1860s for a French photographer.

Nobby Clarke's folly, built in 1892 on what was originally a 15-acre plot on Douglass Street above Eureka Valley, cost $100,000, a princely sum for the time. The materials were the finest available, and the result simply defies description. The entrance doors (right) feature magnificent stained and etched glass panels. Despite all this luxury, Mrs. Clarke refused to live in the house.

Nobby Clarke's folly, at 250 Douglas Street in Eureka Valley, here shown under construction in 1891, was a huge extravagance for its owner, whose humble beginnings could not have foretold such lavish expenditure, estimated at more than $100,000. Apparently Clarke had the luck of the Irish, but his luck didn't hold; the house did not bring him happiness. Today it is divided into apartments. (Courtesy San Francisco Public Library)

This view of the southwest corner of Montgomery Street (at left) and Pine Street in 1860 shows several buildings from the very early 1850s. The American Hotel, the corner building, and the gabled building to its right all appear to be built of rough lumber milled in California. The sidewalks are planked, but the streets are still unpaved. A man in a stovepipe hat leans against the corner, where placards advertise Tuckers' jewelry for sale at cost, a Grand May Festival at Hayes Park, and theatrical events, including Living Tableaux, entitled "Blood, BLOOD!" and "The State Secrets," performed by a man named Moultrie, as well as a performance by George Ladd at another theater. (Courtesy California State Library)

Pine Street west of Dupont (Grant) in 1905 is paved with cobblestones and lined with a variety of houses from earlier decades. On the corner is the Bon Ton Saloon, advertising Kentucky Dew Whiskey. The building, with board-and-batten siding, barge boards, and galleries at both levels, may well have been a prefabricated import. The driver of the wagon, wearing bib overalls, is delivering libations in stout wooden kegs. At far left is a gas streetlight with mailbox attached. (Courtesy California Historical Society)

This view of Second Street looking south from Market Street in 1865 shows the regal elevation of Rincon Hill, where a broad row of mansions looked down on drygoods shops, dentists, and the headquarters of the Temperance Legion in the building in the right foreground. The broad sidewalks are planked and lined with hitching posts; tracks for the horse-drawn streetcar lead to Folsom Street. Second Street itself seems to be paved with cobblestones. (Courtesy California Historical Society)

RINCON HILL
(1854 - 1869)

Of the spoils of time, read and enjoy.
But remember!

— Charles I, upon the scaffold

The story of Rincon Hill and its near neighbor South Park is a cautionary tale, for both locations fell prey to that mindless "progress" which has afflicted San Francisco from time to time. Gold fever had just reached its height when San Francisco's leading families began establishing Rincon Hill as an enclave of Victorian respectability, away from the lawless, incendiary town below. From these auspicious beginnings, Rincon Hill has declined to the state where today it has practically disappeared. Its crest has been graded out of existence and its slopes, which once boasted grand houses set in large gardens, now rest under the steel and concrete stanchions of the San Francisco Bay Bridge.

Once upon a time, the hill and its neighboring park had clear boundaries. Laid out in gridiron pattern, Beale, First and Second Streets sloped up Rincon Hill from Folsom Street to Harrison in one easy rise, then dropped down to cross Bryant and Brannan. A horse drawn omnibus ran along Third Street, crossing the hill's western slope, making Third an important artery

The John Parrott mansion at 620 Folsom Street, built in 1854 of Australian sandstone, was one of the first truly elegant houses on Rincon Hill. As her house neared completion, Mrs. Parrott wrote "I fear that untiring care and unlimited expense can never produce even the shadow of beauty on these eternal sandhills." (Courtesy California Historical Society)

for city traffic. Between Bryant and Brannan Streets, Second and Third was—and is—South Park.

It seems ironic that many of Rincon Hill's most princely residents eventually caused the decline of the area as the city's most fashionable address. These members of Rincon Hill's elite were the industrialists who established their iron foundries and ship-building yards around the Hill's very perimeters. While convenient for business, the proximity of these industrial sites gradually became ruinous for property values.

James Donahue, one of the first industrialists to live in a mansion on Rincon Hill, built on the lower slope of First Street, only a block away from his Union Gas Works. His brother, Peter, a director of the Union Iron Works and later a demonic builder of railroads and locomotives, enlarged the more modest house which importer Faxon Dean Atherton had built at Second and Bryant, just two blocks away. George Gordon, developer of the elegant South Park, built his Vulcan Iron Works at the foot of First Street. Thomas Selby, who built the famous 200-foot Selby shot tower on

First Street below Folsom, built a fine house on the crest of the hill overlooking his factory in 1854. The shot tower was for many years an imposing visual landmark in the San Francisco skyline. At the top was a sieve through which melted lead was poured; by the time the droplets reached the bottom they had hardened into buckshot.

Not all of Rincon Hill's residents were industrialists. There was also a fair sprinkling of bankers, generals, admirals, men of the cloth and southern colonels who said "yes suh" and "no suh." Banker John Parrott's mansion on Folsom Street was among the first elegant houses in the neighborhood. Its walls were of limestone imported from Australia, and its long French windows looked out into lovely gardens. One can imagine the difficulty Mrs. Parrott must have faced in 1854 as she attempted to create a place of grace and charm at a time when the young city was still pulling itself out of the mud.

On the southwest corner of Harrison and Second Streets, another banker, Pedar Sather, built a charming

William Tecumseh Sherman's Gothic style house at 410 Harrison Street was similar to Captain Folsom's house nearby; both may have been pre-fabricated in the East. Sherman came to California as a junior officer in the late 1840s and remained until he was called to serve the Union army in the Civil War. After marching through Georgia, he returned to San Francisco, retired from the army, and became an officer of the Lucas Turner Bank. (Courtesy California Historical Society)

Gothic "Cottage Ornee." Sather is remembered today for the generous donations later made by his wife to the fledgling University of California; the University dedicated its Sather Tower (the Campanile) and Sather Gate in his memory. Directly across Second Street was the Italianate house of Sather's partner, Edward Church.

In a letter to his grandchildren, J. Sather Hutchinson wrote:

My father was a member of the banking firm of Sather, Church and Company. Father was the '& Company' part of the firm. In the Spring of 1854 my parents were married in the large drawing room of the Sather house, at 7:30 a.m.! The reason for such an early hour was that the wedding party was to accompany the bride and groom on the pacquet boat to San Jose, which was about as far as one could go on a honeymoon in those days without experiencing great discomfort. Father gave the minister $20, much to the annoyance of

the minister's wife, who commented, quite audibly, that only a week before her husband had performed a ceremony for a butcher who had given him $50.

The wedding recalls one described by Amelia Ransome Neville:

The bride wore white muslin with a flaring skirt, while her sister, a bridesmaid, wore the same simple fabric. There were no decorations: no display of any sort—it was not yet fashionable.

Joseph Donahoe, founder of the Donahoe-Kelly Bank, was another early resident of Rincon Hill. His first house there was modest, but in the 1860s he moved it to the rear of his large lot on Harrison Street, and in front built a striking mansion in the new Second Empire style, with a mansard roof. His was one of the Harrison Street families that held out and stayed when the rest of the hill was no longer fashionable.

The view from First and Harrison Streets shows Telegraph Hill in the background, with the massive St. Francis Church on its western flank. The houses shown here are modest, and the planked sidewalks narrower than those on Second Street. Gaslights required a nightly visit from the old lamplighter. A horse-car came down to Folsom Street, in the distance. (Author's collection)

Three of the better known members of the military living on Rincon Hill were Generals William Tecumseh Sherman, Henry Wager Halleck, and Albert Sidney Johnston. These West Point graduates had all been stationed in California as junior officers during the years of American occupation which preceded statehood. Sherman had retired from the army to become director of the Lucas Turner Bank. (That fine old brick structure, minus its third story, still stands on the northeast corner of Jackson and Montgomery Streets.) Sherman, never dreaming he was to lead the march across Georgia in the most decisive campaign of the Civil War, lived in a two-story gabled cottage on Beale Street at Harrison.

Halleck, who had learned his skills as an engineer at West Point, financed the magnificent Montgomery Block, and had, in this interim of his life, become an attorney. He and his wife, a niece of Alexander Hamilton, occupied another gabled Gothic Revival house at the northeast corner of Folsom and Second Streets. When the Civil War broke out he was appointed Lincoln's chief military adviser, with the rank of Major General. For two years, Halleck rented his house

to an orphanage for a dollar a year; some of the orphans were said to be survivors of the Donner Party.

Johnston, who lived at 30 Rincon Place, was serving as commander of the Presidio at the outbreak of the Civil War. A native of Kentucky, he resigned his commission, traveled to Richmond, and joined the Confederate Army with the rank of General. He was killed a few months later at the battle of Shiloh. In the 1850s all three men lived peacefully as neighbors and friends on the sunny slopes of Rincon Hill.

Of lesser rank, probably because he died five years before the Civil War broke out, was Captain Joseph Folsom of the Army Quartermaster Corps. Folsom's gabled Gothic style cottage, on Second Street just north of Folsom, was an imported "Boston House." He had shrewdly bought the estate of the deceased Captain Leidesdorff from his heirs in the Virgin Islands, and thus Folsom left his name on a San Francisco street and a town near Sacramento. Folsom, a bachelor *bon vivant*, did much in the early days to promote the reputation of Rincon Hill as a fashionable place to live. His entertainments, featuring elaborate dinners with roast canvas-back duck, made him locally famous.

The only building on Rincon Hill to survive the earthquake was the Sailor's Home at the northwest corner of Spear and Harrison, photographed on May 10, 1906. Built in 1853 at a cost of $250,000, it was dismantled in 1917. (Courtesy California Historical Society.)

It may seem odd that all four of these men owned identical cottages, until we recall that these were probably some of the 25 pre-fabricated dwellings brought around the Horn and purchased by W. D. M. Howard, who also lived in one at the foot of Rincon Hill, on Howard Street.

In later years, Folsom's property, at 240 Second Street, was taken over by John Wieland, who built a large stone brewery just behind the house. Wieland built a little courtyard just off the street where any passerby might enjoy a free beer. A high hedge insured the partaker of his privacy. The gutted walls of the brewery, about all of Rincon Hill that survived the 1906 disaster, were rebuilt, and finally demolished in the 1960s.

To those schooled in the notion that all early San Francisco homes after the Gold Rush were curlicued Victorians, historic photographs of the houses on Rincon Hill come as a revelation. These houses reflected an earlier day in their classical Georgian proportions. Rincon Hill had its share of filigreed Gothic and bracketed Italianate houses, to be sure, but the Nicholas Kittle and Edward Church houses, as well as the twin bow-fronted brick houses of J.O. Eldredge and Bishop

Kip, appear to have been directly transplanted from Boston's Beacon Hill. Just across Second Street from these three stood the William Palmer house, which indeed was transplanted in 1853 from Portland, Maine.

In the earliest views of Rincon Hill, the long side of the Palmer house faced the street, while later views show it with its gable end facing the street. Obviously, a house that could be transported all the way from the East Coast to California could just as easily be turned around on its own lot. (House-moving sometimes became a public nuisance. One letter to the *Examiner* angrily complained about a house that was moved to the busy intersection of Market and Sutter Streets and then abandoned for several days.)

On the wide plot just below the Palmer house was an octagonal house built by William's son, Cyrus Palmer, director of the Pacific Foundry and later the Golden State Foundry, and member of the Board of Supervisors. This octagon was occupied in 1861 by Captain Benjamin Wyman, purser of the Pacific Mail Steamship Company. His wife was a sister of Bret Harte. The exact plan and elevation of this octagon house may be seen in Orson Squire Fowler's book *The Octagon Mode of Building*.

On the crest of Rincon Hill, at 336 and 338 Second Street, lived J.O. Eldredge and Bishop William Kip, who stands on his porch at left. Mary and Grace Eldredge are seated in the buggy; Sarah Lee is on the porch at right, Mrs. Elizabeth Eldredge at the foot of the steps. The flat-roofed house at far left, facing Harrison Street, belonged to Thomas Selby. The picture forms a panorama with the photograph on the facing page.(Courtesy Mrs. James Jenkins)

Vernon Place, which could be entered from Second Street just below the Nicholas Kittle house, was a cul-de-sac with four bow-fronted brick houses like the double Eldredge-Kip house. One of these was the boyhood home of Anson Blake, who eventually became president of both the California Historical Society and the Society of California Pioneers, and who wrote a fascinating memoir describing his boyhood years on Rincon Hill.

Rincon Hill had passed from its glory years by Anson Blake's time, and roving gangs of teenage toughs staged gang wars with one another on its slopes. Apparently, Blake was a charter member of one of these gangs. One of his young pals ventured into the forbidden district around the Pacific Mail docks below Rincon Hill and was shanghaied on one of the ships. He re-appeared a year later, so brutalized that his mind was completely gone. The boy had been just fifteen years old at the time of his disappearance.

In 1875 a giant powder keg at Folger's warehouse, at Spear and Harrison Streets, blew up. The Eureka saloon, the proprietors and customers, the bark *Germania* and its captain all went with it. It blew out every window on that side of Rincon Hill, and set fires on nearby ships that took eight days to put out, according to Anson Blake. Adjoining the atomized warehouse was another, belonging to E. V. Hawthorne, a resident of South Park. Amazingly, the structure suffered only minor damage. With the later addition of a second floor, it stands today. Whether it can withstand the new seismic reinforcement laws is yet to be seen.

In contrast to these tales of explosions and beatings are the peaceful recollections of Alice Hooper McKee, who described a garden filled with fragrant hyacinths brought by a sea captain from the South Pacific. She and her little friends rode in a small basket cart, pulled up and down Harrison Street by a pet goat named

Nicholas Kittle, a merchant from England, built the house at 326 Second Street (left). Rev. William Scott moved into it in 1859. Their Harrison Street neighbor, Mrs. Thomas Selby, rescued Rev. Scott from a lynch mob after he had evoked God's blessing on both Abraham Lincoln and Jefferson Davis in his church on Union Square. The house at right belonged to Henry Halleck, builder of the Montgomery Block and a famed Civil War general.

Billy. The children would pass the grand Jerome Lincoln house with its marble-flagged walks, and in its garden house a parrot which had picked up some colorful language from the Chinese cook, much to the youngsters' delight.

Young ladies at the time of Mrs. McKee's recollections went to Miss Cheever's kindergarten on Essex Street, and later to Madame Zeitska's Seminary in South Park. Many of the older boys attended classes at Huddart's Union College on Second Street at Bryant.

Also on Second Street was the home of Henry George (1839-1897), who in the 1870s wrote the wildly popular *Progress and Poverty*, advocating a single tax on all privately owned land. Not far away, Jack London, a strong advocate of socialism, was born on Brannan Street in 1876, but it is doubtful that the two knew one another.

Adjoining the Parrott house on Folsom Street stood a house whose story epitomizes the rise and fall of Rincon Hill. From its beginnings as a modest cottage set in a large garden, it grew in size with each successive owner. Despite its wholesome appearance, however, each owner experienced some tragic misfortune while living there. Indeed, so pervasive was this seeming curse that, in later years, the press referred to the place as "the Hoodoo House."

Captain Bissell built the original cottage in the 1850s. When "Ophir Jim" Woodworth bought it, his income from the mines was rumored to be a thousand dollars a day. Suddenly, his wealth dried up and he was forced to sell the property.

Senator Milton Latham bought the house from Woodworth; after his first wife died, Latham remodeled the house as a gift for his beautiful new wife, Mollie McMullin. The Senator spent a king's ransom making the house into a California showplace. Shortly

(Text continued on page 176 following photo section.)

The houses above, at 327, 331, and 333 Second Street, between Folsom and Harrison, in 1856 belonged respectively to the William Palmers, the S.H. Harmons, and the William Badgers. The Palmer house, left, came in sections from Maine. The Badger house was built for Palmer's daughter. William Badger founded San Francisco's first YMCA. After 1869, when Second Street was deeply cut, these houses could only be approached from Essex Street, the former carriage road behind them. (Courtesy California Historical Society)

Brick duplexes with stucco surfaces, resembling row houses on Beacon Hill in Boston, lined Vernon Place, south of Second Street. Anson Blake, an early president of the California Historical Society, lived in one of these. (Courtesy California Historical Society)

The Edward W. Church house stood adjacent to the three on the opposite page, finishing the block at the corner of Second and Harrison. The style might be called Georgian, and may have been pre-cut and imported from the East Coast. Church was a partner in the banking firm of Sather and Church. At left was an Italian-style loggia with glass doors, and at right a trellised wing to shelter the garden behind.(Courtesy Mrs. Phillip Landis)

Across the street from the house shown above stood Peder Sather's Gothic cottage, built in the mid-1850s. After the Second Street cut in 1869, the house above was turned to face Harrison Street, and the house below, abandoned and crumbling, became the abode of the poet Charles Warren Stoddard. Robert Louis Stevenson describes the house in his novel *The Wreckers*. (Courtesy Mrs. Phillip Landis)

The Tucker-Coe-Raymond-Earle house, at the corner of Harrison and Essex Streets. Four prominent San Franciscans were to be successive occupants of this delightful house. John Tucker, jeweler and developer of Tucker Town in Pacific Heights, lived here from 1860 - 1865. L. W. Coe, owner of the Imperial Mine in Nevada, was followed by I.W. Raymond, owner of a steamship line. John O. Earle, director of the Ralston Bank of California, lived here until 1876, when he sold the property to cattle baron Henry Miller, who tore down the house to build an ornate chateau with a mansard roof, shown below. (Courtesy California Historical Society)

Henry Miller built this extravagant Second Empire style house at the corner of Harrison and Essex Streets in 1876, after tearing down the more modest house shown above. The Miller family lived in the house until it was destroyed in the 1906 disaster. (Courtesy California Historical Society)

In the early 1870s, after his house on Second Street had been destroyed by the Second Street cut, J. Oscar Eldredge moved his family just down the hill and around the corner to 646 Folsom Street. (Courtesy California Historical Society)

The Horn-Lent-Lincoln house at 555 Harrison Street, a Gothic-style charmer built by Benjamin Horn, an uncle of Gertrude Atherton, was occupied in the 1860s by Comstock silver king William Lent. In 1881 Jerome Lincoln, director of the Bank of California and the Pacific Bank, bought the house. The Lincoln family were still living here in 1906. The front garden boasts a cast-iron fountain and a handsome wrought-iron fence; at the rear is a carriage house with tower.(Courtesy California Historical Society)

Originally the home of Louis McLane, president of Wells Fargo & Company, this house was created by moving two earlier houses together on the large lot. In later years Isaac Friedlander and his family moved here from South Park. Friedlander later lost his fortune in an attempt to corner the grain market. (Courtesy California Historical Society)

The residence of Charles McLane, at 500 Harrison Street, was built in the 1860s in the Second Empire style, with mansard roof, dormers, a central tower with iron cresting, and perfectly balanced bay windows. McLane was an agent of Wells Fargo & Company. (Courtesy California Historical Society)

James Donahue, brother of Peter Donahue, lived at 346 First Street, at the corner of Guy Place. The elaborate fence along First Street, with a gate for carriages, and the double curved stairway leading to the front door, lend elegance to a rather plain house. Two little girls in voluminous dresses march along the sidewalk with their dog, followed by women in pre-Civil War hoop skirts. The Donahue brothers were founders of San Francisco's first gas plant, and also of the Union Iron Works (1849). In later years James Donahue's widow married a man named O'Kane, and the house became known as "O'Kane's House of Plenty." Apparently the good times continued to roll. (Courtesy California Historical Society)

The residence of Philander and Samuel Soule, at 323 First Street, was one of the very few built of brick and stone. It shows a fine restraint and elegance in decoration. (Courtesy California Historical Society)

In 1862, Faxon Dean Atherton, an importer, and later father-in-law of novelist Gertrude Atherton, built what some Victorian scribe described as "A cheerless, unimposing cottage' at Second and Bryant Streets. Shortly thereafter Peter Donahue, president of the Union Iron Works, bought the property. After Donahue's death, his widow Annie and her sister, Eleanor Martin, continued to live there for many years, during which they became the absolute rulers of San Francisco high society. These photographs illustrate the improvements Mrs. Donahue made to the "cheerless cottage," beginning with the addition of a third floor with an ingeniously designed roof. (Courtesy California Historical Society)

The dining room of the Donahue residence, though not large, had everything necessary for elegant entertaining: a heavy silver tureen, multiple wine glasses, silver-shaded candles in candelabra, and a gaslit chandelier, here festooned with smilax. The painting at left, an allegorical subject, is probably a copy of an old master. A Chinese screen shields the doorway from view. (Courtesy California Historical Society)

The settee and high-back tufted chairs in the Donahue parlor were probably the work of New York furniture maker John Belter, who sent his sinuously carved rosewood furniture to every part of the country. Note the carved and gilded center table, a popular feature in interiors of the 1860s. (Courtesy California Historical Society)

The conservatory, with a six-light gas chandelier, displays a photograph of Peter Donahue on an easel. The furniture is an eclectic mixture: another carved and gilded table, with inlaid top; a low round table from China, a Belter chair, and a marble statue, Nydia, the Blind Girl, a very popular figure at the time; the Leland Stanfords had one in their mansion on Nob Hill. Statuary was displayed in virtually every home of this period. (Courtesy California Historical Society)

Left: The rear view of Captain Millen Griffith's house at 569 Harrison Street shows a double stairway leading to the generous veranda, a carefully tended garden, and blooming street trees along the wooden sidewalk. After the family left Rincon Hill the land was donated by the Griffiths for use as a playground. Finally the great concrete stanchions of the Bay Bridge rose from the site.

Below: The Griffith's music room featured both a piano and a pump organ, as well as gas chandelier and wall sconces, comfortable furniture, and Chinese jars. Alice Griffith, the captain's daughter, wrote that no one except Griffiths ever lived on this property. (Courtesy Edward Griffith)

The parlors in the Griffith house look very comfortable, with soft upholstered furniture and floral inlaid carpeting. The wide arched openings gave a charming informality to the rooms. The entrance hall and staircase, below, are sturdy and well-lit, with gaslights on the newel posts. Captain Griffith acquired the polar bear rug through his Alaska shipping fleet. (Courtesy Edward Griffith)

William Babcock, president of the Spring Valley Water Company, lived in this house at 11 Essex Street. The house, with its rustic setting, stood just one block above the city's busy industrial section. (Courtesy California Historical Society)

The low beamed ceiling and compact dimensions of the Babcock parlor suggest a builder conversant with nautical architecture. The large jars and the intricately carved round table apparently came from Asia. At the back of the room a large painting, reflecting the light, looks like a window. Persian rugs are spread on top of floral inlaid carpet. (Courtesy California Historical Society)

This unidentified house, at an unknown address but probably at the crest of Harrison Street, took advantage of its steep site by incorporating a full story below street level, with a large garden and carefully braced trees in front. Is it a hired carriage, or the family's private one? (Courtesy California Historical Society)

The Irving Scott residence at 507 Harrison Street has an older section with gabled roof, and a large addition at right in a very different style. Mr. Scott was general manager of the Union Iron Works, founded by the Donahues. The Scotts lived here from at least 1870 until 1906. Their collection of paintings included Toby Rosenthal's "The Fair Elaine," which caused a sensation in San Francisco in the 1880s. The house of Henry Booth, president of Union Iron Works, is at left. (Courtesy California Historical Society)

The Francis Cutter-Sidney Smith house, at 330 Bryant Street, had a fine garden filled with hyacinths brought from Samoa. Cutter was founder of the Cutter Packing Company, which eventually became a part of Del Monte foods. Smith, who was president of Cutter Packing, later bought the house. (Courtesy California Historical Society)

The view from the end of Bryant Street, with a ship's masts just offshore. The gabled building at left looks like one of W.D.M. Howard's imported Gothic houses. Street trees were carefully protected from careless drivers and runaway horses. (Courtesy California Historical Society)

The Samuel C. Bigelow house, at 26 Laurel Place, with a charming garden, a gazebo, and a view of the waterfront, seems to embody the best of life in the city. The bay windows on the first floor were among the first of their kind to be seen in San Francisco. (Courtesy California Historical Society and Mrs. Samuel Wood)

Laurel Place, with hitching posts. (Courtesy California Historical Society)

Facing page top: The Milton Latham house, at 656 Folsom Street, was regarded as the most elegant in San Francisco. Because tragedy visited each of its successive owners, it became known as the Hoodoo House. The striking interior photographs were taken while Senator Latham was in residence.

Left: Senator Latham's parlor boasted the most expensive mantel in San Francisco, carved of black marble and surmounted by a magnificent mirrored overmantel with a sculpture of a deer's head at the top. The wall decorations and cornice molding add to the air of refined elegance, as does the splendid gas chandelier. A second grand piano, in addition to the one in the library, suggests a deep interest in music. At left of the mantel is the indispensable spittoon.

(Seven photographs, pages 170-173, Courtesy Nancy McNear)

Facing page bottom left: The entrance hall featured snow-white woodwork, most unusual in houses of the period, when wooden trim was normally stained and painted to look like mahogany, oak, or walnut. The steam radiators are a distinctly modern invention. Carpeting was installed in strips which were sewn together by hand during installation. The large doors at left and right led to the front parlor and dining room. Alabaster urns on pedestals gave an air of elegance and balance.

Facing page bottom right: Not one, but two sets of silk draperies flanking a pair of pocket doors guarantee privacy in the family sitting room, which has a splendid white marble mantel and French-style chairs with tufted silk upholstery. The inlaid carpet in a floral pattern was probably imported from England

Above: The library-music room had a huge skylight, a series of rolled maps at far right, a vast center reading table with coal-oil lamps, a writing desk and comfortable chairs, gas chandeliers and sconces, soft carpeting, and another grand piano. Clearly this was the home of cosmopolitan, literate, intellectually curious people.

Facing page top: The dining room table in the Latham house is set for tea; the baronial chairs, upholstered in leather, are set off by a massive sideboard, a truly magnificent chandelier, a statue supporting a gas torchiere, and gas sconces flanking the elaborate overmantel. Even a dining room had to have a spittoon.

Facing page bottom: The Latham house contained her-and-his bedrooms, hers lavishly decorated in the French style, with a canopy bed and tufted silk chairs, while his featured the sturdy walnut furniture common to American houses of the period. The cornice moldings and painted floral ceilings added elegance.

The Silver Street Kindergarten, established in 1878, was the first free kindergarten in the city. Its first director was Kate Douglas Wiggin, author of *Mrs. Wiggs of the Cabbage Patch*. (Courtesy California Historical Society)

A parade at Silver and Third Streets, undated, apparently celebrates the pioneers and their journey across the plains. The covered wagon bears a sign: "Missouri Train, Pike County, Bound for California, 1849." (Courtesy California Historical Society)

Rincon Hill's "back door" was South Beach, the site of a colorful Chinese fishing village. On the heights is the four-story St. Mary's Hospital, established by the Sister of Mercy in 1861 at First and Bryant Streets. A fragment of the old brick retaining wall of this building survives, and is marked by a plaque underneath the approach to the Bay Bridge, just off Bryant Street. (Courtesy California Historical Society)

The Pacific Mail Docks, looking west toward the block between Bryant and Harrison Streets. Both photographs (Courtesy California Historical Society)

after its completion, he suffered so many financial reverses that he was forced to sell the contents of the house and finally the house itself. He died in New York City, bankrupt.

Joseph Eastland, the next owner, was travelling in his private railway car when a collision with another train threw him on top of his little daughter so violently that she was killed. The Bradleys, who became the next owners, failed in business and sold the house to Senator Sharon, who gave it to his son-in-law, Senator Newlands, as a wedding present. Mrs. Newlands died in February, 1882, on the day following the birth and death of their only son.

By the time of the Newlands tragedy, the fortunes of Rincon Hill had also been shattered, and there was no new private owner to be found for the Hoodoo House. The fine old building became first a boarding house, then a boys' school, and then an insane asylum. At one time, one of the inmates climbed on the roof and terrified the neighbors by baying at the moon. Perhaps its destruction in the 1906 fire was regarded by some as a blessing.

THE ELEGANT SOUTH PARK

IN CONTRAST TO the large houses and gardens of Rincon Hill, which looked down on the city, South Park was a small enclave of narrow-fronted houses that looked inward upon a private park, a fenced-in oval of sycamore trees and ornamental shrubs. The elegant little houses, with their stone stoops and English basements, seemed to turn their backs disdainfully on the crudities of the young city on the other side of the hill. This copy of an English oval park between Second and Third, Bryant and Brannan Streets, stood in odd contrast to the windblown hills of rock and sand around it.

George Gordon, founder of South Park, was born in England; in 1849 he settled briefly on the east coast, where he hired a sailing vessel and sold passages to California at a good profit. He also brought a large cargo of finished lumber, realizing the prices such a treasure would bring in San Francisco. Rather than rushing off to the gold fields, Gordon settled his wife and daughter in the new city and invested his nest egg in the Vulcan Iron Works, and later in a sugar refinery. When he became established in the city, he imported some iron warehouses from England, and then in 1854 began planning his South Park development. His architect, George Goddard, laid out a long, fenced-in oval park planted with pleached sycamores, geraniums, fuchsias and English tea roses. Goddard, who was an established London architect before coming to California, followed the pattern established by town planners in London and Bath. The oval was enclosed by a handsome iron fence, and only South Park residents received keys to the gate, separating "the chivalry from the shovelry," as one wag noted.

In 1854, the Alta California's Christmas edition announced the completion of the first quadrant of 17 houses, in what the architect described as the "new English Roman style," an early, more restrained variant of the Italianate. The fact that these houses were of fireproof brick was a great inducement to purchasers who had experienced the uncertainty of existence in a town that had already burned several times. Gordon intended to construct four identical quadrants with 68 narrow-fronted town houses of brick, with stuccoed façades scored to resemble stone. The clay for the bricks was to come from the soil excavated for the English basement each house would feature.

"We doubted," commented the Alta, "that in these dull times Mr. Gordon would find the wide-spread interest which has been evidenced in such an ambitious project." Indeed, the doubts seem justified, for the young city was in the throes of its first major depression. The gold from the Mother Lode, which had showered down on the town in earlier days, had run out. Two of the leading banks were forced to close their doors in 1854, and the streets were crowded with unemployed and disenchanted miners. While the first row of houses quickly found occupants, it was another ten years before Gordon could sell enough lots to begin construction of twelve houses in the second quadrant of the oval.

Ultimately, Gordon built only two of what were to have been four identical rows of houses. When Supervisor Andrew Shrader purchased one of the lots and proceeded to build a brick and frame house of his own design, Gordon took him to court for breach of contract. Shrader won his case by claiming that, in case of a fire, he could run into the brick cellar and, if there were an earthquake, the frame house would be safer. Recognizing defeat, Gordon unloaded his lots to any interested takers, without restrictions. Nevertheless, South Park kept its cachet as one of San Francisco's most select neighborhoods.

The mansions of Rincon Hill (top) loom over South Park's northwest quadrant, built in the "English Roman" style. Few of the later structures followed the original plan. (Courtesy California Historical Society)

Even by today's standards, it must have been an extraordinary surprise to encounter those perfectly matched, handsome little English town houses in the wilds of Gold Rush San Francisco. Each of the row houses, when completed, had a frontage of some twenty-two feet. The basement of each house contained the dining room, whose windows looked out into a semi-submerged areaway a few feet below the street level. Behind the dining room were the pantries and kitchen, as well as a small servant's room. To enter the main floor from the street, one ascended a stone stoop which led to the double front doors. Beyond them stretched the long stairhall, flanked on one side by double parlors, each of which was less than fifteen feet square. A tiny study stood just beyond the stairhall, while the back parlor, or library, presented a pair of long French windows opening into a glassed-in rear conservatory.

It is hard to believe Gordon's sales prospectus for his South Park development, which stated that each of these diminutive houses contained five bedrooms. There was room for two fair-sized rooms above the double parlors, and for two tiny rooms at each end of the upper hall, but where was the fifth bedroom? To be sure, there were larger houses built at each end of the two crescents; perhaps these were the houses advertised.

One may readily imagine a typical South Park interior: the parlor with its flowered Brussels carpet, the ornate suite of high-backed Belter chairs and matching settee covered in velvet or horsehair. There was certain to be a center table and a lamp beneath the prismed whale-oil chandelier, where the light for reading was best. On the marble mantel the inevitable little gilt clock kept time under a glass dome flanked by matching candelabra. Between the windows and over the mantel, tall mirrors reflected the chandelier's light.

Through sliding doors, one stepped into the library, for in most South Park homes the back parlor served this function. Much of the room's furnishings might duplicate those of the parlor; the same carpet and brocaded draperies over lace, with perhaps a heavy Empire-style sofa for reading and napping, and, of course, a tall secretary desk filled with books. There might be classical busts of the Caesars on marble pedestals. Lace curtains afforded a glimpse of the fragrant, flower-filled conservatory to the rear.

Again, there was that question about the bedrooms. How did the residents fit a typical bedroom suite (pronounced "suit" by even the better educated) into a room fifteen feet square? A huge armoire, usually called a "wardrobe," (closets were almost unknown in those

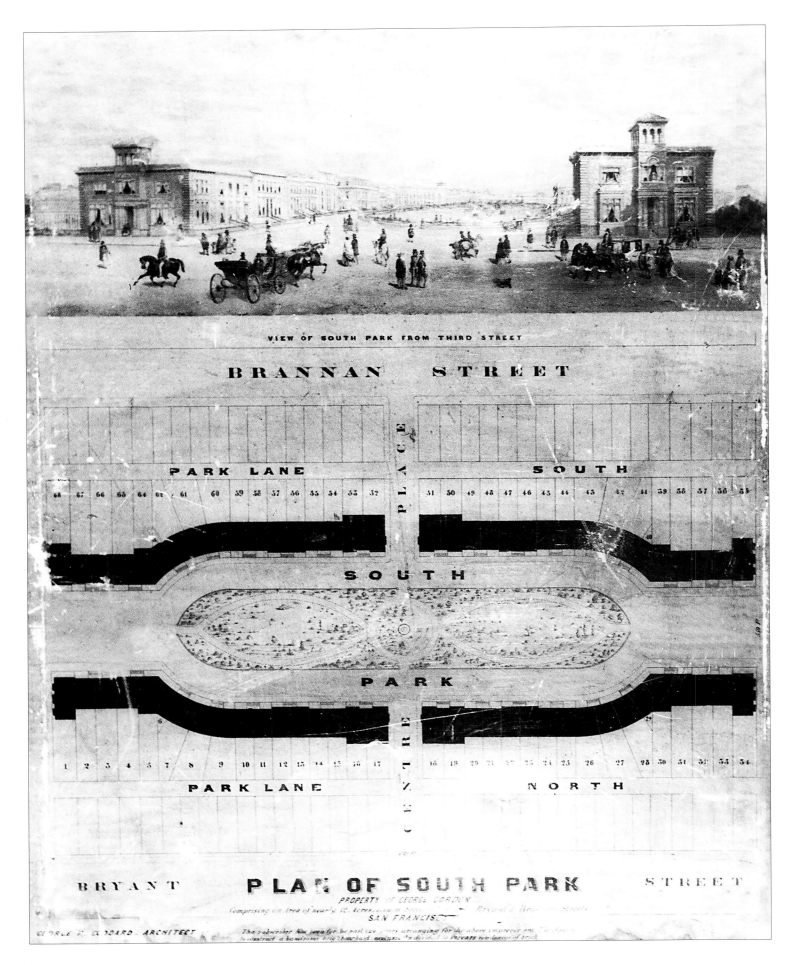

VIEW OF SOUTH PARK FROM THIRD STREET

BRANNAN STREET

PARK LANE

SOUTH

SOUTH

PARK

PARK LANE

NORTH

BRYANT **PLAN OF SOUTH PARK** STREET

PROPERTY OF GEORGE GORDON

San Francisco

GEORGE C. GODDARD ARCHITECT

South Park from Third Street, looking east toward Second Street; the houses on the left were the first group to be completed, in 1855. The horse-drawn streetcar carried riders from South Park to North Beach. (Author's collection)

days), a large chest of drawers, a massive double bed, and the marble-topped washstand or commode, with three drawers for linens and a door to conceal the chamber pot, completed the usual bedroom furnishings. Just bringing these huge pieces up the narrow stairs must have presented a formidable challenge.

Mrs. Mary Greenleaf, daughter of E. V. Hathaway, who lived at 38 South Park, provided photographs of the parlor and library which are offered here. Mrs. Greenleaf recalled that her mother kept the open areaway in front of the basement dining room filled with potted geraniums and other plants. Above the sideboard was a passthrough window from the kitchen, so that diners could be served without being disturbed by the servants.

The Hathaways' servants were two sweet Irish girls, who for years occupied a tiny bedroom adjoining the kitchen. The girls wore calico dresses covered by long,

Facing Page: From the South Park prospectus: George Gordon planned to build his ambitious project on twelve acres bounded by Bryant, Brannan, Second and Third Streets. George H. Goddard was the architect. "Lots will be leased from 10 to 20 years, renewable at 10 per cent per annum on a fair valuation, or sold on three years' credits to parties about to build." (Courtesy Society of California Pioneers)

white, immaculately clean aprons; fancy uniforms for servants belonged to a later, more ostentatious era in San Francisco. Mrs. Greenleaf described how her mother and these girls were forever filling the pantries with canned preserves, a necessary adjunct to life in those days without refrigeration. Her father added one luxury to the house: a bathroom, above the conservatory.

Despite the compact plan of the house itself, there was room at the back of the small lot for a large, two-story barn. Here the Hathaways kept their carriage, two horses, and even a cow. In those days before pasteurization, the cow developed tuberculosis, and Mrs. Greenleaf's little brother died from drinking its milk.

In her first published effort, *The Randolphs of the Redwoods*, (later republished under the title *A Daughter of the Vine*), Gertrude Atherton aptly described South Park life as "having that atmosphere of happy informality peculiar to the brief honeymoon of a great city. The inner park was green and flowered; the flag of the United States floated proudly above. People ran, hatless, in and out of each other's houses, and sat on the doorsteps when the weather was fine."

The leading characters from this novel, thinly disguised by Mrs. Atherton, were quickly recognized by San Franciscans of an earlier generation as Mr. and Mrs. George Gordon and their daughter, Nellie. Mercifully,

This very rare photograph, from the 1870s, shows a South Park parlor with its Italian marble fireplace, gas chandelier, a banjo, and a wealth of Victorian clutter. (Courtesy Mary Greenleaf)

all three Gordons had been dead for years when the young author concocted this Gothic tale of an alcoholic mother, who in revenge against her husband, turned their only child into an alcoholic. No history of South Park can be complete without some reference to this novel, even though evidence weighs heavily against its story line.

As is usually the case, the true stories about South Park make far more interesting reading than any novel. An example is the story of the grand fête held in South Park in 1855 to celebrate the victory of the British, French, Italian and Turkish troops over the Russians in the Battle of Sebastopol during the Crimean War. Apparently, the fine cast-iron fountain ordered from the Colebrookdale Iron Works in Liverpool had not yet been installed, and thus the grassy oval was free for the erection of an enormous tent.

More than three thousand citizens were invited to partake of an elaborate banquet held in the tent. Inside, artists had painted large Crimean scenes on the walls. Evergreens and flags added to the festive scene. Long banquet tables set with delicious viands ranged down the tent's interior. In the center of all this stood a huge roasted ox, replete with horns and hairy shanks, ready to be served to the celebrants. In view of the catastrophe

to come, perhaps the addition of two bottles of wine at each place setting was a big mistake.

Things immediately got off to a bad start when, instead of the expected three thousand guests, some four or five thousand showed up. Then, as festivities progressed, the speakers whom the crowd found to be too long-winded found themselves dodging empty wine bottles. When fights broke out among guests of different nationalities, a riot ensued in which rowdies tore down the flags, broke dishes and smashed a twelve-foot Malakoff cake. Later in the evening, while guests were nursing their wounds and massive hangovers, a small delegation presented an apology to the Russian Consul General, whose residence was in South Park. Next day, the *Alta Californian* stated that the incident was a disgrace to the American name, "committed by the vilest of the vile."

Notwithstanding this disaster, many San Franciscans still take pride in the fact that their ancestors who were early residents of South Park, and like those who claim that their forefathers arrived on the *Mayflower*, the list grows and grows. Not surprisingly, the majority of the park's residents were professional people— lawyers, judges and doctors. A number of military families, both active and retired, also were listed.

The back parlor of the E. V. Hathaway house, #38 South Park, reveals an eclectic mix of Asian, English, and Indian pieces, with plenty of American Victorian bric-a-brac thrown in. A grand piano and a violin suggest that a Sunday afternoon musicale is about to begin. Fitted shutters close out the sun. (Courtesy Mary Greenleaf)

Commodore James Watkins of the Pacific Mail Steamship Line was one of South Park's more famous residents. In those days knowledgeable travelers chose their sailing accommodations according to the safety and comfort afforded by the line, and the reputation of the captain. San Franciscans who planned trips to the Hawaiian Islands or the Orient always made a point of travelling on the ship Commodore Watkins commanded. In the 1850s Watkins' ship, the *Golden Age*, struck a reef near the Quibo Islands, while en route to Panama. Through his wise command the ship was beached, saving more than a hundred lives. One of the passengers was the wife of William Tecumseh Sherman.

Then there was the Reverend Scott. This gentleman, who lived at Number 34, one of the two large end houses fronting Third Street, served at the Calvary Presbyterian Church on Union Square, the site occupied today by the St. Francis Hotel. At the outbreak of the Civil War, the Reverend stood before his congregation and invoked God's blessings on both Abraham Lincoln and Jefferson Davis. While a furious crowd hanged an effigy of Reverend Scott outside in Union Square, Mrs. Thomas Selby, a Rincon Hill woman of known Confederate sympathies, hurried the Reverend into her waiting carriage, which carried him to safety at

the Selby's country house in Atherton. Immediately thereafter, Mrs. Selby's husband, then Mayor of San Francisco, sent his wife to Paris, where she joined other San Francisco women with similar sentiments. Reverend Scott departed for New Orleans, eventually returning to San Francisco after the war.

Perhaps unfairly, Reverend Scott's rashness helped give South Park a reputation as a "hotbed of secessionism." The neighborhood undeniably had a number of Southern sympathizers among its residents, and stories soon began circulating around San Francisco that South Park residents were celebrating Confederate victories behind their shuttered windows. Be that as it may, when news reached San Francisco of Lincoln's assassination, all of South Park was draped in black bunting, the mark of public mourning in the Victorian age.

With these few exceptions, life in South Park was certainly less eventful than it was in the rest of the vigorous young city. There were the usual dinner parties, balls, cotillions and receptions; the Social Register listed Wednesday as the day when South Park ladies were "at home" to receive callers. Gossip often centered on the exploits of a trio of South Park belles who called themselves "The World, the Flesh, and the Devil."

One unique mode of entertainment, known as the "kettledrum tea," was said to have come to South Park via British Colonial India. A kettledrum tea required a young lady to stand by the tea table and lightly tap on a military drum. The exact significance of this fad has since been forgotten, but for a time it was all the rage.

One topic for gossip, according to Amelia Ransome Neville, was the young South Park belle who was locked in her room to prevent her from eloping with her young music teacher. The teacher, saved from matrimony, went on to very considerable fame as a pianist and composer; his name was Louis Moreau Gottschalk.

When in summer the wind and fog blew over the city, fashionable folk customarily adjourned to one of the resorts in the Sonoma or Napa Valleys. A favorite spot in the 1850s and '60s was the White Sulphur Springs Resort, in the Mayacamas Mountains above Napa Valley. Patterned after the White Sulphur Springs in Virginia, the resort featured a white frame hotel with a wide veranda and a score of white cottages nestling in the trees. In the rustic ballroom, lit by colorful lanterns, young ladies with "follow-me-lad" curls, dressed in white muslin flounces, whirled with stalwart young gentlemen to the music of Ballinger's Band.

There were also yachting parties on the Bay, or visits to Mare Island or the Benicia Arsenal, commanded by Julian McAllister, a member of the elite McAllister clan. The San Francisco Presidio also served as a social center, and when a ball or picnic was held there, gaily bedecked launches transported the guests; the Presidio's overland route, running through rough and dusty sandhills, was considered too uncomfortable for ladies.

In their rounds of New Year's Day receptions, young gentlemen made a point of calling at the Gwin and McAllister houses in South Park. "In those dietary dark ages," Mrs. Ransom Neville recalled, "dinners ran to sixteen courses. Terrapin was followed by creamed oysters, a fish course, poultry and game. The accompanying wines would be claret, madeira and champagne. Mrs. McAllister once declared that a dinner of less than four hours in the serving was deemed a failure."

The Fall of Rincon Hill

WHEN GEORGE GORDON died at the age of 47 in 1869, San Francisco's financial and social communities deeply mourned the loss. That year of 1869 turned out to be a pivotal one for other reasons as well. California's overland isolation ended with the driving of the gold spike at Promontory Point, Utah, marking the completion of the Central Pacific Railroad. Shortly afterward, "the Big Four"—former merchants Mark Hopkins, Charles Crocker, Collis Huntington, and Leland Stanford, recent governor of California—moved from Sacramento to San Francisco. It did not take long for San Franciscans to learn that the power and wealth concentrated in these four men extended well beyond their control of the Central Pacific Railroad.

By 1870, the impact of the newly rich "Silver Kings" began to be felt in all California, particularly in San Francisco. The emerging influence of this nouveau riche group was enough to change the face of the city financially, and to create real social upheaval. Nothing pointed up this change more forcefully than the infamous "Second Street Cut," which occurred in 1869.

For four years, the most politically powerful residents of Rincon Hill battled with developers and shippers who wanted to shorten the route from the center of town to the Pacific Mail docks at the foot of Rincon Hill to the south. In the end, the developers won and, in that fateful year of 1869, cut a 60-foot gash directly through the center of the hill. The fact that many of Rincon Hill's residents had established their iron works and ship-building industries at the hill's very back door led to inevitable tragedy.

Mayor Selby, whose Harrison Street house was just around the corner from Second Street, decried the "vandal spirit of the bloodless speculators" and called the $90,000 expenditure "a public outrage." Indeed, the cut turned out to be a greater disaster than even its enemies had predicted, for when the soft interior of the hill was cut through, terrible landslides ensued. As the hilltop soil tumbled into the open gash below, the houses of Second Street, with their flower gardens and trellised summer houses, followed it down into the muddy slough. For years afterward, drivers of heavy drays avoided that route for fear they would create more landslides. Even the blasting of Telegraph Hill in the early fifties was less disastrous, for there, fewer private houses were endangered. So much for that old devil we call progress.

Despite the ruin of the Hill and the growth of heavy industry in the area, some of Rincon Hill's residents clung stubbornly to their homes. At Harrison Street a remarkably ugly bridge, nicknamed "The

The infamous Second Street Cut, made in 1869 to allow easier access between downtown and the Mission Bay waterfront, spelled the end of Rincon Hill as a grand residential neighborhood. Many fine residences lost their front yards and even their porches to the huge gash. On the left is the Macondray house, and behind it the Sather, Kip and Eldredge houses. (Courtesy California Historical Society)

Bridge of Sighs," crossed the Second Street gap, and the houses which did not fall into the gully were turned around to face away from it. Well into the 1880s the city directories continued to list the calling days for the ladies of Rincon Hill and South Park. The Swiss consul, M. Berthon, moved from his house at Number 22 South Park into a seventeen-room mansion which he built at Number 13. On Harrison Street at Essex, Henry Miller, a land and cattle baron, tore down the lovely old Earle house and replaced it with a cumbersome new mansarded mansion, to general disapproval. (It seems paradoxical that a city not twenty years old would already have an "old guard" to look with disdain at the new plutocracy which rose to power in the 1870s.)

Miller's mansion was not enough to stop the decay of Rincon Hill and South Park. Mrs. Phoebe Hearst built a large settlement house in the eastern end of South Park, for the children of working mothers who found employment in the surrounding factories. Kate Douglas Wiggin, author of Mrs. Wiggs and the Cabbage Patch, established the Silver Street Kindergarten, on Silver just below Harrison, for the babies of working class immigrants who had settled in the area. Gangs of teenagers like those Anson Blake described eventually overran Rincon Hill, replacing the well-bred children of an earlier day.

ON THE VERY FIRST DAY of the holocaust which swept San Francisco in 1906, all that was left of Rincon Hill met its demise. Chroniclers of the event thought of the Hill merely as a place of cheap tenements and slums; few registered any serious regret at the passing of this historic quarter. Many even regarded its destruction as a blessing. When the smoke and fire had passed, only one structure had been spared: the old Marine Hospital at Beale and Harrison Streets. Built in 1852, this masterpiece of brick masonry was among the first on the Hill. Its sturdy brick walls stood until 1917, when the building was thought to have outlived its usefulness and was torn down. A fragment of the foundation survives, marked by a bronze plaque under the stanchions of the Bay Bridge, just off Bryant Street.

Since 1860, St. Mary's Hospital, then San Francisco's largest, had been an integral part of Rincon Hill. Even at that early date a number of houses belonging to prominent citizens had been removed for its construction. On the first day of the 1906 fire, patients were evacuated by boats. From the bay they had a clear and final view of the old Rincon Hill, as flames engulfed the entire hilltop and the hospital with it.

After the firestorm of 1906, when refugees were scavenging the sites of their former homes, they came across a hand-painted sign on the site of General Doane's Hawthorne Street house: "Be it ever so humble, there's no place like Rincon Hill."

The story of Rincon Hill and South Park, charming and beautiful places created very early in San Francisco's development, disproves the hackneyed old myth about San Francisco's elite being little more than horny-fisted forty-niners, reformed criminals, former dance hall floozies and mail-order brides. It also warns us to consider carefully what we mean by the word "progress." All the wealth and power of Rincon Hill's residents could not stay the new forces changing the face of San Francisco.

POTRERO HILL

RISING BETWEEN the Mission District and the Bay, with freeways framing it on both sides, Potrero Hill is today a quiet oasis above the swirl of traffic and noisy industry. Once the "new pasture" (Potrero Nuevo) for the mission herds, the hill was granted in 1844 to Ramon and Francisco de Haro, the teenage twin sons of Francisco de Haro. Two years later, the boys, along with their aging uncle Jose Santos Berryessa, were gunned down by Kit Carson, on orders from Captain John C. Fremont during his abortive attempt to become the conqueror of Mexican California. De Haro Street, on Potrero Hill's western flank, is a memorial to the boys' brief tenancy.

In 1848 Governor Mason placed the Potrero lands under protection as a haven for the former mission Indians who had managed to survive the American conquest of the city. This use, plus the natural barrier of Mission Bay, which was used for oyster farming, gave Potrero Hill a few years' respite before the implacable onrush of development reached its shore. Squatters settled in around the fringes of the hill, building houses and pasturing livestock on land which had no single claimant to protest their presence. In 1865 the Long Bridge was constructed across Mission Bay, and soon horse-drawn trams were carrying passengers and goods down to Potrero Point.

When the Second Street cut sliced through Rincon Hill in 1869, it soon became clear that factories, warehouses and shipyards were to be the future of the entire waterfront area south of Market Street. Underwater lots in Mission Bay brought premium prices, and huge sand hills were leveled to fill them in. Mission Creek was forced into a narrow, straight channel, and the once-spacious Mission Bay gradually shrank down to a small cove called China Basin. The shipyards crowded along Mission Creek produced hundreds of sailing ships, steam schooners and scows to carry lumber and bricks for the thousands of houses going up in the Western Addition, as well as hay for the countless teams of horses at work in the city.

Industries also sprang up along the Potrero bayside, with housing for workers on the hills just above. Scotch Hill was the home of immigrant Scottish mechanics who found work in the steel mills. Just next door was Irish Hill, where Irish laborers lived in small hotels and boarding houses. In the era of industrial expansion during World War I, Irish Hill was completely leveled and used for fill along the waterfront. Below these two hills was Dutch Flat, where Dutch immigrants found work in the sugar mill owned by Claus Spreckels.

Nancy Olmsted, in her book *Vanished Waters: A History of San Francisco's Mission Bay*, (1986) sums up the importance of industries at Potrero Point:

> Here the dream of the 1860s is realized by 1884. The Union Iron Works opened in 1882, directly adjoining the Pacific Rolling Mills, the point's first major manufacturing industry, dating back to 1866. The Western Sugar Refinery dominated the southern waterfront of Potrero Point. Within a few years, the Atlas Iron Works would locate here . . . The big mills reverberated day and night, producing mining machinery, pumps, boilers, iron for the railroads, streetcar rails, bridges, marine hardware and big walking-beam engines, iron-clad monitors and cruisers for the Navy. Potrero production was the center of San Francisco's industrial output from 1884 through the first World War.

This view, looking toward Mission Dolores from the western slope of Potrero Hill in 1860, shows fields on both sides of today's 16th Street. Mission Creek flows from left to right under the bridge, toward Mission Bay, while a group enjoys a picnic on a grassy knoll. (Author's collection)

The massive brick warehouses and factory buildings with arched windows, cornices, and imposing portals represented a high standard in industrial architecture. A few of them still function; others stand today, decrepit and empty memorials to the great industries and the workers who kept the city prosperous. Today, touring the district east of Third Street between Sixteenth and Army Streets, one can hear echoes of the clang and roar of industries where thousands of laborers once earned their daily bread.

To the west of Potrero Hill the grazing lands, truck gardens and orchards of the old mission were gradually subdivided and sold to builders. Potrero Avenue, once the eastern boundary of Potrero Viejo, the mission's old pasture, formed a border between the Mission District and Potrero Hill until the building of the James Lick Freeway, which completely isolated the hill from the lowlands.

Butchertown, originally located at Ninth and Brannan Streets, in 1870 was moved south of Potrero Hill, to the banks of Islais Creek. Daily shipments of cattle from the southern ranches were brought here to be slaughtered in the abatoirs, strategically located so that the odorous wastes could be flushed out twice a day by the tides. Tuberculosis patients were sent to Butchertown daily for a cup of hot blood, prescribed by doctors at the time for consumptives. Across the creek to the south, handy to their source of supply, were the tanneries, which smelled far worse than the slaughterhouses. Fortunately for the dwellers of Potrero Hill, on most days the prevailing westerly winds blew the factory smoke and the bad smells out over the Bay to be dissipated.

At the turn of the century a new ethnic contingent settled on Potrero Hill when some two thousand Russian immigrants, mainly from the Volga and Caucasus regions, arrived after fleeing Czarist oppression. Known as the "Molokani," the milk drinkers, they were a puritanical sect who worshiped at a modest little church where the women and men were segregated during services. At the Potrero Hill Neighborhood House, designed by Julia Morgan, the Russians took classes in the English language and learned how to use sewing machines. The charming, brown-shingled Neighborhood House, at 953 De Haro Street, is still in use today as a meeting hall and cultural center. It is an official San Francisco Landmark.

Potrero Hill enjoys the best climate in San Francisco, a city where some 23 different mini-climates have been identified. This fact may have prompted the Crocker family years ago to purchase large chunks of land on the hill, expecting it to become a prime residential area. Their expectations may yet be realized. The sunshine and the stunning,

panoramic views have attracted writers, painters and craftsmen to the hill in recent years.

Two of the most important surviving 19th-century houses on Potrero Hill, the Captain Adams house, at 300 Pennsylvania, and the Richards house, across the street at 301, have recently been lovingly restored, and are designated San Francisco Landmarks. They are shown in the color section of this book.

At Twentieth and Wisconsin Streets, Victoria Mews, a huge compound of apartments and townhouses in the "neo-Victorian" style, has brought a new wave of popula-tion to the north slope of the hill. Nearby, at De Haro and Mariposa Streets, the Anchor Steam Brewery has been completely renovated by Fritz Maytag, who single-handedly saved a great San Francisco tradition. On the south slope of the hill rows of new townhouses, in what might be called the "Neo-Queen Anne" style, look down on Islais Creek and the last remnants of San Francisco's industrial district, now mainly factories and warehouses for building supplies and light industry. The heavy industries that supported a large blue-collar pop-ulation and paid for the city's growth are long gone.

Facing page top: Potrero Hill escaped without major damage in the earthquake and fire of 1906, mainly because the rocky underpinnings of the hill provided a solid foundation for houses there. Hundreds of homeless people, mainly from the devastated south of Market area, lived in tents, arranged in neat rows. St. Teresa's church is in the background.

Facing page bottom: The luckier refugees in 1906 were housed in "Earthquake Cottages," built by the hundreds on Potrero Hill and in the Presidio. The women and children in this picture are beautifully dressed, in spite of their temporary living conditions. One or two little girls seem to be wearing their mothers' hats. The man in the center is unidentified; his clothing suggests that he may be a chef, perhaps in a community kitchen.

The famous drive-in courtyard in the original Palace Hotel allowed guests to peer down from the balconies to see who was arriving. (Author's collection)

THE
BONANZA
ERA

1870 - 1890

THE PALACE HOTEL AND
"THE MAN WHO BUILT SAN FRANCISCO"

*I have made me great works and I have builded me stately mansions and behold! All is
vanity and vexation of spirit. And there is no profit under the sun.
Yea, I hate my labor, for I shall leave it for the man who shall come after me.
And who knoweth if he is a wise man or a fool?*

— Ecclesiastes 2:4

URING THE HEADY YEARS between 1870 and 1890, San Francisco
was like the profligate child who went through one fortune only to
inherit another. As the gold in the Mother Lode began to play out,
a great mountain of silver was discovered in Nevada. Miners devised new
techniques, diverting whole rivers and blasting away mountainsides with
streams of water, or constructing vast networks of tunnels to get at the silver
or gold below the surface. Meanwhile, the trans-continental railroad, completed in 1869, promised new wealth to merchants in San Francisco, as well
as to railroad barons Crocker, Stanford, Huntington and Hopkins, who
amassed staggering fortunes and set new standards in lavish spending.

William Ralston set new records for spending when he built the magnificent Palace Hotel on Market Street, just across New Montgomery from his splendidGrand Hotel, just behind it in this picture. In the foreground is Lotta's Fountain; after 120 years it was carefully restored in 1999. Cable cars on Market had only sparse horse-drawn traffic to contend with. (Courtesy San Francisco Public Library)

Today, many look to this period as San Francisco's Golden Age. Perhaps a better name would be the Silver Age. This time the wealth showering down on the bumptious young town was silver from the Comstock Lode in Nevada. Eventually it exceeded the sum of $300 million.

Unlike gold, silver was not panned from streams or dug out with pick and shovel. The veins carrying silver ran deep under the earth's surface, and miners now had to use expensive machinery to dig long tunnels and bring the ore to the surface. This meant that companies had to be formed, with stockholders willing to pay for the heavy equipment and patiently await the results. In the rush to buy, stocks would go up, up, up, often selling for prices that far exceeded their benefits. Eventually the speculating shareholders would find themselves either out of pocket, or rich—at least until their next venture into the market. The process was similar in many respects to today's lotteries. Everybody was playing. Financiers, clerks, servant girls and dowagers all played the market and prayed that Lady Luck would look their way.

In this atmosphere of boom and bust, certain names rose in the city's financial hierarchy. Mackay, Fair,

Haggin, Flood, Sharon, Ralston, O'Brien, Hearst, Mills, Coleman, Hayward, Baldwin and Sutro all amassed enormous fortunes and entered into the ranks of the city's elite. In 1876 the *Examiner* listed more than 225 San Franciscans worth over a million dollars. Nearly all had started from modest beginnings, so they were popularly regarded as local boys who had made good. In those days of quick fortunes made and lost, San Franciscans looked up to the "Silver Kings" as civic heroes. Their weddings, mansions, jewels, parties, horses and equipages, and even the scandalous behavior of some, became matters of the greatest local interest; of course, journalists gleefully reported every detail of their doings.

If one of these Silver Kings bought his wife a necklace reputed to have belonged to Marie Antoinette, he felt it his civic duty to report how he had acquired it and just what it had cost him. Although some found it vulgar, there was a kind of naive camaraderie in reporting to the press and the city at large just how much one intended to spend on a house one was building on Nob Hill, feeling that such a glorious showplace was a laudable contribution to civic improvement. San Francisco was still a relatively small town, and those who thought

Above: The Garden Court, which has been called the most beautiful dining room in America, took the place of the drive-in courtyard when the Palace Hotel was rebuilt after 1906. The hotel's recent restoration preserved the Garden Court intact. (Courtesy San Francisco Public Library)

The Palace, rebuilt after 1906, is shown here in the 1920s. The hotel has been completely renovated, with great attention to the original design. Knowledgeable pedestrians walking from Market to Jessie Street often detour through the Palace lobby to look at the historical displays and check out the Garden Court. (Courtesy San Francisco Public Library)

Crowds jammed Montgomery Street, between California and Sacramento Streets, on September 16, 1872, when the price of Meadow Valley stock plunged. The Hall and Charles building, at 410 Montgomery Street, survived the 1906 earthquake but was torn down in 1924. (Courtesy California State Library)

that fortune beckoned just around the corner loved reading about anyone who had "made his pile." Perhaps one's own turn would be next. The spirit of the city was never more democratic.

"Our millionaires show no disposition to economize," stated the *San Francisco Newsletter* in January 1876, "and the rage for splendid houses continues unabated. No one will be so envious or unjust as to ascribe any but the best motives to our millionaires, who do not hoard their treasures but are inclined to display them for the benefit of all. It is to be hoped that the fine example of building stately homes which will contribute to San Francisco's name, both at home and abroad, will be speedily imitated by all who can afford to do so."

Today, when our richest and most powerful families barricade themselves against the press in fear and trembling, and furtively arrange their collections of furniture and paintings behind the bland façades of high-rise apartment houses, those old press clippings certainly make good reading.

THE STRONG competitive spirit which had gone into the accumulation of great wealth fired a building boom of staggering proportions. When the Leland Stanfords began building a two-million-dollar villa on Nob Hill, it did not take long for Mary

Anne Crocker and Mary Hopkins to put Jane Stanford in her place. Soon the James Floods were trying to match them, first with a huge country house in Menlo Park, and later with a stone mansion on Nob Hill, surrounded by a bronze fence which alone cost $30,000. When it came to conspicuous consumption, however, it was William Ralston who set the pace.

By the late 1860s, William Chapman Ralston was already established in his grand Italianate mansion on a vast acreage at Belmont, on the San Francisco Peninsula. It was not unusual for Mrs. Ralston to have her plans for an intimate family dinner interrupted by a messenger with the news that her husband was bringing fifty guests to dine and spend the night. With guest rooms to spare, a full larder, and cellars filled with bottles of fine wines, it was no great hardship for the hostess and her large staff to meet such a sudden emergency. On some occasions, Mr. Ralston would commandeer an entire train and fill it with weekend guests. If his party was smaller, he would transport his guests in a huge tally-ho coach pulled by four spirited horses. Leaving San Francisco on even terms with the train, he would race his coach against the steam engine, make a stop or two to change horses, and then dash on to Belmont. To facilitate his portal-to-portal dash, Mr. Ralston placed a device in the road which, when ridden over by the coach wheels, would cause Belmont's entrance gates to swing open. In this way, he could pull up before the entrance of his house without pausing, and disgorge his disheveled, wild-eyed passengers on schedule. If he lost the race with the train, he would be out of sorts all weekend.

All over San Francisco, the forthright iron-shuttered brick and granite business structures of the 1850s gave way in the 1870s to elaborate, wedding-cake affairs. William Ralston, planning to build the California Theater on Bush Street, gave his architects one curious instruction: to find out the size of the largest theater in America, and then design his theater ten feet bigger.

WHEN HE decided to build a new hotel, he hired architect John P. Gaynor, who had come to San Francisco from New York in the 1860s, and sent him east to study the construction of the Sturtevant House and the New Windsor Hotel in New York, and the Palmer House and Grand Pacific in Chicago. Gaynor's design was bigger than any of these, filling two acres. Ralston's Palace Hotel, on which workers began construction in 1874, was the capstone of this era's magnificence, surpassing anything the city had ever seen. Probably no San Francisco building has ever matched the Palace for sheer grandeur in scale or exuberance of detail. True to the bumptious, chauvinistic spirit of the adolescent town, San Franciscans declared the Palace to be the world's most magnificent hotel. They were probably right.

Not that San Francisco lacked fine hostelries. Dating from the 1860s were the Lick House, at Sutter and Montgomery, and the Occidental, just across the way. Just beyond, the Russ House took up an entire block of Montgomery from Bush to Pine. On Market at Powell Street, Lucky Baldwin had just completed his $800,000 Baldwin Hotel and Theater, which seemed to San Franciscans of the 1870s the pinnacle of luxury and style. And Ralston's own Grand Hotel, a splendid $2 million, five-story building, stood just across New Montgomery from the site of the Palace. When the Palace was completed, a footbridge was built above the street, making the Grand simply an elegant annex.

San Francisco was too young to have any strong sense of proportion, so nobody was overly concerned that the new hotel, with 800 rooms, was at least four times too large for its time and place. Rising to a height of 7 stories, at an estimated cost of $6 million, the Palace towered over its surroundings like some giant from another world. San Francisco, with a population of 192,000, of whom 30,000 were Chinese, would need years of growth to catch up to its Palace Hotel.

William Ralston, banker, speculator and silver king, has deservedly been called "the man who built San Francisco." His Palace Hotel brought San Francisco to the world's attention as nothing had since the Gold Rush. Ralston, once a riverboat captain from Ohio, was more than a one-man chamber of commerce. He was a builder and a dreamer, and all of his considerable energies were bound up in making San Francisco a leader among American cities.

The source of Ralston's fortune—and the cause of his ruin—was the Bank of California. As a director, Ralston could draw from his own or from the bank's funds; sometimes the line was not clearly drawn. Nervous board members had begun to think that Ralston's visionary profligacy had gone too far. The Palace had yet to celebrate its grand opening when, on August 27, 1875, they decided to give Ralston his walking papers. On that very day Ralston took his customary swim in the icy waters of the Bay. Shortly afterward his lifeless body washed ashore. Whether his death was an accident or suicide became a matter for his supporters and detractors to debate. The completion of the Palace was left to Ralston's business partner, William Sharon, who would also move into the house at Belmont. The $140,000 mansion which Ralston had just completed at Pine and Leavenworth Streets was converted into a hotel called "The Ralston," the only one of his buildings to bear his name. This too vanished in the flames of 1906.

In the boastful '70s, every American believed his city or state to be the crossroads of God's universe, but few could compete with San Francisco when it came to civic pride. Whatever the shortcomings the young city had at that date—and it had many—San Franciscans needed only to take visitors into the Palace's seven-story marble-columned court, large enough to permit a turnaround for carriages, to make their point. They could marvel at the four elevators, the 365 slanted-bay windows, the 800 guest rooms with 15-foot ceilings. If this alone was not sufficient, the visitor could sample the hotel's superb cuisine, prepared by thirty world-renowned chefs. Even the place settings were magnificent: the china was Haviland and the plate was by Gorham. W. & J. Sloane of New York had opened a branch store in San Francisco just to supply the Palace's acres of fine carpets. Most strikingly, at a time when San Franciscans still needed to import most of the refinements of life, Ralston had established factories in San Francisco to supply the splendid furniture, linens, and even mattresses for his Palace. Even the carriages which drove into the courtyard may have come from the carriage factory which Ralston had established locally.

In the building's first years, San Franciscans could take their guests to the Palace's lavish bar, or relax in one of the elegant lobbies while pointing out some bonanza king whose wealth exceeded that of an Arabian sultan. Of course, it was "the thing" for a gentleman of affairs to take a large suite at the Palace when business called him to San Francisco.

For 31 years the Palace Hotel enjoyed its world fame. When the 1906 fire swept down Market Street the Palace held out for a time, thanks to two huge water cisterns, built for just such an emergency. Then, when the water supplies had been used up in fighting neighboring blazes, the magnificent hotel succumbed.

After the disaster the Sharon estate, still the owners, spent $100,000 to tear down the solid, fire-blackened brick walls of Ralston's Palace Hotel. Sharon's son-in-law, Francis Newlands, commissioned a New York firm, Trowbridge and Livingston, to design a new "earthquake- and fire-proof Palace Hotel." George Kelham, a young member of the firm, was sent to San Francisco to supervise the work. He stayed on, to become one of California's leading architects.

In 1909 a stunning new Palace held its grand reopening. The guest rooms no longer boasted fifteen-foot ceilings, but the lobbies and public rooms were undeniably handsome. Best of all, the old carriage court had now become the Palace Court, with a magnificent art-glass ceiling. Many believe it is the most dazzlingly beautiful public dining room in America. After 90 years of use, the hotel, now owned by a Japanese conglomerate, has undergone a complete, careful renovation. William Ralston's dream, in modified form, is ready for the 21st Century.

Paradoxically, the rambling frame *palazzo* Ralston built at Belmont, with its silver doorknobs and mirrored ballroom, still stands today, housing the College of Notre Dame. It is the sole visual reminder of Ralston's many contributions to San Francisco. The mansion in Belmont, and scores of San Francisco mansions yet to come, mirrored the dashing self-confidence, the individualism and the vigorous inventiveness of the Victorian Age in America.

Nob Hill in the 1870s

Build me a castle, forty feet high
So I can see you, as you ride by.

— "Down in the Valley," American folk song

THE STEEP, wind-blown eminence long known as "Fern Hill" or "The Hill of Golden Promise" might never have become famed as the home of California's "Nabobs" were it not for Andrew Hallidie's timely invention of the cable car. Hallidie, moved by the plight of horses dying from over-exertion on the horse-car lines, devised his preposterous contraption to free public transportation from dependence on horses. On August 1, 1873, Hallidie and his backers assembled at the foot of the Clay Street hill to test the world's first cable car.

The celebration following the success of this venture was hardly over when Hallidie was summoned to appear at the offices of Governor Leland Stanford, one of the four owners of the Central Pacific Railroad. Stanford, always fascinated by mechanical gadgets, was in the midst of building an enormous palazzo on the steep southeastern slope of Nob Hill. Not only would Hallidie's cable car make the mansion more easily accessible; if it worked, it would escalate the property values of the relatively inaccessible crest of the hill. By 1876, thanks to Hallidie's and Stanford's efforts, the Comstock millionaires were joining the railroad kings in creating a faubourg which made the name Nob Hill synonymous with grandeur, wealth, and high-flown pretension.

In his support of the California Street Cable Railway, Stanford shrewdly multiplied the value of his square block (bounded by California, Mason, Pine and Powell Streets) from the $30,000 he had paid for it. Indeed, "Hallidie's Grip," as the cable car was then known, played a major role in the settlement of the Western Addition when lines were extended out Hayes, Sutter, California, Washington, Jackson, and Pacific Streets, benefitting thousands of real estate investors.

As we have seen, despite difficult access, there were several comfortable houses along Taylor Street a decade before the arrival of the cable car and the "Nabobs." In 1872, financier James Ben Ali Haggin built the first of San Francisco's truly colossal mansions on Taylor

The Colton-Huntington house, designed by Samuel Bugbee & Sons, was the most restrained and elegant of the great Nob Hill mansions, with noble proportions, a fine balustrade around the top, and white marble lions by the front steps. (Courtesy Roy D. Graves Collection) **Below**: Collis Huntington, from an old newspaper photograph.

Street. Haggin employed architects Henry Kenitzer and Edward Raun to design the French Renaissance structure, with 60 rooms, crowned by the newly popular Mansard roof. With two full floors above a high basement, plus a third floor in the mansard, the house reached a height of fifty feet. Rising another thirty feet above all this was what came to be known as "the millionaire's tower," soon to be an almost obligatory feature of grand houses.

One journalist described the exterior detailing of Haggin's mansion as "a happy medium between excess elaboration and niggard simplicity." Within the mansion, however, simplicity and restraint took a back seat. "All rooms," continued the journalist, "will receive every possible finish. The plaster is of Monterey sand mixed with marble dust. All ceiling moldings, cornices and center medallions are to be made on the premises by Mr. Zellar."

The Haggin lot was one block square, reaching from Clay to Washington Street, and from Taylor to Mason, allowing room for a stable large enough to hold forty horses and eighteen carriages. No doubt Haggin's stable, like those of other bonanza kings, had polished mahogany floors and silver fixtures. He was remembered as a dashing man who often drove a handsome tally-ho coach filled with guests out to the Cliff House for a party. His wife was said to be rather reclusive in her opulent house. One society scribe stated, "As a hostess, Mrs. Haggin was best known for her occasional teas and *conversaziones*."

NEXT TO BUILD a great Nob Hill house was General David Colton, a lawyer for the Big Four, who was sometimes referred to as "the half" of "the Big Four and a half." The 1872 Colton mansion, at California and Taylor, was reportedly built from the plans of an Italian palace brought to America by Colton's friend Milton Latham. But it was of frame construction, painted to resemble white marble, perhaps because the memory of the earthquake of 1868 was still fresh in the minds of the architects, Samuel Bugbee and Sons. The imposing white lions and the front stairs were the only real marble used on the exterior.

To an age which had become convinced that somber earth tones were the only fashionable colors for houses, Colton's classical white house must have been something of a shock. Even more surprising, it lacked the usual "millionaire's tower."

Not long after the completion of his house Colton, at age 46, passed on to another mansion in the sky, and his widow found herself in the courts fighting the Big Four for her inheritance. What had been a warm friendship with neighbor Charles Crocker suddenly cooled. Hiring J. Frank Smith, one of the few local attorneys not in the railroaders' pocket, the Widow Colton was able to produce letters, soon known to all as "the Colton Papers," revealing the Big Four's scandalous business tactics, such as their buying of legislative votes. The anti-railroad public was delighted to see the railroad men squirm, but Colton's former partners refused to back down.

Four panels of a rare panorama made by Eadweard Muybridge in 1877 show (from left) Pine Street, California Street with cable car lines laid out, the Tobin house on the left side, the Crocker and Colton/Huntington houses on the right side. A small cottage sits at one corner of the otherwise empty lot where James Flood would later build his brownstone mansion.

Chief shark in the attempt to relieve the widow of her bankroll seems to have been Collis Huntington. Just a few years later he carried on the same sort of battle with the recently bereaved Jane Stanford. The press turned out reams of copy decrying the scoundrel Huntington; local wags said he felt neglected when an occasional issue of the papers forgot to include some scathing comment about "nefarious Mr. Huntington, the crocodile."

As scandalously as he behaved in this episode, Huntington managed further to astonish San Franciscans a few years later by buying and moving into Colton's house. Here he amassed a superb collection of paintings and French antiques, which were lost when the house, boarded up after Huntington's death in 1901, shared the fate of its neighbors five years later. Huntington Park, the site of the house, is the sole physical reminder that the house was ever there.

Even more bizarre, Huntington's nephew, Henry, after his uncle's death, chose Collis Huntington's widow, Arabella, as his second wife; at least she didn't have to change the monogram on the family linens. The Henry Huntingtons lived in Pasadena, where he

established the famous Red Car Line, an electric train system serving dozens of southern California cities, and said at the time to be the world's finest public transit system. Henry Huntington spent much of his earned and inherited wealth buying rare books and manuscripts at an unheard of rate, and building a great library to hold them. After their death the Huntingtons' San Marino mansion, with its world-class art collection, became the Huntington Gallery, and with it went a bequest to sustain the famous Huntington Library, perhaps the most valuable in the world.

Directly across California Street from the Colton-Huntington palazzo, Joseph Tobin, founder of San Francisco's Hibernia Bank, built a mansard-with-tower house in 1872. The press dutifully reported that this magnificent structure was fifty feet square, three stories high plus mansard, with a 75-foot tower. One entered through an octagonal vestibule ornamented with marble statues of the Four Seasons. On the second floor, a wide hall opened into a family chapel ornamented with fine stained glass windows. Unlike their plutocratic neighbors, the Tobins apparently led a very pious, reclusive life; their daughter Agnes wrote poetry, and a

A pile of lumber blocks Mason Street, and at far right a few cottages, with stairs leading down to California Street, occupy the steep lot that will eventually become the Fairmont Hotel. The large rocky outcroppings had to be blasted away from these lots in order for Flood and the Oelrichs to begin construction. (Courtesy Roy D. Graves Collection)

son, Richard, later served as a distinguished minister to the Netherlands.

The Charles Crocker house was completed in 1876 on the block now occupied by Grace Cathedral, near the very top of Nob Hill. Its architects, Raun and Taylor, claimed that the building was in the French Renaissance style. While they may have taken a few liberties with the definition, no one contradicted them. With its curved pediments, Mansard roof and bull's eye windows scattered about, one might say that the Crocker house had some remote kinship to the French Renaissance style, but any other resemblance was purely coincidental. The house, with 12,500 square feet and a 75-foot tower, was undeniably a bold and inventive expression of what Charles Crocker wanted it to be: the house of a very rich man.

Crocker fully intended to live up to this grand creation. In 1877, when the completion of his house and his silver wedding anniversary coincided, he and his wife held a grand reception to which they invited 500 guests; the house was so large that no one felt crowded.

With the same enthusiasm he put into building his million-dollar house, Crocker also set about filling its vast painting and sculpture gallery. His greatest pride was a canvas which he described to visitors as "the only Meissonier on the Coast." Crocker had paid $25,000 for this picture of an old man smoking a pipe. Another of his favorites, entitled "The Butcher Shop," depicted an old woman chasing a dog who had stolen a piece of meat from her shop. Crocker himself once said, while showing a visitor his collection, "Actually, I'm not a kanoozer." Connoisseur or not, Crocker's tastes were in perfect step with his times. Some of today's slick art magazines are once again advertising "narrative paintings," those same Bougereaus and Meissoniers which men of Crocker's generation so admired.

Charles Crocker later built another mansion, adjoining his own, for his son William. San Francisco legend has it that the elder Crocker's majordomo managed to rescue only Millet's "Man with a Hoe," Corot's "Dance of the Nymphs," Rousseau's "The Oaks," and a few tapestries from William's house when the flames of 1906 swept Nob Hill. Less well known is the fact that the fire also claimed 35 Degas paintings and a Rubens, also from the younger Crocker's collection.

Only in recent years have people again learned to cherish the works of California's early-day artists, once admired by the great collectors of the state. A generation ago, the work of men like Virgil Williams, the Nahl brothers, Thomas Hill, Albert Bierstadt and William Keith, to name a few, enjoyed only second class status. Today, such paintings, when available, bring prices that would have made even the Nob Hill tycoons gasp.

ANOTHER MEMBER of the Big Four to lead the mansion building contest was California's former governor and later senator Leland Stanford. Completed in 1875, his California Street house, exclusive of its million-dollar retaining wall, cost more than three million pre-inflation dollars. Following the Powell Street grade and enclosing the back of the Stanford lot along Pine Street was a 30-foot-high retaining wall of gray basalt blocks topped by granite. This wall has withstood both earthquake and fire, not to mention 125 years of wear. Chances are that it will outlive the Stanford Court and Mark Hopkins hotels, which it continues to support. Credit should go to versatile Arthur Brown, Sr., the Central Pacific engineer who designed and oversaw the wall's construction. (Arthur Brown, Jr., a graduate of the Ecole de Beaux Arts in Paris, was the architect of San Francisco's beautiful new Civic Center after the destruction of the old one in 1906.)

In 1887, when the Stanford house was twelve years old, the *San Francisco Newsletter* described it as "still the most elegant home in America." Occupying one of the city's most commanding sites, the Stanford mansion's huge plate glass windows encompassed a view that swept from the Coast Range Mountains to the fading reaches of the Pacific Ocean.

The mansion, designed by architects Samuel Bugbee & Sons, was intended to resemble an Italian palazzo. The rusticated sandstone first floor alone was eighteen feet high, while above it rose redwood walls which served as a foil for every manner of Italian Renaissance detail, from pedimented windows and paneled recesses, to heavily bracketed eaves upholding the crested, low-pitched roofline. The architects described it as "a conservative expression of Italian Renaissance." Those less kindly disposed said it looked like a giant packing case.

Whatever one felt about the exterior, the interior, designed by the New York firm of Pottier & Stymus, was breathtaking. From California Street, the visitor mounted a broad granite staircase to an elaborate Corinthian portico. Through massive doors of rosewood and mahogany, one passed into a vestibule paved with mosaic tile. The second entryway, lined with mirrors eight feet wide, led to a circular atrium three stories high and forty feet in diameter, crowned by a huge amber stained-glass dome. Pairs of red granite columns guarded each of the wide doorways leading to the rooms at each side of the rotunda, whose marble floor was inlaid with the signs of the zodiac.

The reception room was frescoed in the popular "East Indian Style"; the library was paneled in the English Gothic Style, and the billiard room was Eastlake. (Charles Eastlake was one of several Victorian reformers in England who attempted to improve the lot of the lower classes by designing inexpensive, cottage-industry furniture and houses. He was aghast when he learned what the Americans were creating in his name.) The furnishings of the Pompeian drawing room were from the Centennial Exposition at Philadelphia, and were a gift to the Stanfords from the people of California. Even the butler's pantry was described as being in the "intermediate Gothic Style." Of particular interest was a large artificial tree in one of the drawing rooms: on its branches sat mechanical birds which, at the touch of a button, would burst into song. Another device in the mansion was a mechanical "orchestra" which produced symphonic effects at the pull of a lever on its great mahogany and glass case.

For a time it seemed there would be no end to Stanford's extravagance. The original Stanford mansion in Sacramento was superseded by the Nob Hill house, then a 9,000-acre farm on the peninsula for breeding blooded race horses, containing two race tracks and employing 150 attendants. The relatively modest house which George Gordon had originally built on the property was remodeled into a luxurious manor house. Stanford also acquired a 55,000-acre farm in the Sacramento Valley, where he began a vineyard with three million grapevines. He built the town of Vina, and imported French vintners to help him supply the world with wines that for sheer quality would outdo the best that Europe could produce.

All this extravagance came to a sudden and tragic halt with the death of the Stanfords' only child, Leland Jr., age fifteen. The boy who was to have inherited all the Stanford enterprises fell victim to typhoid fever, contracted while traveling with his parents in Italy in 1884. As a memorial to their lost son, the heartbroken couple set out to establish the most costly enterprise of all, the Leland Stanford, Jr., University, declaring that "the children of California will now become our children." Frederick Law Olmstead and H.H. Richardson were commissioned to design the grounds and buildings for the campus in Palo Alto. From then on, the Stanford fortune was funneled into the organization and staffing of a university that was to become world-class.

The James ben Ali Haggin mansion, occupying one whole block on Taylor between Clay and Washington, was the first to sport a "millionaire's tower," and featured a Mansard roof. (Courtesy Alex Brammer)

The Charles Crocker mansion, at California and Taylor, with 12,500 square feet and a 75-foot tower, seems to have been specifically designed to eclipse the Stanford mansion, two blocks east. (Courtesy Alex Brammer)

Immediately after the Senator's death in 1893, the Stanford fortune was frozen in litigation. A mountain of problems began when the notorious Collis Huntington claimed that Jane Stanford's inheritance was the rightful property of the Central Pacific Railroad. As for her expensive project in Palo Alto, Huntington publicly referred to the University as "the Stanford Circus." Unfortunately, the late Senator's countless investments were scattered over the country, and it took years for Stanford attorney Sam Wilson and his sons to locate and settle these diverse holdings.

Meantime, to cut down on expenses, Jane Stanford and her loyal secretary, Bertha Berners, moved into two rooms of the Nob Hill mansion. Over time, Mrs. Stanford reduced the household staff until only a single servant remained to take care of their needs, quite a sacrifice for one accustomed to incredible luxury. She paid the Stanford professors out of the household allowance established for her by the court. Bertha Berners, in her biography of Jane Stanford, fondly recalled the one-on-one conversations Mrs. Stanford used to have with her God at this time. When her feelings were hurt she would say, "Really, God, is this necessary?" or "God, did you hear that?" Apparently God listened; Jane Stanford triumphed over her trials, and the University survived.

When the fortune was finally unfrozen and the future of the University seemed better assured, Mrs. Stanford went to New York specifically to call on Mr. Huntington. To his amazement, she walked into his office, took the chair he offered her, and announced, "Mr. Huntington, you and I are two old people and shall probably never meet again; therefore, I have come to make my peace with you." Then and there the hatchet was buried and the two parted, never to meet again on this planet.

Jane Stanford died in 1905; one hopes that her spirit did not witness the destruction of her Nob Hill mansion and all of its contents in the following year. Happily, photographers had made a complete record of the house's interior, and the glass plates had been sent down to the university in Palo Alto for safekeeping. These photographs proved invaluable when the university made insurance claims, for here was a complete record of what had burned. Then again, possibly Mrs. Stanford's spirit did have something to do with the photographic plates' survival: the earthquake left many of the university buildings in ruins, but the plates

The Stanford mansion (1875), at California and Powell Streets, was long regarded as the most beautiful house in America. While the scale of the Nob Hill mansions is difficult to convey in a photograph, the two men standing near the steps give an idea of the size of this enormous dwelling. The spectacular interior included the Pompeian room (left) and the dining room—the largest in San Francisco—where the table could be expanded to seat a hundred guests. The ceilings were eighteen feet high. (Author's collection)

escaped entirely unharmed. They remain a visual record of one of California's grandest houses.

Another legend, perhaps apocryphal, says that when Governor Stanford purchased his block-square Nob Hill lot and told his wife of his plan to build a house on it, she thought the lot seemed much too large to hold just one house. "Why don't you ask the Hopkinses if they wouldn't like to buy the other half of the lot?" she asked her husband. "I think Mary might like to build a nice little cottage next door."

At the time of this proposal, the Hopkins family was living in a modest $35-a-month cottage on Sutter Street, where wealthy "Uncle Mark" was happily raising his own vegetables. Realizing that the other half of the Stanford lot would be a nice investment, he told his wife Mary, twenty years his junior, to go right ahead and build her little dream house on it. Mrs. Hopkins called in architects Wright and Sanders and outlined for them what she had in mind. As her husband watched with amazement, an incredible 70-room melange of Gothic towers, bay windows and Moorish conservatories rose on the steep hillside. The story goes that Mark Hopkins referred to the house as "The Hotel de Hopkins," and swore that he would rather be dead than live in such a place. Unfortunately, his wish came true. On May 20, 1878, as the house he hated was nearing completion, his frail body gave up the ghost. He was laid to rest in Sacramento, in a great vault of rose marble, reputed to have cost $80,000—a final irony for a man who disliked ostentation of any kind.

What kind of house in 1878 would suit the whims of America's richest widow? Her wealth, combined with her romantic notions (Mary Hopkins was an avid reader of romantic Victorian novels) provided the answer. No building in San Francisco more perfectly illustrated the word "fantastic." The *Newsletter* described it as a happy meeting of the Norman French, Gothic, and English Tudor Styles. However, when a house of this period turned out to be like nothing on land or sea, the contractor or architect would usually say, "When we don't know what else to call 'em, we call 'em Queen Anne."

Even the reporter of the *Newsletter,* accustomed as he had become to describing the architectural eccentricities of the town's new rich, now collapsed into polite vagaries: "Mrs. Hopkins' dwelling is filled with many graceful irregularities." Dutifully, he enumerated such features as "the Moorish room decorated in a style in vogue during the Middle Ages," and the great entrance hall and vestibule, eighty feet long and sixty feet high, which featured a thirty-foot Gothic arch

Mary Hopkins. (Courtesy Bancroft Library)

with an allegorical sketch representing "Home." The library was furnished in German black walnut; the dining room in English oak, and the grand salon was "frescoed in the East Indian style and made to harmonize with the French Gothic." Around the upper reaches of the great hall were more paintings. A group at one end represented "Fine Art," while a group at the opposite end illustrated "Poetry and Music." As the reporter described it, "extending around the entire circuit of the hall were portraits of famous painters, sculptors, architects, musicians and poets." All of this excess apparently drove the exhausted artist, Jules Tavernier, to take off for the South Seas and the solace of drink. His contributions to the Hopkins mansion were never completed.

Regrettably, there is no record of Mrs. Hopkins' filling the thirty guest rooms, "done in the Queen Anne Style or that of Louis XV." Nor are there tales of her holding court in her great bedroom, copied after a room in the palace of the Grand Duke of Milan, with padded blue velvet doors, amorous cherubs on the ceiling, and walls of ebony inlaid with ivory and precious stones. Quite unexpectedly, and to the horror of her adopted son, Timothy, the Widow Hopkins eloped with Edward

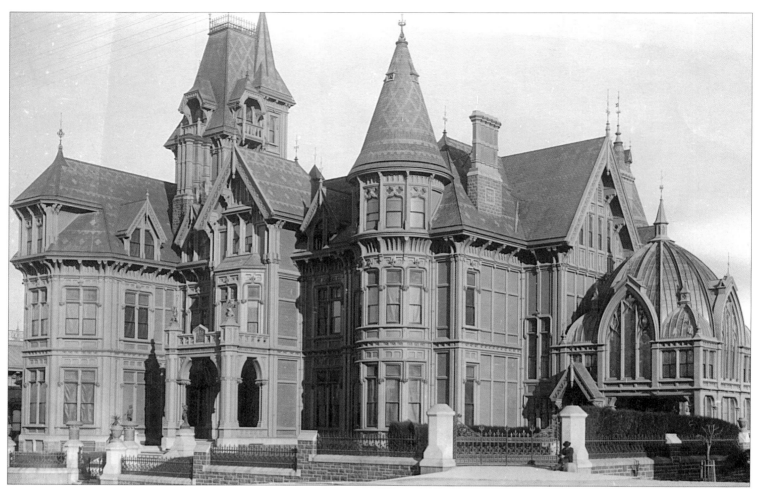

Mary Hopkins could easily look down on the Stanfords from her seventy-room aerie at California and Mason Streets. This house was described by contemporaries as "a happy blending of the Norman, French, English Gothic and Moorish styles." The tower, capped by a Mansard roof, suddenly erupts into a spire. The two white stone gateposts at the corner were replaced by ceramic ones at the entrance to the Mark Hopkins Hotel. The conservatory on the right side of the house was built above the carriage entrance, while the main entrance was at the top of a flight of stairs leading up from California Street. The Stanford house beside it seemed almost conservative in comparison. (Courtesy Alex Brammer)

The maple room held a large painting of soldiers with cannons, and a rustic fireplace.

The rear view of the Hopkins mansion, looking north from Pine and Mason Streets, shows the carriage entrance and the drive down to the stables, the roof shown at bottom right. Perhaps a housemaid, peering out through the narrow window at the top of the highest tower, enjoyed the view that would eventually entrance countless visitors to the Top of the Mark. This view shows why the design of the house was simply unclassifiable. (Courtesy Bancroft Library)

The original dining room, here photographed after the house became an art school, had a magnificent parquet floor and a coffered ceiling. It was described by a contemporary as following a style "in vogue during the Middle Ages." (Courtesy Bancroft Library)

203

The grand entrance hall (opposite and left), featured a pipe organ, as well as murals and paintings intended to express the owner's profound interest in the arts. It was clearly designed to be the last gasp in San Francisco architectural splendor. No one can be sure whether the paintings hanging in the great entrance hall were painted by members of the Hopkins Art Institute, or whether they are the remnants of Mary Hopkins's original collection. When the fire approached the Hopkins house in 1906, the paintings were torn from the walls and piled on the lawn of the Flood mansion, across the street. There the sparks ignited them, and they in turn caused the spread of the fire which destroyed the interior of the Flood house. (Courtesy Bancroft Library)

The conservatory, built above the porte cochere, looked almost like a Victorian birdcage, paneled in clear and colored glass. The amazing carpentry skills required to build this vast mansion, in an era before power tools, are exemplified here in the delicate curved ribs of the conservatory framework. Nothing like the Hopkins house will ever be built again. (Courtesy Bancroft Library)

Searles, a decorator from Herter & Co. of Boston, who was twenty years her junior.

After buying and remodeling the late Mrs. Manson Minturn's New York town house at 60 Fifth Avenue, the former Mrs. Hopkins and Searles sat down in earnest to design a great stone castle in her old home town of Great Barrington, Massachusetts. In 1891, only four years after her marriage to Searles, the elderly woman felt the hand of the Lord upon her. She planned an elegant funeral at which all the security guards, hired to hold back the crowds, were to wear white monks' cassocks. The costumed guards proved superfluous, for few people actually came to her funeral.

Immediately upon Searles' inheritance, there followed the inevitable lawsuit by Timothy Hopkins (born Timothy Nolan, he had been adopted by the childless couple). The ensuing trial brought large crowds to the courthouse in Salem, Massachusetts, but spectators were disappointed, on the second day of the trial, when Edward Searles decided to make a $10 million settlement on Timothy rather than expose himself to further public ridicule. In 1892 he donated the Nob Hill house to the University of California, which in turn made it the headquarters for the Mark Hopkins Art Institute (today the California School of Fine Arts). When Searles died, it is said, he left his entire interest in the Hopkins millions to an obscure young New York art dealer named Walker. The new heir was informed of these glad tidings by mail because he couldn't afford a telephone.

In those years, before the Mark Hopkins Art Institute was consigned to the flames in the 1906 holocaust, the building served as the center of San Francisco's artistic and Bohemian life. The grand rooms of the first floor were a perfect setting in which to display collections, while the rooms on the upper floors were converted into studios. Here the beautiful, statuesque young Alma de Bretteville posed for painters, photographers, and sculptor Robert Aitken, who used her as a model for the figure atop the Dewey Monument in Union Square, never dreaming that she would eventually marry Adolph Spreckels and give the city its finest art museum, the Palace of the Legion of Honor.

Once a year, the huge grey house on Nob Hill would come to life when artists held their Mardi Gras Ball. There, couples dressed in gay period costumes would crown a king and queen of the Mardi Gras and dance until dawn, bathed in the light of glittering chandeliers. Today's revelers pass through the mansion's replaced gateposts on their way to the Top of the Mark or the Peacock Court.

WHEN IT CAME to building spectacular Nob Hill mansions, the Crocker, Stanford and Hopkins houses were difficult to outdo. Sam Wilson, Leland Stanford's attorney and one of the founders of the national Republican Party, built a house on Pine Street just east of Powell Street, but for all its grand porte cochere and fancy Italianate furbelows, it simply fell into the "also-ran" class. Then, just as it seemed that the race was over, the silver king James C. Flood entered as a dark horse.

Even before building their Nob Hill mansion, the Floods were well known to San Franciscans, for the genial and handsome pair had once been proud owners of the popular Auction Lunch Saloon on Washington Street. Originally from New York State, where Mr. Flood had built fine carriages, they had moved to San Francisco during the Gold Rush. On the dignified premises of the Auction Lunch, Flood and his partner William O'Brien tended bar while Mrs. Flood supervised the production of those fine collations which San Francisco's saloons always proffered along with the purchase of a nickel glass of beer. No doubt everybody rejoiced for this hard-working trio when Flood's and O'Brien's investments in the Comstock Lode paid off. Flood became the founder of the Bank of Nevada, with headquarters on California Street.

Most Californians thought that the Floods had already made their architectural statement some years before when they stunned the Old Guard down the Peninsula at Menlo Park. In the midst of this sacred enclave of "old" San Francisco society rose the Floods' Linden Towers, an immense white frame mansion that resembled nothing so much as a huge wedding cake. Now, with his bold addition to the Nob Hill palaces, Jim Flood had struck again.

"Yielding precedence to none," said the *San Francisco Newsletter*, "this massive mansion standing on California Street, between Mason and Taylor, is a monument to wealth!" Architect Augustus Laver included every luxurious detail that Comstock silver could buy. This new building stood out in startling contrast to its wooden neighbors, for its walls were of dark, reddish-brown Connecticut sandstone. The house was long celebrated as the only brownstone dwelling west of the Rockies, but its most outstanding feature was a magnificent $30,000 bronze fence. Tradition has it that the Floods retained a servant whose sole duty was to keep this fence polished to a dazzling brightness. Otherwise, the exterior was a model of restraint compared with the appointments within.

Once again, the *Newsletter* reporter went into paroxysms of delight. The grand entry hall boasted vaulted

The James Flood mansion at California and Mason Streets, built of Connecticut brownstone and surrounded by the most expensive bronze fence in the city, survives today in altered form as the Pacific Union Club. After the interior burned in 1906, Willis Polk designed substantial changes: he placed curved wings on the sides and added a third floor, replacing the squat tower on the original. (Courtesy California Historical Society)

Samuel Wilson, attorney for the Big Four, built this house at 711 Pine Street, between Stockton and Powell. With three stories above a basement, a carriage entrance, and a fine view to the south, the house was lavish by any normal standard, but paled by comparison to the enormous mansions at the top of Nob Hill. (Courtesy George Cadwallader)

The grand salon in Sam Wilson's house (top two pictures) may have been smaller than Stanford's or Crocker's, but it bowed to no one in matters of taste. The informal family sitting room (lower left) featured flowered curtains and plenty of statuary. The white marble fireplace was draped in an exotic fabric. A decorator quoted in the *Examiner* in 1893 said, "If your mantel is of white marble, paint it. If that seems too drastic, there are many handsome fabrics available to make a suitable drapery for it." The billiard room (lower right) doubled as an art gallery, with paintings and statuary ranged beneath a splendidly painted ceiling. Oddly enough, the draperies are in a large plaid pattern. (All pictures courtesy George Cadwallader)

Sam Wilson's dining room held two chandeliers with gas candles, a massive mantel clock with statues of a hunter and wild animals, and plenty of shaded candles. The table, draped with a brocade cloth, holds a bouquet of lilies. Ceilings were fifteen feet high. (Courtesy California Historical Society)

glass ceilings upheld by enormous, carved caryatids. Naturally, there were the requisite silk-hung walls, acres of jewelled art glass, marquetry floors and sliding doors which could be thrown open to create one vast salon of the entire ground floor. The whole effect was indeed overpowering. (Laver, also the architect of San Francisco's disastrous 19TH-century City Hall, did a much better job on the Flood mansion.)

During the 1906 fire, it was hoped at first that the thick stone walls of the Flood house would withstand the flames, but unfortunately the many paintings and furnishings moved from the neighboring Hopkins Art Institute and piled on the Flood lawns by the militia spelled the doom of the Flood house as well. The art works were ignited, and the fire leaped to the mansion. The walls survived, but the interior was destroyed, leaving a masonry shell.

After the fire, the members of the Pacific Union Club purchased the Flood property. Willis Polk, by then one of San Francisco's most prominent young

architects, convinced the club directors to spare the ruined walls. By adding a third floor, Polk modified the awkward "millionaire's tower" with an elevated roof line. He also extended the rooms to the right and left of the central mass into rounded wings. Despite the restraint used in the redesign, the sheer scale of the interior is still overwhelming. The imposing house with its bronze fence is the only pre-fire Nob Hill mansion still standing today.

ALTHOUGH not nearly so dramatic as the Flood house, another fine house on Nob Hill belonged to Senator James G. Fair, yet another Comstock silver king. The Fair mansion, a long, two-story Italianate Style house (with tower, of course) stood on a lower slope at the northwest corner of Pine and Jones Streets. As bonanza mansions went, this imposing house could hold its own, but its most talked-about feature was a large painting by the popular San Francisco artist, Toby Rosenthal. Entitled "The

Seminary Alarmed," it depicted a scene of pandemonium which occurred when a mouse got loose in a young girls' seminary. The painting, a gift to Fair from Irving Scott, manager of the Union Iron Works, in thanks for huge orders, cost $75,000.

Both Fair sisters were married in this house: Virginia Fair to William K. Vanderbilt, and Theresa (Tessie) Fair to Hermann Oelrichs, scion of a New York family.

The lot on which the present Fairmont Hotel stands was originally purchased by the James Fairs in order to build a house which would have aroused the envy of its neighbors. Unfortunately, the couple separated; Mrs. Fair (nee Theresa O'Rooney) sued the Senator on grounds of "habitual adultery," and the dream house never became a reality. A few years later Tessie Fair and her husband, Hermann Oelrichs, used the lot, which was a part of her dowry, to build the magnificent Fairmont Hotel.

The doors of the new Fairmont had not even opened when flames swept through its unfinished marble halls during the 1906 disaster. After the fire, the property was purchased by the Law brothers, makers of a popular patent medicine. They held a grand ball there to celebrate the complete restoration of the hotel, just one year from the date of the 1906 conflagration. For many years, a number of former Nob Hill home owners displaced by the disaster made the Fairmont their new address. This restoration project was one of Julia Morgan's first large commissions.

Julia Morgan, who belongs in the pantheon of great San Francisco architects, was not only the first woman to graduate from the school of architecture at the University of California; in 1896 she became the first American woman to graduate from the Ecole des Beaux Arts in Paris. Like a number of other creative San Franciscans, she owed her further education to the generosity of Mrs. Phoebe Apperson Hearst. When, in later years, Mrs. Hearst's proteges wanted to repay her, she asked that they use their money to assist other young, creative persons.

Julia Morgan, like such predecessors as Maybeck, Coxhead and Polk, was a strong practitioner of the Bay Area Shingle Style, as well as creating buildings in the historical styles of the Beaux Arts school. Among the seven hundred structures attributed to her during her long career (she retired in 1950) were William Randolph Hearst's San Simeon, and his mother's enormous estate, Wyntoon, on the McCloud River. The campanile at Mills College, the Women's City Clubs in San Francisco and Berkeley, and a number of Y.W.C.A. buildings are among her better known projects. Many towns around the bay boast houses by Julia Morgan. Shy and reclusive, she stipulated that all her drawings

and floor plans were to be destroyed after her death. She died in 1959 in her modest combined home and office on Divisadero Street.

SENATOR WILLIAM SHARON, who was soon to inherit William Ralston's estate in Belmont, felt called upon to build a house which would be a cornerstone of the Sharon dynasty. On the south side of Sutter Street, between Powell and Mason, Sharon bought from William and Honoria Sharpe a comfortable house set on a wide lot and surrounded by a large, terraced garden. By the end of 1874, when Sharon had had the house remodeled to his own tastes, he had created a structure 110 feet long and three stories high, plus the usual 60-foot "millionaire's tower."

Within were the expected walnut and mahogany staircases with bronze figures of Ceres and stalwart Roman soldiers to grace each newel post. News reporters of the day went into ecstasies describing such features as the immense double drawing room, nearly seventy feet in length. Its five large bay windows were hung with draperies of gold satin which had cost $2,000 per pair, a sum which one reporter noted could build a cozy cottage elsewhere in San Francisco. The three immense crystal chandeliers in this salon had fifty gas jets apiece, each jet mounted with an etched glass globe bearing the Sharon crest. The effect of these blazing fixtures, when lighted for festive occasions and accompanied by lighting from numerous similar side lights, gave the great chamber the effect of a blazing sunset. The chandeliers had cost $2,100 each (perhaps $50,000 in today's dollars). The axminster carpet, woven especially for the room, measured something like 250 square yards.

None of this grandeur was wasted on the Sharons. The coming-out parties and weddings of the two Sharon daughters were covered by local scribes in acres of newsprint. Clara Sharon's wedding to Senator Frank Newlands, an enormous display of wealth, heralded "a new era in grand entertainments." Flora Sharon's equally spectacular wedding to Sir Thomas Fermor Hesketh was held at the Ralston showplace in Belmont; the couple led a charmed existence in England, leaving many prominent descendants.

The last two years of Senator Sharon's life were troubled by scandal. A widower, he was sued in 1883 by Sara Althea Hill, who claimed he had married her secretly, kept her in style at the Grand Hotel, and then abandoned her. She claimed half his property, on the basis of a nuptial agreement which he claimed was a forgery. The trial went on for fourteen months, with all the sensational testimony gleefully reported in the newspapers, before the judge finally ruled in Sara's

Senator James J. Fair, one of the Comstock million-aires, built this house at the corner of Pine and Jones Streets, on the steep southern slope of Nob Hill. The unpaved street and the wooden sidewalk have a small level dip to allow carriages to enter through the gates. Daughter Tessie Fair and her husband Hermann Oelrichs built the Fairmont Hotel. (Courtesy Alex Brammer)

William Crocker built this house for his bride in 1886, at California and Jones Streets, just west of his father's enormous mansion, on the site of today's Grace Cathedral. Curlett and Cuthbertson were the architects of this "Queen Anne Cottage." Willis Polk said its only substantial feature was the stone entrance arch. The flames of 1906 proved his point; only the granite stairs and the arch remained standing. (Author's collection)

favor. Sharon took the case to the federal court, but he died in 1885, before the court declared the marriage contract a forgery. The splendid rooms of the Sharon mansion were thrown open again while the Senator lay in state. The floral displays were said to be as elaborate as those for his daughters' weddings.

The house was passed on to William O'Brien. He lent it to his sister, Maria Coleman, whose pretty twin daughters became leading belles of local society. Once again the great drawing room blazed into life at the wedding of Cecilia Coleman and Harry May. After O'Brien's death the property was sold to Abigail

Parrott. The house's final blaze of glory went unrecorded when the flames of 1906 swept it, along with its neighbors, into oblivion.

There were more Nob Hill mansions built in the 1880s, when the Hearsts, Whittells, Bourns, Sherwoods, and other millionaires joined the exalted ranks of hill dwellers, but then, for a decade or so, there was a lapse. By this late date, most of the original bonanza kings had moved on to more heavenly mansions, and their progeny generally chose to spend their inherited millions in New York, Newport, or Europe, hobnobbing with a more established, older aristocracy.

One exception to this exodus was W. H. Crocker, who, with his wife, moved out of the family mausoleum to a slightly more modest house on California Street, just west of his father's house. The new house, designed by Curlett and Cuthbertson, was of roughly-dressed sandstone, in the latest "Richardson Romanesque" style. Here, and later on at their handsome Peninsula estate (today the Burlingame Club) the Crockers entertained local and visiting luminaries. In the 1890s one entertainment at the Crockers' outraged the sensibilities of the San Francisco *Argonaut's* social editor: a breakfast at which the guest of honor was the actress Sarah Bernhardt. The scribe expressed shock that this chaste Christian home should momentarily shelter an actress, a woman who was an affront to decent society.

In the 1890s, young Willis Polk, who was devoting his efforts toward liberating San Franciscans from the old "Victorian dragon," wrote of the young Crocker's Nob Hill house,

> It would be hard to assess the school of architecture to which this building belongs. It is not Colonial. It is not Assyrian, it is not Byzantine, it is not even Early English, although the imitation timbers in the gables warrant this assumption. Perhaps the elastic term 'Queen Anne' would best classify this production of 'modern' architecture. The Assyrian lions, when combined with the medieval gryphon, which are consigned to guarding the massive entrance, make a truly terrifying spectacle. The great arch above the entrance surely denotes strength and will surely stand, thanks to the cement . . . This is the only house in this excessive neighborhood which represents a legitimate application and use of the materials.

Such faint praise was rare from Polk, who trained his critical eye on houses throughout the city. Of the Tobin house, for example, he remarked that "the architect has amused himself with a Norman porch, Gothic detail, a French roof and a lot of his own imagination."

Despite his architectural objections to "inferior" work, Polk was philosophical about his city. "In recent years a great deal of criticism has been levelled at these Nob Hill houses," he concluded. "One thing, however, may be said in their defense and that is that they cost a great deal of money!" Polk was later retained by the Crockers to modify some of the more excessive details of their mansion.

IN DECEMBER 1892 a reporter from the San Francisco *Examiner* noted some mysterious activity taking place on the corner of California and Jones Streets. "Two pretentious houses, formerly the homes of Mason Rathbone and of Hugh Whittell, have bitten the dust, and in their place a new residence is underway which is predicted to make the ghost of Queen Anne walk nightly to protest that her name ever be mentioned in this Nob Hill precinct again."

The reporter seemed a little put out because the prospective owner of this new house had made no statement to the press as to the cost or size of his dwelling. Such reticence was entirely contrary to the usual preliminaries to building a Nob Hill house. However, the reporter was permitted to see the drawings by the architect, A. Page Brown, formerly associated with the celebrated New York firm of McKim, Meade and White. The new house, Page informed the reporter, was to be in the latest Colonial Revival Style, which Stanford White was introducing to his Eastern clients. A workman carrying a hod of narrow yellow bricks said they were called Roman Bricks "because they came from San Jose."

Anson Towne, the house's new owner, reportedly began life as a humble brakeman for the Southern Pacific Railroad, and had risen to the presidency of that railroad after winning the esteem of the sole surviving member of the Big Four, Collis Huntington. Unlike the Nob Hill families of an earlier day, the Townes did not share their private lives with the press. Thus we have no record of what went on behind the dignified marble portals of the Townes' house. Indeed, those portals have come to make that house truly noteworthy, for they became the famed "Portals of the Past," preserved in Golden Gate Park since 1906.

For all the derision which in later days has been aimed at these Nob Hill palaces, they did represent the very quintessence of wealth and power. Their owners were among those hardy pioneers who had survived the migration West, had seen their first efforts wiped out by fires, floods, and financial panics. They had played at Fortune's madly rocketing wheel and come out winners. Their Nob Hill mansions were a gaudy, exuberant celebration of success.

California Street just above Grant, in this undated photo, has a cable car running uphill, exactly as it does today. Passengers could admire the neat, modest houses—including a very chic Mansard-roofed house, beautifully proportioned and finished. The street is cobbled, and the sidewalks are newly laid with cement. Gaslights still line the street; the poles were probably for telephone lines. (Author's collection)

CALIFORNIA STREET CABLE CAR RIDE
CIRCA 1890

TO PRESENT-DAY San Franciscans and to millions experiencing the city for the first time, a trip on the California Street cable car is still one of the most enchanting features of a beautiful city. Imagine what it was like in the 1890s!

The ride began, as it still does, at the corner of Market and California Streets. Cutting through the heart of the financial district, the cable car began its trip by passing before such majestic banking houses as Ralston's Italianate Bank of California on the right and the ornate Nevada block to the left. At the corner of Montgomery Street, the feverish center of it all, stood the famous Parrott Block, which had held the offices of Wells Fargo until the 1860s,

when Wells Fargo built their own building across Montgomery Street.

With a grand flourish of bells, the little car commenced its steep ascent up Nob Hill. The old pioneer structures at the beginning of the rise could hardly be described as prepossessing, but they offered fascinating reminders of the town's earliest attempts at permanence and respectability. At Dupont Street (now Grant Avenue) stood the rose-brick walls and tower of old Saint Mary's Cathedral, just as they stand today. As the car halted, passengers had a brief, fascinating glimpse into the heart of old Chinatown.

Arnold Genthe, a pioneer in bringing artistry to photography, left in his *Pictures of Old Chinatown* a priceless

213

This view of old Chinatown before 1906 shows how Chinese decorations were added to buildings that followed the conservative designs of the 1860s and 1870s. The building on the corner, across the street, shows the window design (six over six) most common in the 1860s, before large panes of glass were available. (Courtesy California State Library)

record of that exotic world which vanished forever in the flames of 1906. Cleverly concealing his camera, for many Chinese regarded those black boxes as instruments of the Devil, Genthe captured in his lens all the unbridled color of the area. Here was the wealthy Chinese merchant in his silken robes, or one of the seldom-seen upper-class Chinese ladies leaning on the arm of a serving woman as she moved painfully along on tiny bound feet. "And the children," wrote Genthe, "hope of heaven and of everlasting worship to their fathers . . . no raiment was too bright or beautiful for them."

Otherwise, the scene was rather a somber one, for the men of Chinatown usually wore black. A black, western-style hat, black suit, and black Chinese slippers made up the standard uniform. Indeed, the very walls of Chinatown – former commercial buildings of the pioneer city – were of dark, decaying brick, generally cast in shadow by overhanging balconies. At night, however, the streets of the entire quarter would take on a festive appearance, for the only lighting came from gaily colored lanterns suspended in rows from the balconies overhead.

Even in daylight, the shadowy streets of Chinatown presented an exotic mood, which gave rise to tales of Tong wars, opium dens and dark, secret passages down into the bowels of the earth. A visit to one of those nefarious hideaways was one of San Francisco's biggest tourist attractions for generations. It wasn't until the Fire of 1906 levelled the entire quarter that most of the city's population learned that the alleged network of passageways penetrated no deeper into the earth than any normal basement would.

With the passage of time, and the lessening of the perceived "Chinese menace," San Francisco's residents slowly came to recognize Chinatown as more than simply a congested slum. Genthe's superb photographs reveal old Chinatown as a place of exotic and dark beauty. From the California Street cable line, one could contemplate disembarking and entering an entirely different world. The clanging bell roused passengers from Oriental reveries, and the little car would lurch forward, up the steep slope of Nob Hill's east side. To the right and left were narrow-fronted houses with towering staircases, more reminders of the city's pioneer days, when the regrading of streets left these houses high and dry.

At the southwest corner of California and Jones Street stood the neo-classical house of A.N. Towne, a director of the Southern Pacific Railroad, and one of the few Nob Hill residents who did not publicize the cost of his house and furnishings. The entrance hall (above) suggests a tasteful restraint. After the 1906 fire, all that remained were the marble pillars flanking the entrance (left), framing the view of the old city hall. The pillars were taken to Golden Gate Park, where they now stand as the Portals of the Past (see page 243). (Courtesy California Historical Society)

General David Porter's imposing Italianate house and garden, on the northwest corner of Powell and California Streets, was built in 1871, four years before Leland Stanford built across the street. The landscaping is meticulously designed, with the driveway curving up from the carriage entrance at the left, on California Street. The house was removed before 1906 to make way for the Fairmont Hotel. If that had not been done it would have burnt anyway. At left is the Flood mansion. (Courtesy Alex Brammer)

At the Stockton Street corner stood Grace Episcopal Church, with its dark brick walls, stone buttresses and slim, truncated belfry. Fronting Stockton Street, just opposite Grace Church, the galleried frame house of Colonel Jonathan Stevenson clung to the hillside. Stevenson had once commanded the New York Volunteers, a regiment that arrived in California in 1846 during the Mexican War. Although these troops saw no military action, they were lucky enough to be on hand when the Gold Rush struck. Whether or not they profited during the boom days, most of these men remained in the area and became part of the fabric of early Californian settlement. Colonel Stevenson himself lived to a ripe old age, and for years his jaunty figure and high-peaked Mexican war cap were a familiar sight on San Francisco's streets.

The cable line's climb along California Street from Stockton to Powell becomes even steeper, then, as now, thrilling for riders clinging to the hand-rails. Fronting Powell Street, on the right side of California, was a long, low building which served as Senator Stanford's stables. Just across Powell, rising from terraces above a high retaining wall, was the bay-windowed Italianate mansion of General David Porter. The general was also an attorney, and judging from the size of his imposing house, he must have been a figure to be reckoned with

in San Francisco society. His house was later replaced by the terraced gardens of the Fairmont Hotel.

The steepest ascent of all, from Powell to Mason Street and the crest of Nob Hill, swept past the wondrous Stanford mansion on the left. Just above it, at the very crest of the hill, were the spires, galleries and Gothic-domed conservatory of the Widow Hopkins' mansion. Next on the right was the somber brownstone of James Flood, reminiscent somehow of a giant plum pudding, its austerity relieved by the highly polished bronze fence which surrounded its lawns on all sides.

BEYOND THE FLOOD mansion stood the stately Colton (later Huntington) house, its classical portico and white wooden walls contrasting boldly with its somber neighbors. Across California Street from the Flood and Colton mansions were houses which in any other area would be regarded as fairly handsome, but here they were hardly noticeable, overpowered as they were by their imposing neighbors. One-time Mayor Edward Pond remodeled the Bentchley cottage in the middle of the block, and the Tobin family's mansarded mansion clung to the slope where Taylor Street makes its southward plunge.

Next, on the right, were the two Crocker mansions. At one time, the Irish "sand-lot agitator," Dennis

This view, taken from high up in the Charles Crocker house by photographer Carleton Watkins, shows the Colton-Huntington house at left, and the modest but very handsome home of the Tobin family, with Mansard roof and tower. At least one full story is below street level on this steep site. To the left of the Tobin house in the background are the enormous Palace Hotel and the twin minarets of Temple Emanuel Synagogue, on Sutter Street. (Courtesy California Historical Society)

Kearny, brought a pick-axe brigade to the top of Nob Hill, where he threatened to burn down the "palace of the railroad mogul," Charles Crocker, who had imported Chinese laborers to California. Kearny, whose slogan, "The Chinese Must Go," was known to all San Francisco, enjoyed popular sympathy from the local Irish laboring class. He might have commanded still more support if his tactics had extended beyond the attacks that he and his gang made on defenseless Chinese laundries. Kearny's threat toward Crocker, the real malefactor in this matter, was brought on not so much by the Chinese question as by Crocker's imperious gesture against a little man in building a "spite fence."

When Charles Crocker was buying out the small property owners in the block to build his mansion, a certain Mr. Yung (who, incidentally, was not Chinese) held out for a price which Crocker felt to be exorbitant. Yung was an undertaker, and his narrow, two-story house fronted Sacramento Street above Taylor. After making several overtures to his stubborn neighbor, the frustrated Crocker erected a forty-foot-high solid wooden fence which completely enveloped the undertaker's house on three sides. In retaliation, Yung used his front windows to display coffins. After Crocker's death Yung settled, finally, for $6,000, the amount of the original

offer, and Crocker's heirs were able to remove the offending house and its high stockade. After the 1906 fire they immediately donated the devastated block for the construction of Grace Cathedral. The stone gateposts along Sacramento Street are all that remain of the Charles Crocker mansion.

As construction began on this magnificent church, workers discovered a wide tunnel running from the Crocker house to the Flood house, passing under the Huntington mansion and making a right angle turn under California Street. To this day, no evidence has ever come to light to indicate why the tunnel was built. Some speculate that it was to serve as an escape hatch in the event of another popular uprising similar to the incident when Dennis Kearny "got his Irish up."

On the southwest corner of Taylor and California stood the Anson Towne mansion, whose yellow Roman brick walls made giant steps down the slope. Beyond it was the "Modern Gothic" wonder of Robert Sherwood's house, built in the 1880s. It was a match, for sheer ornateness, of any house on the hill, with its nervous aggregation of angles, towers, balconies and bay windows. Its balconied tower became the signature of the architect, William Curlett. In dramatic contrast was the white, foursquare Italian palazzo built by the George Whittell family in 1892 on the northwest corner of Jones and California. Ernest Coxhead was the architect.

A Whittell Building still stands on Geary Street east of Stockton; a Whittell mansion also stands in Woodside where a younger Whittell added a zoo, complete with its own elephant house. By far the most enduring monument to this family, however, is a large pyramidal headstone bearing a remarkable epitaph written by Hugh Whittell, who established the family fortune in California. Originally this stone stood in the cemetery at Lone Mountain, but it was later transferred to Cypress Lawn Cemetery. Those who seek it out may enjoy the following inscription:

HUGH WHITTELL

In the five divisions of the world I've been
The cities of Peking and Constantinople I've seen.
On the first railway I rode before others were made
Saw the first telegraph operate, so useful to trade.
In the first steamship, the Atlantic I crossed;
Suffered six shipwrecks where lives were lost.
In the first steamer to California I did sail,
And went to China in the first Pacific Mail.
After many endeavors my affairs to fix,
In a short time I'll occupy less than two by six.

Just past the Whittell mansion stood the home and the spacious stables of "Lucky" Baldwin, whose Baldwin Hotel once occupied the site of the Flood Building on Market Street. The Baldwin Theatre, built as a part of the hotel, gave a young San Franciscan named David Belasco his start. Anna Held, on the advice of her manager, Florenz Ziegfeld, took her famous milk baths at the Baldwin Hotel. To these names can be added a scattering of such immortals as John Drew, Otis Skinner, Maude Adams, Minnie Maddern Fiske, Sarah Bernhardt, Richard Mansfield and Sothern and Marlow: all made their appearances on the Baldwin's stage before its final curtain fell in the flames of one of the city's most spectacular fires of the 1890s, taking four lives. For a short time, it seemed that this would be the final performance for Lucky Baldwin as well. Suffering from some financial "over-extensions," he had not renewed his insurance policy, and the fire left him nearly bankrupt. However, one of his "over-extensions" was his investment in lands on which the city of Pasadena now stands. They didn't call him "Lucky" for nothing.

As the cable car coasted down the western slope of Nob Hill, the dwellings on either side became less and less impressive. At the bottom lay Polk Street, where Frank Norris' fictional dentist, McTeague, had his office. Polk Street has always been a place of flats and small businesses, with nothing of the glamour of Nob Hill or of the grand parade which once greeted the cable car riders at the next block, Van Ness Avenue.

VAN NESS AVENUE

THERE WAS no streetcar line on Van Ness Avenue. Principal residents kept their own carriages, and if servants and lesser folk wanted to reach the rarefied portals of the Avenue's mansions, they could take the cable cars which crossed Van Ness at various points but did not run up or down its length. West of Van Ness Avenue, Pacific Street became Pacific Avenue, thanks to its immediate proximity to that fashionable boulevard. Indeed, Van Ness and Pacific Avenues, Franklin and California Streets and Broadway were the most stylish streets in San Francisco in the 1880s.

In the early 1850s, James Van Ness, a cultivated New England attorney, established a comfortable country place for his family in the wilds of what is today the vicinity of Hayes Street and the avenue which bears his name. His chief fame came from his authorship of the Van Ness Ordinance, a bill which helped untangle the land claims and counterclaims which had obstructed the westward expansion of the young city. Van Ness Avenue already bore his name when, in 1855, he became San Francisco's sixth mayor.

During Van Ness's administration the citizens, tired of corruption among police and city politicians, established the Second Vigilance Committee. Although Van Ness seems to have had a clean slate, he later found it prudent to remove himself to the calmer atmosphere of San Luis Obispo in 1861. Another decade passed before the grand boulevard named for him began to realize its future as one of the most fashionable parts of the city. During this period the prestige which encroaching industry and ruthless speculators had robbed from Rincon Hill and South Park attached to new locations. Westward from the crest of Nob Hill, up and down Van Ness Avenue, in the sandy wastelands of Pacific Heights and the bowl-like valley west of city hall, an amazing profusion of wildly ornate mansions proclaimed the new wealth of their owners. By the late 1870s even the profligate display of the Nob Hill mansions

Van Ness Avenue, the widest street in the city, was ideal for parades. This one, at Van Ness and Post in 1893, featured a float with huge swans, a four-horse carriage, and a marching band. (Author's collection)

was being rivaled by the enfilade of bay-windowed wooden castles along both sides of Van Ness Avenue.

Beneath its workaday commercialism, San Francisco, with its carefree Latino history and melting-pot population, was quick to put aside daily cares to celebrate, with flags, parades, fireworks and oratory, even the most trivial event on the calendar. Whether it was the arrival of a President, a saint's day, or some ethnic holiday, there was sure to be a parade. And what spot was more suitable than broad Van Ness Avenue—a few feet wider even than Market Street—with its fine houses, green lawns and flowers? The logical starting place was Augustus Laver's grand $7 million City Hall, 29 years under construction, east of the avenue, where the new Main Library stands today. On the west side, at Hayes Street, the Jesuits, squeezed out of their former location at Market and Fourth, in 1878 began building Saint Ignatius Church and College, which San Franciscans claimed to be "the finest church of the Jesuit Order in the world."

St. Mary's Cathedral, a giant red-brick Gothic pile on the northwest corner of O'Farrell and Van Ness, was rescued in 1906 by the heroic efforts of Father Charles Ramm, who, before a gaping crowd of refugees, climbed to the very top of the steeple to extinguish with his bare hands a flame that was just beginning to threaten the entire structure. When he had won, he clung dizzily to the pinnacle, disappearing from time to time in the smoke which billowed about him. Finally some of the beleaguered firemen who had witnessed the heroic act helped him descend. The great church stood until 1962, when it was destroyed by an arsonist. It was replaced by the spectacular but controversial new St. Mary's Cathedral at Geary and Gough Streets, finished in 1971. Even those who think it resembles a huge washing-machine dasher on the outside cannot deny the power and majesty of the interior.

VAN NESS AVENUE was not all mansions and churches. South of California Street, the few big houses were interspersed with more modest dwellings, and an innovation in housing called "French Flats." Before the 1870s most Americans considered it improper for two families to dwell under the same

(Text continued on page 224)

Claus Spreckels, patriarch of the large Spreckels clan, built this house on the southwest corner of Van Ness Avenue and Clay Street, on a design by the Reid brothers. It was said to be in the French style, although it looks more like a German *Schloss*. The lavish salon (below) was undeniably French, decorated in the Victorian version of the style of Louis XV. The chairs and sofa give an idea of the enormous scale of this house, which towered above all the other houses on the avenue. With massive walls of sandstone and a slate roof, the house survived the flames of 1906 with severe interior damage; while it was being restored, Claus Spreckels died in 1908, and the house became first a boys' school, and later an arts club. (Author's collection)

When Aimee Crocker, daughter of E.B. Crocker of Sacramento, married R. Porter Ashe, of a distinguished North Carolina family, her parents built this astonishing house at Van Ness and Washington for the happy couple. Aimee, a true eccentric, sometimes welcomed guests in her entrance hall with a large boa constrictor draped around her neck. Chafing under the staid social rules of the time, she divorced Ashe and married a Russian prince, and then went on through countless wild adventures and four more marriages. Her memoir, *And I'd Do It Again*, is a rare collector's item today. (Author's collection)

Charles Holbrook's house, on the northwest corner of Washington and Van Ness, was in the "Modern Gothic" style, with high peaked gables, an open balcomy at the rear with witch's hat turret, and fine iron cresting along the ridge. The front steps were of pure white marble. The bulbous top on the slender chimney, very common on houses of the era, was a great liability in earthquake country. The Holbrook house survived the 1906 cataclysm. (Courtesy Charles Marrow)

Portier curtains augment sliding doors in the Holbrook dining room (left). The Holbrooks clearly had a great enthusiasm for pattern— in textiles, wallpaper, and carpeting. (Courtesy Charles Merrill)

Below: Three young ladies of the Holbrook family pose in a flower-filled parlor on a special occasion — possibly a coming-out party — in the 1920s. (Courtesy Charles Merrill)

The staircase in the Holbrook house was a spectacular demonstration of the carpenter's and plasterer's arts, with a stained-glass skylight and Gothic arches which echo those on the house's exterior, shown on page 221. (Courtesy Charles Merrill)

The Jonathon Merrill house, on the east side of Van Ness Avenue, featured turreted bays on each corner, with windows lighting a very large attic. (Courtesy Charles Merrill)

roof, and the use of the term "French" in this context suggested something racy or wicked. But in wicked San Francisco, the French Flat found immediate popularity. By the early 1890s there were more than a thousand such multiple dwellings in the city.

Shortly before the turn of the century, the city's first high-rise apartment house, the Marie Antoinette Apartments, rose to a dizzying seven stories at Van Ness and Sutter. This complex and its twin, the Lafayette Apartments, built on Sacramento Street and fronting Lafayette Park, were considered to be the ultimate in stylish modern living. The Marie Antoinette was destroyed in 1906, but the Lafayette survives today.

Another survivor is the old Richelieu Hotel at Van Ness and Geary. Although it was destroyed in 1906, the replacement, frequently remodeled, is the only pre-1906 commercial institution on Van Ness Avenue still in operation at the same address.

On the corner of Eddy and Van Ness the foursquare mansard-roofed Wallace mansion overshadowed its more modest neighbors. Standing on the west side of the the avenue, it escaped the flames of 1906, and was remodeled into quarters for Tait's Restaurant. In keeping with Tait's naughty reputation, the new restaurant had a long canopy which extended from the front door to the edge of the sidewalk, so that patrons could pass unseen from their carriages to the private dining rooms within.

From California Street northward, the grand procession of ornate frame houses, each with its own half-block frontage, proceeded toward the Bay amid shrubs and rolling lawns. Many residents belonged to the Van Ness Avenue Protective Society, which in 1892 quashed a proposal for an electric trolley line; members stated they might consider horse-drawn cars, but the notion of unsightly overhead electric power wires was unacceptable.

One might say that San Francisco set its best foot forward here. Indeed, the list of Van Ness Avenue mansions and their distinguished owners is far too large to permit a description of any but the most outstanding. At 1519 Van Ness, at the southwest corner of California Street, stood an amazing conglomeration of spires, finials, arched windows, stained glass, and every imaginable curlicue, the mansion of hide merchant

Across Van Ness Avenue from the Holbrook house was the more modest Merrill house (opposite), also with shining white marble steps. The interior views of the library/music room, entrance hall and parlor show typical 1890s taste: heavy portiers, enormous mirrors, and statuary. All these pretty things were destroyed when the Merrill house was dynamited, along with all the others on the east side of Van Ness, in 1906. (Courtesy Charles Merrill)

Jacob Johnson. Even in this collection of Victorian marvels, this house, of which nothing else is known today, was a real prize. Just across California, the mansarded mansion of Mrs. Emily Pope, of the powerful Pope-Talbot Lumber clans, would have been of major importance in any other locale, but on Van Ness Avenue it was merely an also-ran. On the northwest corner of Sacramento and Van Ness, J.H. and David Neustadter, importers and manufacturers of men's shirts, built a striking house with a collection of rounded towers, parapets, pointed dormers and elaborately decorated chimneys. Except for its Romanesque front entry and its wood-frame construction, it was a reasonably faithful example of the French Gothic style. This marvel was in one of the few blocks on the west side of Van Ness that burnt in the flames of 1906.

One of the most opulent of all the Van Ness mansions was the great German Baroque *schloss* (described as a "French chateau") built by sugar king Claus Spreckels in 1897 on the southwest corner of Van Ness and Clay Street. This three-story structure, one of the first steel-framed dwellings in the city, was faced with red sandstone; its 40-room interior included such elegant touches as gold-plated hardware, a large pipe organ, and bathtubs of Numidian marble. A large marble rotunda doubled as an art gallery. Such luxury was only fitting for the man who had made his fortune in sugar, shipping and real estate, who gave the band shell and colonnade for the Music Concourse in Golden Gate Park, and whose descendants left their mark in the city.

The Spreckels palace boasted an enormous gabled, crested roof, which in itself added another three stories to an already impressive height. Covered with slate, the roof withstood the flames of 1906, even after they had gutted the interior walls. In fact, the structure's roof and stone outer walls remained stable enough to support an entirely new interior, designed by the Reid brothers, its original architects. Claus Spreckels died in 1908, before the renovation was completed. The mansion was used as a boys' school, and for a brief period served as the home of The Seven Arts Club. It was finally demolished in 1928, to make room for the Spreckels Mansion Apartments.

JUST ACROSS Clay Street James B. Stetson, president of the California Street Railway and a member of the firm of Holbrook, Stetson and Merrill, built a house that, by today's standards, might be regarded as the prettiest of the Van Ness Avenue mansions. With its crested mansard roof and judicious distribution of ornament, the house, painted pale grey and white, looked like a charming Victorian valentine.

The Jacob Johnson residence, at the southwest corner of Van Ness Avenue and California Street, looks almost like a conventional Victorian house with a chapel built on its roof. The spire and the many finials seem to reach for the sky. The right side of the house shows it to have been very large indeed. (Author's collection)

Stetson, a doughty old pioneer, left a personal account of the 1906 disaster, in which he registered his indignation at members of the Army Militia who drove him out of his house at the point of a bayonet several hours before the fire reached Van Ness Avenue. As soon as the militia left, Mr. Stetson went back into his house and used seltzer bottles and water from his bathtubs and flower vases to save it from the flames. Despite the crashing plate glass windows broken by dynamiting across the street, even when the heat caused the paint on the exterior walls to blister and peel, the old man stubbornly continued his battle. In fact, he claimed with some justice to have saved not only his own house but all those north and west of it as well, for the fire did not spread beyond the corner where his house stood.

Just north of Mr. Stetson's house was a huge and exotic building whose architects, Curlett and Cuthbertson, classified it as "East Indian" in style; it boasted a Venetian Gothic porch, swelling bays, and, between two gables, an observation tower that rather

James B. Stetson's house at Clay and Van Ness survived the 1906 disaster because Stetson refused to allow it to burn. The house is richly but tastefully ornate, with arched windows, strong window caps, a Mansard roof with imposing dormer windows, topped off with metal cresting. It was a great contrast to the Spreckels house, (shown on page 220), just across Clay Street. (Author's collection)

resembled a ship's pilot house. The *San Francisco Newsletter* confessed that the house could not be adequately described even in the full page allotted to it. It was built by Judge and Mrs. E.B. Crocker of Sacramento; he was a brother of Charles Crocker and an attorney for the Central Pacific Railroad. The Judge Crockers built the magnificent Crocker Art Gallery adjoining their Sacramento home, perhaps that city's chief ornament today.

The house on Van Ness was built as a wedding gift for their daughter, Amy (she spelled it Aimee and pronounced it Ayemay), when she married R. Porter Ashe, an attorney and bon vivant sportsman. It must have suited the young lady's exotic tastes. Aimee began to create sensations at a tender age, and continued to keep the publishers of yellow journalism happy as "the madcap heiress" until her death in 1941, when she was in her late eighties. Married six times and widowed once, she wrote her memoirs under the title *And I'd Do It Again*, in which she recalled posing as an exotic dancer at William Hammerstein's Manhattan Roof Garden

Theatre. She wrote of being kidnapped by a love-starved Asian, and of the week she spent in a Turkish harem. Then there was a magnificent dinner party she gave in honor of "the Maharajah of Kaa," a four-yard-long, eight-inch-thick boa constrictor which Aimee draped over her bare shoulders. His majesty kept his head and tail nestled cozily in the train of the heiress's evening gown.

In later years, Aimee's fantastic house became the home of the silver king Walter Hobart. After the 1906 disaster it became the temporary home of the City of Paris department store. Clerks sold ladies' evening clothes, fans and opera cloaks in the elegantly appointed drawing room. Men's outer garments were displayed in the library, while such items as ladies lingerie, nightwear, linens and underwear were sold in the bedrooms. Customers passing from one room to another could pause in the great hall to admire some of the large paintings which the owners had left behind. The mansion was demolished in 1918 to make way for a parking lot—an ominous sign of the times.

227

The Henry Bothin house was a typical but rather sober Queen Anne of the 1890s, with corner tower and ponderous chimneys, and an open balcony at the front. Contrast this style with the Stetson house on the previous page. The Bothin house was blown up by the soldiers in 1906. (Author's collection)

One long-time survivor on the northwest corner of Van Ness and Washington was the "Modern Gothic" mansion of Charles Holbrook, of Holbrook, Merrill and Stetson. His partner, Jonathon Merrill, built a similar house just across the avenue on the northeast corner. In 1906, when houses on the east side of Van Ness were dynamited to check the flames, the Merrill house was among those blown sky high. Miss Olive Holbrook watched its destruction, along with the homes of friends and neighbors, the Bothins, the Wenbans, the David Walters. "These houses," she recalled, "did not explode all over the street, but rather simply folded up within the confines of their own foundations."

The architect of the Holbrook, Stetson and Merrill houses was '49er Henry Macy, of the Nantucket Island Macys. Both the Holbrook and Merrill houses were fitted out with a new invention, the pneumatic clock, which made use of a free and plentiful commodity: air. Herman Wenzel, its inventor, patented the device in 1877 for use in institutions such as banks, school houses and hotels. In this system, several clocks could be operated and controlled from one central instrument, a complicated device which included inverted glass bells covering other glasses filled with liquid. Pipes installed in the walls carried the air from this central point to each of the clocks, which could be designed to match the decor of each room.

Unfortunately, the pneumatic clock was not well-suited for San Francisco. Any disturbance in the walls, such as settling or earthquakes, could discombobulate the whole system. In the 1906 quake, the tubes snapped and the glass bells were smashed. What was worse, all of Wenzel's drawings and patterns were destroyed as well. The earthquake and the invention of electric clocks spelled the doom of this unique device.

Van Ness Avenue's future as a grand residential boulevard was doomed, like Rincon Hill, though it owed its demise primarily to earthquake and fire, not to greed and stupidity. With the eastern side of the avenue destroyed, either by dynamiting or by building crossfires to stop the onrushing holocaust, and the mansions on the west side converted into restaurants, stores and business houses, the character of the broad thoroughfare was changed forever.

Within a few years after 1906, when the department stores and offices downtown were rebuilt, Van Ness Avenue became San Francisco's automobile row and a neighborhood of apartment houses. The great houses which had required at least a dozen servants to maintain them were no longer economically feasible, so one by one they went. The Holbrook mansion, kept in mint condition by members of the family, stood until 1946; it was a touching sight to see one of the Holbook daughters out sweeping the marble stairs that led to the street. Finally the house was demolished to make room for a used-car lot; today a motel completes the cycle.

Within recent memory a large, square house with a semi-circular portico and Palladian windows stood on the northwest corner of Broadway and Van Ness, where another motel stands today. On the lot adjoining to the north stands the last of the great Van Ness Avenue mansions. This house and its former corner neighbor were built by banker Daniel Meyer as wedding presents to his two daughters; Moses Lyon, an associate of Willis Polk, was the architect of both. The surviving house, with its unspoiled interiors and columned classic façade, reflects the more restrained taste that came to San Francisco in the late 1890s. Behind the large foyer and rococo reception room is a Gothic-style stair hall, replete with a minstrel's gallery where musicians, seated amid a forest of potted palms, once held forth at receptions and balls. Extending from the dark-paneled dining room is an elegantly appointed chamber which once served as a library. Used for years as quarters for the International Institute, the house has recently been restored.

ON THE EAST SIDE of Van Ness Avenue, north of Lombard Street, is a row of large, three-story town houses in the Roman Revival or neo-classical style, which began to prevail in San Francisco in the 1890s. The most interesting house in this row, 2826 Van Ness, is a fine Italianate with a small Doric porch from a later era. This house, originally on Larkin Street, was moved to its new lot on Van Ness and thus saved from the 1906 fire.

The burning of St. Mary's Cathedral in 1962 left the handsome stone St. Bridgets, on the corner of Van Ness and Broadway, as the only surviving pre-1906 house of worship on the avenue. The First Presbyterian Church, affectionately known as "Old First," and St. Luke's Episcopal Church at Clay Street were rebuilt after the disaster, as was the Jewish Concordia-Argonaut Club, founded in 1864, at Post and Van Ness.

A postlude to the story of Van Ness Avenue's glory and decline is the story of its last parade. When the Panama Pacific Exposition held its grand opening in 1915, thousands of citizens, with bands playing and flags fluttering, marched joyously down Van Ness Avenue to the site of the exposition. Ostensibly, the 1915 Fair was to commemorate the completion of the Panama Canal, but to the people of San Francisco, who had rebuilt their wrecked city within a miraculously short period of nine years, this was a moment to celebrate the promising future of their beloved city by the Bay.

Today, with automobile agencies moving out, the run-down look that Van Ness Avenue has presented for many years is gradually changing. The old Masonic Temple just above Market Street has been converted into offices and little theaters which luxuriate in marble splendor. Further north, the Spanish-Moorish headquarters of the San Francisco Unified School District stands peeling, dirty and neglected, just south of the sparkling new Davies Symphony Hall.

Davies Symphony Hall and the new State Office Building at McAllister Street were intended to complete the west portion of the Civic Center by framing the Opera House and Veterans' Building. The contrast between the French Renaissance style and the Post Modern style shows the truth of a familiar observation: that San Francisco was lucky the great earthquake and fire happened in 1906 rather than 1976. When the San Francisco Museum of Modern Art moved to its new location south of Market, it left behind the twisted mass of bronze pipe, dubbed "The Plumber's Nightmare" by wags, which has stood for decades in front of the Veterans' Building.

Further north, the massive Opera Plaza complex, spawned by the Redevelopment Agency, proves conclusively that more is less. Across the avenue an old muffler shop has become a chic restaurant. McDonalds and Burger King have replaced Doggie Diner as the spots where latecomers can grab a quick bite on the way to the Opera. Further north, the Cathedral Hill Hotel, which local residents still call the Jack Tar, exemplifies all that is worst about the architecture of the 1960s, although its original checkerboard colors have been painted off-white. Across the street the studios for KRON-TV have replaced St. Mary's Cathedral. At Post Street a huge condominium complex, Daniel Burnham Court, has raised its post-modern greenhouse lobbies and red-tiled gables over what must have been the largest hole ever excavated in San Francisco, now a parking garage.

At Sutter Street the new Galaxy movie theater, a stack of glass cubes at the corner, insults the splendid Scottish Rite Temple across the street. At Pine the high-rise Holiday Inn convinces one that the modest motels along the avenue are not so bad after all.

A little steam train carried passengers and new settlers out to the Hayes Valley, shown here in an engraving from the 1860s. At right center is the amusement park built by Colonel Thomas B. Hayes, at Hayes and Buchanan Streets. On the hill at left is the Protestant Orphan Asylum, built by General Henry Halleck at Haight and Laguna Streets. The building later became the home of the first California State Teachers' College, the progenitor of San Francisco State University. Today the site is occupied by the University of California Extension. (Courtesy California State Library)

THE WESTERN ADDITION

THANKS TO THE courageous last stand of San Francisco's fire-fighters, the flames of 1906 penetrated only a few blocks beyond the west side of Van Ness Avenue. Their success ensured that today, despite the inroads of the Redevelopment Agency in the 1950s and 1960s, we still have a good idea of how the Western Addition must have appeared in its prime. Indeed, enough remains to support author Charles Caldwell Dobie's assertion that the entire quarter was "a delirium of the woodcarver."

Established in the settlement of early land disputes by the Van Ness Ordinance of 1855, "The Western Addition" included the entire area west of Larkin Street, from Fort Mason southward to the slopes of Twin Peaks. The ordinance even established the sites for parks and streets which would one day follow the grid plan laid down for Yerba Buena by Jasper O'Farrell. For twenty years after 1851 the area was shown on city maps as "The Big Sandy Waste." Sometime before the turn of the century, fashion-conscious developers renamed the east-west ridge overlooking the Golden Gate as Pacific Heights. Official city maps still do not identify Pacific Heights and its western neighbor, Presidio Heights, as geographical entities; the Western Addition encompasses both districts. Thus there is understandable confusion as to the boundary lines. We follow here the custom of regarding California Street as the dividing line between Pacific Heights and what most people today call the Western Addition.

Stretching westward from Van Ness to Presidio Avenue and southward to Market Street, the Western Addition encompasses more than four hundred city blocks. Of the approximately 14,000 Victorian houses to be found in San Francisco at least half are in the Western Addition, ranging from the Gothic Revival, Italianate, Eastlake, and Queen Anne styles through the Stick Style, Richardson Romanesque and even the French Second Empire style, occasionally combining elements of two or three of these styles in a single house. Fifteen of these houses and three churches have been named official San Francisco Landmarks.

The earliest development in the Western Addition was the work of an Irishman, Colonel Thomas B. Hayes. As a true son of the "auld sod," Hayes, immediately upon his arrival in San Francisco, became a member of the city hall crowd. His political career received a setback when it was learned that he had served as a second to Judge Terry, who shot the popular Senator David Broderick in a duel in 1859. But Hayes did serve as a California delegate to two Democratic National Conventions in the 1860s; he died in Panama in 1868 en route to a third convention. Before his death he left an indelible mark on the city, giving his name to a street and to the valley which forms a part of the Western Addition.

Immediately after the passage of the Van Ness Ordinance, Hayes acquired 168 acres stretching from Van Ness Avenue westward to Buchanan Street and south to Market. He rented out most of his acreage to Irish immigrants, who raised vegetables on his lands and who made the Hayes Valley a bulwark of Irish solidarity. The tenants were not all of the "lace curtain" variety; the term "hoodlum" originated in the district. John Cleary sold water from a pushcart, and a man named Corbett ran a livery stable, where his son James was born. "Gentleman Jim" Corbett grew up to beat John L. Sullivan and win the heavyweight championship of the world in 1892.

Colonel Hayes helped to build the Market Street Railway, a little steam engine with passenger cars which went all the way out Market Street, past mountainous sand hills, to Valencia, with a branch turning out Hayes Street west to Laguna. This was the first of a series of trains, horse-cars, and cable cars which eventually led west along Oak, Hayes, Fulton, McAllister, Geary, Sutter and California Streets, making the Western Addition accessible to middle-class families. A huge car-barn once stood at Fulton and Masonic, where a supermarket is now being replaced by a large apartment complex, surrounded by blocks of Victorian houses.

At Buchanan and Hayes Streets, Hayes created an amusement park in 1860, with a music pavilion, a beer garden, a bowling alley, and charmingly landscaped grounds for picnics and strolling. In 1872, four years after Hayes' death, the park was destroyed by a fire. Seven years later Laura Mowry, a large property holder in the area, built the block-square opera house known as Mowry Hall, which served as the seat of city government in the months after the 1906 disaster, and which stood long enough to be photographed for the Junior League's splendid book, *Here Today*. The book's title in this case was prophetic: Mowry Hall fell to the Redevelopment Agency's wrecking ball in the 1960s.

This building, probably a school or orphanage, had just been built in the Great Sandy Waste at Geary and Franklin Streets when this picture was taken in 1864. The view is toward the northeast, with Nob Hill in the background. (Courtesy California State Library)

The style of this magnificent structure, with Mansard roof, tower, and two grand entrances, could best be called French Second Empire. It boasted 125 windows on its two street façades, besides an unknown number at the back. The building was an innovation in Victorian San Francisco, a multiple-family apartment house which sacrificed nothing in the way of fashion. Franklin Street is at right; at left is Golden Gate. (Courtesy California State Library)

Near the southwest corner of Hayes' property a new Protestant Orphan Asylum was built in 1860. Established originally as a haven for the orphans of the Donner Party, it had enjoyed temporary quarters in the Rincon Hill home of General Henry W. Halleck, builder of the Montgomery Block. When the orphanage outgrew his house, Halleck and a group of charitable citizens arranged for the construction of a much larger orphanage out in the sandy reaches of Market Street, at the corner of Buchanan and Haight. Years later the orphanage moved again, and the huge old brick building left behind became the California State Teachers' College. Rebuilt in the 1920s, the site became the home of San Francisco State College. Since 1954 it has been the University of California Extension in San Francisco; a portion of the campus is now used by the private French-American Bilingual School.

Hayes Valley suffered tragedy when a woman, early on the morning of April 18, 1906, started a blazing fire in her kitchen stove to cook breakfast, unaware that

The Theodore F. Payne house, still standing on Sutter between Franklin and Gough Streets, has a rare open balcony under the corner tower and a carriage entrance at left. The house underwent a thorough restoration in the 1990s, when it was to become an elegant gay men's club. It has recently been dwarfed by the mammoth "Sutterfield" condominium complex looming over it at the right side. (Courtesy California Historical Society)

the chimney had collapsed in the 'quake. The "Ham and Eggs Fire" began on Hayes just west of Gough Street, spread east and south into the Mission District, destroying a larger area than any of the other blazes started by the earthquake. St. Ignatius College and the heavily damaged city hall were two major casualties of the Ham and Eggs Fire.

Among the lucky survivors of the fire is the John Nightingale house at 210 Buchanan Street, unique because of its horizontal appearance in a neighborhood of vertical houses. Its design incorporates elements of several styles: a tower with a mansard roof, Stick-Eastlake ornamentation, fish-scale shingles, and other details hard to classify, all combined in a design of remarkable unity. The house, built in 1882, illustrates the versatility of the architect, John Marquis.

Nightingale, a forty-niner, was a real estate agent and city supervisor who helped choose the site for the 1870 city hall. He built the Buchanan Street house for his daughter and her husband, a member of the aristocratic Page family of Virginia. When Mrs. Page died in 1890, Page finished raising their daughter in the house; the family name survives in Page Street, one block north. The house was one of the first to be designated as a San Francisco Landmark, #47. (See page 130)

Before 1870, only one street ran west of Larkin. The owners of the Stanyan cottage, which still stands at 2006 Bush Street, collected a toll from those travelling the road to the cemeteries located on or near Lone Mountain, known for a time as "Laurel Hill." In those days, a visit to the cemetery was often considered a pleasurable Sunday family outing, rather than a mournful duty. Many families would continue on west to Ocean Beach over the Point Lobos Toll Road, along what is today Geary Boulevard, for a picnic. After clearing the dunes away, workers laid a road all the way out to the Cliff House on Point Lobos, and sports driving their ladies in rented buggies could wave cheerily at Nob Hill millionaires and their wives in shining carriages drawn by perfectly matched teams.

THE WESTERN ADDITION grew in direct proportion to the rest of San Francisco during the 19TH century. In 1850, the city's population was 57,000. Ten years later, it had increased to 149,000, and by 1890 to 300,000. By 1900 the Western Addition was more or less filled up with elaborately ornamented cottages, row houses, flats and mansions. On almost every corner were storefront buildings, with flats upstairs for the storekeepers' families, to provide residents with

The Conley-Fortmann house, with two entrances, one on Gough Street (at right) and one on Eddy, stood until the 1960s. Not long before it was demolished the house had its moment of fame in the movie *Vertigo*, when James Stewart looked up to see Kim Novak standing at the window above the Eddy Street entrance, only to find when he ran inside that she had disappeared. When this photograph was taken the gaslight at the corner was still in service. (Courtesy California Historical Society)

groceries, meats and drygoods within easy walking distance. This pattern of building established the character of the Western Addition, where even today many people walk to a corner store for daily necessities. A few residents kept their own horses and buggies in carriage houses at the back of their properties. A knowledgeable walker today can still spot these structures, some with the projecting beam for lifting feed into the haymow above the stable, by peering down a narrow driveway on Haight, Waller or Page Streets. But most people who wanted to take a spin in Golden Gate Park or drive out to the Cliff House rented their horses and carriages; one or two old livery stables, long since converted to auto repair shops, still survive.

Divisadero and Fillmore Streets were built as commercial thoroughfares crossing the Western Addition, offering a wider variety of shops, often with strong ethnic flavors. Jewish bakeries and kosher markets centered on southern Fillmore and along McAllister Street. The south end of Fillmore was Scandinavian, with Swedish bakeries and specialty shops spilling northward from Market Street. A beloved novel describes the lives of Norwegian immigrants in this district: *Mama's Bank Account*, by Kathryn Forbes, became *I Remember Mama*, a long-running play in which the young Marlon Brando played his first role on Broadway, and eventually a memorable movie starring Irene Dunne. Today the handsome Swedish-American Hall

The McMorry-Lagan house, at 198 Haight Street (here shown from Laguna Street in a photograph taken in 1964), remained in one family from 1883 to 1983. Designed by architect Thomas Welsh, it is a superb Italianate with a mansard roof at the attic level, which contained quarters for Irish servants. The original carriage house, at left, with an upper door for hay, still contains U.S. Army blankets from 1906, when soldiers used it as an emergency dormitory. Now carefully restored, the property is San Francisco Landmark #164. (Courtesy James Scott)

and the sturdy brick Danish Lutheran Church on Church Street are the last echo of a population long ago assimilated and scattered. Farther west, near Duboce Park, German immigrants settled around the ornate wooden German Hospital, rebuilt in red brick in 1916 as Franklin Hospital, and finally replaced in the 1960s by the massive concrete Ralph K. Davies Medical Center.

For at least forty years, drivers racing north on Franklin Street have been intrigued by a blackish-green Italianate Victorian slowly moldering away at 807 Franklin Street, its blank south façade perched on a retaining wall above a gas station, and seeming to have been overlooked in the rebuilding of the neighborhood. Rumors said that the house was haunted, or that it was the home of elderly, eccentric sisters who never set foot out of doors. Its large side yard, originally a garden, was used as a parking lot. Pigeons roosted on its handsome portico and on the graceful, arched window casings. It seemed a foregone conclusion that the house would eventually be demolished, swallowed up in the rush to build high-rise condominia around the Civic Center.

The house was built, probably in 1872, by Max Englander, a German immigrant who arrived in California before 1850 and who led the small Jewish congregation in Marysville, where he was a pioneer farmer, before moving to San Francisco. The architect, Wildrich Winterhalter, was also a German immigrant. The Englander family is buried in the Jewish cemetery in Colma.

The Englander descendants leased the house to Julius and Bertha Hedges, who used it as an elegant rooming house during the Depression, and who raised their daughters, Julia and Gwendolyn, in the house. Gwendolyn married, but later returned to live with her sister. Julia, a stunningly beautiful woman, entertained troops during World War II as a flamenco dancer, but never married. The Hedges sisters finally bought the house in 1950, and lived there for years with only a care-taker to keep the place together. After her sister's death, Julia Hedges lived on alone until 1982, when she died, leaving the house to the First Baptist Church.

After years of delay in clearing the title, the house was finally sold in 1991 to a buyer who plans a thorough restoration of one of the most beautiful houses in the Western Addition. The interior details are largely unchanged: the ornate staircase, the onyx mantel in the dining room and a monumental gilt-framed mirror in the parlor have been perfectly cared for since the 1870s.

Eddy Street, in the block between Van Ness and Franklin, once lined with palm trees, still contains some noteworthy survivors. The house at 819 Eddy, built for the Stadtmüller family in 1880, remained in the family until 1951. Then, like many another house in the Western Addition, it became a boarding house. In 1963, new owners painstakingly restored the house to its original beauty, making it one of the most note-worthy Victorian survivors in the city.

On the northwest corner of Eddy and Gough stood a spectacular, bay-windowed Italianate palazzo,

The German Hospital, with grounds filling one square block at Castro and Duboce Streets, was the third built by German immigrants; two earlier ones were south of Market Street. This large frame building had the latest hygienic and scientific equipment, with a large and well-trained staff. Many Germans settled in the neighborhood around this hospital. It was torn down, to be replaced by a handsome brick hospital with stone trim, and was renamed Franklin Hospital in 1916, at the height of anti-German sentiment. In the late 1960s the brick buildings were demolished to make way for the massive raw concrete blocks of the Ralph K. Davies Medical Center, now the California Pacific Medical Center. (Courtesy Ralph K. Davies Medical Center)

surrounded by lawns and graced by two porched entrances. The house was once owned by Henry Fortmann, president of the Alaska Shipping and Packing Company. By the 1950s it was a rooming house, with most of its original wallpaper, carpeting and light fixtures intact. It was demolished in the 1960s to make room for a soccer field. Fortunately we can see the house today by renting a copy of Alfred Hitchcock's film *Vertigo*, in which Jimmy Stewart follows Kim Novak into the house, only to find she has vanished; perhaps she slipped out the second entrance.

West of Gough Street at Eddy is Jefferson Square. After the 1906 holocaust, it was filled with tents and shanties flung together by the refugees. All of the dwellings around the square fell before the bulldozers of the Redevelopment Agency in the 1960s.

Next to the Phelps House (see p.66) on the right, at 1153 Oak Street, is the Mish house, San Francisco Landmark #62, built in the 1880s for Phineas and Sarah Mish, who were successful merchants. This handsome blend of Stick-style and Italianate design once had a mansard roof, making it even more hybrid. The decorations over the windows are exceptionally refined, and the house is of noble proportions. It was nearly lost in the early 1970s, when it stood empty for years, its front doors gaping open. Squatters moved in and began stripping the house of its interior ornamentation, including hardware, fireplace mantels, and doors. Neighbors report that they even built campfires in some of the rooms. Vandals had begun stripping the exterior when authorities cleared out the building and secured it so that restoration could begin.

ALAMO SQUARE, the park bounded by Fulton, Hayes, Scott and Steiner Streets, is a treasure trove of well-preserved Victorians, so notable that they now comprise the Alamo Square Historic District, registered with the National Trust. The square might be called the architectural and geographic epicenter of the Western Addition.

The row of Queen Anne houses along Steiner at Grove were built in the 1890s by Matthew Kavanagh, who built the house on the far left, at the corner of Grove, for himself. These are without doubt the most famous group of Victorians in the city, not only because of their carefully tended beauty, but also because of their dramatic contrast to the towering skyline of modern San Francisco rising just behind them. The "postcard houses" are surely the most photographed architectural subject in the entire West. Day after day, tour buses line up at the crest of the Hayes Street hill, disgorging hundreds of tourists who argue, in German, Swedish, French, Chinese, Japanese, Italian, Spanish or Portuguese, about the best spot to stand for the classic photograph. This view is now instantly recognizable to people all over the world.

One block south of the square at 601 Steiner is a large Queen Anne house whose location at the crest of a hill, with gardens, stone retaining walls, and decorative iron fence, sets it apart, giving it the air of a mansion. There is no evidence to support the legend that this house was the lair of Boss Abe Ruef and Mayor Eugene Schmitz, who were tried for political graft in 1907; the house best identified with these men was at 2849 Fillmore Street. This gabled, bay-windowed house was built in 1891 by James Scobie, a railroad contractor. In 1900 it was sold to Nicholas Ohloff, whose grandson James Broughton used the house as a setting for one of his highly entertaining movies, "How Pleasant It Is To Have Money." In 1958 the Episcopal Church bought the house and has used it since as a rehabilitation center, necessitating the fire escapes which partially obscure its handsome design.

At 926 Grove Street, just east of Alamo Square, is the John Koster mansion, set sideways to the street on six lots and facing east, with a massive porch and a terraced lawn below leading down to what is now a parking lot. Built in 1897 on a design by Ferdinand Martens and Alfred Coffey, the mansion is a graceful embodiment of Beaux Arts classical symmetry, with soaring columns, beautifully scaled pediment and balustrades, and four round corner bays. It looks remarkably like a limestone structure, but its exterior is entirely of redwood. The entrance is paneled in variegated rose marble, with an intricate beveled and leaded glass panel in the door. In the large foyer are a fireplace and a glori-ous rose-tinted art glass window on the stair landing. The basement was originally a ballroom.

John Koster was a successful merchant of cigars, liquors, vinegar and pickles; he very sensibly also owned the California Barrel Company, as well as the Mt. Hamilton Vineyards and a steamship line running from Eureka to San Francisco. In 1921 the house became the Jewish Community Center, with a Hebrew school, whose director was Moishe Menuhin, father of the child-prodigy violinist, Yehudi Menuhin. The Menuhins lived at 732 Hayes Street. In 1929 Rose Fritz, a physician, purchased the mansion, which remained in her family's possession for 63 years. The federal government commandeered the house during World War II for military housing; the splendor of the rooms apparently did not impress the army, for during this period the paneled woodwork was painted green, and many interior ornaments and fixtures were lost. The house, now divided into apartments, has recently been renovated by a new owner.

Further east on Grove, below Fillmore, is a block of superb Italianate houses which were among the first in the city to be restored, beginning in the 1950s. One of these, at 822 Grove, once the home of opera star Maude Fay Symington Powers, has been maintained in pristine glory since the 1870s. Next door at 824 Grove, Richard Reutlinger, a founder of the Victorian Alliance preservation society, has accomplished one of the city's most remarkable restorations, including extravagantly furnished and authentically decorated Victorian interiors. Flanking both sides of Grove Street, with graceful trees along their sidewalks, these houses comprise a splendid example of the architectural styles prevailing in the 1870s and 1880s, giving the visitor the feeling of having stepped back in time to those decades.

COMMANDING THE UPPER, northwestern corner of Alamo Square, at 1198 Fulton, is one of the best-known Victorians in the city, an exuberant blend of Italianate and Stick styles with a monumental square tower rising above it (see pages 122-123). It was designed in 1882 by Henry Geilfuss, a native of Germany, who built many surviving houses in the area, as well as St. Mark's Lutheran Church at 1135 O'Farrell. Victorian architecture buffs make a great point of recognizing Geilfuss's designs.

The Fulton Street house was built for William Westerfeld, a German confectioner and baker, for $9,985, several times the cost of an ordinary house because of its lavish interior and 14-foot ceilings. When Westerfeld died in 1895, the house was appraised for $15,000 and sold to John Mahony, a building contractor who built the St. Francis Hotel, the post-quake

The famous "postcard view" from Alamo Square, of the row of Victorians on Steiner Street below Hayes, with the modern city skyline behind them, draws an endless stream of tourists from all over the world. (Courtesy James Heig)

The "other" Victorians on Steiner Street above Fulton show a considerable variety in their architecture, from the Stick style to the exuberant turreted Queen Anne. (Courtesy James Heig)

Palace Hotel, the Greek Theater and other buildings on the UC Berkeley campus. In 1928 it became a rooming house, welcoming Russian emigres, who established a nightclub called "Dark Eyes" in the basement ballroom. So many Russians flocked to the house that it became known as "The Tsar's Embassy." Today many people quite seriously maintain that it was once the Russian Consulate: untrue. In the 1960s, during the hippie invasion of the city, a commune called the Calliope Company moved in and was immortalized by

Tom Wolfe in *The Electric Kool-Aid Acid Test*. Next came film-maker Kenneth Anger, whose friend, Anton LeVey, head priest of the Church of Satan, brought a pet lion into the house and kept 500 candles burning night and day in the tower room.

When the hippies moved out they took with them marble fireplaces, stained- and etched-glass windows, light fixtures and doorknobs. Since 1970 the house has gone through at least three renovations; it was a bed and breakfast for some years, and now is a private

The John Koster house, placed sideways on Grove Street below Steiner, is a monumental Beaux Arts mansion with four round corner bays, a large portico with balcony, and an elevated site that provides wonderful views. After a long and sometimes troubled history, the house has been renovated as apartments. Its spacious grounds provide a proper setting for this very important building. (Courtesy James Heig)

house, lovingly restored, lavishly decorated and furnished in Renaissance Revival furniture. It is occasionally open for house tours, allowing visitors to marvel at the splendid woodwork and the fine views from the tower windows.

Two blocks east, at the corner of Fulton and Steiner, is the mansarded-roofed mansion built in 1904 for Archbishop Patrick Riordan and designed by architect Patrick Shea (San Francisco Landmark #151). Its broad frontage opposite the park is a study in Beaux Arts sobriety and elegance, contrasting with its flamboyant Eastlake and Queen Anne neighbors. The house has 15 bedrooms, first- and second-floor parlors, a dining room that seats 50, and 18 fireplaces. The vast hall holding the curved, three-story staircase is by itself larger than most houses. After many years' service as a home for troubled youths, the building was splendidly restored in the 1980s as a bed and breakfast, called "The Archbishop's Mansion."

One block north of Alamo Square, along McAllister Street, are some startling survivors the 19th-Century fashion. At the southeast corner of Scott and McAllister is a handsome double house in the Italianate style, with especially refined proportion and ornament, including carved classical heads as window decorations. Stretching eastward is a row of Stick Style houses so ornate as to defy description. One block further east, at 1347 McAllister, is a curious building in the French Baroque style, built as flats in the late 1890s, with *oeil de boeuf* windows in the mansard roof, carved faces and caryatids, ornate French windows, and

a canopy over the entrance. (See page 125) James F. Dunn, its architect, did three or four other structures in the Parisian Belle Epoch style: one on Franklin Street north of Vallejo, one on Haight opposite Cole Street, and the Chambord Apartments at Sacramento and Jones Streets, built after 1906.

The magnificent Chateau Tivoli, at the corner of Steiner and Golden Gate, has a history almost as arresting as its gold leaf decorations, its 22-color exterior paint scheme, and its roof of colored slates laid out in diamond patterns and stripes. Even the iron roof cresting, removed from Victorian houses for scrap during World War I, has been replaced on this house. *Painted Ladies Revisited* describes the house as "one of the finest Victorians in the city, as well as being the greatest painted lady in the world." (See page 126)

Daniel Jackson, an Oregon lumber baron, commissioned William Armitage, a leading San Francisco architect, to design this house and two adjoining apartment buildings to the west in 1892. Jackson and his wife Maria lived here until 1898. In 1905, Mrs. Ernestine Kreling, widow of two Kreling brothers and owner of the Tivoli Opera House, bought the 22-room house and lived in it until 1917. In this interim she married William "Doc" Leahy, who succeeded her late husband as manager and operator of the Tivoli. Many world-famed opera singers, including Luisa Tetrazzini, were among Leahy's discoveries.

In 1917 the mansion became a center for various Jewish cultural organizations. In 1929 the Yiddish Literary and Dramatic Society established a cultural

Three houses, all near Alamo Square, are an interesting contrast in style.

Left: Perched high above Hayes Street, on the south side of the park, is a classic San Francisco Italianate, with slanted bay windows decorated with incised carving and dentil moldings, a bracketed cornice, and a portico supported by corbels and surmounted by a small balcony with urn-shaped finials. The simplicity of the design is most pleasing.

Middle: This house on Steiner Street between Fulton and McAllister, combines the Italianate and Stick Styles. The square bays are decorated with classical colonettes and keystones at the top of the arched windows. The portico is bit of neo-classical splendor, with Corinthian columns and a sunburst pediment; the window above it sports a bonnet pediment, for a very rich, lavish effect. This house became famous in the 1960s as the home of fans of the Grateful Dead, who had it painted in a multicolored patchwork design, with a life-size alligator climbing up the façade.

Right: The ornate Italianate at 824 Grove Street is the headquarters of the Victorian Alliance, one of the city's largest preservation groups. The interior is lavishly decorated in the Victorian style.(Courtesy James Heig)

center, school, and restaurant in the house, where members of the Jewish intelligentsia who had fled Russia during the revolution could preserve their culture in America. For the next 32 years the house was filled with music, art, and drama, maintaining an operatic tradition originally established by Mrs. Kreling. Bernard Zakheim, painter of the Coit Tower murals, taught art here.

From 1961 to 1975 the building was a rooming house. Then it was purchased by a New Age psychologist, who built a hot tub in the basement and established the Center for Release and Integration, with training in such disciplines as postural integration, rebirthing, and pelvic release. Since 1985 it has been meticulously restored as a bed-and-breakfast inn, with public rooms available for weddings and events.

"The Bonanza Era" continues on page 277, following the Color Plates section.

Color Plates

These columns, dubbed "Portals of the Past," originally were at the entrance of the Anson Towne residence on Nob Hill. After the 1906 conflagration, they were all that remained of the house. They were placed in Golden Gate Park as a memorial for all the magnificent houses that once graced the crest of the richest hill in America: Stanford, Hopkins, Huntington, Crocker, Flood, Tobin, Whittell, Haggin, Tevis.

The Park Lodge, usually called McLaren Lodge, was designed in 1896 by Edward Swain, and was intended as a residence for superintendents of Golden Gate Park. It is recognized as the best extant example of the Richardson Romanesque Style in California. After many years' service as administrative offices for the Park & Recreation Department, it is now being restored as a museum for the history of Golden Gate Park.

On the northeast slope of Potrero Hill are three notable houses dating from the 1860s. The Richards house, at 301 Pennsylvania (above), a simple but handsome flat-front Italianate, is now used for commercial purposes. The Adams house, across the street at 300 Pennsylvania (see page xiv), is a private residence. The Prentice Crowell house (left) at 400 Pennsylvania is now a duplex, with a beautiful side garden. It was requisitioned for use by the U.S. Navy during World War II.

The Ellinwood house, on the southeast corner of Pacific and Divisadero, is the best documented old house in San Francisco; the architect's drawings, drawn on linen, have always been on the premises. After standing empty for fifty years (1928 - 1978), the house was meticulously restored by Anne Ellinwood, granddaughter of the original owner, who spent a fortune bringing the house back to its former glory, only to lose it in foreclosure.

The glory of the perfectly restored interior of the Ellinwood house is this stairway, leading to an enormous mirror on the second floor. Visible in the mirror's reflection is a part of a stained-glass dome, eighteen feet high, unique in San Francisco. Miss Ellinwood spent more than $100,000 to restore the dome. She also had the stair carpet woven in England, to match the original pattern installed a hundred years earlier.

The Atherton mansion, on the northeast corner of California and Octavia Streets. Dean Faxon Atherton made his fortune as an importer. After his death his widow left their country estate, Valparaiso Park (now part of the town of Atherton) and built this astonishing house, which is described in the writings of Gertrude Atherton, her daughter-in-law. In later years the San Francisco chapter of the Junior League was founded here.

On the north side of California Street between Octavia and Laguna is a row of splendid Italianate houses which were restored in the 1960s. Shingles have covered the original siding on the house at far right, above. The portico and bay window of the middle house (detail at left) show the lavish but tasteful ornamental carvings that make this house unique.

The Vedanta Temple, at Webster and Filbert Streets, was built in 1905 for the Vedanta religious order, which practiced the ideal of inclusiveness. All faiths were welcome at the temple; each tower symbolizes a different Eastern religion. To the conventional design for a two-story Edwardian house the designer added exotic window and door decorations on the first floor, a beautiful gallery surrounding the third floor, and a roof design marvelously eclectic.

The Clay Street Row (above), comprised of these five houses plus a house at the corner of Steiner street, are known as the very earliest examples of Victorian preservation in San Francisco. In the late 1930s, attractively painted in light colors, they made the point that Victorian architecture need not always be gloomy and peculiar. A mixture of flat-front and slanted-bay Italianates dating from the 1870s, the houses have a modest scale that makes them cozy and comfortable.

Paul Verdier and his sister, Madame Tessin, were fourth generation San Franciscans, and heirs to the beautiful City of Paris department store. Mme. Tessin's house, on Pacific east of Divisadero, a large Queen Anne with fine art-glass windows, has kept its tall chimney with a bulbous top; most such chimneys were lost in the 1906 quake.

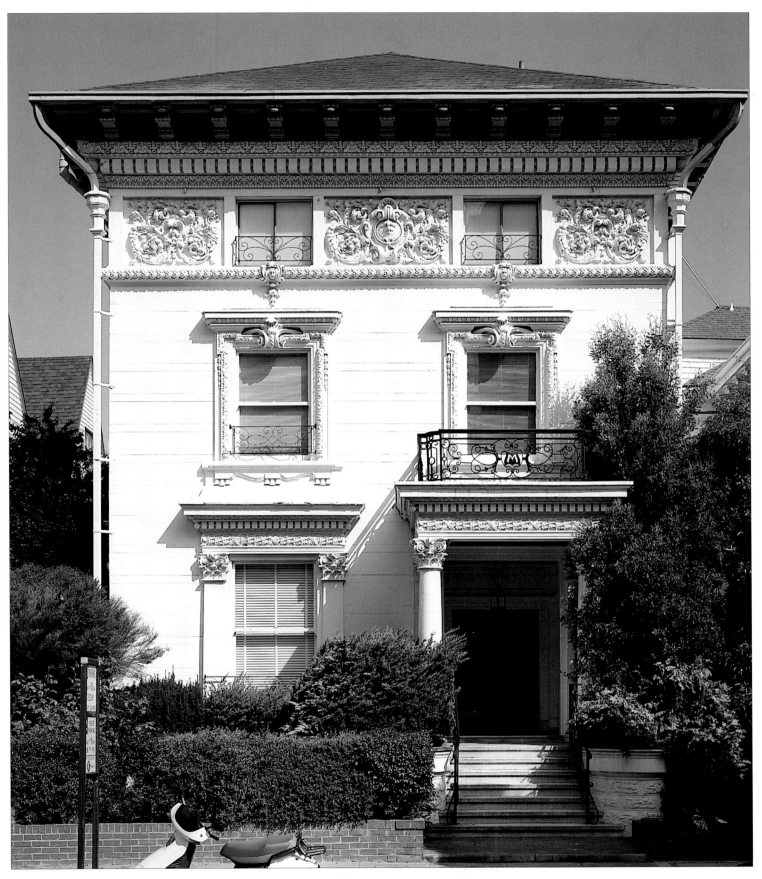

This house at 2250 Vallejo Street, a turn-of-the-century Italian palazzo, with superb plaster and wood ornamentation and wide overhanging eaves, is unique in Pacific Heights. The interior includes an oval dining room running the width of the ground floor, with equally elaborate plaster decoration. This house has always been impeccably maintained.

The James L. Flood, mansion at 2120 Broadway, built in 1902, has long housed the Sara Dix Hamlin School for girls. Flood's father built his brownstone mansion on Nob Hill, now the Pacific Union Club. The younger Flood obviously admired his father's famous bronze fence; he installed a slightly more modest version of it around this house, with splendid entrance gates (left). James Jr.'s widow, Maude Flood, liked to say it was unusual for a woman to have a daughter born in a men's club and a son born in a girls' school. An interior detail (near left) shows the excellent craftsmanship of the house in an intricate mosaic wall with a fine bronze sconce.

The dining room of the Flood mansion, perfectly preserved today, is of noble proportions, with lavish mahogany woodwork, an exotic marble fireplace with ormolu decoration, and gilded plasterwork. The Floods lived in this house only six years. In 1908 they built a vast $3 million white marble palace with a private chapel, further west on Broadway, now the Sacred Heart Convent School. Maude Flood grew tired of palaces, and moved into the penthouse of the Fairmont Hotel to finish her days.

This mansard-roofed beauty at 1776 Vallejo Street boasts a matching pair of slanted bays in front, while the columned entrance is on the side, a very unusual arrangement for San Francisco. Captain Ephraim Burr, native of Rhode Island, became a popular mayor of the city (1856 -1859), known for his frugality, which led to his success as the head of the first savings union in California. He built this house in 1878 as a wedding present for his son, who was a chemist. At the back of the property Burr built an iron house as a laboratory, so that his son would not blow up the rest of his family with one of his experiments. Burr was a financial backer of "Hallidie's Folly," the cable car.

In 1909 Leon Roos, owner of Roos Brothers clothing store, set out on his honeymoon, leaving architect Bernard Maybeck with a commission to build a house at 3500 Jackson Street. The result is regarded as a Maybeck masterpiece, a curious blending of Tudor style half timbers, carved Gothic decorations, and dizzying roof lines, with a suggestion of Japanese influence. The house, impeccably maintained, has remained in the Roos family for 92 years. Its drawing room, in the lower, right-hand section in this view, is one of the most beautiful rooms in San Francisco, with a superb view of the bay.

William Bourn, who was head of the Spring Valley Water Company, had made a fortune from his Empire Mine near Grass Valley. In 1897 he commissioned young Willis Polk to design this handsome town house in the Carolingian style, at 2550 Webster Street. It is a masterpiece of the bricklayers' and stonemasons' arts, with beautifully carved decorations and fine fixtures, such as the bronze lantern (above). Nothing like it was being built in the city in 1897. Polk also designed the offices and main residence at the Empire Mine, and contributed much of the design for Bourn's magnificent estate, Filoli, on the Peninsula.

Ernest Coxhead, who came to San Francisco from England, designed this true English Queen Anne house at the corner of Pierce & Jackson Streets for Irving Scott, who gave it to his daughter Elizabeth as a wedding present. This is one of the earliest houses by Coxhead, who designed many fine buildings in the Bay Area. The main entrance (below) is especially handsome.

This turn of the century house at Vallejo and Fillmore is a precursor of the Craftsman style that would later sweep the country. The wide overhanging eaves and the simple but sturdy design, a radical departure from the ornate Victorian styles of earlier decades, are relieved by the delicate tracery of the window panels, the inlaid design in the brick façade, the little Palladian window in the attic, and the generous, beautifully crafted front door.

Designed by James Dunn, this pair of flats at 2415 - 2417 Franklin Street is the utmost in refined French style, with beautifully formed windows, Louis XV cartouches, delicate filigree balcony railings, and two strong male figures holding up the cornice. Compare this with another Dunn design at 1347 McAllister (page 125) and 1677 Haight (page 135).

This house at 1814 Vallejo Street may be the most graceful Queen Anne in the city, with curved glass in the windows on both levels of the round tower, a sunburst in the front gable, fishscale shingles, and graceful garlands in the frieze, highlighted by a first-rate color design and blooming wisteria.

It is difficult to believe that this extremely ornate house is not Victorian; its design is curious combination of neo-classical and baroque elements, with Palladian windows at the third floor level. It was built in 1912 for a prominent member of San Francisco's French community, John Andrew Bergerot, at 3340 Washington Street.

A classic San Francisco firehouse stands at Washington and Baker Streets, with the date of its founding (1893) proudly emblazoned within a coiled fire hose in the gable. The tower features louvered panels, designed for drying heavy canvas fire hoses after use. Interior designer John Dickenson bought and restored the building about 1960; it was later the residence of former Governor Jerry Brown.

The house at the entrance to St. Francis Wood (above), on St. Francis Boulevard, was built for a prominent San Francisco attorney, around 1916, when the Mediterranean style was the height of fashion.
Another favorite style of houses in St. Francis Wood is this Colonial Revival house (left) on Santa Paula Avenue, built about 1920. The architect's name was Knipscher.

The "Rain Barrel House," at 61 San Andreas Way in St. Francis Wood, is a picturesque cottage, reminiscent of the Cotswolds, designed by Henry Gutterson, who designed several of the houses in the development. The flagstone walk, the quaint tiled roof, the simple, massive door, the plain wooden shutters, the copper gutter and downspout, and of course the rain barrel itself combine to make a single, charming impression.

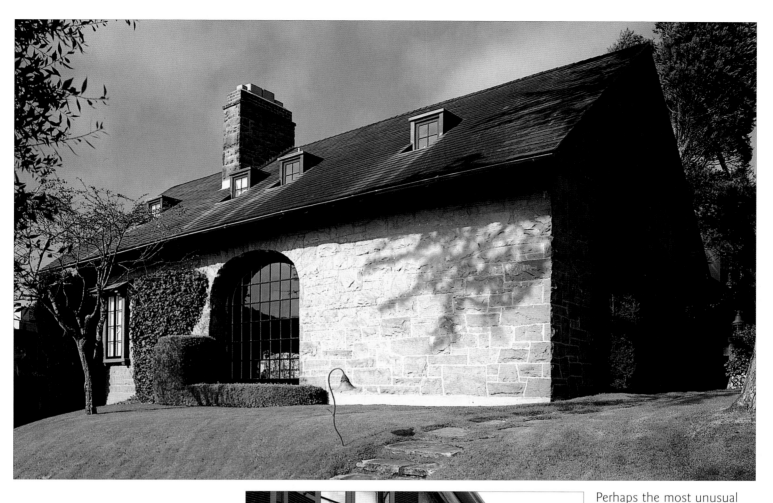

Perhaps the most unusual house in St. Francis Wood is this cottage at 85 Santa Monica Way, one of 65 houses in St. Francis Wood designed by Henry Gutterson, and built in 1925 for D.C. de Graff. Its great blocks of rough-cut Boise sandstone are perfectly fitted, while the projecting beams and rafter pole have a home-made look. The chief extravagance is a magnificent multi-paned window in a recessed archway; at first glance it seems incongruous, but on reflection perfectly appropriate to this modest masterpiece.

A Spanish-Moorish house at the top of St. Francis Boulevard features interior and exterior woodwork in striking designs, made of exotic woods imported from South America. The aim of many architects in the late teens and early twenties was to achieve picturesque effects, suggesting faraway places. This house certainly satisfies that goal.

Ingleside Terrace, built in the 1920s, allowed architects to indulge almost any fancy for picturesque effects, varying from quaint English cottages to Spanish haciendas to miniature French chateaux. This house defies classification, although it is interesting to compare it to the house at 2550 Vallejo Street, shown on page 253. The extraordinary decoration seems influenced by the work of Louis Sullivan, the famous Chicago architect who was Frank Lloyd Wright's mentor.

269

The Erlanger house is classic Maybeck, reminiscent of his best houses in Berkeley, with brown shingle and brick exterior, sweeping rooflines, multi-paned windows, and a thoroughly woodsy feeling, right down to the lichen growing on the roof.

The rustic setting of Forest Hill seems made to order for Bernard Maybeck's informal country houses. Three of his buildings were built here. The C.C. Young house, at 51 Sotelo Drive, was the first, in 1913. Second was the impressive S.H. Erlanger house, at 270 Castenada, shown here. Finally, the Forest Hill Association Club House was built in 1919 by residents of the enclave. This view shows the enormous polygonal sleeping porch with leaded-glass windows in a lattice design, surmounting a wide entrance door set into a massive brickwork arch.

The houses in the district between Sloat Boulevard and Eucalyptus Avenue are free-standing, rather than abutting one another as in the Sunset district, and have alleys behind them in the middle of the block, allowing for detached garages and eliminating the necessity for the garage door under the picture window. Houses and gardens in the area are uniformly well kept and immaculate, making the district most attractive. These five pictures show a great variety of interpretations of the "Spanish Revival" style (the one at center left is actually French) but the similarity of size and scale make the whole neighborhood feel like a town unto itself.

In 1925, California "went Spanish," with the creation of an architectural past that was supposedly based on the California missions, and which was enthusiastically embraced by developers, real estate promoters, architects and builders all over the state. Hollywood also played a significant role in popularizing the style. The houses shown here are fairly restrained examples of the prevailing style, with traditional tiled roofs, white or cream-colored stucco walls, artistic windows, and stubby towers or turrets at the roofline.

In the 1980s and 1990s, with the redevelopment of the South of Market district, Rincon Hill has again become a residential area. The apartment house shown here, built adjacent to a buttress of the Bay Bridge at 38 Bryant Street, harks back to the Art Deco style, with streamlined forms and sleek, finely crafted fixtures. The building looks a little like a luxury liner, with round windows suggesting portholes. Large windows frame a view of the bay, across the street, where the *Jeremiah O'Brien* was docked at the time this picture was made. The building stands at the beginning of Bryant Street and the end of Main Street. (Courtesy Hildegard Kleinen)

The Alex Boyd house, on the corner of Washington and Octavia Streets, was a five-story wonder with turrets, art glass windows, marble steps, balconies, and plenty of windows to take advantage of the spectacular views in all directions. This house was only about twenty years old in 1913, when Adolph Spreckels bought it, along with several others (two are visible in the background); he had all of them moved away to make room for the enormous mansion he built for his beloved wife, Alma, who had given him two daughters and a son. Alma's white stone mansion stands today, the residence of a very famous novelist. (Courtesy California Historical Society)

The Haas-Lilienthal house, at 2007 Franklin Street, now the home of the San Francisco Heritage Foundation, is perfectly preserved, with the original furnishings in most rooms. Designed by Peter Schmidt for William Haas, it still has its ample side yard and wrought-iron fence. It is open to visitors on Sundays and Wednesday afternoons. This photograph is from *Artistic Homes of California*, published in 1888, which contains photographs of 38 San Francisco houses; only three remain standing. (Author's collection)

The Majestic Hotel, at the corner of Sutter and Gough Streets, offered accommodations to visitors who preferred to be away from the noise of the city center in the late 1800s. The hotel later became a rooming house, then a gay bath house-hotel brazenly called "The Brothel." It was carefully restored in the 1980s, and features a restaurant decorated in the Victorian style. (Author's collection)

BELOW PACIFIC HEIGHTS

Standing in solitary grandeur at 1409 Sutter Street is an island of elegance crouching in the shadow of an immense concrete high-rise completed in 1992. The house, one of only two remaining in San Francisco with an open "widow's walk" cupola at the top of a tower, was built in the early 1880s by pioneer merchant Theodore Payne (see page 233). Shorn of its original neighbors, it has served at various times as a restaurant, an alcoholic treatment center, a decorator's studio, and a private club for gay men. The contrast it makes with its huge new neighbor to the west, which borrows several Victorian design elements, shows us where 110 years have brought us.

Fronting Octavia Street between Bush and Sutter is a block-long row of ancient eucalyptus trees. Once upon a time they cast their mournful shadows across the façade of a four-square mansarded mansion in the

French Second Empire style, set in a 300-foot-wide garden and known to everyone in San Francisco as "The House of Mystery." The name was fitting, for even in its heyday the mansion's tall windows were shrouded against the gaze of the curious. Few people felt comfortable passing by its ominous portals, and onlookers seldom saw anybody leave the house other than an imperious looking black woman wearing a red shawl, her strong features obscured by a large black poke bonnet. This was the notorious figure known to turn-of-the-century journalists as Mammy Pleasant. Historians and novelists have long attempted to understand the character of this myth-enshrouded woman and the couple whom she kept under her domination in the gloomy old mansion on Octavia Street.

Born of a white slave-master and a voodoo queen, Mary Ellen Pleasant escaped slavery and studied under

277

Mammy Pleasant's "Mystery House" stood on the west side of Octavia between Sutter and Bush (this view is from Bush Street). The photograph was probably taken during the 1920s, when the house was used as a young men's rooming house. The eucalyptus trees along Octavia Street, here only adolescent, are now giant; they are a San Francisco City Landmark, but the house was torn down shortly after this picture was taken, to make room for Green's Eye Hospital. (Author's collection)

New Orleans' voodoo priestess, Marie Laveau. Active in the "underground railroad," she was also, in later years, a large contributor to the cause of the martyred liberator, John Brown. When her abolitionist activities came to light in New Orleans, she fled to San Francisco.

Using the funds left her by her late husband, a black abolitionist from Boston named Pleasant, Mary Ellen began her San Francisco career by operating two boarding houses for the Gold Rush crowd. One was for clerks and working-class men, the other for the more affluent. Mary Ellen Pleasant, or "M.E.P." as she was then known, offered employment for young, attractive women who found themselves stranded and without funds in San Francisco. Women were scarce in the city, and M.E.P. might hire them as "entertainers" in her fancier boarding house, or in a lavishly furnished cottage, where a young lady in an imported Parisian gown might entertain a succession of carefully selected and well-to-do gentlemen callers. M.E.P. often could

arrange a profitable marriage between one of her beautiful young protegees and one of those gentleman callers. Through such alliances, she came to hold a strong influence over some of San Francisco's most prominent families. She had no need to stoop to blackmail; Mammy would simply let certain powerful men know she needed a favor, and it was done. She soon became one of the richest and most powerful women in the growing young city.

Thomas Bell, a multi-millionaire and major stockholder in the New Almaden Quicksilver Mines, was one of the men who fell victim to M.E.P.'s cunning. Using his money, she built the imposing house on Octavia Street. She hired an architect-builder named Lane, who employed the firm of Mozetti and Trezoni to fresco the walls and ceilings. She bought the costly furnishings, most of which came from the Philadelphia Exposition of 1876. Pairing Bell off with Theresa Clingin Percy, one of her protegees, she moved the couple into the house, where they began a strange and frightening existence. Mammy Pleasant acted as house-keeper for the pair, hiring, firing, and occasionally eliminating their servants when they learned too much. At her bidding, Thomas Bell would now and then adopt some waif who Mammy declared was another of his and Theresa's children. The Bell mansion, it is said, was riddled with secret passages and hidden peep-holes from which Mammy could keep her "family" under surveillance. She kept them virtual prisoners in the house, while she went out shopping in the handsome Bell carriage.

This strange state of affairs went on for years until finally, after finding Thomas Bell more of a hindrance than a help to her endless schemes, Mammy got him out of the way. On a dark, foggy night the servants, huddled in the kitchen, heard a cry and then a thud from the front hall. One courageous housemaid, determined to know what was going on, stepped into the darkened passage. The front doors were wide open, and the fog enshrouding the gloomy eucalyptus trees drifted into the house. At the foot of the stairs lay Thomas Bell, his skull crushed. The maid later testified that while she did not see Mammy Pleasant at the scene of the accident, she had seen a red shawl hanging on the upper railing of the staircase.

Despite the accusations levelled at her by the newspapers, Mary Ellen Pleasant was never tried for Bell's murder. In time, Theresa Bell was able to escape Mammy's bondage. Sure of her hold over Theresa, Mammy had placed all of her property in the Bell name. Theresa claimed the house and all that remained of Mammy's fortune. By this time Mammy had grown too old and feeble to fight the claims, and she died penniless, in the arms of strangers. Theresa Bell's troubles did not end here, however. Knowing her story, few respectable San Franciscans would have anything to do with her, and she drifted from one district to another, always hoping to find a friend among her coolly distant neighbors. Theresa died in 1917. The House of Mystery, after serving for years as a boarding house, had one moment of glory just before it was torn down in 1927, when it was used as the setting for the classic horror movie, *The Cat and the Canary*.

The row of eucalyptus trees on Octavia Street now has landmark status, and may stand for another hundred years as reminders of the old house and its sinister occupant. Out in Napa's Tulocay Cemetery the Society of African Americans has placed a marker over Mammy's grave which simply states, "She was a Friend of John Brown."

Aside from the eucalyptus trees the only reminder of Mammy Pleasant in today's San Francisco is a handsome four-square Classical Revival house at 2016 Pine Street, said to have been built for one of Mammy's favorite wards, Rebecca Howard Gordon.

At the northeast corner of Sutter and Octavia Streets is a many-gabled, bay-windowed building, appropriately known as the Queen Anne Hotel. Built in 1890, when the Queen Anne style was at its peak, this ornate structure served as quarters for Miss Lake's School, which trained young ladies to become leaders of San Francisco society. In 1899 it became the Cosmos Club, an exclusive club for gentlemen. In later years it was sold to the Episcopal Diocese to become The Girls' Friendly Society Lodge, a haven for young working women. During the 1920s, when the House of Mystery across the street had become a boarding house, some of the young male boarders would climb on the roof of Mammy Pleasant's house on dark nights, carrying sheets and flashlights. When the hysterical girls down the street would summon police, the boys would disappear into the maze of secret passages in the House of Mystery.

The Queen Anne was for a time a nurses' residence, then a rooming house. In 1980 it was vacant, and vandals were moving in for the kill. At the last minute the building was saved, its fine woodwork and plaster intact, for restoration as a luxurious Victorian bed and breakfast inn.

At 1825 Sutter Street, not far from Japan Town, is a handsomely restored Italianate built in 1878 for Captain and Mrs. John Cavalry. The house and the story of its building are recorded in Kathryn Hulme's book about the Cavalry family, *Annie's Captain*, the story of a devoted family man from the time of his courtship until the end of his life. The book lends the house on Sutter Street a particular charm. The present owners keep the place as ship-shape as the Captain would have wanted it. Out in front is a small plaque reading, "Built in 1878 by Captain John W. Cavalry."

BY FAR the oldest house in this area is the pre-fabricated Stanyan house (San Francisco Landmark #111) at 2006 Bush Street. This is a true "Boston House," shipped in sections around the Horn to California and built in 1852. The original occupants were the family of San Francisco Supervisor Charles Stanyan, who helped the city acquire the lands for Golden Gate Park, and gave his name to the street on the park's eastern border. When the house was built, Bush Street was a toll road, so the Stanyons may have been toll collectors during the time when the costs of the road were being met. The Junior League book *Here Today* offers a charming view of the Stanyon place before its gardens on the east were subdivided. It remained in the Stanyan family for more than 100

This ornate set of flats on O'Farrell Street between Fillmore and Steiner was demolished by the Redevelopment Agency in the 1960s, soon after this picture was taken. Any old house preservationist would have loved to restore such a fine old building. (Courtesy James Scott)

The rather unusual neo-classical house, with a Palladian window arrangement on the upper floor, swags and garlands as decoration, and an elegant arched entryway, has been restored, and stands on Webster Street between California and Pine Street. (Courtesy James Scott)

years. Around the corner, at 1307 Buchanan Street, is a little Italianate cottage which was moved in 1875 from its original site at Hyde and Bush Streets, and thus escaped destruction in 1906.

The owners of two adjoining houses at 1828 and 1832 Pine Street made immeasurable contributions to San Francisco's musical life. These were originally the homes of Jacob and Frederick Zech, born in Durkheim, Bavaria, and early immigrants to San Francisco. While still in his twenties Jacob Zech built the first piano actually manufactured on the West Coast, a six-octave square grand. In the 1860s the two brothers made to order grand pianos with magnificent cases of California laurelwood. By 1867 the brothers had built 494 pianos and organs, nationally honored with medals for superiority. In the 1870s William Ralston ordered several of their pianos for the Palace Hotel, and some for himself. A Zech piano is proudly displayed today at the

Convent of Notre Dame, which occupies William Ralston's mansion in Belmont.

August Zech, son of Jacob, while in Europe served as a pianist for the Royal Court at Leipzig. The oldest son of Frederick also became a distinguished musician, eventually teaching at the famous Kullak conservatory in Berlin. He returned to San Francisco in 1882, to teach and compose; in 1902 he directed his own symphony concerts here. He wrote five symphonies, five symphonic poems, two operas and other shorter works.

William Zech, Sr., youngest son of Frederick, gained fame as a violinist, a teacher of violin and piano, and a musical director. In 1901 he organized the Zech Orchestra, which for a period of 35 years served as a training ground for musicians, especially for members of the San Francisco Symphony, which the Zechs, in fact, helped to found. San Francisco State University has established a scholarship named for William Zech, in memory of his many years of teaching music there.

The beautifully maintained Italianate house at 1900 Webster dates from 1884, when Simon Berges commissioned a well-known architect, Bernard Henricksen, to design it. Berges's descendants, who still occupy the house, have the original plans and elevations, drawn on linen. A unique touch are the beautifully detailed blind windows. The owner was afraid that too many windows would interfere with the arrangement of furniture, so the architect fell back on the blind window, a device employed by architects of the Italian Renaissance.

Further to the west, at 1901 Scott Street between California and Pine, is the family home of the late Dr. Albert Shumate. Built in 1870 by Dr. Shumate's grandfather, John Frederick Ortman, this Italianate house, with its fine garden, still occupies half of the 100-vara frontage, 187 feet along Scott Street. The house, which once had its own windmill, is one of the very few Victorians in San Francisco still in the families of their original owners. The Ortmans used to picnic on the land just east of the site, where rows of later Victorians now stand; an old real estate publication identifies the area as a picnic ground.

HOUSES OF WORSHIP

ALONG WITH ITS RICH collection of Victorian houses, the Western Addition has a number of noteworthy churches. The oldest of these is Old St. Patrick's, built about 1852. Early photographs show it standing on Market Street, on the site of the Palace Hotel. In 1873 the little rectangular church was moved, first to Eddy Street near Laguna, and re-christened St. John the Baptist Church. A few years later it was moved again, to the north side of Eddy, between Scott and Divisadero, where it stands today. For eight more years it served as the Holy Cross Parish Church, until a fine new church was built on the adjoining lot. Since then it has become a parish hall. It is the only surviving specimen of the Greek Revival Style which once prevailed in Gold-Rush San Francisco.

St. Mark's Evangelical Lutheran Church (San Francisco Landmark #41), at 1135 O'Farrell Street, is a stone and red-brick version of the Richardson Romanesque Revival Style popular in the 1890s. Designed by German architect Henry Geilfuss for a German congregation, the church has a superb interior and especially fine stained glass windows. Like many older churches, it has excellent acoustics, and is used occasionally as a concert hall. It has served an active congregation for more than a hundred years.

Just north, at Franklin and Geary Streets, the First Unitarian Church (Landmark #40), replaced the original Unitarian church on Union Square, where Nieman Marcus now stands. An early pastor, Reverend Thomas Starr King, one of the most influential clergymen in San Francisco history, was best known for his eloquence in convincing San Franciscans to prevent California from joining the Confederacy at the beginning of the Civil War. He was to enjoy his fine church on Union Square only a short time before he died in

1864, at age 40. His congregation built a handsome crypt for him in front of the church; his was the only burial permitted within what were then the city limits. When the new church was built on Franklin Street, the crypt was taken along and installed to the left of the entrance, where it remains one of the city's treasured landmarks. The beautiful church, designed by Percy and Hamilton, completed in 1879, features magnificent stained glass. In the 1960s the need for expansion led some church members to consider tearing the old church down. In 1968 architect Warren Callister designed an addition without harming the original structure. His skilful design harmonizes beautifully with the old church.

Trinity Episcopal Church, at Bush and Gough Streets, is a great granite structure in the English Medieval style, said to be influenced by England's Durham Cathedral. Its architect, A. Page Brown, was commissioned by Bishop Kip in 1892. The fortress-like exterior belies the delicacy of the vast interior space, where the bronze angel supporting the lectern and two of the stained glass windows were designed by Louis Comfort Tiffany.

Smaller but equally interesting is the Old Cathedral of the Holy Virgin, at 864 Fulton Street, near Fillmore. It was built in 1880 as St. Stephen's Episcopal, and its fine stained-glass windows commemorate early parishioners: Wooster, Chalmer, Menzies, Quackenbush, Hinkels. The Russian Orthodox refugees from the 1918 revolution bought the church in the 1920s, and still conduct services there.

For 103 years, on the southeast corner of Eddy and Gough Streets, stood St. Paulus German Lutheran Church, designed by architect Julius E. Krafft, possibly in homage to Chartres Cathedral. Built entirely of

This house, with a fine porch and gallery, stood on Eddy Street between Scott and Divisadero, with the Holy Cross parish church behind it. When the house was demolished by redevelopment, the little Old St. Patrick's church became visible—the oldest surviving church in the city. Originally built on Market Street in 1854, where the Palace Hotel stands today, it was moved twice, and thus escaped destruction in the 1906 disaster. (Courtesy James Scott)

St Paulus Lutheran Church, gracing the corner of Gough and Eddy Streets, was called the largest wooden structure in the West; built by German shipwrights, it was supposedly modeled on Chartres Cathedral in France. It burned in November, 1995. (Courtesy San Francisco Public Library)

wood by German shipwrights in 1892, it was a master-piece of Victorian Gothic carpentry stunning to behold, one of the largest wooden structures in the country. The construction cost was $65,000. Inside, the beautifully curved vaulting beams, the pillars, and the elaborate woodwork were all of redwood, while the entire ceiling was covered in cedar shingles, perfectly aligned. The stained-glass windows were exceptionally fine. This delicate, fragile-looking masterpiece suffered almost no damage in the 1906 or 1989 earthquakes. After the 1906 quake the church was used as a hospital, where some 13,000 people received treatment. The church, San Francisco Landmark #116, burned to the ground in November 1995, leaving a painful vacancy.

This group of fine Italianate houses, at Webster and Fulton Streets, fell to the bulldozers of the Redevelopment Agency in the 1960s. Block after block of houses like these were demolished, at enormous expense to the taxpayer and with total disruption to residents. Even a casual observer can see that the houses were in excellent condition, needing only a careful restoration. Instead they were replaced by expensive, monotonous houses whose shingled exteriors and flat roofs require high maintenance. (Courtesy James Scott)

REDEVELOPMENT

IMMEDIATELY AFTER THE 1906 destruction, Van Ness Avenue and Fillmore Street became commercial centers. Once the city was rebuilt, the larger stores returned to their original sites, leaving smaller businesses in place. Few people cared to live in an area that was both crowded and out of style. Many bought Model Ts and moved to the Richmond district, and later into other developments west of Twin Peaks. In their place came a flood of Japanese immigrants, who settled in the blocks from Sutter to Oak Street. After the tragic internment of the Japanese at the beginning of World War II, the neighborhood became home to thousands of blacks who had come to work in the defense industries.

By the 1920s the ornate Victorian houses had begun to look dowdy and run-down, and the first wave of remodeling began. Wooden gingerbread trim and cornices were stripped off, and façades were stuccoed and often trimmed with Spanish tile rooflets over the bay windows, in an effort to follow the fashion for "Mission Style" architecture. Some years later the salesmen for Johns-Manville asbestos shingles hit the area, and more Victorian masterpieces were stripped and hidden behind supposedly "fireproof" sheathing.

Among the casualties of redevelopment in the 1950s were these sturdy representatives: (top) O'Farrell at Franklin Street, (middle) Franklin near Geary Street, and (bottom) flats on Geary west of Gough Street. Built in the days of horses and buggies, these houses fell to the needs of motorists speeding up Franklin and west on the Geary Expressway. (Author's collection)

Still, thousands of 19th-century houses remained remarkably intact, because the Depression and then the war years made remodeling impossible. In the 1950s the restoration of older houses was still an isolated and haphazard phenomenon. Long before there was anything resembling a preservation movement, Urban Renewal came to the Western Addition, and with the aid of federal funds began tearing down block after block of supposedly sub-standard buildings.

In time, the area from Franklin to Divisadero and from Bush south to Haight came to look like a virtual war zone, resembling the aftermath of the London Blitz. Block after block of sturdy Victorian houses and flats, many of them very well maintained, were indiscriminately bull-dozed and replaced with public housing of unrelieved architectural monotony. The loss to San Francisco is incalculable.

The city Landmarks Board, then in its infancy, was powerless to stop the wholesale destruction. Justin Herman, affable chief of the Redevelopment Agency, would attend Landmarks Board meetings and assure members that an important building would be preserved, and two days later the building would be reduced to matchwood. Justin Herman Plaza, across from the Ferry Building, has as its chief adornment the infamous Vaillancourt Fountain, which reminds many San Franciscans of the wreckage of the Western Addition.

Just one example of the loss was the total eradication of the rows of second-hand stores along McAllister Street between Gough and Webster. Thousands of San Franciscans remember a foray in McAllister Street in the 1950s as a fascinating and vital experience. Here one could browse for days through mountains of antiques, hideous old furniture and clothing, discovering treasures, weighing costs, haggling with the delightfully adversarial proprietors, many of whom were World War II refugees from Europe. The shopkeepers all knew each other, knew the stock and the prices of their competitors. Husband and wife would often argue in Yiddish about what to charge for a choice item, while informing the customer, "Honey, it just come from the governor's palace." Very likely this was true. Such an excursion was wonderfully enriching, even if one didn't buy anything. Thanks to redevelopment, the shopkeepers were dispersed, the buildings were bulldozed, a way of life and learning came to an end. Where today would one go to find, for ten cents, a book called *Men, Women and Tenors*? Or to hear a shopkeeper proclaim, as one longingly fingered the dusty marble top of a commode, "For twenty dollars you can't get beveled!"

The Redevelopment Agency gradually accumulated thousands of remnants – wooden and marble fireplaces,

The wreckers proceeded apace on Sutter Street near Franklin in 1960, to make way for the Geary Expressway, the western portion of which followed the path of the old toll road leading out to the Cliff House. (Courtesy James Scott)

This row of flats with storefronts below stood on O'Farrell Street between Fillmore and Steiner, with the lower windows boarded up. After the redevelopment agency bought and vacated buildings like this one, vandals broke in and smashed windows, stole doorknobs and marble mantels, and often set fires in the buildings. (Courtesy James Scott)

The wholesale devastation wrought by the Redevelopment Agency uprooted thousands of residents in the Western Addition. People moved out just ahead of the wrecking ball. (Courtesy San Francisco Public Library)

Even the redevelopment agency recognized the quality of the double house at right, on Scott Street between Eddy and Ellis; it was saved from destruction and restored in the 1970s. An early flat-front Italianate building with exceptionally fine window treatments and a handsome double portico, this house is unique in San Francisco. (Courtesy James Scott)

overmantels, corbels, columns, brackets, elaborate picture moldings, plaster rosettes and classical heads, marble sinks, newel posts, even whole stairways — and stored them in a warehouse watched over by a man named "Woody," who suddenly became very popular with people who were beginning to restore old houses. Midnight scavengers would comb through the wreckage of buildings, saving what they could before the debris was loaded onto trucks and hauled to the dump the next morning. One man and his helper, six hours ahead of the wrecking ball, liberated more than 200 sets of handsome bronze door knobs and escutcheons from a nine-flat Italianate building on McAllister Street; the next day all the doors were piled up and hauled away to the dump.

Whole blocks were cleared and left vacant, some for twenty years or more; people planted vegetable gardens in empty blocks along Fillmore and Steiner Streets.

Where the Princess Theater had once drawn crowds to watch vaudeville stars, corn and tomatoes flourished; string beans grew where kosher delicatessens had tempted the passersby. "Urban Renewal" plodded along for four decades; long before it was completed the reinforced-concrete high-rise apartments built in the 1950s along Scott near Ellis had become unlivable and had to be razed and replaced—at incredible expense—with low-rise apartments in a style that might be called Minimalist Neo-Victorian. If federal funds had been used to restore the original buildings rather than clearing them out, thousands of families could have stayed where they were, a vital architectural tradition would have been preserved, untold millions of taxpayers' dollars would have been saved, and San Francisco wouldn't be stuck with a stingy imitation of what was there in the first place.

Asbestos shingles, aluminum windows, and a complete stripping of Victorian ornamentation made this cottage, in the 700 block of Waller Street, look as if it were beyond repair. But an energetic and knowledgeable young couple bought the house, found an old photograph, and restored the façade precisely to its original design. The cottage is one of a row of eight very similar cottages in the block. (Courtesy James Heig)

Luckily, while the destruction was occurring, it dawned on some of the Federal agencies that a few of the old houses might be spared to break up the desolate, look-alike projects which were strangling the lower Western Addition. A few of the smaller, more manageable Victorians were moved to various new sites and attractively restored. The most important of these is at 1737 Webster Street, where an exuberantly decorated house with a hat-shaped false turret, designed by the Newsom brothers, came to rest after having stood for a century on Turk Street near Franklin. Several more landed on the west side of Scott between Eddy and Ellis. Along Golden Gate and McAllister Streets a few blocks of pleasant look-alike shingle houses were built to cover up the blight. With tree-lined streets, these structures help to alleviate the terrible sadness of the wholesale destruction.

Geary Street, once lined with splendid Victorians, has been converted into a sunken raceway which pedestrians may cross at just one point by an overhead bridge. Japan Town, a mixture of pseudo-Japanese-style structures mixed with some of the Victorians left standing, reflects the gradual slowing down of the reconstruction madness which threatened the entire Western Addition. To the south an elevated freeway for three decades vomited speeding cars from its exits, the resulting noise and dirt making several blocks of sturdy Victorians almost unfit for human habitation. Yet the old houses stand, stuccoed, shingled, peeling, or newly restored, still giving shelter after more than a hundred years of service.

This row of ten Italianate houses, on Golden Gate Avenue at Scott, were once perfectly matched; seven of the ten retain their original façades, while three have been stripped, stuccoed and "Spanishized," with red tile roof decoration. The row shows the beauty that can be achieved by uniformity tempered by small variations in design. (Courtesy James Heig)

ROW HOUSES

SAN FRANCISCO's Victorian row houses were a vital part of the fabric of the pre-earthquake city. Row houses, which present a rank of identical façades lined up like soldiers along the street, often consist of several two-story double houses with mirror-image façades and floor plans; sometimes each duplex was squeezed into a 40-foot frontage, leaving just 20 feet for each dwelling. Usually built on speculation by a contractor or building association as a less expensive alternative to the free-standing single-family house, some row houses had common walls, while others were completely separate but touching, with setbacks carefully arranged to admit light to the interior rooms.

Many row houses were destroyed by the Western Addition Redevelopment; a particularly fine Italianate row along Laguna south of Bush Street was demolished to make room for a Japanese temple. A few rows remain, and have become special treasures for those who value richness regulated by uniformity. Along Webster Street south of California is a row of Italianates of which one or two were stripped and

shingled; all have now been restored. Further north, a famous row of tiny Italianates marches along Webster between Clay and Washington; these houses were prefabricated in Chicago in the 1870s. Along Scott Street, north of Bush, is a row of miniature Italianate cottages, so small they look like studios, with slanted bays, bracketed cornices, and pediments over the windows and doors. A stick-style row with particularly beautiful porticoes and exterior detailing is on the north side of Golden Gate at Steiner. Another row of Italianates, separate houses with identical façades, once lined an entire block along Golden Gate east of Scott Street. Ten of the original row of sixteen houses remain; of the ten, three have been desecrated, but seven have more or less their original façades, showing clearly what a handsome effect can be achieved by the repetition of classic simplicity.

Another striking row, this one of beautifully preserved flat-front Italianates, lines the south side of Bush Street, just east of Fillmore. Designed with English basements containing dining room and kitchen, they

Perhaps the prettiest surviving row houses in the city are these on Golden Gate above Steiner. They were built as seven perfectly matched two-story attached houses, with low turrets capped by finials, blending elements of the Italianate and Stick styles; the façades and porticos display a highly refined decoration. (Courtesy James Heig)

recall the houses of South Park. At the east end of this row, running south to Sutter, is a famous little walkway called Cottage Row, with planting along one side and a row of tiny two-story cottages along the other, rather like an English mews. Such houses, with parlor and kitchen on the first floor and two small bedrooms tucked under the steep gable, once abounded in San Francisco. Intended as working men's cottages, they were sometimes euphemistically called "brides' houses." A number of such houses, having escaped the wrecking ball, are to be found along some of the smaller streets in the Mission District. Their compact dimensions and easy maintenance make them as desirable today as some of the larger Victorian houses.

Other important blocks of Victorian houses show how variations on a style can produce a charming line of houses, each slightly different from its neighbors, but all harmonious with one another. Laguna Street between Bush and Pine is Italianate on the east side, showing the charm of classical restraint. Directly across the street the exuberant Stick Style asserts itself, with wildly imaginative porches, window trim, and hat-shaped turrets.

The first block of Scott Street, between Duboce and Waller, moves northward from late Italianate through what might be called experimental Stick Style, in which the builder seemed to be trying out all the latest advances in bay window design, and down to Queen Anne at the end of the block, where a single-family house with a round turreted balcony abuts a massive two-family house with an octagonal turret. A few radically remodeled houses in this row show how the tastes of the 1930s, 40s, and 50s were superimposed on Victorian styles.

Although present-day detractors describe Victorian houses as being "drafty, gloomy and peculiar," their spacious, well-lighted interiors, high ceilings, handsome woodwork, elaborate plaster cornices and rosettes, marble mantels, and tall doors with elegant bronze hardware have made them eminently desirable for city living. Unlike their eastern counterparts – the dignified, somewhat lugubrious brownstone row houses of New York – San Francisco's row houses are now recognized as perfect embodiments of that frivolous and romantic spirit which is the essence of the city we all love. Over a hundred years have passed since the Western Addition was in full flower. The passage of time has restored public regard for the Victorian style, and the Western Addition is again a vital part of the color and beauty that make San Francisco unique.

In 1885, when M.H. Hecht built this shingled Tudor-style house at the corner of Washington and Octavia Streets, at the crest of Pacific Heights, the area was still regarded as a countrified suburb. The design of the house was a departure from the customary Gothic revival, Italianate, or Queen Anne styles popular in the period, and in fact looks rather like an informal shingle-style country house (Author's collection)

PACIFIC HEIGHTS AND COW HOLLOW

Pacific Heights is the area west of Van Ness and north of California Street on the heights above the Bay. Its boundaries follow an east west ridge along the city's northernmost flank. This neighborhood has long been one of the most beautiful in San Francisco. The area south of Washington Street offers an occasional cityscape, but the area north of Pacific Avenue drops off to provide magnificent panoramic views of the Bay, past the Marin Headlands, and out to the Pacific. Below the ridge, where numerous springs and rivulets once drained northward, is Cow Hollow, a former dairy farm, with Union Street as its main thoroughfare.

In the 1860s, Pacific Heights' northern slopes were a network of nurseries, small vegetable farms and open fields called Golden Gate Valley. A great sand bank separated Black Point (Fort Mason) from Washerwoman's Lagoon, bounded by Franklin, Lombard, Laguna, and Filbert Streets, and useful not just for laundry but also as a source of fresh water for livestock.

The oldest house still standing in this area–dating to the early 1850s, and thus a rival of the Abner Phelps house for the title of oldest dwelling in San Francisco–is the two-story Black cottage. This modest frame house with a cantilevered balcony stands at the end of a little cul-de-sac known as Blackstone Court, opening on the west side of Franklin Street, just half a block south of Lombard. The house once stood on the bank of Washerwoman's Lagoon. Early records

Leander Sherman, founder of the Sherman & Clay music company, had excellent taste in decoration as well as in music. Many famous musicians performed at his house at 2160 Green Street, built in 1886. This picture, taken from the ballroom, shows the double stairway leading to the parlor level of the house. It is now a deluxe bed and breakfast inn. (Author's collection)

decorations, it has been described as "A meeting of the mysterious East and the uninhibited West."

As early as the 1860s, a few fine houses began appearing on the steep slopes of Pacific Heights. The first and grandest of these was the house Henry Casebolt built in 1865-66 for his wife and eleven children. (Casebolt brought the balloon horsecar to San Francisco.) Every detail of the façade – the rusticated corners, the heavy brackets under the wide eaves, the arched windows set in pairs and crowned with wooden pediments – serves as a textbook example of the Italianate Style. The exterior was flecked with black paint to create a stone-like effect. Built to last, this house boasts massive ships' timbers at each of its four corners, and equally heavy beams are placed diagonally to offer reinforcement. Casebolt sold the house in 1893, and it has passed down through a number of owners who have maintained the old place in perfect condition. It stands above a high retaining wall at 2727 Pierce Street, and while it no longer enjoys an uninterrupted view past windmills and farm houses down to Washerwoman's Lagoon, it does overlook the rooftops of modern dwellings and apartment houses that now surround it.

Nearby, at 2450 Union Street, is another quaint farmhouse whose façade boasts a central pediment in the German baroque style. Originally, this building stood on a knoll in the center of a large square block, with access to Union and Filbert Streets. When the lot was subdivided in the 1890s, the owner, George Bowman, moved the house to the Union Street side. Remaining in the original lot, however, is a deep, old-fashioned garden with large trees and a shingled annex, built to house both the servants and the kitchen. The date of construction of these structures is not known, but the mansard and Italianate window detailing suggest the mid 1860s. Two former owners believe that the original structure dated to the 1850s.

As the 1860s passed into the 1870s, the Pacific Heights area became dotted with fine country estates. On the western slope of Russian Hill, just east of Van Ness, stood the large New England style country house of Captain Ephraim Burr, with its picket fence, made from bed slats rescued from a sunken ship. Burr lost this house in 1891, when the city extended Van Ness Avenue. A little west, at 1772 Vallejo Street, Burr built a splendid mansard-roofed house for his son in 1875. The house, with its graceful side porch and garden, has been carefully restored, and serves today as law offices. One feature of this property was a separate cast-iron house, probably shipped from England, which Captain Burr erected for the scientific experiments of his son, Edmond. In this shelter Edmond might blow himself

concerning land disputes in this area show a man named Black as the owner of the property before 1852.

A little further to the west, above the lagoon, on what is today Union Street, was George Hatman's dairy. Surviving houses include 2038 Union Street, the mansion of dairy rancher James Cudworth, who built it in the 1870s, and 1980 Union, the matching "brides' houses" Cudworth built for his two daughters. All three have been converted into shops and restaurants.

One of the most unique structures in all San Francisco is the Vedanta Temple, at 2963 Webster Street, built for the Vedanta Society in 1905. (See page 251) With its towers, onion domes, minarets, crenelations, and a Moorish arcade, all perched atop a fairly conventional two-story house with curious window

Franklin Street was lined on both sides with enormous houses that rivaled those on Van Ness Avenue. This house was built for William H. Martin at 2015 Franklin, next door to the surviving Haas-Lilienthal house, which is today Franklin Street's crown jewel. (Courtesy California Historical Society)

up, reasoned the old man, but at least the family would be spared. The iron house has vanished without a trace.

In 1856, Captain Burr won the San Francisco mayoral election; legend has it that it took a thousand armed men and a police wagon at each polling station to purify the election. Burr had a reputation for honesty – indeed, for penny-pinching – that appealed to voters. He established the San Francisco Accumulating Fund, commonly known as the Clay Street Bank, California's first savings and loan company. As mayor, Burr was foresighted enough to back Andrew Hallidie's invention of the cable car with $30,000 in 1873.

One of the oldest houses in Pacific Heights is the Captain Leale house, at 2475 Pacific Avenue. Set back from the street on a high rise of land, the house is thought to have been built in the 1850s, when it served as the farmhouse for a 25-acre dairy. In 1883, Captain Leale, a popular ferry boat captain, purchased this house and apparently added the bracketed false front, trimmed with wooden finials. In his back garden, Leale built a little house which he fitted out as a study and furnished with ship's fittings to resemble a pilot house.

Another of Pacific Heights' grand country houses was the mansarded Leander Sherman house, at 2160 Green Street, built in the 1870s by the founder of San

Francisco's greatest music store, Sherman, Clay & Co. A huge ballroom occupies the entire west wing of the house, and in this skylighted, three-story room is a platform on which such great musicians as Paderewski and Madame Schumann-Heink performed. Lotta Crabtree, who lived just west of the Sherman House, also entertained Sherman's guests in this music room. The house has recently been lavishly restored as a bed-and-breakfast inn.

Another reminder of urban change in Pacific Heights is the house at 2828 Vallejo Street, which was moved to that address from its former site at 2222 Broadway in 1912, when James L. Flood chose the Broadway site for his sumptuous marble Italian Renaissance palazzo. The owners of the 1880 Victorian, Dr. Brigham and his wife, moved the old house in sections to its present Vallejo Street address.

At 2209 Jackson Street is a comfortable, one-story Victorian, much the oldest house in the area, which stands as the single remnant of a housing tract created by a pioneer San Francisco jeweler, John W. Tucker, between 1861 and 1863. (Tucker lived at the time on Rincon Hill.) His housing development, then out in the sandy wastes of Pacific Heights, was called "Tuckertown."

The L.L. Baker house, at Washington and Franklin, was built for the founder of Baker & Hamilton Hardware, one of San Francisco's earliest and most successful businesses, with large brick warehouses still standing south of Market Street. The house was later occupied by Antoine Borel, Swiss founder of a banking dynasty that continues today. (Author's collection))

FRANKLIN STREET — By the mid 1870s, the future of Pacific Heights as a quarter for splendid dwellings had been assured, as the houses along Franklin and Gough Streets testified. In particular, Franklin Street, from California to Pacific Avenue, was lined on both sides with houses as impressive as the Van Ness Avenue mansions. A number of these houses were occupied by the German Jewish merchant and banking families, who historically had been the great leaders in San Francisco's financial and cultural development.

Of the scores of impressive houses which faced one another across Franklin Street, only two or three remain standing today. The 1906 fire broke through to the east side of Franklin, from California Street to Clay, and all of those houses that managed to escape have since been replaced by modern apartment buildings and flats. The Blanding (later Hotaling) house, on the Clay Street corner was the last to go, torn down in the 1960s. The L.L. Bakers' modern Gothic mansion, on the northeast corner of Washington and Franklin, was purchased by banker Antoine Borel at the turn of the century. He remodeled its interior in the Venetian style with a vaulted, marble-columned interior gallery; the house was demolished in 1907.

The William Talbot mansion, on the northeast corner of Jackson and Franklin, met the same fate. This house boasted elaborate flower gardens and terraces running all the way down to Pacific Avenue. William Talbot, of the great lumbering firm of Pope and Talbot, had a strong preference for northeast corners, perhaps due to his northeastern origins; he was a native of Maine. Sadly, this great old house went the way of nearly all of its opulent neighbors.

Directly below Talbot's house, on the northeast corner of Pacific and Franklin, stands the house Talbot built as a wedding present to his daughter when she married Henry Dutton, son of the founder of the Fireman's Fund Insurance Company. In the 1950s, banker Paul Hardman purchased this elegant Italianate house with the specific intention of preserving it from the fate which had befallen all its neighbors. It was among the first Victorian restorations in the city.

For years, the William Martin house, which towered over the southwest corner of Jackson and Franklin Streets, stood as an arresting San Francisco landmark. The onion-domed tower and its four Juliet balconies caught everyone's eye, but the tattered curtains hanging at its unwashed windows gave the place a grim and eerie look. Travelers on the Jackson Street cable cars referred to the deserted old house as "The Charles Addams Mansion." This house was once occupied by the Washington Dodge family, who survived the Titanic sinking. In the 1960s it met the fate of its Franklin Street neighbors, and fell to the wrecker's ball.

A happier fate awaited its adjoining neighbor, the Haas-Lilienthal House. This perfect specimen of San Francisco Victorian design, described by its architects Schmidt & Shea as "Modern Gothic," was built in 1886. Because of its red brick "Colonial" chimneys, Gothic, bay-windowed tower, and several Elizabethan appurtenances, one is tempted to describe it as "Queen Anne." Members of the Haas family donated this wonderful house on Franklin Street to serve as headquarters for the Foundation for San Francisco's Architectural Heritage.

The Haas family, which established its early fortune in wholesale groceries, and the Lilienthals, who established theirs in banking, were among the most prominent members of San Francisco's Jewish aristocracy. Through intermarriage, this community became one big, though not always happy, family. The results of the many confusing alliances of Haases, Hellmans, Sterns, Branstens, Koshlands and Lilienthals may be perplexing, but all these families contributed greatly to San Francisco's cultural development. In 1887, the *Examiner* noted "were it not for the large Jewish patronage, we should seldom see a First Class tragedy or famous opera rendered in our Thespian temples." This patronage has continued to the present.

On the northwest corner of Franklin and California Streets, and running up California, are three superb Victorian mansions which still enjoy their original settings of rolling green lawns and handsome plantings. When Edward Bransten wanted to tear two of them down in 1974, the San Francisco Landmarks Board, the Pacific Heights Association and the Foundation for San Francisco's Architectural Heritage joined forces to prevent their destruction.

At the top of this group, 1834 California Street, the home of pioneer grocer Isaac Wormser, the "W" in S &W products, was built in 1876. In 1895 it was sold to John C. Coleman, a gold miner, who hired the firm of Percy and Hamilton to add the fat tower and enlarged other portions of the house, somewhat blurring its original Italianate style. Next on the slope below, the house at 1818 California Street, a classic Italianate, was built in 1876 by Louis Sloss as a wedding present for his daughter, Estelle, and her husband, Ernest Lilienthal. Later, it was sold to Judge Orville Pratt, whose wife, Emily Wilson Pratt, was a granddaughter of Samuel Wilson, a founder of the American Republican Party and third president of the San Francisco Bar. This

house was tastefully restored as a bed-and-breakfast, and is now a private home.

The third house, at 1701 Franklin Street, was built in 1895 by Edward Coleman. Along with his brother John, Coleman had made a fortune mining gold at Grass Valley. *Here Today*, the San Francisco Junior League's inventory of historic San Francisco buildings, describes this house as "triumphantly Queen Anne." This house, having escaped the wrecker's ball, has been restored for use as law offices.

LAFAYETTE SQUARE — Lafayette Square, the highest point in Pacific Heights, bounded by Gough, Sacramento, Laguna and Washington Streets, was known as Holladay Hill when it was the site of Ben Holladay's house and grounds. Holladay made millions from his ownership of the Overland Stage Line. Built in the late 1860s, Holladay's white-painted frame house was reached originally by long flights of stairs reaching all the way to to Van Ness Avenue. A carriage drive from the western side made for an easier approach. Amelia Ransom Neville describes the interior as "charming in the manner of the 1860s, with long French windows draped in cobweb lace, long oval mirrors, crystal chandeliers and pale carpets with great medallions of roses."

Mrs. Holladay, a member of the aristocratic Ord family, was one of the great beauties of San Francisco society, and her polish and social accomplishments stood out in contrast to the tastes of her rough diamond husband, a former stagecoach driver. After enjoying a European success and marrying her daughters to the Count de Pourtales and Baron de Boussiere, Mrs. Holladay brought them all back from Paris and across the continent in a private railroad car. All this was too much for old Ben, who, after their arrival in San Francisco, fled to the wilds of Oregon.

At the turn of the century, city developers, wishing to cut Clay and Octavia Streets through Ben Holladay's estate (today's Lafayette Park), declared Holladay a squatter. For years the claims of the city and Holladay's counter-claims went through the courts. During this period Holladay grew a beard, vowing that he would not shave it until the property rights were settled in his favor. Holladay's lengthening beard gradually became one of the more spectacular sights of the city. The Holladay house was dismantled in 1928; by this time Holladay was long dead. Finally, in 1935, the city paid the Holladay estate $200,000. During the lengthy litigation Holladay had sold off a chunk of land on the Gough Street side of his parcel to Alexander Wilson, who in 1908 built the splendid apartment house at 1925

Built for John Sabin, a director of the Pacific Telephone Company, in the mid 1880s, this house still stands at the corner of Pierce and Pine Streets. It was a most unusual house for its day, with a unique portico design and sinuously curved brackets separating the windows, giving the house a clean, modern look by comparison with many contemporary houses. The 1887 description notes that "Electric appliances are used throughout the house"—a rather unusual departure from the gaslights of earlier years. (Author's collection)

Gough Street, now a co-operative. The residents have a beautiful view of Lafayette Park, with no fear of any encroaching buildings.

Opposite the park on Sacramento Street, just above Gough, there stood, until the 1960s, a square white house that greatly resembled the Colton-Huntington mansion on Nob Hill. In later years there was much speculation from the neighbors, who noticed that the rooms were lit only by gaslight after dark. When the house was being demolished, local newspapers stated that it had belonged to the reclusive Miss Frances Molera, who, in her will, left the historic Cooper-Molera adobe in Monterey to the National Trust for Historic Preservation. Frances Molera's Spanish father, Joseph Molera, a well-known San Francisco architect, designed the house on Sacramento Street, and lived there until his death in 1932. Other than that, no one has troubled to learn about the house and its mysteri-ous occupant. The apartment building that took its place is singularly uninteresting.

The Great Mansion of Michael De Young

The blocks along California Street from Van Ness to Divisadero were crowded with the usual San Francisco lots with frontages of just twenty-five feet. Despite the resultant restrictions of space, there were many elegant mansions along this stretch. Some of these houses still stand today, most notably on the north side between Octavia and Laguna, and on the south side between Laguna and Buchanan. But one of the most spectacular mansions ever built on California Street, that of Michael De Young, is gone.

Located at 1919 California Street, on the south side between Gough and Octavia, the De Young lot had a frontage of some two hundred and fifty feet. The house was a classic example of the popular Italianate style,

Michael De Young, owner of the *Chronicle* and founder of the De Young Museum, built a classic Italianate mansion at 1919 California Street, with the usual stone lions at the top of the entrance stairs, and a pair of griffons guarding the steps up to the front door. The garden was immaculately kept, with designs worked in flower beds facing the street. (Courtesy San Francisco Public Library)

boasting two-story slanted bays on either side of a marble columned entry. For years, the elaborate furnishings and decorations of these rooms were on display as "Pioneer Rooms" at the De Young Museum, but they were removed for the additions made to house the Brundage Collection of Asian art; one bedroom is still on display.

This great palazzo was the showplace of one of the most powerful men in San Francisco, the owner of the San Francisco *Chronicle*. De Young helped raise the city from an economic slump by sponsoring the California Midwinter Exposition, held in Golden Gate Park in 1894, over the vociferous protests of John McLaren, who wanted to keep all buildings and statuary out of the park. When the Chicago Exposition of 1893 made its final bow, De Young, along with a group of other

wealthy San Franciscans, bought, borrowed or leased the exhibits and had them shipped out to San Francisco, where a "Midwinter Fair" was intended to show the world what an ideal climate prevailed here. The Japanese Tea Garden, the pleached sycamores which ornament the music concourse, and the museum which still bears De Young's name, all are reminders of that exposition. Even Little Egypt, the sensational hootchy-kootchy dancer who had thrilled and scandalized visitors to the Chicago Fair, was brought out to whet the appetites of San Franciscans for the exotic.

After the Midwinter Fair was over, De Young built a large gallery onto the east side of his California Street mansion to display the collection of paintings he had gathered from all over the world. After his death, the collection went to the De Young Museum. Many San

The dining room of the De Young house shows some features not previously seen in San Francisco houses: a great decorative arch setting off the fireplace niche, with the arch echoed in a mirror over the sideboard, furniture in the baronial 17th-Century style, and most radical of all, a row of electric light bulbs set into the cornice molding. (Courtesy San Francisco Public Library)

Franciscans recall the twenty-foot bronze vase which stood in front of the museum entrance. This huge Art Nouveau piece, crawling with nude babies, came from the atelier of Gustave Dore in Paris. It was displayed for years in the California Palace of the Legion of Honor, built by De Young's enemies, Alma and Adolph Spreckels. Today, the vase is in Golden Gate Park.

Other works from De Young's private collection which helped to form the artistic tastes of generations of San Franciscans were a copy of Napoleon's throne, a life-size statue of King Saul, and an immense canvas entitled "A Russian Wedding," which has finally been rescued from years of oblivion, carefully restored, and placed again on display at the Legion of Honor, where it will doubtless dazzle future generations of art lovers.

A financial report to the Board of Supervisors from the Board of Park Commissioners, dated June 30, 1899, gives an interesting inventory of the contents of the De Young Museum, and shows why Alma Spreckels, busy building her own museum in Lincoln Park in 1921, dismissed the De Young as "that warehouse in Golden Gate Park." The De Young had only one curator, whose duties that year included recording and numbering the objects recently donated: gelatin slides of California food fishes, stuffed birds, and mineral samples. Cases were being prepared to exhibit a native deer, one for gnawing mammals, and three for birds of prey. Collis Huntington had contributed 22 valuable oil paintings. Michael De Young, founder and planner of the museum, had given a collection of old Mexican pottery, as well as relics of the Spanish American War, sent from

Mrs. Faxon Dean Atherton's house at California and Octavia looks rather like a collection of smaller houses clusterer together, with a fat tower thrown in for good measure. Carpenters and builders, working with hand tools, must have been taxed to the limit by the odd angles and arches of the roof and the curved trim. And yet the house is obviously finished to perfection. Today it contains several apartments. See page 250. (Courtesy San Francisco Public Library)

the Philippines. The museum included a Napoleon Room, an Old German Room, a Wells Fargo & Co. Pioneer Hall, a model and map room, a musical instrument collection, and a library. All this was enough to keep the single curator busy.

Mike De Young, like most newspaper owners in the Old West, had a stormy career. His brother, a co-owner, was shot and killed by Milton Kalloch, son of Mayor Isaac Kalloch. And Michael himself was shot and wounded by Adolph Spreckels after the *Chronicle* ran a story impugning the honesty of the family patriarch, Claus Spreckels. Stephen Birmingham, in his *California Rich*, states that the De Young mansion was acquired from one of California's more prominent families without any money being exchanged, perhaps in return for not printing some scandalous information.

De Young had four daughters, who during their prime ruled San Francisco's high society like princesses of the realm. From the great house on California Street they all made brilliant marriages. Helen married George Cameron; Phyllis became Mrs. Nion Tucker; Constance married Joseph Tobin, and Kathleen married Ferdinand Theriot. These families have retained controlling

interests in the *Chronicle*, one of the few local newspapers to survive the depredations of time and corporate mergers. In 2000, the Hearst Corporation purchased the *Chronicle* from the De Young heirs.

For over a decade after De Young's death, his heirs continued to maintain the old place for family gatherings. When the building was torn down in the 1940s, the workmen left one of the huge granite fence posts, which is all that marks the site today. On one part of the property, however, is a massive Tudor townhouse with a large bay window and one-half of an elegantly tall Gothic arch, intended to be a carriage entrance. The other half of the arch was to be a part of a matching house to be built by another De Young daughter, who exercised her woman's prerogative, and changed her mind.

OTHER CALIFORNIA STREET HOUSES

At California and Octavia Streets, on the southern slope of Holladay Hill, Mrs. Faxon Dean Atherton built a mansion in the 1880s. Even in a day when tastes for the exotic were allowed to run rampant, this house took every prize. A huge, squat corner tower, an eclectic collection of wall treatments crowned by gables and an incredible roofline, all contributed to a spectacular effect. Queen Anne was on display here at her most riotous.

Gertrude Atherton, in her autobiography, *Adventures of a Novelist*, leaves us a fine image of her mother-in-law, builder of this house and descendant of an aristocratic Chilean family. Gertrude's husband George met an untimely demise on a Chilean navy ship, and rather than burying him at sea, the captain had George's remains shipped home in a barrel of rum. The shipment arrived with a request from the crew to have their rum ration replenished. Following her husband's death, Gertrude Atherton escaped the boredom of country life at Valparaiso Park, the house which gave the town of Atherton its name, and came to live in San Francisco.

Like her daughter-in-law, Mrs. Faxon Atherton was a strong-minded woman who built according to her own notions. Her house on California Street extended to the sidewalk, so, to prevent passersby from gazing into her front windows, she had the sills placed at a high level. As a result, the occupants were unable to see out without standing on tiptoe, a medieval effect which was later corrected. The house also contained a two-story central hall, with a balcony, that served as a ballroom. Recalling the view from the balcony of bare-shouldered ladies in voluminous skirts, Gertrude Atherton wondered if perhaps the yardage might not have been better distributed.

Two blocks of California Street hold a number of very fine Victorians (see page 252). Between Octavia and Laguna on the north side are splendid Italianates, and on the south side between Laguna and Buchanan are several Italianate and Stick Style houses of noble proportion and especially fine ornamentation. On the northeast corner of California and Buchanan is an early example of "French Flats," or multi-family housing, in the classic Italianate style, a very large, imposing building. In the 1960s the destruction of the fire house in this same block became the immediate cause of the founding of the California Heritage Council. The fire house's Gothic façade was ornamented with fire-fighting symbols and portrait busts of fire chiefs, all carved by firemen.

At the northeast corner of California and Webster Streets is Temple Sherith Israel, which can trace its origins to Gold Rush times. Five successive temples preceded the present one. This synagogue, in the Romanesque style, with its mighty dome and huge rose window, was dedicated on Washington's birthday, 1904. Temple Sherith Israel was one of the few great public buildings to survive the 1906 disaster intact.

Many passersby have wondered about this odd structure in the 1900 block of California Street, built by Michael De Young as a wedding gift to one of his daughters. Its grey façade and Gothic Revival design are unique in the city, but the mysterious half of a Gothic arch makes people wonder whether part of the building was demolished. Actually, the second half was never built: Mike De Young's second daughter simply changed her mind. (Courtesy James Heig)

As a result, it was used temporarily as a court house and for other civic functions until the city was rebuilt. Political boss Abe Ruef, Mayor Eugene Schmitz and the entire Board of Supervisors were tried for corruption here in 1907. Rabbi Nieto gloomily watched the trials, which he felt were a profanation of his holy temple.

Albert Pissis, architect of the Flood Building, the Emporium, and the Hibernia Bank, designed this massive edifice in the shape of a giant cube with huge pendentive arches supporting a dome some ninety feet above the floor. Today Sherith Israel, especially noted for its fine library, is a place of prayer, study, and fellowship for a large congregation. It is California Landmark #42.

Claus Spreckels and his sons built at least seven mansions in the city. This house, built by John D. Spreckels, of white limestone, with four immense Corinthian columns on each side, stood at the corner of Pacific and Laguna Streets. It survived the 1906 earthquake with only slight damage, but was later demolished. Across Pacific Street Spreckels built a beautiful house in a more delicate Beaux Arts style, for his attorney; this house served for many years as the library of the California Historical Society, and has recently been restored as a private residence. (Author's collection)

Turn of the Century Pacific Heights —

In the 1890s, several colossal houses in the latest neo-classical style were built in Pacific Heights. John Spreckels built two of these, facing each other across Pacific Avenue at Laguna Street. Spreckels lent one house to his lawyer, Samuel Shortridge, who later became a U.S. Senator. One served for years as the library for the California Historical Society; the other was demolished in the 1920s. A third Spreckels mansion, on the northwest corner of Pacific and Gough Street, was built by John's brother, Rudolph. It too was torn down in 1965 and replaced by a particularly repellent church building.

The great white stone mansion built in 1913 at Washington and Octavia Streets by Adolph Spreckels and his formidable wife, Alma De Bretteville Spreckels, is one of San Francisco's most beloved landmarks, and is the largest single-family residence in the city. The architect, George Applegarth, a graduate of Paris's Ecole des Beaux Arts, also designed the California Palace of the Legion of Honor, the Spreckels's magnificent gift to the city. With its huge lawn sweeping down to Jackson Street, Alma's private palace replaced half a dozen large houses which she had moved to new

locations – an expensive way to clear out the back yard. The five-car garage facing Jackson Street had a turntable in the floor so that no car ever had to back out. In 1931 Alma opened a salvage shop in the garage, thereby qualifying as the inventor of the garage sale. For more than thirty years she collected choice items from her friends and sold them to benefit her various charities. Just behind the house, at the top of the lawn, is an enclosed swimming pool with a retractable roof, designed by architect George Livermore, where Alma liked to skinny-dip. The turbulent life of the fascinating Alma Spreckels is related in Bernice Scharlach's superb biography, *Big Alma*.

At the northeast corner of Jackson and Laguna Streets is the red sandstone mansion which for years served as headquarters of the California Historical Society. William Franklin Whittier built the house in the mid-1890s as a gift to his wife, who was killed in a carriage accident shortly before the house's completion. Despite this unhappy beginning, the 30-room house became a San Francisco showplace.

Among the first San Francisco stone houses to boast a steel frame, the Whittier mansion was fitted out with all the requisite touches of the day. The entrance hall,

This red sandstone mansion, at Jackson and Laguna Streets, was built in 1896 for William Whittier, a mercantile, railroad and shipping millionaire, at a cost of $152,000. It was the first house in the city to have a steel frame. The Whittier house featured a "Turkish Corner" smoking room, very much in vogue in the 1890s, in the northwest round bay. In the 1930s the mansion housed the German consulate, and later became the headquarters of the California Historical Society. It is now a private residence. (Courtesy California Historical Society)

The Irwin house (left) and the Dunphy house (right) shared the crown of Pacific Heights, on Washington Street between Octavia and Laguna. The Dunphy house was demolished in 1912; the Irwin house was razed after a fire in 1956, to make way for a high-rise apartment building. This picture was made in 1906, when refugees' tents dotted Lafayette Square, across the street. (Author's collection)

24 by 32 feet, is paneled in carved oak; the large drawing room and its adjoining, octagonal smoking room (with a Mudejar ceiling), are paneled in mahogany. The dining room paneling is a rare wood called tamanu. The hardware in all the main rooms is of hand-wrought German silver. Downstairs is a ballroom measuring 36 by 54 feet.

The Whittier mansion was sold in 1940 to the German government. The house served as the German consulate and was the setting for numerous lavish functions given by the popular local consul, Fritz Wiedemann, who had been Adolph Hitler's commanding officer in World War I. Herr Wiedemann burnt all his secret papers in the furnace and fled the country after the outbreak of World War II. For the next decade, the house and its contents were under the jurisdiction of the Alien Property Custodian. It then became the home of Mortimer Adler's Institute for Philosophical Research, before it was passed on to the California Historical Society. It is now a private residence.

Built in 1886 to crown the crest of Pacific Heights, the Dunphy mansion, on Washington Street west of Octavia, must have been one of the most livable in the city. It featured a mansard roof, an octagonal tower, marble walks, an enclosed deer park, and of course a ballroom. Unfortunately Jim Phelan, one of San Francisco's most beloved mayors and benefactors, liked the splendid view from that location. In 1912, Mayor Phelan's sister and brother-in-law, the Sullivans, removed the old Dunphy house and replaced it with the long, buff-colored brick Italianate house which still stands in the 2100 block of Washington Street. For years Phelan kept a *pied a terre* in this building, while his chief residence was at Villa Montalvo on the peninsula.

Further west, at the northeast corner of Washington and Laguna Streets, was a turn-of-the-century mansion to end all mansions. Sugar baron William Irwin and his wife, the former Mrs. Ben Holladay, Jr., built their house within view of the old Holladay mansion. In the popular neo-classical style, of stone with a steel frame, the Irwin house was decked out with six engaged ionic columns and a grand double staircase, with stone lions and colossal urns, sweeping up to the massive entrance. An enormous hall filled the entire southeast corner of the house. In a side hall, a grand staircase, twelve feet

Top: The Irwin house featured magnificent entrance stairs and great Doric pilasters on the front. The interior (above and left) was equally splendid; the stairway was the model for one in the last scene of "Gone With the Wind," when Rhett Butler tells Scarlett that he doesn't give a damn, and she collapses on the stairs. In the background of the top picture is the Richardson Romanesque house of Templeton Crocker. (Author's collection)

A very large house on a very steep lot at Washington and Gough Streets appears at first glance to be a two-family house, but is actually the home of the William F. Goad family. It features an ample front porch with white marble steps, and a surprising asymmetrical design for the 1880s: the right wing has slanted bays, while the left wing is flat. (Courtesy California Historical Society)

wide, led to a landing lit by an immense Tiffany window. The 60-foot drawing room, in the Louis XV style, opened at the back to an equally large, paneled library, adjoining the immense dining room, with a huge curved window taking in the panoramic sweep of hills and bay. All these rooms opened into one another with wide sliding doors, thus forming one vast space some ninety feet square.

Built in 1904, the house made a perfect setting for the wedding, in 1911, of the Irwins' daughter, Helene, and Templeton Crocker, the grandson of Charles Crocker. Apparently neither of the newlyweds' families wanted to be outdone in bestowing lavish gifts upon the couple, and the results made for interesting reading. Local papers described such items as million-dollar checks from both sides, automobiles with chauffeurs, diamond necklaces and other similar ornaments for the bride, and a staggering array of silver, crystal, china and linens. Unfortunately, these gifts

could not ensure marital happiness, and the marriage was a brief one.

Templeton Crocker and his sister Jennie fell heir to the St. Francis Hotel, and on several occasions were ready to sell it, only to have the buyers, after making improvements, go into receivership. Each time, the Crocker heirs got to keep their down payments and got back their hotel, with its new improvements.

For some years following the deaths of the Irwins, their huge "wedding house" served as headquarters for the San Francisco Medical Society. During World War II the large ballroom housed the Irwin Memorial Blood Bank. The house was demolished after a fire in 1956. A large, modern apartment house occupies the site today. As an ironic touch, a single plaster lion stands at the new apartment building's entrance—a reminder of the pair of great stone beasts which once guarded the site.

At 2622 Jackson Street, just a few houses east of Scott, is a handsome Italian-style mansion designed by

The Classical Revival house at 1901 Jackson Street was built for Baron Edward S. Rothschild about 1902, on a design by Frank Van Trees. It became a boys' school in 1910, and then for many years was a residence club, the Chateau Bleu. Finally it was a nursing home, and then stood empty and deteriorating for several years. In September 2001 a thorough restoration of the house is nearly complete, including replacement of the wide white marble front stairs, renovation of a splendid 10' x 12' Tiffany art glass window on the west side, and magnificent plasterwork on the ceilings. This enormous house is now divided vertically into two three-story townhouses, each with five bedrooms.

Willis Polk for capitalist George Gibbs. Built in 1894, this beautifully proportioned house, with its stone walls and semi-circular portico, was one of Polk's first San Francisco dwellings. It bears no resemblance to the rustic city houses which he would design later. Some people argue that the inspiration for its round porch came from a design by Raphael for the Temple of Vesta. The true inspiration, however, was the work of McKim, Mead and White, and the years Polk spent in New York. The house for many years served as headquarters for the San Francisco Institute of Music and Arts.

Just east of the Gibbs house, on the northwest corner of Jackson and Pierce, stands one of the most arresting dwellings in Pacific Heights. Built in 1896, it was one of the first houses to create a mood of "countrified elegance" in the city. Irving Scott, president of the Union Ironworks, commissioned Ernest Coxhead to design this house as a wedding present for his daughter, Elizabeth.

Although the term "Queen Anne" was tossed about loosely in Victorian times, this house is an example of the true English Queen Anne style of the early 18th century. Of tapestried red brick, it commands the corner with a high gabled roof and towering chimneys. On the view side, overlooking the Bay, is a huge bay window; the other windows on the street sides are smaller, grouped in pairs, with lead mullioned panes. In contrast to this rustic informality, the massive front entry, with clusters of Corinthian columns, upholds a handsome curved pediment and an elaborate carved cartouche overhead. The lack of any further embellishments on the entire façade, other than a heavy stone cornice above, further dramatizes the effect. (See page 259)

Within, handsomely paneled rooms are dimly lit by the grouped windows, creating a tranquil mood. In the living room is a huge open hearth, surrounded by panels bearing carved Grinling Gibbons garlands. The fine collection of 18th-century paintings and antiques further

heightens the feeling of an ancient English country house. Here one sees the happy result of cooperation between an excellent, innovative architect and a client with good taste.

In the same year that he built the Gibbs house, 1894, Willis Polk was commissioned to build a house on Webster Street, between Washington and Jackson, for William Bourn, who later built the fabled Filoli in Woodside, now a property of the National Trust. Bourne's Georgian-style townhouse of klinker brick, with massive chimneys, seems a bit ponderous by modern standards, but, like the Gibbs house, it makes an impressive statement. (See page 258)

These two Polk houses had an undeniable influence on builders in San Francisco. A local newspaper of that day, *The Wave*, noted that "the unpretentious solidity of Polk's work cheapens the gabled and turreted mansions around them." No longer would San Franciscans be content with bay-windowed, begabled redwood "villas" squeezed onto city lots.

No reference to the unique architecture of Pacific Heights would be complete without mention of the Swedenborgian Church of the New Jerusalem, located at 2107 Lyon Street, the northwest corner of Washington Street. It was established in 1893 by Reverend Joseph Worcester, occupant and designer of one of the rustic Marshall cottages on Russian Hill. The design of the church was partly inspired by sketches of a tiny village church in the Po Valley near Verona. These sketches, made by Bruce Porter, were left for young Bernard Maybeck to interpret when he was employed in the offices of A. Page Brown.

The hand-made maple chairs, instead of pews, the cheery fireplace, the heavy tile roof and vine-clad walls are symbolic expressions of the elemental nature of the Swedenborgian viewpoint. The delicately modeled campanile, or bell tower, overlooking an inner courtyard, combined with the low, beamed ceilings, creates an atmosphere of truly disarming rusticity. Murals painted by Bruce Porter and William Keith contribute to the prevailing mood of peace and dignity. Today's reader will be surprised to learn that all of this was created within a budget of $9,000, of which $4,500 built the church itself, and $4,500 was expended on a residence for the minister.

Facing Page: The Louis Schwabacher house, on Clay Street between Van Ness and Franklin, narrowly escaped destruction in 1906 when the fire was stopped just across Clay Street. This house has a distinctly French flavor, with its mansard roof, the cheery tower with decorative inset dormers, and fine iron cresting along the roof. (Author's collection)

TIME WAS WHEN Broadway west of Van Ness Avenue was regarded as nothing more than a rustic backwater, much of it too steep to permit residential development. But by 1890 it had become one of the most stylish and favored locations for mansion-builders. In 1900 James Leary Flood, son of Comstock millionaire James C. Flood, built a lavish wooden palazzo at 2120 Broadway. (See pages 254-255) Its columned Renaissance façade, its marble entrance guarded by stone lions, its ornate drawing room and conservatory have been carefully preserved. In the dining room is a magnificent ormolu-trimmed mantel of purple-veined marble. The Sarah Dix Hamlin School now occupies the house.

After only six years in his first palazzo, Flood built an even grander marble one, in the Italian Renaissance style, designed by Bliss and Faville, architects of the St. Francis Hotel. This house is so monumental–the rear wing has a very large private chapel, beautifully decorated and lined with magnificent stained glass windows–that it is hard to imagine its being used as a private residence from 1912 to 1939, when Maude Flood gave it to the Catholic church and moved to the Fairmont Hotel. Today this splendid structure, one of the most lavish houses ever built in San Francisco, houses Sacred Heart Academy, which has expanded into the two neighboring mansions as well. Next door to the west is the austere red brick Stuart Hall, formerly the mansion of railroad and lumber magnate Arthur P. Hammond, built in 1905. And on the other side, at 2200 Broadway, is the stunning English Regency style house, built in 1914 by banker Adam Grant and designed by a New York architectural firm, Hiss and Weeks. The architect had thought the design was for an enclosed city lot. When he finally visited the site, construction was well under way, and he saw the sweeping views the house commanded. He immediately ordered the number of windows to be doubled. These three houses comprise a major architectural treasure, and Sacred Heart Academy is to be commended for preserving them.

Just across Webster Street, east of the Grant house, there stood, until recent years, the Romanesque Revival mansion of Mrs. Phillip Van Horne Lansdale. Her parents, the Sidney Smiths, early San Francisco pioneers, had built a fine house at 333 Bryant Street, on Rincon Hill. They were among the last to surrender to the encroaching industries in 1890, when they built on Broadway in what was then a rural wasteland. Sidney Smith was president of the Cutting Packing Company, which became a part of Del Monte Corporation. The lower two floors of their house were of the stone construction so favored by proponents of the Richardson Romanesque style. The upper floors,

The Andrew Thomas Little house, at the southwest corner of Pacific and Buchanan, was one of the earliest in Pacific Heights. It was built in 1875, in a style reminiscent of New England houses, with terraced gardens leading down the hill. The gardens shown here are still quite young, suggesting an early date for this picture. In the dining room (below) the table is set for a lavish feast, with decanters, candlesticks, and heaps of fruit, below a two-globe gas chandelier, with everything reflected in a splendid gilt-framed mirror. (Courtesy California Historical Society)

with bay-windowed towers crowned by a steep gabled roof, were of wood frame.

After the death of her husband, Lt. Phillip Van Horne Lansdale, in the Samoan uprising of 1899, their daughter Ethel returned to her parents' home, where she lived until her death in 1962. Lansdale must have been an outstanding officer, for three destroyers were named in his honor. His widow never remarried.

The maple woodwork, typical of the period, the series of parlors connected by wide sliding doors, and the collections of Victorian furnishings from the Rincon Hill house, mixed with Mrs. Lansdale's collection of fine antiques, all added to the majesty of this aging house, hidden behind a screen of vines. Among the treasures was a tiger-skin rug, given by the king of Korea to Lt. Lansdale in appreciation for being taught to ride one of those towering "penny-farthing" bicycles so popular in the 1880s.

After Mrs. Lansdale's death in 1962, the house stood vacant, or so it was thought, until horrified nuns from

The Andrew J. Pope house, a 35-room mansion at the northeast corner of Divisadero and Pacific Avenue, was built in 1889 on a very large lot. It was extensively remodeled in 1913 by San Francisco's leading architects, Willis Polk, Albert Pissis, Arthur Brown, Jr., and Howard White. The house was lavish, even for its time. In 1929 it was completely destroyed by fire, but not before interior photographs had recorded its splendor. (Courtesy Pope family album)

the Sacred Heart convent discovered that a commune of hippies had moved in. The commune leader held a news conference in the oak-paneled dining room and announced that his little community was made up of twelve men and five women from Los Angeles, with a common interest in writing, health, food, nudism and the great outdoors. Apparently they were shown the great outdoors, for shortly thereafter the fine old house fell to the wrecker's ball, to be replaced by a large apartment house of no architectural interest whatever.

Further east, at 2040 Broadway, stood another great house which, like the Lansdale mansion, was built by refugees from Rincon Hill. In 1894, the formidable Mrs. Peter Donahue, formerly owner of a mansion at Second and Bryant Streets, commissioned the young architect A. Page Brown, newly arrived from New York, to design a house suitable to her social standing in the city. The result was a three-story Italian Renaissance palazzo which Mrs. Donahue shared with her sister Eleanor (Mrs. Edward Martin), who lived on

The foyer of the Pope house left no doubt as to its owner's taste or financial standing. The interiors were designed by Albert Pissis, Willis Polk, and Arthur Brown, Jr., the city's leading architects. (Courtesy Pope family album)

The library (top) of the Pope house featured a huge Renaissance fireplace, flanked by two enormous mirrors. The drawing room (below) by Willis Polk shows a fine restraint in decoration, avoiding Victorian flourishes for a dignified neo-classical style. (Courtesy Pope family)

The dining room of the Pope house was richly paneled in dark wood, with a three-dimensional, sculptural frieze above. The coffered ceiling had a truly novel feature: small light bulbs in each square, enclosed in little crystal sacs. The baronial sideboard holds a collection of silver, while family portraits look down from the walls. All this was lost in a fire in 1929. (Author's collection)

in the house long after Mrs. Donahue's death. Eleanor became the chief social arbiter of San Francisco. She and Percy Greenway organized the Saturday Night Cotillions, at which the daughters of "acceptable" families were presented to society. Invitations to her dinners and balls were highly coveted. She entertained Alice Roosevelt Longworth and her husband, among many other notables. Indeed, at the age of 102, she was still giving grand dinner parties in her palatial dining room. She might doze a little at the head of her table, but her guests were always happy to be invited. Mrs. Martin's beautiful palazzo has long since joined that flock of ghostly mansions which once lined Broadway.

A T THE CROSSING of Pacific and Divisadero Streets is the highest hill in Pacific Heights. on the northeast corner, lumber baron Andrew Pope built a 35-room brick and stone house in the Queen Anne style in 1889. On a December evening in 1929 a fire spread through the Pope house, enveloping the second and third floors in minutes, and then reaching the basement, where a gas water heater exploded. The Popes and their ten servants were able to escape, but they were unable to save anything. Paintings by old masters, rare tapestries, Oriental rugs, sculptures, and priceless specimens of European and Asian art were consumed. Gone too were the fine interiors which had been lavishly redone in 1913 by Albert Pissis, Willis

Polk, and Arthur Brown, Jr. A fortune in family jewelry, locked in a fireproof safe, was later recovered. All else was lost in a fire which old-timers still recall as the most spectacular blaze since 1906. Today four handsome houses occupy the Popes' site.

Directly across, on the southeast corner, a pioneer physician, Dr. C.N. Ellinwood, one of the founders of Stanford Hospital, built a spectacular frame mansion in the transitional Queen Anne–Colonial Revival style (see pages 248-249). The architect was Eugene Freeman, whose later work included the famous Dunsmuir House in Oakland. The Ellinwood house, with its noble columned portico and classical symmetry, stood empty for fifty years, from 1928 to 1978, resisting the deterioration and demolition which have been the fate of so many priceless neighboring landmarks. Anne Ellinwood, the doctor's granddaughter, spent eighteen years and some $2 million in carrying out a complete restoration of the house, which she then tragically lost to foreclosure. Along with the treasured original furnishings and fixtures in the 28-room mansion Ms. Ellinwood found the original floor plans and elevations, done on linen, and all of the construction bills, checks, receipts and letters, thus making this the best documented pre-1906 building

left standing in San Francisco. Visitors from the East Coast or Europe may scoff at the historical pretensions of so young a city as San Francisco, but what a wealth of memory has already been lost in this colorful place.

One of the last great houses to be built in Pacific Heights, just prior to 1906, was Marcus Koshland's Petit Trianon, so-called because the façade was an exact copy of Marie Antoinette's original playhouse at Versailles. Mrs. Koshland, a notable San Francisco art patron, was also a great music lover. Many San Franciscans have enjoyed listening to chamber music in the glass-domed interior court. Although the façade was badly damaged in the 1906 earthquake, it was perfectly restored and may be still admired at 3800 Washington Street.

The beautiful C.O.G. Miller mansion, at the corner of Pacific and Baker Streets, was similarly damaged by and rescued from the 1906 disaster. It was still under construction when the quake hit, and its toppling brick walls had to be completely rebuilt.

Scores of Pacific Heights houses which pre-date 1906 bear testimony to the fact that, while a few were damaged by the quake, hundreds survived. Of course, they were relatively new, they were well-built, and they stood on solid ground, rather than landfill.

MANSIONS IN THE MISSION:

BETWEEN 1860 AND 1880 the population of San Francisco quadrupled, to 234,000 people. Hordes of immigrants from Germany and Ireland swelled the perimeters of the Mission District from the foot of Rincon Hill southward into smaller subdivisions, past the Potrero and up the slopes of Twin Peaks. Here lived the men and women who made the city function. Besides the Irish and Germans, there were sprinklings of Finns and Scandinavians, seasoned with Greeks, Mexicans, Scots and Latvians. Whole volumes could be written about the ethnic history of this district, which was also home to those dwindling Hispanic families who had established the Dolores Pueblo before there was a San Francisco.

By the mid-eighties, the Mission District and the other neighborhoods south of Market Street had become home to half of San Francisco's residents. After the advent of the cable car down Market Street, the whole district became known as "South o' the Slot." In other parts of the city, the Chinese had their quarter, the French and Italians theirs; but South o' the Slot was San Francisco's true melting pot. Here in

the sheltered mission valley which the padres had chosen as the only habitable spot on the San Francisco peninsula was a world that was more cosmopolitan than any other part of the city.

Miles Overholt, who grew up in the district, wrote a poem about it:

"Whether you know your locations or not,
The heart of the city is South o' the Slot!
That is the spot,
True to the dot,
The heart of the city is South o' the Slot."

The poet's enthusiasm, shared by many thousands of people in his district, is only intensified by his impoverished rhyme scheme.

The most important building in the district was the magnificent United States Mint at Fifth and Mission Streets, replacing the old mint on Commercial Street. English-born architect Alfred Mullett was commissioned by the U.S. Treasury Department to design this building, the first of several similar commissions. Begun in 1869, five years under construction, the new mint

These pictures of the Old Mint, built in 1855, were made in 1906, during and after the great fire. Looking south on Fifth Street on the first day of the fire, a crowd has gathered to see the flames engulfing an apartment building on Mission Street, where the Chronicle building stands today. Meanwhile employees stand on the roof of the U.S. Mint, hoping to put out any fires caused by sparks. Their efforts were successful; the Old Mint's thick stone walls and the efforts of workers saved the building, which is today the only structure in the downtown area dating from the 1850s. When the fire had passed, the Old Mint, shown here from the back, with its tall chimneys for smelting gold, stood alone, miraculously intact. The building was a Gold Rush museum until the early 1990s, when it was closed for lack of federal funding. (Courtesy San Francisco Public Library)

The first of seven mansions built by the Spreckels family in San Francisco stood at 21st and Howard (now South Van Ness). Like everything the Spreckelses built, this house was of the finest materials available, with solid walnut doors, exotic wood trims, and fine stone details. The house was built for Claus Spreckels, who gave it to his oldest son, John, when he was 32 years old. Claus Spreckels moved back to this house after his Van Ness Avenue mansion was damaged in the 1906 fire; he lived here until his death in 1908. The house was demolished in the 1930s. (Author's collection)

was built to last. Its walls were of solid granite and limestone; it boasted a copper roof, wrought-iron girders brought from Philadelphia, and six columns thirty feet high, each weighing thirty tons and cut from a single piece of stone. Little wonder that it withstood the 1906 fire. "For seven hours," recalled a mint employee, "a sea of fire surged around this grand old Federal edifice, attacking it on all sides with waves of fierce heat. At length the Mint was pronounced out of danger, and a handful of exhausted employees stumbled out on the hot cobblestones."

The beautifully proportioned classical building, still a property of the U.S. Treasury Department, was for many years a museum, displaying gold and silver coins struck there in the 19th century, as well as gold nuggets and other important items from the Gold Rush era. Collectors all over the world treasure coins struck in this building, identified by a tiny "s" on one side.

Two historic houses stand side by side just north of Mission Dolores, at 214 and 220 Dolores, between 14th and 15th Streets. These are the Tanforan cottages, probably named for the family of Toribio Tanforan, who settled in the Dolores Pueblo in 1840, according to Bancroft's *Pioneer Record*. Dr. Hugh Baker, a former occupant of one of the houses, believes that No. 214, the older of the two, was a pre-fabricated house brought

Frank M. Stone built this house around 1885, when it would have been regarded as the very latest style: Queen Anne, radically asymmetrical, with every inch of its façade covered with decoration. The interior featured magnificent stained glass, different exotic woods in all the rooms, and frescoed ceilings. This house, at 1348 South Van Ness, is one of only four survivors out of fifty houses shown in the book *Artistic Homes of California*, published in 1887. The interior of the house is remarkably well preserved inside and out, with a hall fireplace, superb woodwork, original wallpapers, and fine art glass windows, including one depicting the "legendary Wahoo bird, of the Japanese, which ever seeks the rising sun." (Author's collection)

round the Horn. With their large garden plots and comfortable porches, these houses suggest a way of life long since vanished from the crowded city.

The Mission District has had more than its share of celebrated residents over the years. David Belasco, a Mission District lad, once trod the boards of the magnificent Baldwin Theater, built for him by his boyhood friend, Lucky Baldwin. In 1890, when the Baldwin went up in flames, Belasco set out for New York, where he attained great fame as a producer. The beautiful actress, Lily Langtry, lived for a time on 21st Street before purchasing a ranch in Lake County. Alexander Graham Bell was married in a house still standing at 58

Liberty Street. Theatrical producer David Warfield was a South of Market boy, as were mayors Angelo Rossi and "Sunny" Jim Rolph, who grew up at 21st and Guerrero and eventually became governor of California.

South of Market becomes the Mission District at 13th Street (now called Division), under the piers of the freeway, where all the streets turn a 45-degree angle and aim due south. Also at this juncture South Van Ness, which until the 1920s was called Howard Street, extends for twelve blocks until it comes to a dead halt at Army Street. Howard street was for several decades one of the smartest addresses in the city.

Earthquake damage in the northern Mission District was especially heavy in 1906, when scores of houses and hotels built on the soggy bed of Laguna Dolores were tossed from their foundations or sank into the mud. Valencia and Mission streets were devastated. And on the next day the fire swept across 12th Street and rushed through some 27 blocks until it was stopped along Dolores Street on the west and 20th Street on the south; Capp and Howard Streets, in an irregular stepped pattern, were the eastern limits of the flames. The fire-fighters, aided by scores of refugees equipped with towels and sheets dipped in water, beat out the flames with their bare hands.

Outside the perimeters of the burnt area are many survivors of the 19th century. Time has not been kind to most of them. They have been hemmed in by commercial structures, stuccoed, asbestos-shingled, converted into auto repair shops with rooming houses above. A few still sit in overgrown gardens, seeming to shrink back from the ugliness and noise that threaten to envelop them. A gaping vacancy shows where a handsome dwelling, intended to last for generations, has been smashed up and carted off, leaving only a stone coping along the sidewalk to show that it ever existed at all.

One striking survivor, at 573 South Van Ness (see page 121), rises above the rooftops of its more modest neighbors, a marvelous confection of deep pink with delicate plaster traceries all picked out in white. Its swelling bays and a domed tower once looked out over spacious lawns with circular flower beds and a carriage drive. In 1906 its owners must have watched, terrified, as the houses across the street went up in flames. Today its nearest neighbor is a garage painted scarlet, perhaps in a whimsical attempt to keep up with its splendid neighbor.

Three blocks further south, the 800 block shows clearly that survival for these houses is a win, lose, or draw proposition. At 880-882 is the Queen Anne style Remensberger house, unfortunately covered with asbestos shingles. Next to it is the ugly Builders' Exchange, surrounded by a huge parking lot extending to Capp Street; at the center of this large parcel was once an imposing Italianate house. At 825 South Van Ness is a Queen Anne built in the early 1890s by Fred Howard, (no relation to William D.M. Howard, for whom the street was named.) Fred Howard, employed by provision merchants Norton, Teller & Roden, hired architect Charles Rousseau to design this beauty.

Possibly the greatest loss to the neighborhood was the big foursquare Italianate mansion of Claus Spreckels, the Sugar King, at the northwest corner of 21st and South Van Ness. (See page 315) Here the four Spreckels

sons grew to maturity, each leaving his mark on the city and on the whole state. Their father, when he moved into the great stone mansion he built at Van Ness and Clay Streets, handed the house over to the eldest son, John. When his new house was gutted by fire in 1906, Claus Sr. returned to this house, where he died in 1908. Built in 1884, it cost some $70,000, at a time when $7,000 built a very imposing house, and a workman's cottage cost $700. When it was demolished in the 1930s the onyx mantels and the rooms paneled in mahogany, walnut and cocobolo wood were either scattered to the four winds or fell under the wrecking ball. By then the neighborhood had long since fallen into decline, and the heirs to the Spreckels dynasty were finding their own mansions (there were actually seven of them in San Francisco) too cumbersome to maintain.

The 900 block of South Van Ness is a treasury of striking Victorian design, showing some of the wild inventiveness and variety created by architects, builders, and owners, who often chose embellishments from catalogs furnished by planing mills.

AT 919 SOUTH VAN NESS a curbed Flemish pediment crowns a small mansard roof, complete with a swagged bull's-eye window. (See page 318) Below these the curved bay windows, balusters, colonettes and baroque pediments complete a façade that has no known prototypes in San Francisco, perhaps in the world. Built in 1900, the house does bear a slight resemblance to the baroque town houses in Amsterdam, with their narrow brick fronts and curvaceous pediments reflected in the canals. But Robert Zimmermann, who designed this house for his brother Charles, apparently was uninterested in the classical serenity of the Dutch baroque. The Zimmerman house marks a gradual transition from Victorian exuberance to Beaux Arts eclecticism, all happening here on a 25-foot frontage. It must be seen to be believed.

The John and Wilhelmina English house at 943 South Van Ness, built in 1885, has the classical unity of the Italianate style, but the boards at the corners are more typical of Stick Style, while the carved, mannerist window pediments suggest Eastlake and Queen Anne. The architect, Peter Schmidt, also designed the Haas-Lilienthal house at 2007 Franklin Street, as well as the Stadtmüller house at 919 Eddy. This house is now a lavishly furnished bed-and-breakfast inn, with a hot tub and a secluded cottage in the beautiful rear garden.

The John Coop house at 959 South Van Ness is a pure, whiz-bang example of the Queen Anne style, with several patterns of shingled siding, a hexagonal

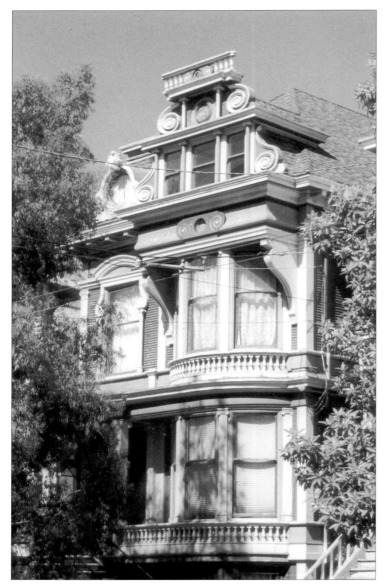

Robert Zimmerman designed this house at 919 South Van Ness, built in 1900, by which time the Queen Anne style was becoming passé. The builder borrowed elements from Flemish, Dutch, and French styles to create a house completely unique in San Francisco. (Courtesy James Heig)

A mixture of Italianate and Stick styles, this house at 943 South Van Ness, designed by Peter Schmidt for John and Wilhelmina English, was built in 1889. Carefully restored, it is now a bed and breakfast inn. (Courtesy James Heig)

tower rising to become cylindrical and ending in a round witch's cap turret. Inverted baseball-bat columns support the front porch, and a medieval gable tops it all off. The ornamentation may be explained by the fact that John Coop was the proprietor of the San Francisco Planing Mill on 5th near Brannan Street. He later became secretary of the Belvedere Land Company, owners and developers of an expensive island in San Francisco Bay.

The splendors of the street do not stop here. Further south, on the west side, 1348 South Van Ness is a

mansion commissioned by attorney Frank Stone in 1886. The designer, Seth Babson, one of California's leading architects, is also responsible for the Stanford and Crocker mansions still standing in Sacramento, as well as a superb Victorian at 1920 Union Street in Alameda. His other San Francisco houses are all demolished.

The Frank Stone house (see page 316) was one of 52 mansions chosen for illustration in the 1888 publication, Artistic Homes of California, recently republished as *Victorian Classics* by Windgate Press of Sausalito, with an introduction by architectural historian Alex

A stroll along Guerrero Street south of 24th Street lifts the heart of anyone who cares about preserving old houses. A strong restoration movement is going on in this once affluent neighborhood. The 1880s Stick Style is predominant, as shown by the two houses on the right. The house on the left, probably somewhat later, shows elements of the Classical Revival, lightened by the charming cupola at the attic level. All three houses are in superb condition, with striking paint colors. Other houses in the same and neighboring blocks are equally well done. (Courtesy James Heig)

Brammer. The interiors of the Stone mansion are today almost exactly as described in the 1888 publication. The frescoed parlor ceiling depicts a sunburst and a legendary Japanese bird, the "Wahoo." In the grand entrance hall is a fireplace of cocobolo wood. Of the 52 houses shown in *Artistic Homes*, once the pride of northern California, only five remain standing today. This one is San Francisco Landmark #74.

Across the street, 1381 South Van Ness is a florid Italianate house with square bay windows topped by a curved pediment. It was designed in 1884 by Charles Havens, who was for several years an official City Architect. Sporting a spectacular new paint job, this house is now San Francisco Landmark #125. Unfortunately it has lost its handsome carriage house.

THE SIDE STREETS in this area, such as Capp and Shotwell, (see page 118) are built out in relatively simple Italianate or Stick Style rows, in contrast to the mansions along South Van Ness, which are nearly all Queen Anne. The consistent scale of the small houses makes the rows wonderfully pleasing to the eye.

The location of this interesting house is unknown, but it appears to be on the northern slope of Bernal Heights in the Mission District. Nine people appear in the picture, including the pater familias standing on the unique spiral staircase. All are carefully posed, with the servants standing at the side of the house, decently removed from the family. The house probably dates from the 1860s, to judge from its four-paned windows and its elegant, simple design. It has its own water tower, a large clock at the top of the carriage house, an astonishing number of matching finials on the roof and the gates, and what must have been the most meticulously trained garden in all San Francisco; every plant is pruned and plucked and made to stand rigidly upright. One can't help thinking the family must have been German. They apparently brought their house and garden to a point of proud perfection, and then called in a photographer.
(Courtesy California State Library)

St. Charles School, built in 1875 on 18th Street at Shotwell, is a masterpiece of elegant, restrained design, beautifully maintained. Designed by architect Charles J. Devlin, it is a rare example of a large, early wood-frame schoolhouse. (Courtesy James Heig)

Shotwell between 21st and 22nd Streets is a delightful surprise, planted with fruit trees, and lined with houses that give it the sense of a small community in itself. The real prize in this block is 715 Shotwell, a one-story Italianate house with handsome arched windows looking over a generous, beautifully planted garden.

The tall steeples of two churches punctuate the sky-line at either end of a long row of Capp Street cottages. The United Presbyterian Church, built in 1890 at 23rd and Capp, is in the Romanesque Revival style which was a trade mark of its architects, Hamilton and Percy, who also designed the Unitarian Church at Geary and Franklin. St. John's Lutheran Church at 22nd and Mission Streets, built in 1900, served the German com-municants who lived in the area.

A walk through this district makes one think back to the days when there were no speeding cars crashing through the streets, no low-riders throbbing with the latest rap beat amplified to inhuman sound levels, no ghetto-blasters, motorcycles, semi-trucks, diesel buses,

or jet planes overhead. Only the sound of horses' hooves on the unpaved thoroughfares, and the low rumble of wheels of coaches, buggies, drays and carry-alls disturbed the sunny afternoons. Human voices were audible: vendors calling out their wares, women calling to their children, who called to each other. At sunset the lamp lighter would pull his horse to a stop before every street lamp, which he lighted with his long flame-tipped stick, and silence descended.

Guerrero Street, two blocks west of Mission, is a boulevard which may well be described as high, wide and handsome. As a consequence it attracted several man-sion builders in the 1880s and '90s. South of the fire line at 20th Street, Guerrero is lined with imposing Victorians. Two survivors have recently received city landmark status. The John McMullen house (see page 116) at 827 Guerrero, a cottage remodeled into a sizeable Queen Anne by Samuel Newsom, has been carefully renovated and blessed with a beautiful blooming garden. It is Landmark #123. Next door, the classic flat-front

Left: This flat-front Italianate house at 1556 Revere Street dates from 1865; its design, with exceptional window treatment and a broad veranda, is unique in San Francisco, since no similar houses survived the 1906 fire. It is now an antique shop. (Author's collection)

The John Coop house, at 959 South Van Ness, an exuberant Queen Anne house with a steep witch's hat tower, was built for the owner of a wood planing mill. His artistry is amply demonstrated in this house, on which the entire façade is ornamented with the planer's handiwork. (Courtesy James Heig)

The so-called "Romeo flats," with outside stairways recessed into the façade, originated in North Beach, but good examples exist here and there elsewhere in the city. This one is on Chattanooga Street, near 23rd Street, in the Mission District. (Courtesy James Heig)

The Picturesque Style, which was all the rage in the 1920s, reached its San Francisco pinnacle with this charming English cottage at the corner of 21st and Sanchez Streets, at the very crest of the 21st Street hill. It is a rare example, not only because of its superb design, but also because of its beautiful landscaping and spectacular views. It was built in 1930 for James Rolph III, son of Mayor Sunny Jim Rolph. (Courtesy James Heig)

Italianate house known as the Kershaw house, Landmark #136, is of unknown date, but is generally recognized as the oldest house in the Liberty Hill area.

The flat-front Italianate Edwards house at 1366 Guerrero and the elaborate Queen Anne Hellwig house in the same block are both beautifully maintained and architecturally noteworthy. A house simply known as "the Flood mansion" at the southwest corner of Guerrero and 21st is most impressive, despite the later addition of a box-like third floor. The large Queen Anne at 778 Guerrero is approached by a stone staircase leading to a handsome columned porch with a Palladian window above. Its corner tower is crowned by a dome with lunette windows, rather like a tiara on this doughty old dowager.

At 102 Guerrero Street is a house boasting one of architect Henry Geilfuss's most refined façades. Geilfuss, a native of Germany, was responsible for many fine houses in the Western Addition, but this seems to be the only example of his work in the Mission District. In 1980 the house was restored by architect Roy Killeen.

Liberty Street, in the blocks to the east and west of Guerrero, abounds with handsome houses set off with luxuriant plantings, and is one of the few streets lined with unaltered single-family Victorians. The large double-bay-windowed mansion at 58 Liberty, painted in reddish-browns, resembles an elaborate plum-cake. Alexander Graham Bell is said to have been married in this house.

The present owners of 159 Liberty, west of Guerrero, proudly display an invitation to a reception at the house, dated March 27, 1896, to meet Susan B. Anthony, famed suffragette; the owner at that time was Judge Daniel J. Murphy. The house boasts a purely classical porch with Corinthian columns and a broken pediment, in contrast to the Victorian baroque façade. Equally handsome is the 1870 flat-front Italianate house on a large double lot at 106 Liberty. The remarkable baroque pediments over the first-floor windows give distinction to an otherwise simple design.

Noe Valley, Eureka Valley, Castro Valley, the 21st Street hill are all districts which make up the largest

Dolores Street has a fine mixture of styles, including this Queen Anne with a round tower above a very large and beautiful art glass window. The house was carefully restored in the 1980s. (Courtesy James Heig)

A very different kind Queen Anne rules the corner of Fair Oaks and 24th Streets, with an octagonal tower, fine art glass windows inset at the center, and a sturdy balustrade above the porch entrance. (Courtesy James Heig)

and oldest residential part of the city. Literally hundreds of houses in these neighborhoods are worthy of mention; old-house buffs who know these streets all have their favorites. A complete list would fill a large volume. Since our purpose is only to stimulate, not completely satisfy, an interest in the city's architectural history, we can mention only a few of the more striking examples.

Possibly the largest and most expensive house ever built in the district is the mansion at 250 Douglass Street, known as Nobby Clarke's Folly, San Francisco Landmark #80. Starting out as an Irish sailor boy, Alfred Clarke came to San Francisco and worked as a

drayman, then joined the police force. He worked his way up to become assistant to the chief of police, a position which he held for some thirty years. How he was able to afford a project on the scale of this house is a matter for speculation. Construction began in 1891, and took well over a year to completion. More than half of the $200,000 Clarke had been accumulating since vigilante days went into the mansion. The house, with a 17-acre park for its setting, was a marvel of lavish paneling and spindlework within, and a Queen Anne triumph without, featuring several kinds of towers, gables, fancy shingling on the walls, and what today might be called a "drop-dead" entrance porch.

The materials throughout were the finest money could buy. (See pages 146-146)

Stories, true or false, inevitably grow up about such a place. One is that Nobby's wife didn't approve of the neighborhood and refused to live in the house. Yet an incomparably lavish house with a 17-acre garden makes this an unlikely reason for her refusal. A directory for 1903 lists an Alfred Clarke living at 1713 Broderick; apparently he himself didn't live in his extravagant house. In 1904 the place was converted into the California General Hospital, advertised as "A commodious hospital with large grounds sheltered from the cold west wind." In later years, its grounds sold off, it served as a boarding house for employees of the Standard Oil Company. It has since been converted into apartments.

SCATTERED HOUSES IN AND NEAR THE MISSION DISTRICT

At 196-98 Laidley Street, near Miguel, is a mansard-roofed mansion built in 1872 by attorney Cecil Poole. In 1900 the property was bought by Theresa Bell, the ward whom Mammy Pleasant had married off to Thomas Bell and who had subsequently lived as Mammy's prisoner in the House of Mystery. After Mammy Pleasant's death, Theresa was ostracized by polite society, and spent her later years a lonely woman. It is said that when someone did befriend her Theresa would buy a house near to her new friend. The mansion at 196 Laidley was but one of several San Francisco houses she owned before she died in 1914.

On Potrero Hill, at 18th and Pennsylvania Streets, two mansions dating to the late 1860s stand directly across the street from one another. The Captain Adams house, a classic Italianate at 300 Pennsylvania, once sat on a 13-acre parcel, with the house at its highest corner, commanding a wide view of the city. Perhaps it was to keep their old family home intact that Captain Adams's descendants sold the property, furnishings, portraits and all, to a couple who have served as sympathetic custodians ever since. They have spent years carefully restoring the old place to its original charm (see page 245).

The Richards house, across the street, has been less fortunate. Shorn of its colonnaded Corinthian porches and its octagonal observation tower, it served as headquarters for an ambulance service. Solidly built, it may yet fall into the hands of an owner who can restore it

to its former glory. It is a rare example of the Italianate style, particularly early for San Francisco, and numbers among the oldest remaining residences in the city.

Down Third Street to the south is a district once known as Butchertown, for very literal reasons. Near the waterfront were the slaughterhouses and tanneries that kept San Francisco supplied with fresh meat, shoe leather, and harnesses. On the gentle hills above were modest houses where the workers lived, in one of the best weather areas in the entire city. Many streets in this more elegantly renamed Bayview District are still lined with small 19th-century cottages, some brutally altered with stucco, shingles, or plywood, but many still more or less intact.

On Palou Avenue at Newhall Street is All Hallows Church, a Gothic Revival wonder built in 1886 by carpenters who obviously were masters of wood-frame construction and ornament.

On a triangular gore where Newcombe Avenue meets Third Street is the old South San Francisco Opera House. The title is rather a misnomer, since the structure, now City Landmark #8, is not in South San Francisco, nor was it ever really an opera house. Built in 1888 as a Masonic Lodge, it was called an Opera House as were many auditoriums in the Old West. Actually it was used for traveling vaudeville and medicine shows. After the 1906 disaster it was listed as the only theater still standing, besides the Chutes on Fillmore Street. Its auditorium, with a small stage still boasting velvet hangings and some canvas backdrops, is occasionally open to the public.

A few blocks further south is San Francisco Landmark #61, at 1556 Revere Street, a large square house of two stories over an ample basement, standing like a racehorse among Shetland ponies. It was built for the Sylvester family in 1865 by Stephen Piper, builder of the South San Francisco Opera House. The Sylvester brothers used the 8,000-square-foot mansion as the center for a vast dairy operation in the Bayview and Hunter's point area. In 1911, the house was moved from Quesada Street, one block north, to its present location. Linda Blacketer, the present owner, calls it her dream house: a big Victorian in a sunny neighborhood. Ms. Blacketer, an antiques dealer, has deeded the façade to the San Francisco Heritage Foundation, to ensure its preservation. A specialist in American Victorian pieces, she holds the house open on the third Saturday of each month.

Three of San Francisco's most powerful families erected major commercial buildings on Market at Third Street in the last decade of the 19th Century, all three to house newspapers. Michael de Young's Chronicle building, with a rather clumsy clock tower (left) was the earliest, followed by William Randolph Hearst's Examiner building directly across Market Street. But Claus Spreckels outdid them both by building the city's first real skyscraper, 18 stories high including the ornate dome with bulls-eye windows, and a fine lantern with a flagpole on top, to house his newspaper, the *San Francisco Call*. All three buildings survive today, in much altered form, thanks to their steel frames. This photograph, taken in 1904, shows the city at its prosperous best, with streetcar and cable car lines on Market Street and not a single automobile in sight. (Courtesy San Francisco Public Library)

THE
FIN DE SIECLE
CITY

1890 - 1906

THE GILDED AGE: CHAMPAGNE DAYS

WHEN SAN FRANCISCANS raised their glasses to welcome a new century on New Year's Eve, 1900, they held the same youthful optimism that had always marked the City by the Bay. In just fifty years, San Francisco had weathered boom and bust, fire and Gold Fever, earthquakes and social upheavals which could have proved ruinous but somehow never did. During the 1890s the city, still bumptious and wicked and frivolous on the surface, gradually achieved cultural and economic maturity.

The California Midwinter Fair, the gold rush to the Klondike, the waves of immigration from Europe and Asia, and the Spanish American War all added immeasurably to San Francisco's wealth and importance in the 1890s. California's phenomenal agricultural riches, the railroads, an expanding shipbuilding industry, and trade with the Orient brought more money into the city. Evelyn Wells, in her captivating book *Champagne Days of San Francisco*, described life for the city's fortunates during a time when wealth spoke in loud, imperious tones.

The lavishly furnished parlor in Tessie Wall's boarding house at 147 Powell Street, with a gilded fireplace mantel, was a suitable showcase for Tessie's girls, who greeted gentlemen callers on tufted and fringed couches and poured champagne on the Louis XV center table. All these lovely furnishings brought hot bidding at an auction in the 1920s, after Tessie's death. (Courtesy San Francisco Public Library)

The book's three leading characters, the Banker, the Senator, and the Judge, are fictional (or are they?); all other characters are thinly disguised portraits from the real life of the city. One was "Bessie Hall," who could put away copious amounts of champagne and who wore diamonds as big as eggs. Was it pure coincidence that a woman named Tessie Wall operated a lavish "boarding house" at 147 Powell Street? It couldn't have been an ordinary boarding house, for after Tessie's death in the 1920s half the town attended the auction in which her gold-plated bed, her tasselled draperies and other valuable possessions were sold to the highest bidder. These treasures probably came from Tessie's post-1906 town house, still standing at 535 Powell Street. C.A. Meussdorffer, architect of the neighboring Family Club, was its architect.

Some years earlier Tessie, in an alleyway leading from Market to O'Farrell Street, had gunned down her lover, Frank Darrioux. She was quoted in the press: "I did it because I loved him, God Dammit!" Fortunately her aim was poor, and she only winged him.

Evelyn Wells also describes the "Cocktail Route," for decades a part of San Francisco legend. The town's tycoons, like the Senator, the Banker and the Judge, met in the early afternoon at Lotta's Fountain, to adjourn for refreshments at such great watering places as the Palace bar, where the city's bonanza kings might rub elbows with local celebrities like the English nobleman, Lord Talbot Clifton, and his pal, White Hat McCarty, a horse trainer from Boston, who in 1898 won $100,000 backing a fifty-to-one shot in the American Derby at Chicago. McCarty's white beaver hat and a heavy gold watch chain were the only reminders of the fortune he had flung away on bets and high living. At the Baldwin Hotel, which enclosed a magnificent theater, guests could bend an elbow in the rich red-plush-and-gilt splendor of the bar while scanning the current playbill. At the Montgomery Block people ordered Pisco Punch, whose formula was thought to have died with Duncan Nicol, the saloon-keeper; the recipe was found again about twenty years ago.

One could spend hours on the Cocktail Route because each saloon provided a huge collation of turkeys, hams, breads, relishes, and jellied and creamed dishes. If the evening proved to be truly gala, these gentlemen, leaving their wives waiting in the great scrolled mansions on Nob Hill, might repair to one of the fine restaurants nearby. Most favored of these were the Pup, Marchands, the Maison Doree, Gobey's Oyster House, and of course the Poodle Dog. The most likely story is that the restaurant was called Le Poudre d'Or, (Gold Dust), and that its customers, being a little shaky in their French, called it the Poodle Dog, and the name stuck. The "wicked" Poodle Dog, a subject of much ill-rumor, was a respectable family restaurant on its main floor; it was the upstairs rooms which gave the establishment its risque

The St. Germain on Ellis Street was one of several popular French restaurants which drew crowds of diners in an age when families dined out often, for the grand sum of 65 cents per person, wine included. (Courtesy San Francisco Public Library)

reputation. The saying was that no girl went upstairs at the Poodle Dog to say her prayers. An old California Architectural Record, circa 1900, shows photos of the Poodle Dog's top floor, revealing not just a small cabinet for dining, but a completely furnished dining parlor with an adjoining bedroom.

To be sure, thousands of people in the Mission District drank beer and not champagne, and for them the grandeur of Nob Hill was only a matter of surmise. But even for those hard-working folk, life was better in the mild climate of San Francisco than it would have been in any other large American city. Golden Gate Park and Ocean Beach were accessible to anyone with the leisure to enjoy them, and it was a tradition for families to come home to a big Sunday dinner after a long day of frolicking on the beach. Scores of restaurants offered a complete "table d'hote" dinner, accompanied by a bottle of good California wine, for sixty cents.

In a city which took its pleasures seriously there were many innocent pastimes. Everyone loved a good parade. The Scottish Caledonians marched to the skirl of bagpipes. The German Turn Verein, fostering physical fitness, organized frequent parades which ended with a great picnic at an outdoor resort. The French held a parade on Bastille Day. The Irish on St. Patrick's Day were joined in their grand parade by the city's Jews and Italians, just as many different groups marched with the Italians on Columbus Day, when a man

dressed as Columbus "discovered" North Beach, and a beautiful girl reigned over the festivities as "Queen Isabella." Many of these traditions are still alive and healthy, and have since been joined by the great Chinese New Year parade and the Gay Freedom Parade, which draw crowds numbering in the hundreds of thousands.

Theater and musical performances were a vital part of San Francisco's culture from the Gold Rush onward. Readers who have a special interest in the subject should read the excellent two-volume historical study, *The San Francisco Stage*, by Misha Berson, published by the San Francisco Performing Arts Library and Museum, giving a lively, detailed account of theater, opera, vaudeville, minstrel shows, and other divertissements in San Francisco from 1849 to 1906. Ms. Berson's study shows us that musical and dramatic fare was far richer, more exciting, more daring, more controversial in the 19TH century than anything we see today.

San Franciscans had enjoyed opera as early as the 1850s in theaters around Portsmouth Plaza. The lavish Wade's Opera House, opened in 1876 at Mission and Third Streets, had 2,500 seats, a stage more than 100 feet wide, and reportedly the biggest crystal chandelier in the United States. The theater changed names and ownership several times, and finally, as the Grand Opera House, was managed by Sigmund and Charles

The dining room at the famous Lick House, one of the city's earliest restaurants, achieved a grandeur far exceeding today's eateries. The room was lit by two enormous crystal chandeliers hung from 25-foot ceilings. (Courtesy California Historical Society)

Ackerman, who kept in their office one of the finest theatrical libraries in the world—David Garrick's prompt books and other priceless treasures—all of which crumbled to ashes in 1906.

During its high seasons, the Opera House stage was graced by such musical luminaries as Emma Calve, Adelina Patti, Edward De Reszke, Scotti Nordica, Madame Sembrich, Luisa Tetrazzini, Madam Ernestine Schumann-Heinck, and Nellie Melba. On opera nights the 30-foot chandelier glittered above a Diamond Horseshoe, years before New York's Metropolitan Opera had a Diamond Horseshoe. In low season melodramas took the stage: "Bertha, the Sewing Machine Girl," "East Lynne," "The Two Orphans," "May Blossom," and "The Old Homestead." Sarah Bernhardt and Ellen Terry appeared there. And the great Enrico Caruso sang at the Opera House on the evening of April 17, 1906; early the next morning he ran from his room at the Palace Hotel and joined the crowds of panicked citizens in the streets. Understandably, Caruso refused ever to return to the city whose performance outdid his own best efforts. A few hours after his final performance in San Francisco, America's biggest crystal chandelier lay a twisted wreck in the fire-blackened rubble of the old Opera House.

It is amazing to learn that a city as small as San Francisco supported as many as 35 theaters, all operating simultaneously. These ranged in quality from cheap vaudeville houses to such splendors as the California Theater, built by William Ralston on Bush Street above Kearny for $250,000, or the opulent Baldwin Hotel and Theater on Market Street. Traveling stock companies brought the leading stars of the theatrical world to these venues. Among the traveling companies, there was a saying: "If they like you in 'Frisco, you're all right."

At the Tivoli Gardens, opened in 1875 at Sutter and Stockton Streets, patrons sat at little tables sipping German beer and listening to light classical music. Joseph Kreling, the owner, built the new Tivoli Opera House on Eddy Street near Market, and in 1879 launched a phenomenally successful 27-year run of Gilbert and Sullivan shows and other light opera.

At the Orpheum, on O'Farrell, performances featured both locals and touring performers from the Orpheum Circuit. Each Thursday a matinee launched a new production. Just before curtain time on Thursdays, Tessie Wall and her girls, sporting the latest Parisian fashions, would parade down the center aisle to their reserved seats in the front row. Many San Francisco ladies got their fashion tips from watching this fashion show, so it wasn't only men who fought for tickets for the Thursday matinee.

All of these legends of young San Francisco merely suggest the quality of life in one of America's most effervescent cities. Old photographs show San Francisco in this period to be one of the country's most attractive cities as well. The views from the hills and the incomparable setting were ample compensation for the rows of bay-windowed houses marching over the hills in gridiron-pattern, the planked sidewalks and the treeless streets. But there is also clear evidence of San Francisco's expanding industries and burgeoning prosperity.

Architectural development, which is the socio-economic barometer of any time and place, was astonishing. In the years between 1898 and 1906 no less than 36 major new commercial buildings rose to unprecedented heights; 32 of these buildings still stand. Those early buildings were all locally financed. The skyline was transformed even more dramatically than in our own times, when major financing comes from outside the Bay Area.

The elevator, of course, made such buildings possible. But not until a group of young Chicago architects introduced the steel frame and poured concrete construction could buildings over six stories tall become practical. Indeed, the Chicago firm of Burnham and Root designed the first eight-story building in San Francisco: Mike de Young's Chronicle building at Market and Kearny, in 1889, which stands today, shorn of its clumsy clock tower and sheathed in a blank modern skin. Within two years the same firm was commissioned to design the Mills Building on Montgomery, which, despite many alterations, still boasts its handsome Romanesque entrance portals.

The Reid brothers designed the Claus Spreckels Building, also known as the Call Building, San Francisco's first true skyscraper, originally eighteen stories tall. Lost in a boring remodeling in the 1930s were its grand arcaded entry and its exotic dome, pierced by rows of bull's-eye windows. The Crocker Building,

Top Right: The original Poodle Dog restaurant was housed in this modest building on Montgomery Street. It was replaced by four later Poodle Dog restaurants, each larger than the preceding one. The last one had five stories, with intimate dining rooms on the upper floors. (Courtesy San Francisco Public Library)

Bottom Right: The Heidelberg Inn, a popular German restaurant at Ellis and Market, appealed to the romantic tastes of its customers by selling postcards reminiscent of popular operettas. On the reverse: "Youth is the Springtime of life, budding and blooming in the effulgence of happiness. . . . *Prince Karl Heinrich and Käthie in Old Heidelberg.*" (Courtesy James Heig)

The splendidly ornate Odeon Cafe, at Market and Eddy Streets, featured vaudeville shows in addition to a very ambitious menu. This picture is from a postcard dated 1915. (Courtesy James Heig)

designed by A. Page Brown in 1892 for the triangular wedge at Post and Market Streets, featured inviting shops at the street and basement levels. It was demolished in 1960, to be replaced by the McKesson building, apparently designed to keep people out.

Further west on Market Street, between Fourth and Fifth, the monumental Emporium Department Store, with its great Roman dome, was designed in 1892 by Albert Pissis and his English partner, William Moore, for Abby Parrott, daughter of pioneer John Parrott. After the 1906 Fire, only the splendid stone façade remained standing; the great art-glass dome which crowned its rotunda lay in a twisted heap of metal on the floor. Fortunately an entirely new structure, in keeping with the old, rose behind the original façade, and the building, once described as "the largest department store in the world," is essentially as it was at the turn of the century. The Emporium closed forever in early 1996, ending a century of service to San Franciscans of every class and walk of life. It was the last of three great San Francisco family-owned department stores to be dismantled, following Paul Verdier's City of Paris and Raphael Weill's White House.

Directly across Market Street from the Emporium stands the equally monumental Flood Building. Like the Emporium, it was designed by Albert Pissis, although some say that the elegant marble lobby was designed by the great Stanford White. The Flood Building was threatened by the wrecker's ball a few years back, but developers abandoned their plan when they realized how costly the removal would have been. In 1992 the country's largest Woolworth's store, housed for decades in the Flood Building, closed while the building underwent renovation. Today the building, splendidly restored inside and out, is again an architectural gem.

In varying degrees, these buildings were influenced by the work of Boston architect Henry Hobson Richardson, the first American architect accepted by the ancient and honorable Ecole des Beaux Arts in Paris. Through his accurate detailing and proper use of materials, Richardson set a revolutionary standard for American architects. He insisted that if builders used ancient building traditions for their inspiration, as most Victorians claimed to do, they had to dignify their sources by employing the stone and marble of the originals and not ignore centuries-old rules for correct scale and proportion.

Richardson began this movement by designing buildings of rough cut stone, employing squat columns and arches patterned after those of the Romanesque churches of provincial France. The style, taken up by American architects, has been labeled as "the 3 R's: Richardson's Romanesque Revival." Often applied to brick or wood frame construction (Victorian taste was slow to die), Richardson's edicts about honest use of materials were first heeded only by the more serious American designers. And despite their good intentions, these architects were not always successful in their first interpretations. Willis Polk described one

The Hibernia Bank building (1889), designed by Albert Pissis, was a particularly tasteful example of the widespread practice of building banks to look like classical temples. This elegant building survived the 1906 earthquake, and continued its use as a bank until the 1970s, after which it stood empty for several years. It is now used as the Tenderloin police station. (Courtesy San Francisco Public Lilbrary)

Richardson-influenced building in San Francisco as "an inebriation in stone."

Nevertheless, Richardson's movement caught on across the country. At the moment of the Victorian Era's full flower in the 1880s, the disciplines of the Beaux Arts school suddenly began to make sense to people. No longer would there be cheerful misinterpretations of historic styles. Inventiveness, which had been the best quality of Victorian architecture, was still admired, but it was now to follow the ancient disciplines, which had, after all, taken centuries of trial and error to evolve.

Richardson's Romanesque forms seemed a bit heavy, even for some Victorian tastes, but his influence was evident when American architects began to adapt the Roman orders to their designs at the end of the century. This in turn led to the adoption of the regal Italian Renaissance Style, first taken up by the Beaux Arts-trained New York architects, McKim, Mead and White. Ideally suited to grand buildings and palatial houses, both in town and country, the Renaissance and Roman Revival Styles, as adapted to Beaux Arts disciplines, continued to dominate American architecture from the 1880s well into the 1920s.

In California, the buildings of the quadrangle at Stanford University are an early and very successful adaptation of the Richardson Romanesque style. Because of their heavy arcades, they are often thought to reflect the Spanish Mission Style, but this is erroneous. The Mission Revival Style came many years after the Stanford buildings went up in the 1890s.

All of the aforementioned San Francisco buildings followed this Richardson influence, as tastes emerged from the Romanesque to the Classical Roman. The Crocker Building, with its arcaded portico, and the Mills Building serve as excellent examples of Richardson Romanesque, while the Emporium and Flood Buildings, with their Roman arches and engaged columns, reflect the newer Roman Revival Style.

The Hibernia Bank, also by Albert Pissis, was regarded in its time as a gem. In his praise of this new structure, architect Willis Polk complimented Pissis "for defying popular taste by not employing every material and known style into one commission." The bank, completed in 1890 at the corner of McAllister and Jones Streets, was the first structure of any kind in the city to follow the Beaux Arts disciplines. Albert Pissis was the first graduate of the Ecole des Beaux Arts to work in San Francisco since Belgian architect Peter Portois came here in the 1850s. Pissis could never have foreseen that his beautiful temple of finance would be used as a Tenderloin police station in the 1990s.

In the decade before 1906, several San Francisco millionaires broke with the local redwood tradition in domestic architecture to build themselves mansions boasting steel frames. Strongly influenced by the great Renaissance Revival mansions which McKim, Mead and White were building in New York, these dwellings clearly reflected the return of classicism which hadn't been seen in Bay Area domestic architecture since the late 1850s. Because they were all located in Pacific Heights, all survived the 1906 disaster (the Claus Spreckels house on Van Ness was gutted by fire) only to be demolished in later years. Only the Whittier house at Jackson and Laguna still stands.

This return to academic classicism, known today as the Beaux Arts movement in American architecture, marks the beginning of the end of the Victorian revivals which had dominated all San Francisco architecture for the previous forty years.

WILLIS POLK AND "LES JEUNES"

WHILE SAN FRANCISCO has never been regarded as a great creative center for the arts, it has from time to time had some outstanding moments. One of these occurred at the turn of the century when a group of young rebels calling themselves "Les Jeunes" lent to San Francisco a brilliance which has never quite been duplicated. Numbering San Francisco's brightest journalists, painters, poets and architects, "Les Jeunes" could be found of an evening enjoying the 25-cent dinner, with plenty of wine and spaghetti, at Sanguinettis on Front Street or at Poppa Coppa's in the old Montgomery Block.

Several of these "Bohemians" joined forces to put out a little publication called The Lark, just four and a half by five and a half inches, printed on colored bamboo paper from Chinatown. Its title defines it exactly. The three publishers were Gelett Burgess, a writer, Porter Garnett, a poet, and designer Bruce Porter. Sometimes the colored ink ran on its pages, but this only added to its artistic appearance. Charming illustrations by Florence Lundborg or Bruce Porter were mixed with bits of utter nonsense and shrewd bits of advice.

Gelett Burgess was best known, unfortunately, for his "Ode to A Purple Cow," which may have reflected the drinking habits of his clique:

I've never seen a purple cow,
I hope I never see one,
But ah, my foes, and ah, my friends,
I'd rather see than be one.

The verse was quoted so often that Burgess printed a second quatrain in a later issue:

Ah yes, I wrote the 'Purple Cow'
I'm sorry now I wrote it;
But I can tell you anyhow,
I'll kill you if you quote it.

The Lark sold for five cents a copy or for a yearly subscription of one dollar (Burgess said that mathematics had never been his strong point). Among its earliest contributors were Ernest Peixotto, Bruce Porter and Willis Polk, one of San Francisco's most promising young architects.

To put it mildly, Willis Polk was a satirist. His frequent critiques of San Francisco's domestic architecture—Nob Hill houses in particular—plus the fact that he was a fiendish practical joker, did little to advance what became a brilliant career. One of Polk's early contributions to The Lark was an advertisement for his forthcoming book, to be entitled *Architecture Moderne*, an edition limited to three copies, each to be "handsomely bound in half chicken leather." Polk, only five feet two inches tall, soon became the *enfant terrible* of San Francisco architecture, delighting the public with his scathing descriptions of the ostentatious piles built by millionaires. But in the field of Bay Area architecture he became a giant.

Born in Kentucky in 1865, Polk was the son of an architect-house builder; his father had been severely injured during the Civil War, and the impoverished family moved to St. Louis, where his mother had to find employment to help support the family. Willis, at the age of five, cooked meals for his parents and little sister. Polk loved architecture at an early age; he would draw pictures of houses on fences, scraps of paper or anything else that came to hand. In 1882, when he was just 17, he won a competition for the design of an Arkansas school house. When he confronted the judges for his reward, they took him to be an office boy. When he proved his identity as the prize winner, they told him to go out and play until they had completed the business at hand.

After gaining experience working for his father, he designed some houses in Kansas City. Then, still in his twenties, he went to New York to work for A. Page

Brown, a graduate of the Ecole des Beaux Arts, who had begun his architectural career in the offices of the esteemed McKim, Mead and White. At Brown's office and at Columbia University, where he studied the new Beaux Arts influences on American architecture, Polk became a devotee of the new school. When Brown came to San Francisco in 1889 to design the new Ferry Building, Polk came with him. "Architecture and I hit San Francisco about the same time," Polk remarked later. He wasn't far wrong.

Information on this period in Polk's life is sketchy at best, but we do know that he and Addison Mizner, a young dilletante architectural designer, moved in together in an old house on the peak of Russian Hill. The house had recently been purchased by Oakland financier Horace Livermore, whose family lived in a large house which would one day become Oakland's Claremont Country Club; they felt no need to move into an old San Francisco house dating to the 1860s. Following a recommendation from the Reverend Joseph Worcester, who had just moved from Piedmont to build four shingled houses across the way, Livermore bought the old Russian Hill house and with it a 50-vara lot. He invited Polk and Mizner to live there rent free, if they would undertake to make it a more habitable place. (See page 142)

Indeed, the two young men did such a creditable job on the old house, creating a beautiful redwood room with beamed ceilings, fluted ionic columns, and huge windows to encompass the magnificent view, that Livermore finally brought his family over to live in the place, leaving Polk and Mizner to find new quarters. Mizner's colorful career led him to Palm Beach, Florida, where he soon became famous for designing elaborate Mediterranean-style houses for the newly rich. Polk found quarters on the top of Russian Hill, and stayed on to become one of San Francisco's most revered architects.

Fronting Vallejo Street, on the crest of Russian Hill, were the three rustic cottages which the Swedenborgian Reverend Joseph Worcester, an amateur architect, designed for one of his parishioners, Mrs. David Madison. One of these three houses was the home of Colonel Rowan, who, in the Spanish-American War, gained fame by carrying the message to Garcia. At the end of the row, Reverend Worcester built a fourth cottage for himself. These four houses, two of which survive, influenced Willis Polk in his introduction of the rustic city house to San Francisco.

Polk built a house in a similar rustic style across from Reverend Worcester's cottage for Mrs. Williams, widow of Virgil Williams, the founder of the California Institute of Design. Traditionalists felt that this precipitous site

Willis Polk (Courtesy San Francisco Public Library)

would be impossible to build on, but Polk took on the challenge, waiving payment in exchange for the property's remaining twenty-foot frontage. Polk's parents purchased this part of the property and his father did much of the actual construction. The resulting modest shingle house revolutionized San Francisco's domestic architecture, for not only was it in the informal shingle style (strongly influenced by the Eastern "cottages" of Stanford White) but it also was designed on several levels to fit the contours of the steep hill.

This handsome house, standing today at 1013-1014 Vallejo Street, is a tribute to Polk's skills, for its 40-foot frontage drops down the side of the hill to a depth of 40 feet. With its high gables and small leaded windows, it is one of the few Polk houses influenced by medieval building traditions. Most of his other dwellings, whether shingled or stuccoed, are in the Mediterranean or Georgian styles.

In 1893 the Atkinson house, an Italianate villa at 1032 Broadway, built in 1853 of materials brought around the Horn, suffered extensive damage from a fire. Polk was commissioned to repair it. Thanks to his sensitive rebuilding, the character of the original house was retained, although one of his major revisions was to cover the exterior wooden walls with stucco. In keeping with the romantic spirit of the old house is Polk's fine redwood interior woodwork, which adds to the rustic, countrified mood. (See page 137)

Luckily, this house, which once knew such luminaries as Mark Twain, Robert Louis Stevenson and Ina Coolbrith, was rescued by its owner from the flames of 1906. Even the garden, designed by Bruce Porter, is as it was then. Thanks to those generations who have since been its occupants and custodians, it remains one of San Francisco's cherished landmarks.

The shingle style house which Willis Polk built on Vallejo Street, at the crest of Russian Hill, is modest and plain by comparison with the elaborate Victorian era houses that preceded it. One of the first Shingle style houses to be built in San Francisco, it was defiantly asymmetrical, rustic, informal, both inside and out. (Courtesy California State Library)

San Franciscans in the 1890s were learning to celebrate the beauty of the Bay Area's unspoiled scenery. Going together as organized groups or as single families, they rode the ferries to Marin County or the East Bay where they enjoyed camping and picnics in the wilds of Mt. Tamalpais or the Berkeley hills. It was natural, then, that the new Arts and Crafts movement would find an enthusiastic local following. Soon houses of redwood shingles, with interiors of paneled, polished natural redwood, began to spring up in the cities and towns around the bay.

Actually the shingled house was a part of vernacular American architecture; all along the Eastern seaboard are houses covered with hand-split cedar shingles, dating back to colonial times. In the late 1880s and '90s the firm of McKim, Mead and White designed huge shingled houses, modestly described as "beach cottages." Young architects like A. Page Brown, Bernard Maybeck, Ernest Coxhead and Willis Polk, all newcomers to the West Coast, began introducing shingle styles to both Los Angeles and the San Francisco Bay Area. Indeed, the style became so popular in San Francisco that it could easily have been mistaken for a local regional style. William F. Knowles, Albert Farr, and Julia Morgan were other important practitioners of the Shingle style.

Polk, Coxhead and Maybeck were soon designing rustic city houses out in the "new" Pacific Heights, as well as in other towns around the bay. While Maybeck liked to use Gothic or medieval elements in his designs, Polk preferred to juxtapose handsome Georgian details with his redwood shingle surfaces. Some of the most successful examples of this style are to be found along the Presidio Wall, in the 3200 block of Pacific Avenue. This row of shingled houses, ingeniously planned to conform to the shallow, irregularly shaped lots—the narrowest end is only 16 feet deep—are a credit to the ingenuity of their designers. Ernest Coxhead, an English Beaux Arts graduate who designed numerous shingled houses and rustic churches, was the architect of 3232 and 3234 Pacific.

Bruce Porter, Polk's artist friend, contributed strongly to these designs; he lived at 3234. He also had a hand in designing 3203 Pacific, across the street from this wedge-shaped row. Eli Sheppard, owner of the House of the Flag on Russian Hill, built this house as a wedding present for his daughter. When the engagement was broken, Sheppard sold the house to Bruce Porter, who in turn commissioned Willis Polk to remodel it. Polk changed the entire structure while maintaining its rustic appearance. Later Sheppard's daughter became Mrs. William Hilbert, and with the help of Bruce Porter designed her own rustic house at 3343 Pacific. Bernard Maybeck designed 3233 Pacific a few years later. This block of houses facing one another across Pacific Avenue is one of the most arresting areas in San

The interior of Polk's own house was mostly of natural redwood, making for a rather dark but cozy effect. The house, one of several that escaped the flames of 1906, follows the contours of the steep hill sloping down to Taylor Street and Broadway. (Courtesy California State Library)

Francisco. Most of the houses predate the 1906 fire, and thus dramatically mark the end of the eclectic Queen Anne style, dominant in San Francisco architecture until the turn of the century.

This change from Victorian to Beaux Arts architecture must be mainly attributed to the three men—Polk, Maybeck and Coxhead. They arrived in the wake of A. Page Brown, who met an untimely death in a carriage accident. Brown's most significant local contributions were the Ferry Building, the Crocker Bank Building on Market Street, now demolished, the grand Renaissance palazzo of Mrs. Peter Donahue, which once graced Broadway, and Trinity Episcopal Church at Bush and Gough Streets. But his disciples designed houses from Petaluma to Palo Alto, from Pacific Heights to Berkeley. Maybeck's superb English Tudor house at 3500 Jackson Street, built in 1909 for the Roos family, has a manorial Gothic great hall and beautifully executed carvings (see page 257). It is considered Maybeck's *tour de force*. His Palace of Fine Arts, built for the 1915 Fair, is discussed in a later chapter.

Willis Polk's first grand San Francisco house was the Italian mansion he designed in 1894 for George Gibbs at 2622 Jackson Street. For decades it housed the San Francisco Music and Arts Institute; it has recently been carefully restored, and is again a private home. Its beautifully detailed façade and interiors indicate Polk's ability to work in an academic style

equal to that of any finished Beaux Arts graduate, which of course Polk was not.

Another grand town house by Polk is the William Bourn house, built in 1894 at 2550 Webster Street (see page 258). This massive Georgian style house shows Polk's astonishing versatility. The Georgian style town house of klinker brick, with massive chimneys, seems a bit ponderous by modern-day standards, but it makes an impressive statement. Obviously the Bourns liked his work, for they commissioned him to design a stone house at the Empire Mine, which they owned, near Nevada City, as well as a large country house, "Madrono." Finally they called him in as a consultant for their magnificent country house, Filoli, built in Woodside in 1917, now the property of the National Trust. At about the same time (1916) Polk was busy with the design of Carolands, the enormous mansion built by Harriet Pullman in Hillsborough, which has perhaps the grandest stair hall in the Bay Area.

Polk's houses had an undeniable influence on San Francisco builders. *The Wave* noted that "the unpretentious solidity of Polk's work cheapens the gabled and turreted mansions around them." No longer would San Franciscans be content with bay-windowed, begabled villas crowded onto city lots.

There are far too many examples of Polk's work to enumerate them all, but one of his most successful projects was the handsome Mediterranean style house he designed in 1900 for Fanny Osborne, widow of Robert Louis Stevenson, on the northwest corner of Hyde and Lombard Streets. Although considerably enlarged, it has not been altered beyond recognition. Its arched entry and paired, arched windows are Polk's signature details (see page 141).

Of particular interest to this brief account of Polk's life and work is the house which still stands at 2139-2141 Buchanan Street, which he remodeled at the turn of the century for his new in-laws, the Frederico Barredas. Gertrude Atherton, in *Golden Gate Country*, devotes pages to the "romantic Barredas." Señor Barreda had brought his family to the U.S. when he had been appointed the minister from Peru. He had also served as Peruvian minister to Spain, France and England. After his retirement, Barreda had built a great house on Madison Avenue, New York, and a great country house, "Beaulieu," at Newport.

In the 1870s some colossal debacle wiped out Barreda's fortune, and he moved his family to San Francisco, where he felt he might better recoup his losses. The New York mansion was sold at a profit, and "Beaulieu" was purchased by Mrs. Astor, a close friend of Madame Barreda, "for sentiment's sake." Of course, the remarkable Barredas were lionized by San Francisco society. There were four beautiful daughters and a son. Christina, the youngest daughter, became Mrs. Willis Polk in 1900. She was to share Polk's triumphs and frequent vicissitudes until her husband's death in 1924.

Polk's work included scores of San Francisco homes and some of the city's major buildings. Less well known is the influence he exerted in the effort to preserve San Francisco's architectural history.

One of Polk's major contributions was the preservation of the James C. Flood mansion on Nob Hill. After the 1906 fire only the exterior walls of the house remained. The Pacific Union Club bought the property with the intention of finishing the demolition and building a new clubhouse. Polk convinced the building committee that the old walls were stable. By adding an extra floor he modified the awkward tower which projected above the front, and by adding the curved wings on each side he provided the additional space the club needed. Thus he preserved the sole survivor of Nob Hill's bonanza mansions, actually improving the design in the process.

Another example of Polk's enthusiasm for San Francisco's past comes from his restoration of Mission Dolores in 1916. Polk carefully studied the techniques in which the mission Indians had been trained to build the California missions—the old ways of making roof tiles and fashioning the ancient beams. In those days, when restoration was done at all, it generally followed the whims of the restorers, who often cared little for authenticity. Polk employed a method of proper, even scientific restoration. So subtle was his work that the mission's biographers often claimed that it had never been restored at all. If he had done nothing else, Willis Polk's preservation of some of the city's most treasured landmarks deserves the highest commendation and gratitude.

During this period, America's eastern architects were creating a colonial revival style, and California's architects were determined to unearth an architectural tradition which was unique to the West. In this search for a historic style, the Mission Revival was born. Californians are only too aware of what this movement led to. It began with railroad stations, such as those put up by the Southern Pacific and Santa Fe. It was carried on into the creation of "Mission Style" bungalows with roughly plastered walls and fake beams. There was even a "Mission Style" in furniture design, which produced a popular version of the Morris chair. These effusions grew out of the Arts and Crafts movement in which, for the first time, styles were created for home makers of modest means. It was an era of klinker brick fireplaces, board-and-batten paneling, "airplane roofs," and redwood logs hollowed out for hanging ferns on the front porch.

Next, in dramatic contrast, came the "Spanish colonial" revival. This style was first seen at the San Francisco and San Diego Expositions of 1915. By borrowing from the great baroque cathedrals and palaces of Spain and Mexico (certainly not from any local historic models other than the missions), Californian architects "recreated" a style which supposedly harkened back to California's elegant Spanish manorial past. Their efforts, which had absolutely no basis in fact, met with varying degrees of success. In truth, however, it must be acknowledged that red tile roofs, pastel stucco and arcaded patios were well suited to the Mediterranean light and climate of California, and this revival style ushered in a trend toward indoor-outdoor informality which characterizes California life today. The Presidio has a number of Mission Revival structures dating from the 1920s. Countless schools and colleges were built in the style. Although no longer as exuberant as it was in the 1920s, when all of California seemed to "go Spanish," this movement continues to this day. Currently, architects are likely to call it "Early California."

If Willis Polk ever regretted the role he played in this Mission Revival movement, he never said so explicitly. However, he did suggest once in an architectural journal that adapting religious architecture created by missionaries and natives to the needs of modern civilization could only invite ridicule.

No discussion of Willis Polk and his contributions to the "San Francisco Renaissance" should overlook his designs for and modification of San Francisco's commercial buildings. To list just a few, the Kohl or Howard Building at 400 Montgomery Street (1904), the Insurance Exchange, 433 California Street, the San Francisco Water Department, 425 Mason Street; the Hobart Building, 582 Market Street (1914), the Merchants' Exchange at California and Montgomery, (1902), and the Mills Building (1908).

Polk's most famous commercial design is the Hallidie Building at 130 Sutter Street (1917). The all-glass façade, generally recognized as the introduction of the glass curtain wall which has become a cliche of modern architecture, was actually an effort on Polk's part to create an attractive façade within a low budget, and quickly. The glass façade was hung, curtain like, away from the actual structural frame of the building, in a separate frame of elaborate cast iron, with ornate fire escapes at either side. The ornamental iron fretwork relieves the cold severity of an all-glass wall, and the result is highly decorative. The Hallidie Building was commissioned by the University of California, and has always been painted in blue and gold. It was renovated in 1979 by Kaplan, McLaughlan & Diaz, architects.

In this radical departure from the Beaux Arts tradition, one may surmise what influence Polk's genius may have had on the architecture of a later day. Willis Polk died in 1924.

THE CITY MOVES WEST

FOR THREE DECADES after 1855, the lands west of Divisadero Street, the border of the Western Addition, remained an empty wasteland, inhabited mainly by rabbits, raccoons, and seagulls. A few farmers struggled to grow produce in the moist pockets between sand dunes, and the gravediggers and gardeners who worked at the cemeteries built cottages for their families far out in the country. A number of these cottages remain today, along McAllister Street west of Parker; a particularly interesting cottage stands at the corner of McAllister and North Willard, with a truly magnificent California Buckeye tree in the front yard. And there were other, more important signposts of the westward movement of a burgeoning population.

In the 1860s, seven decades before the sand dunes became covered by endless rows of houses the developers called "Junior Fours," when the Richmond and Sunset districts were as yet unheard of, even before Golden Gate park became a reality, the Point Lobos Toll Road was built to carry adventurous travelers out to Ocean Beach and Seal Rocks. It was a difficult and expensive project for those who laid out the first macadam street in San Francisco. Over 800 kegs of blasting powder were needed to clear away the sand hills.

These were the days when San Franciscans, visiting one of the far-flung farmhouses west of Van Ness Avenue, packed an overnight bag. Travel on the horse trails, which often disappeared under shifting sands, was especially hazardous after sunset, when highwaymen sometimes stopped the traveler to relieve him of cash or a gold watch and chain. Today it hardly seems possible that the broad, heavily traveled Geary Boulevard was once the Point Lobos Toll Road.

Lone Mountain Cemetery, established in 1853, was what first drew San Franciscans to venture far west of the city limits, which were first at Taylor, then at Larkin Street, and still later at Divisadero. Before that date, the dead were buried where they fell, or in the back yard, or eventually in Yerba Buena cemetery, at today's 8th and Market Streets. By the time the Western Addition was laid out in 1855, it was already clear that commercial development would make the old cemetery land too valuable. Several far-sighted investors bought some 350 acres west of the Bush Street termination at Presidio Avenue.

Bush Street, the only road leading west of Taylor Street, became a toll road for visitors to the new cemetery, bounded by today's California, Presidio, Geary, and Arguello Streets. Other cemeteries were soon established around the base of Lone Mountain. In 1860 the Roman Catholics purchased the acreage now bounded by Turk, Masonic, Geary and Parker Streets. In 1864, thirty acres were set aside for the Masonic Cemetery, bounded by Turk, Parker and Arguello Streets.

In the Victorian age, when pleasure and sorrow were not considered mutually exclusive, weekly visits to the family burial plot were an established custom. Virtually every family had relatives underground, in an era of large families, high infant mortality, and low life expectancy. Patterned after Boston's Mount Auburn, or Brooklyn's Greenwood Cemeteries, Lone Mountain, with a huge cross at its summit, visible from the distant

A row of Stick Style cottages, lining McAllister Street west of Parker, is a pocket of history overlooked by many San Franciscans, who concentrate instead on the magnificent St. Ignatius Church across Parker Street. These one-story houses, built in the 1880s and 1890s, when the area around Lone Mountain was filled with cemeteries, very likely housed the families of gravediggers, gardeners, and other workers in the fields of the dead. The cottages form the westernmost row of Victorians in the city, although individual houses — for farmers or entrepreneurs along the Geary Street highway, may predate these. (Courtesy James Heig)

city, gradually became a park-like place of winding paths, dotted by the showy family crypts of the affluent. Families brought picnics out to the cemetery and spent an enjoyable afternoon strolling the flower-bordered paths and pointing out the graves of old friends and famous or notorious city characters. It was generally hoped that the visit would not be marred by the sight of an actual funeral. The name "Lone Mountain" seemed to many to be too mournful, so in time it was changed to "Laurel Hill."

Many visitors, having come this far west, wanted to continue their journey to the sparkling waters and clean sands of Ocean Beach. Developers began planning the paved road which headed more or less straight west to the bluff above the Cliff House. By the 1870s there were horse-drawn omnibuses, and even a little steam train, to carry the multitudes

heading west to the beach. Lone Mountain and its sepulchral neighbors were now, more often than not, only stopping-off places for the fun-loving citizens of the young city.

Then, in 1900, the Board of Supervisors passed an ordinance which forbade the burial of dead within the city limits. In January, 1917, the Board of Health declared that Calvary, Masonic, Odd Fellows, and Laurel Hill cemeteries were "a public nuisance, a menace, and a detriment to the public health and welfare." These cemeteries, along with Nevi Shalome and Gibbath Olom, the Jewish cemeteries in what is now Dolores Park, were to be closed, and the dead removed from San Francisco, within fourteen months. The caretakers of Calvary, Masonic and Odd Fellows complied, and the disinterred bodies were reburied outside the city, mainly in Colma, in San Mateo County. The

The San Francisco Columbarium, an architectural treasure unfamiliar to many residents, stands at the end of Loraine Street, off Anza. Built in 1898, it houses the ashes of a number of prominent early San Franciscans, including the very accomplished Klumpke sisters and their father. One stone tablet reads: "Dorothea Klumpke Roberts, Astronomer, 1861-1942. She loved the stars too fondly to be fearful of the night." (Courtesy James Heig)

proprietors of Laurel Hill, however, held out against the ordinance for 28 years. Finally, on a vote of the citizens of the city, the last cemetery was closed in 1940. Those remains who had no families to claim them were buried in a mass grave at Forest Lawn Cemetery in Colma. Today the only reminder that these burial sites ever existed near Lone Mountain is the beautiful domed San Francisco Memorial Columbarium, which stands at what was once the entrance to the Odd Fellows Cemetery.

The elegant Columbarium, built in 1898 to house cremated remains, technically was not a burial site, and so did not fall under the ordinance prohibiting burials within the city limits; it escaped demolition when the surrounding cemeteries were removed. Its architect, B.J.S. Cahill, created a domed circular temple in the Roman Baroque style, with a rotunda reaching a height of 75 feet. At the apex is a stained-glass cap some twenty feet in diameter. After many years of neglect, the Columbarium was acquired by the Neptune Society, and has recently been beautifully restored and painted. Memorial services and even concerts and weddings are held in the magnificent rotunda, one of San Francisco's least-known architectural treasures, at 1 Loraine Court, off Anza.

Gertrude Atherton, in My San Francisco (1946), referred to the "giants" who built San Francisco: "The very ground trembled at their tread, and now they lie forgotten in Lone Mountain Cemetery." Not only were their remains moved away, even their tombstones were used by city engineers to build a seawall along the Marina Green. On days when the water is calm and clear, one can read inscriptions on some of the stones.

This famous photograph of the third Cliff House, taken on December 29, 1896, is sometimes mistakenly assumed to show a lightning bolt at upper left. Actually the sky is full of roiling clouds, backlit by a sun low in the west. (Author's collection)

The Cliff House

Four successive structures have been built on the bluff at the end of the Point Lobos Road, overlooking Seal Rocks and the natural arch formed by crashing waves. The first building on the promontory, known as Seal Rock House, was erected in 1858. The first Cliff House opened October 15, 1863. It burnt a year later. The second began as a four-square little structure housing a restaurant and bar, but in time wings for guest rooms were added. The proprietor, Captain Junius G. Foster, formerly of the Pacific Steamship Service, took great pains to maintain a respectable clientele. "It was like a family gathering," he later recalled, for in a city as small as San Francisco, all the better families who came to his resort knew one another.

About two miles south of the Cliff House, another resort, the Ocean House, was built of timbers from ships that had piled up along the coast. It enjoyed an unsullied reputation until the mid-1860s, when the Ocean View Racetrack was built on a site near today's Sloat Boulevard, from 26th to 34th Avenues. The patrons were members of a "fast set," given to hard drinking, gambling, and other sorts of fast living. Some of them came to the Cliff House. While Captain Foster frowned on such conduct, he could hardly turn patrons away. Many of them were members of San Francisco's most affluent and prominent families.

The builders of the Mission Toll Road, which had been enormously successful, in 1864 set about building the Point Lobos Toll Road, a macadam thoroughfare leading from the city in the east through the sand hills of the Western Addition, past the cemeteries at Lone Mountain and on through the shifting sand dunes to the promontory above Seal Rocks. No longer was the six-mile trip an all-day ordeal, with the danger of being swamped in treacherous sandslides. Beside the main

Adolph Sutro's Cliff House, an utterly fantastic hotel and restaurant perched on rocks above the sea, seems to be built for the ages, but it lasted only eleven years, from 1896 to 1907. (Courtesy Roy D. Graves collection)

road, near today's Clement Street, the builders laid down a clay raceway, almost two miles long, where adventurous riders or drivers could show off their horses and make wagers to be paid off at the Cliff House bar.

Soon, on a fine day, those mournful processions heading out Bush Street toward the cemeteries had to swallow the dust of gentlemen, wearing high hats and elegant riding clothes, astride their blooded horses, and the equipages of San Francisco's elite, bowling along the Point Lobos Road for a pleasant sojourn at one of the beach resorts. Everyone recognized James Ben Ali Haggin's six-in-hand tally-ho coach, or the carriage of Mrs. Peter Donahue with its high glass windows and a team of matching bays, or Mrs. Latham's brown, satin-lined carriage with yellow wheels, or the blue sea-shell carriage carrying Mrs. Hensley and her friends. And there were neat broughams and basket phaetons with sleek Dalmatians trotting behind. Merchants, stock-

brokers, bankers, and men about town, perhaps after an evening of revelry, would be seen next morning taking the fresh sea air. Those who followed the cocktail route, beginning at the Palace or Baldwin Hotels, often ended up in the wee hours of the morning over "a cold bottle and a hot bird" at the Cliff House.

With the advent of the transcontinental railroad in 1869, tourists began coming to San Francisco in greater and greater numbers, to see for themselves all those unbelievable things they had heard about the gilded city by the Golden Gate. The Cliff House, with its magnificent view of the Pacific and the noisy sea lions basking on the rocks below, became an essential part of the San Francisco experience, and a fitting climax to the tedious train ride from the East Coast. The Cliff House became so popular that as many as 1200 teams and carriages were often tied up at the hitching rails stretching along the Cliff House road. The men drank cocktails in

Horses and buggies face a small army of pedestrians on the way from Ocean Beach up to Adolph Sutro's magnificent Cliff House. The rocky cliff on the right side of the road is the alarmingly unstable underpinning of Sutro Heights; Sutro eventually had the hillside surfaced with naturalistic concrete rocks to stop frequent landslides. The surfacing survives today. (Courtesy Roy Graves collection)

the bar, while the ladies sat in the glass-enclosed porches, watching the sea lions below and sipping champagne or sherry or milk punch, a mixture of whiskey or brandy, milk and sugar, thought to be great restorative. On special holidays, throngs lined the Cliff House terraces to watch the fearless James Cooke or the daring Rose Celeste walk a tightrope stretched above Seal Rocks and the booming surf below.

Some tourists came only for the view. Captain Foster liked to recount the story of 170 tourists from Massachusetts, who ordered more than 200 glasses of water and three lemonades. "Hell," he said, "two prospectors and their girls spend more money for one dinner than the whole state of Massachusetts does in an entire day."

Gradually the growing crowds of tourists–and the bank crash of the 1870s–kept Captain Foster's best customers away. He began to allow a less elegant, rowdier crowd to patronize the place, and the Cliff House lost its status as a resort for the "right people." Still, while the boys from the mining camps might be allowed to drink and scuffle with their Barbary Coast lady friends in the private dining rooms, a man could always take his family there to dine with complete propriety. Thus Captain Foster hung on until 1883, when Adolph Sutro bought the Cliff House and brought in a new manager.

Then, on a January night in 1887, the schooner *Parallel*, containing forty tons of gunpowder, crashed onto the rocks directly below the Cliff House porch. The resultant blast was reportedly heard a hundred miles inland, and the Cliff House lost most of its north wing. Repairs were made, and business continued as usual until Christmas, 1894, when fire from a defective flue reduced the entire structure to ashes within minutes.

The energetic Adolph Sutro held a competition, won by C.J. Colley and Emil S. Lemme, for the design of the spectacular third Cliff House, completed in 1896. Fronted by a Gothic-arched porte cochere, it rose a full six stories above its rocky eminence. With its glassed-in verandas, towers, and fancy pinnacles, crowned by a bright blue roof, it looked like the most ornate sandcastle ever devised, projecting over the crashing surf with a kind of giddy assurance. At the time of the 1906 disaster, the eastern newspapers claimed it had fallen into the sea. This was untrue, but the following year it did burn to its stone foundations.

In 1908 the fourth Cliff House rose within the stone walls which had once supported the great wooden castle. With its heavily corniced flat roof, the new replacement conveyed at least a certain dignity. Some thirty years later the Whitney brothers, owners of Playland at the Beach, remodeled it in a style which can only be called unfortunate. Only the finely-proportioned dining room overlooking Seal Rocks remains, a happy reminder of an old and honorable tradition in San Francisco. The property is now owned by the Golden Gate National Recreation Area.

Adolph Sutro stands in front of his beloved house on Sutro Heights, on the hill above the Cliff House. Sutro, a brilliant and tireless engineer, inventor, builder, politician, and rare book collector, allowed nothing to stand in his way in the creation of a splendid recreation center for all San Franciscans. (Courtesy San Francisco Public Library)

ADOLPH SUTRO

THE BUILDER of the third Cliff House, Adolph Sutro, was a generous benefactor to the city, and one of the most colorful men of his era. He was more daring and far more interesting than any of the Silver Kings or the Big Four. Born of a wealthy Jewish family in Aachen, Germany, he began his career as a cigar merchant in San Francisco in 1850, at the age of twenty. But he was well educated, and his background in engineering was not to be wasted. In 1864 he approached William Ralston with a scheme to run a four-mile tunnel under Nevada's Mount Davidson, where the Comstock millions were being mined, in order to remove the water and poisonous gases which constantly took the lives of miners. At first Ralston, director of the Bank of California, supported Sutro's novel position that the miners' safety might be just as important as the stockholders' dividends. But the bank's directors, unwilling to share their wealth with this newcomer, took a strong stand against Sutro's plan. He spent fifteen years getting financing and building his tunnel before finally selling his interest in 1880 for something over $1 million.

Sutro next bought several miles of sand dunes on the northwestern slope of Twin Peaks, and planted what is today Sutro Forest. On a sunny afternoon in 1879, capitalist Adolph Sutro and his daughter, Emma, were out driving together toward the hillside above the Cliff House, when they came upon a white cottage set in a deep garden. "Never have I seen a view to equal this!" cried Sutro. "If the house is for sale, I want it." A knock on the door brought the owner, Sam Tetlow, the well-known proprietor of the Bella Union gambling house, saloon and theatre on Portsmouth Plaza. Business at the Bella Union wasn't what it once had been, and Tetlow agreed to the immediate sale of his house and acreage. Four years

The entrance stairway of Sutro Baths, flanked by gardens of fern and palm, led down to the dressing rooms and promenades. An enormous mirror at far right allowed visitors to be sure their dress was proper for the festive occasion. (Courtesy California State Library)

later Sutro bought the Cliff House, along with surrounding acreage, and began years of work on improvements at Point Lobos. Sutro Heights, on the high hilltop just east of the Cliff House, was his 21-acre estate, with a sweeping view over the Pacific, from the Marin headlands down the sandy length of Ocean Beach. At this point Sutro owned about one-twelfth of the land in San Francisco.

His house was not as ostentatious as the Nob Hill palaces of the Silver Kings. With its glassed-in porches and observation tower, it was more comfortable and functional than showy. But Sutro spent a fortune on his gardens, lining the winding paths and geometric flower beds with scores of carved and cast stone or plaster statues. He bought so many statues at once that they were shipped from Belgium as ballast on the sailing vessels coming around the Horn. The gardens were startling, to say the least. At first glance, a visitor might think he was in a cemetery. There were centaurs and fauns, as well as figures of every deity known to mythology. Graceful dancing girls modeled after Canova's works stood a few feet from Laocöon and sons ensnared by pythons, while nearby several Venuses circled the

Apollo Belvedere at the top of a flowered hillock. Mixed with these noble figures were characters from the novels of Charles Dickens or the fairy tales of the Brothers Grimm. At the end of a long, palm-lined allee were huge, elaborate wooden entrance gates, flanked on either side by great stone lions. A public-spirited man, Sutro did not keep his treasures locked away. On any pleasant day from nine to five, the gates were thrown open, and scores of San Franciscans enjoyed strolling through his gardens.

While his splendid new Cliff House was going up, Sutro, a Populist, went into politics. Crusading against corruption and championing the working man, he was elected mayor of San Francisco in 1894, in spite of strong opposition from the newspapers. He donated 26 acres of land for the site of the University of California, San Francisco, on the north slope of Twin Peaks. He amassed "the finest private library in America," much of which was destroyed in 1906; the important collection on California history is now at San Francisco State University.

And just north of the Cliff House he built Sutro Baths, the architectural wonder of its time, with seven

The Sutro Baths, here shown near the end of construction, opened in 1896, to the astonishment of all visitors. With acres of glass overhead, seven swimming pools, and countless amenities, events and attractions, the baths were unique in the world. (Courtesy California State Library)

indoor pools (six with salt water, one with fresh), a two-acre roof made of 100,000 panes of glass, stained-glass windows, 517 dressing rooms, nine clubrooms, huge potted palm trees, and a museum full of paintings, photographs, stuffed birds and animals, totem poles, mummies, knights' armor, and a collection of mechanical wonders. Construction was completed in 1894, but Sutro delayed the official opening because of a dispute with the Southern Pacific Railroad, which wanted to charge a fare of ten cents for the ride out to the ocean. Sutro insisted that was too dear. He built his own electric tram line, the Sutro R.R. Co., to Point Lobos, charging five cents fare. Only then, in 1896, did the baths officially open.

In architectural daring and ingenuity, the Sutro Baths attempted to outdo the original Palace Hotel, and they were far more popular with San Franciscans. Adolph Sutro was a curious combination of inventor, idealist and showman. He devised a complex pumping and filter system to bring two million gallons of sea water into the pools each day. "I've always held swimming to be the very best exercise," he said. "It requires the use of all the members of the body, it is invigorating and pleasureful and keeps the circulation free and quick. The ocean water is particularly stimulating." The baths supplied bathing costumes and towels for all patrons; its laundry could handle 20,000 suits and 40,000 towels per day. Live music was provided, not only at the baths but also on the electric train bringing customers from the city. Thousands of people thronged the million-dollar natatorium, to swim, to listen to music, to watch famed Australian swimmer Charles Cavill swim around seal rocks (who would do it today?) and then perform his "famous Monte Christo act" in 1897. A "Monster May Day Festival" in 1897, advertised as "Lots of fun for the little folks, a beautiful queen, triple May poles, 1000 children in grand march and the butterfly ballet," brought 9,000 spectators to the baths. There was an amusement park with thrilling rides, as well as endless contests, exhibitions, celebrities, ceremonies. The Sutro Baths were the equivalent, for their time, of Marine World or Disneyland, except that the patrons were far more actively involved, rather than being mere passive observers. And admission was only 25 cents for adults, 10 cents for children, plus the 5-cent train fare.

The largest pool in the entire Sutro natatorium was often the scene of swimming and diving competitions with hundreds of competitors and thousands of spectators. The judges, sitting on a floating platform, had a good view, but often got splashed. (Courtesy California State Library)

Sutro's death in 1898 placed responsibility for the Cliff House, Sutro Heights and Sutro Baths, along with the rest of his real estate holdings, on his family. Upkeep was an enormous burden, and without Adolph's enthusiasm and drive the baths gradually lost their appeal. The family tried unsuccessfully to persuade the city to buy the million-dollar bath house for $687,000 in 1912, and in 1919 offered the business for sale for $410,000, but there were no takers. In 1934 the biggest pool was converted to an ice-skating rink, and other improvements were made to attract new customers. Finally, in 1952, the Sutro family sold the baths to George Whitney, owner of Playland at the Beach, for $250,000. Whitney kept the skating rink open until 1966, when he closed the place for good. A few months later fire destroyed the bath house where so many thousands of San Franciscans had found healthy recreation and excitement for seventy years. The Golden Gate National Recreation bought the site for $5.5 million in 1980. Today throngs of visitors line the sidewalks where the entrance used to be, look down into the huge scooped-out bowl of earth and rock, and try to tell their children and grandchildren what a visit to Sutro Baths meant to San Franciscans growing up in the early years of this century.

Adolph Sutro's support of Mike De Young's efforts to bring the Midwinter Fair to Golden Gate Park in 1894 earned him the eternal enmity of John McLaren, who hated to see any buildings or statuary intrude into his hard-won oasis of greenery. Years after Sutro's death, when his heirs generously donated Sutro Heights to the city as a public park, crusty old John McLaren had his revenge. He had Sutro's collection of statues, which McLaren called "stuckies," hauled off to be used as fill. The public assisted in the depletion: it was a popular San Francisco pastime for those winding up a rowdy drinking party to say, "Let's go out to Sutro's and steal a statue!" Very probably at McLaren's instigation, Sutro's house was leveled. Today, what remains of the romantic Sutro Gardens is still open to the public as a city park.

The Japanese Tea Garden, beloved of millions of visitors, began as an exhibit, shown here, at the 1894 World Exposition in Golden Gate Park. This picture is from an 1894 color lithograph. (Author's collection)

GOLDEN GATE PARK

IN A BOOK DEDICATED mainly to San Francisco architecture, it may come as a surprise that Golden Gate Park should be mentioned at all, and yet the park has several pre-1906 structures worthy of note.

Frederick Law Olmstead, designer of New York's Central Park, was invited to San Francisco in 1866 to discuss a proposal for a park in the western reaches of the city. A large acreage was set aside in the area then designated as "Outside Lands" – that is, lands not yet included within the official city limits. Engineer William Hammond Hall, the first park superintendent, drew up a magnificent plan for a park in accordance with Olmstead's principles of design, with roads and pathways following the natural contours of the terrain. To his eternal credit, Hall laid out a superbly landscaped park in the midst of sand dunes.

The city in 1866 hardly seemed large enough to warrant the grand expenditure of $1.3 million (the surprisingly high official appraisal value of the land) for a park. The city actually paid out $810,565 to squatters whose claims to the land were probably spurious anyway. Graft, corruption, and crooked politics added to the difficulties. In the 1870s the huge park gradually took shape. Then John McLaren came to work as an employee in the park in the 1880s. In 1887 he was elevated to the position of park superintendent. Despite his reputation for irascibility, "Uncle John" was beloved by most citizens for his 57 years of dedication to what he called "my park." Anecdotes about his devotion and his ingenious planting methods are legion. When city officials asked him what he would like for his 90th birthday present, he asked for 10,000 yards of good manure.

The Conservatory of Flowers was built in 1879 with donations from a number of contributors, including James Lick, whose name is also attached to the Lick Observatory on Mount Hamilton, near San Jose, and (unfortunately) to a freeway. The Conservatory was closed because of storm damage in 1996, but is currently being renovated. (Courtesy San Francisco Public Library)

McLaren constantly battled to keep benevolent societies and ethnic organizations from putting statues all over his park. When a statue was installed he tucked it into an inconspicuous spot and planted greenery around it which would conceal it entirely. Even the life-size statue of McLaren is not easy to find. He fought against the Midwinter Fair of 1894 because it brought buildings into the park which he feared would become permanent; his fears were justified. The De Young Museum and the Japanese Tea Garden were both remnants of the 1894 Fair.

The two windmills at the park's western edge serve as excellent examples of McLaren's ingenuity, for not only were they quaint and decorative, they pumped thousands of gallons of underground water each hour, thus alleviating a serious water shortage. The first windmill, no longer operable, was built in 1902. The northern one, erected in 1905, donated by Samuel Murphy and named in his honor, has been restored, thanks to a campaign led by the late Eleanor Rossi Reno, daughter of former mayor Angelo Rossi. The huge sails, an impressive feature of the windmill, have not been used to pump water since 1927, when an electric pump was installed.

McLaren Lodge, built in 1897 to serve as the superintendent's residence, is a fine example of Richardson Romanesque design, popular in the 1890s. (See page 244) Its mellow sandstone walls harmonize with the rustic setting; the interior and the furnishings complement the exterior design. Edward Swain was the architect. The lodge is currently being converted into a museum and information center for Golden Gate Park

Also in the Richardson Romanesque style is the Children's House, built in 1885 with funds donated by William Sharon, a Comstock millionaire. This jewel of stone masonry was designed by the firm of Percy and Hamilton, with William Hall as consulting engineer. The interior was badly burnt in the 1960s, but has been rebuilt and carefully restored as a center for arts and crafts. The building overlooks Children's Playground, the first such facility to be built in the United States. Old photographs show families in full Victorian dress, enjoying themselves in giant swings, or riding the carousel, recently restored to magnificent condition.

The Midwinter Fair of 1894, sponsored and promoted by Mike De Young and the *Chronicle*, left the exquisite Japanese Tea Garden, whose moon gate, pagoda, arched bridge, and beautiful plantings have delighted visitors for more than a hundred years. The band concourse with its pleached sycamores and handsome Roman arched and colonnaded band stand were gifts of Claus Spreckels in 1889.

The Conservatory of flowers, a little reminiscent of London's great Crystal Palace, is the earliest and certainly the most spectacular contribution made by private citizens to the park. The building, containing some 15,000 square feet, was ordered from New York in 1876 by James Lick, an early philanthropist, who had built a luxury hotel downtown. Lick later built the great Lick Observatory on Mount Hamilton, above San Jose. He was a man of modest personal habits, but his strong interest in horticulture led him to order this huge conservatory for his otherwise modest country place in San Jose. Lick died before the conservatory could be built, and his will provided that it be left to the Society of California Pioneers. Through the generous contributions of 27 wealthy San Franciscans, the conservatory was erected in Golden Gate Park in 1879. In 1883, when it was devastated by fire, Charles Crocker and others contributed funds for its restoration. A storm in the winter of 1995-96 did millions of dollars of damage to the glass building. Repairs are not complete as of this writing.

Sigmund Stern Grove — Another important element of the San Francisco Parks system is Sigmund Stern Grove. Sloat Boulevard west of 19th Avenue was the site of a race track shown on an 1868 map of San Francisco. Just to the north was a small pond, which today, drained and partially filled, is the site of the amphitheater in Sigmund Stern Grove. This grove of massive old eucalyptus trees conceals in its depths a charming little glade and the former Trocadero Inn, the only remnant of the old days of horse races and the bon vivants who patronized them. Dating to the 1880s, the one-story Victorian cottage with wrap-around porches was owned and developed by George Greene, a pioneer who named it the Trocadero Rancho. The inn, which has witnessed many notable gatherings, is best remembered by old-timers as the last hideout of Abe Ruef, the corrupt political boss who was sent to prison in 1907.

Mrs. Sigmund Stern, a beautiful, wealthy, civic-minded member of the playground commission, used to take drives with John McLaren in search of sites for new playgrounds. He took her to see the Trocadero Inn with its enchanting vale below the house. Mrs. Stern promptly bought the parcel and presented it to the city as a memorial to her husband. In 1938 Mrs. Stern, aided by other subscribers, established the Sigmund Stern Grove Festival Committee, whose purpose was to provide, free for all who cared to attend, the best in symphony, opera, ballet and concert music. Enormous audiences of 10,000 or more have made the Stern Grove summer concerts Mrs. Stern's crowning achievement.

THE PANHANDLE DISTRICT

FILLING A WHOLE BLOCK bounded by Fell, Lyon, Hayes and Baker Streets, is the former Southern Pacific Hospital, built in 1907, a monumental example of Neo-Classical architecture, perfectly balanced and nobly columned, and surrounded by an exceptionally fine iron fence. The architect was Daniel Pattarson. The huge central building, along with the dependencies behind it, has recently been splendidly renovated for use as a retirement center. The complex is San Francisco Landmark #191.

Across Hayes Street at the corner of Baker is one of the more important Queen Annes surviving in the city. The old mansion served for some years as a funeral home. It has recently been carefully restored and its side garden replanted, as the Brahma Kumaris Meditation Center.

At 301 Lyon Street, at the corner of Fell, is the Thomas Clunie house, built in 1897 and designed by William Curlett, one of San Francisco's favored architects. Clunie, a lawyer, politician and real estate speculator, went to considerable expense to install one of the first telephones in this house. One of only two surviving Queen Annes with an open balcony in the tower (the other, designed by Curlett, is at 1409 Sutter Street), this house is city landmark #128. It is now a bed-and-breakfast inn.

The earliest structure in this area was a roadhouse called "Sans Souci" (translated as "without sorrow" or "carefree"), standing on the bank of a small lake of the same name, near Divisadero and Fell Streets. Popular throughout the 1850s, the resort consisted of a ten-room house, a stable, hen house, dovecote, coach shed, flower garden, greenhouse, ox shed, swing, and bowling alley, according to an 1856 inventory. It belonged to Dutch merchant William Fell. Newspaper columnist Edward Morphy described the resort in glowing terms:

A great resort for gentlemen who appreciated pleasant dinners and other comforts of that kind. Game abounded all about. Quail and ducks were plentiful in season; delicious broiled chickens were always available, and the cellars were amply stocked. The only way of getting there was on horseback or by Shank's mare; but sometimes ladies, duly escorted by admiring swains, found their way thus far from the haunts of the city; and generally it was a pleasant time with delicious memories.

In the winter of 1861-62 Sans Souci Lake burst its banks and flowed away to the southeast, inundating Francois Pioche's country estate, the Hermitage, and other houses near Mission Dolores. With the lake gone, the resort became a private home, surviving at least until 1918. When the city limits were extended, public transportation followed, with car lines extended westward along Hayes and McAllister Streets in the 1880s. By 1890 people had begun building large houses on what had been open fields around the Sans Souci resort. One of the city's largest clusters of Queen Anne Victorians, many of them with turrets, is centered near the intersection of Fulton and Broderick. Those facing Broderick Street on the hill toward McAllister are especially noteworthy for their variety and ingenuity of decoration. The houses in this area form a kind of textbook of the Queen Anne style. (See pages 132-133)

Of particular interest here is the architectural transition which began in the 1880s near the Panhandle, where the Queen Anne and Stick styles mingle, with Queen Anne becoming dominant above Haight Street. Further up the slopes the dwellings of the Craftsman era begin to take precedence, with many notable examples of shingle-style houses, plus one or two striking Art Nouveau designs. Still further up, the neighborhoods show a mixture of stuccoed Mediterranean-style villas, half-timbered Tudors, and American Colonials, most dating from the 1920s and 30s. Finally there are the duplexes and single-family houses of the post-WWII years, when developers and contractors built, often without benefit of an architect, and often on lots that had previously been considered too steep to allow construction, in a style of Spartan simplicity. Sometimes the older houses, originally built on large lots in a semi-rural neighborhood, lost their side yards to newer construction, so that one finds a Queen Anne manor shoulder to shoulder with a Craftsman cottage or a pair of Mediterranean flats from a much later era. Here, then, in this one small area, one can see virtually every aspect of San Francisco's architectural, social, and economic change for the past century.

At 400 Clayton Street, on the corner of Oak, is a handsome neo-Georgian house, replete with engaged columns, pedimented windows, and a formal entrance. This house catches the eye because its sober exterior stands out among the riotous Victorians nearby. Designed in 1895 by Ernest Coxhead for one Alonzo McFarland, the house is an early example of the Beaux Arts style which would sweep the city after the turn of the century.

One block south is a pair of rather nondescript flats, at 1890 Page Street, where James L. Flood, son of the Comstock king, lived with his wife, a former chorus girl from St. Louis. Their adopted child, Constance, in later years became the center of a series of court hearings which lasted for twenty years. When the first Mrs. Flood died, Jim married her sister, Maude, who apparently didn't care for Constance. The girl was sent to a convent school in Santa Barbara, where she stayed for years without ever being allowed to visit her father. When she graduated and was preparing to go to college, she was told she had no relatives. She had only a dim recollection of her adoptive parents. Wanting to establish her own identity, she sued the Floods to claim her proper place in the family. After years of litigation, the Floods conceded that she was indeed their child, and made a sizeable settlement on her. Within a year, Constance, still a young woman, died of exhaustion caused by the strain of all those hearings. Her story is recorded in a book entitled *The Strange Case of Constance Flood* (1956), by Willa Iverson, still occasionally to be found in good used bookstores.

Across Page Street, at 1901, is an ornate Colonial Revival house, designed in 1896 by architect E.J. Vogel and once occupied by novelist Kathleen Norris. With its elaborate, swagged cornice and Corinthian entrance porch, it is a smaller version of the mansion at 737 Buena Vista West, by the same architect.

The Haight-Ashbury contains, in addition to mansions, some outstanding row houses. One row of ornate Queen Anne flats is at 500 - 508 Cole Street, at the corner of Page. Cranston and Keenan, who built many houses in this district, were the builders, in 1896.

On the southeast corner of Oak and Lyon is a row of six Queen Anne houses, built by the Rountree brothers and designed in 1891 by William H. Lillie, who did a similar row on Washington Street at Buchanan, in the Romanesque style inspired by H.H. Richardson. The Rountree houses, which have similar floorplans, show an amazing variety of decoration on their asymmetrical facades.

At 91 Central Avenue, just above Haight Street, is an apartment house that must be seen to be believed. The heavily rusticated ground floor has arched doors and windows. Above this are three bracketed balconies which support six two-story Corinthian columns, framing three-sided bay windows. A grand baroque pediment crowns the whole thing. The color scheme picks out each of the six mammoth plaster faces under the brackets. Built in 1904, this building rather puts one in mind of the long façade of the Winter Palace in St Petersburg. The rococo ironwork at the entrance is truly a work of art, equivalent to the ironwork found in Russia.

All Saints Episcopal Church, at 1350 Waller Street, is another architectural gem (see page 135). This half-timbered cottage-like structure has an arched entry, above which is a small rose window fitted into the gable facing the street. It is a little surprising to learn that so modest a church carries out masses in the High Church manner. During the years in which All Saints stood at the very heart of hippiedom, it became the community church of the "flower children." Like many other churches in the city, it reached out to the thousands of young people who flocked to San Francisco with little but the clothing on their backs. The beloved rector, Reverend Leon Harris, sent out a letter reminding his flock that the church was not a private club, but rather a regiment of Christian soldiers dedicated to supplying food, clothing, and comfort to those in need, "and hippies need these things."

At 1080 Haight Street, corner of Baker, a large, very ornate mansion with a Romanesque porch and a soaring corner tower stood for years as a dispirited, unpainted hulk. John C. Spenser, the original owner, had a distilling plant built in to purify water for the house when it was built in 1895. Frederick Ravin, a native of Germany, was the architect. In the dining room was a large, built-in fish tank with a glass front, so that each member of the family could select his own fish or crab for dinner. After so many years of neglect, it seemed impossible that so large a house could be rescued for contemporary use.

At last in 1975 the house was offered for sale, with furniture included; in the basement were a forest of Victorian floor lamps, half a dozen roll-top desks, chests, bureaus, chairs, sofas, and tables, the residue of an owner who also ran a furniture store at the turn of the century. Today the house, splendidly restored by Barbara Chambers, is in frequent demand as a location for movies and television shows. The interiors are featured in Randolph Delahanty's excellent book, *In The Victorian Style*. (See page 136)

BUENA VISTA PARK

THE NAME BUENA VISTA dates from Spanish times, when the earliest settlers rode up to enjoy the spectacular views of the Pacific, the Golden Gate, the entire length of San Francisco Bay, and the hills of Contra Costa (the opposite shore). As early as 1860, the city set aside Buena Vista Park because of the view it afforded the stroller. To climb a hill to enjoy a "prospect" was one thing, but to build a house with a view in mind seems to have been a rarity. In the horse-and-buggy days a hilltop locale was valued more for its privacy and prestige than for the view it offered from inside the house. The important rooms generally looked out on the street, and windows were heavily draped.

Before the advent of the automobile, the carefully graded streets around Buena Vista Park were as Olympian a spot as one could find in San Francisco. Yet enormous houses were built, especially along the curved blocks of Buena Vista East. The builders of those mansions must have urged their teams to the utmost effort to bring lumber and masonry supplies up to that hilltop aerie.

At 1081 Haight Street, the very first house at the corner opposite the park is fitted ingeniously into its narrow triangular lot. The name "flatiron house" seems far too mundane for this charming bit of Victorian fantasy, whose corner tower serves as a kind of exclamation point at the bottom of Buena Vista East. Like a number of other houses in the city, this one seems to consist almost entirely of windows, with narrow strips of wall to separate them. The house and its delicate iron fence look so fragile that it seems a miracle they have survived at least two major earthquakes, not to mention the vicissitudes of time and fashion.

Along Buena Vista East are a number of imposing Victorian and Edwardian houses, some radically altered or converted into apartments, some original single-family homes of outstanding design and quality. In their midst is one Art Deco high-rise apartment house, a classic design from the 1920s. At the top of the first long block, at 181 Buena Vista East, is a monumental late Victorian house of exceptional quality, for decades the home of the Adolfo de Urioste family. The fat, rounded turrets of the house afford spectacular views of the Bay and the Berkeley Hills (see page 134). Built on seven lots, it contains a ballroom in the lowest floor. The current owner has completed a thorough renovation, including the addition of a large artist's studio at the rear, designed by the architectural firm of Tanner and Van Dyne.

The massive old St. Joseph's Hospital, designed by Bakewell and Brown, at the very top of Buena Vista East, has been converted into an elegant condominium complex, Park Hill, whose occupants enjoy superb views of the Bay (see page 135). The dependencies behind the hospital, including the original nuns' quarters and the power house, have also been converted, and the large chapel is now used as a social hall for residents, who can play bridge or Trivial Pursuit under the watchful eyes of Jesus and the angels shining down from the tall stained-glass windows on the sides. The chapel, built in the style of small Byzantine churches in Italy, is a cube, capped with an octagonal top on the exterior, to accommodate the magnificent domed interior, which retains its original decoration. God's eye looks down from the very center of the dome upon the card players below. No cheating! The delicate peach-colored tint of the exterior makes the huge hospital building, built in the 1920s, resemble something transplanted from Amalfi or Sorrento. The entire complex is listed on the National Register for its architectural distinction.

At the corner of Buena Vista West, Upper Terrace drops down one short block to Masonic. At the top is a shingled colonial house dating from the 1920s, with a picket fence, looking like a bit of New England set down in a tiny urban lot. Just below, on a triangular lot facing Masonic, is a striking and unique house in the Tudor style, built of clinker brick, a good example of a design perfectly in harmony with its setting. Until 1942 this house was used as the Japanese consulate; a few remnants of a classical Japanese garden survive in the manicured front yard (see page 134).

Back up on Buena Vista West is a collection of houses belonging to every known style, from classic brown-shingle Craftsman houses to stately Roman villas. Dominating it all is a block-buster high-rise apartment house in the Spanish style, boasting a huge, ornate entrance porch covered with plataresque decorations, inspired by early designs done in silver repousse. The work of a clearly un-Spanish architect, H. C. Baumann, it was built in 1925, an outstanding example of the neo-Churrigueresque apartment houses built all over San Francisco in the Roaring Twenties; several of these were Baumann's. The apartments on the northern side enjoy one of the finest views in the entire city, of the Golden Gate, Mount Tamalpais, and beautiful St. Ignatius Church.

At the next corner, where Java Street drops down to Masonic, 601 Buena Vista West is a very unusual Victorian with a rounded tower, more Queen Anne than anything else, with a carriage house intact behind it. The house has long since been converted to apartments. and suffers the indignity of unsightly wooden stairs built onto its northern side. Further down at 701 Buena Vista West, at the corner of Frederick, is a classic Beaux Arts Roman Villa, with arched windows, wide steps leading to a columned entrance, and small iron balconies below the second-story windows. The bracketed cornice is a hold-over from the Victorian Italianate style. (See page 135)

Further down, at 737 Buena Vista West, the four-square mansion of Richard Spreckels, a grandson of old Claus, dominates its neighbors. Richard Spreckels, who was for a time in charge of the family sugar refinery, commissioned German architect E. J. Vogel to design this house in 1896, in the latest Colonial Revival style, a precursor to the Beaux Arts movement which was just beginning to emerge in San Francisco. The architect designed a similar but more modest house for novelist Kathleen Norris, at 1901 Page Street; both houses have literary associations, for Jack London and Ambrose Bierce had studios in the Spreckels house. The perfect symmetry of this house, including even matching chimneys on the sides, is a clear departure from the asymmetrical Queen Anne style dominant in 1896. If the house seems considerably more ornate than a true colonial, with its columns, bulls-eye windows, and fancy Corinthian portico, it was because the late Victorian age found real colonial houses much too plain. This one boasts fanlighted windows, festoons and garlands decorating the frieze under the eaves and on the entablature of the curved front portico. A magnificent iron gate leads to the side yard and the carriage house. The house, restored some years ago as a bed-and-breakfast inn, has just undergone another extensive renovation by a new owner.

Among the interesting houses in this district is one of Bernard Maybeck's charming rustic cottages at 1526 Masonic. Its simple, sweeping roof line testifies to Maybeck's ability to give even the most modest of his houses a unique style. Just across the street, Piedmont

This resolutely symmetrical house on Buena Vista West, designed by E. J. Vogel for Richard Spreckels, features fanlights over the windows, a noble portico, and perfectly matched chimneys. It served as a bed and breakfast inn for several years, and has recently been renovated as a single family residence. (Courtesy James Heig)

Street drops down to Ashbury. On the south side, at 11 Piedmont, is the oldest house in the neighborhood. Built around 1860 as a farmhouse for a goat farm in the lowlands to the north, it was moved to the upper corner of the farm when the Panhandle was laid out in the 1880s. The old house was completely renovated in the 1960s by architect Donald Clark and his partner, Dr. Robert Aycock. With its carefully planted hillside frontage, it is a historical grace note in this densely built-up neighborhood.

The entire hilltop aerie surrounding Buena Vista Park is a study in sheer ingenuity, in which later houses are packed into the former gardens of larger, older places. Despite the countrified look of the Queen Anne castles, Tudor cottages, Roman villas, and rustic Craftsman houses, this is emphatically a cityscape. The exuberant individualism of these houses makes the neighborhood, with its sweeping views, a phenomenon that could happen only in San Francisco. When San Francisco's boundaries had been extended

westward to the Pacific and southward to the San Mateo County line, another hilltop park, about a half-mile west of Buena Vista Park, was dedicated to mark the geographic center of the city. This tiny nipple, grandly named "Mount Olympus," was fitted out with a pyramid-like structure surrounded by benches and topped with a statue. At the time the western half of the city was a sandy wasteland. Today the site might serve as a center of population as well as geography, for almost half of the city's people live west of it. Yet local newspapers recently printed an article requesting information as to the exact locale of this lost landmark. Even those living near the park had no idea what it represented. The statue has long since disappeared, and the legend carved in stone has eroded away, but the park is still there, in a little circle at the very end of Upper Terrace. Crowding around it are apartment houses, some built on lots so steep that they are one story fronting the street and three or four stories at the rear.

A classical villa on Roosevelt Way, reputedly built for silent screen star Norma Talmadge, is unique in San Francisco. The one-story façade is deceptive; the rear of the house, on a steep lot, is three stories high. (Courtesy James Heig)

Twin Peaks

THE OFFICIAL MAPS of San Francisco make no designations of the countless little neighborhoods which exist within the larger districts. Their borders, and sometimes even their names, are known only to the people who live in them. This is particularly true of the sprawling northern slopes of Twin Peaks, where even the residents themselves cannot always say just where one neighborhood begins and another leaves off.

In what is roughly a one-square-mile area, we find portions of Upper Market, Mount Olympus, Clarendon Heights, Edgewood Terrace, the Haight-Ashbury, Ashbury Heights, the Panhandle, Sutro Forest, Parnassus Heights, Buena Vista Park, and Buena Vista Hill. Some of these names were supplied by real estate developers, but most of them have come into use merely through habit. Often the residents form small neighborhood associations, such as one in the Upper Market area which calls itself the East Twin Peaks Association. To enjoy the full flavor of these individualistic little enclaves, one should explore, preferably on foot, the steep, tree-lined streets, the postage-stamp-size gardens, and the astonishing variety of architecture, ranging from the smallest improvised vernacular cottage to the grand villa, and spanning well over a hundred years of building and rebuilding.

Before Twin Peaks Boulevard was graded from Market Street to follow the rising contours of *Los Pechos de la Choca*, Corbett Street, overlooking Eureka Valley, was the road used to get around the eastern slopes. As an outlying extension of the Mission District, the steep hillsides were lined with simple cottages built for working-class families who often found room to keep a goat and a few chickens, and to raise a garden. Today these simple Victorian cottages, interspersed with small flats and later houses, are worth their weight in gold because of the splendid city view they afford. Members of the East Twin Peaks Neighborhood Association strive to keep developers from ruining the rural charm that has always marked this section of town.

Clinging to the sides of the hills, this almost vertical neighborhood is one which the eager explorer cannot afford to miss. Of all the houses which show the individualistic tastes of their owners, perhaps the former home of silent screen star Norma Talmadge, at 439 Roosevelt Way, is the most arresting. Built in 1910, it appears to be a "Wedding Cake" classical villa of one story. A portico of Corinthian columns anchors it to the sidewalk, while the rest of the deceptively large house follows the steep hillside behind it. Startling as it may be at first glance, it nevertheless fits quite comfortably into the eclectic neighborhood.

Ord Street, and its extension, Ord Court, are like the narrow, winding streets people love to explore in Italy or France. Mars, Saturn and Uranus Streets are all lined with picturesque little houses which cling by their toenails to the steep slopes; almost every one has a porch, a cornice, or some small decoration to endear it to its owner, and to the passerby. At the corner of 17th Street and Uranus a small grocery store, more than a hundred years old, still serves the people of the neighborhood.

Some of the streets as originally laid out were too steep to grade, so the houses along them are reached by long stairways. The Vulcan Stairway, leading upward from the dead-end Ord Street just north of 17th Street to Levant Street above, offers what must be the ultimate in residential seclusion in San Francisco. Residents of the half-dozen houses built along the steps must carry their groceries and supplies up, or down, hundreds of steps every day. Moving is a nightmare, and yet at least one of these houses has a large grand piano in the parlor.

High above Corbett is Burnett Avenue, leading to a honeycomb of short blocks with such evocative names as Christmas Tree Terrace. The slopes above Market, rising toward Twin Peaks, are dominated by the Post-WWII "Modern" school of architecture: layered apartments with glass walls and balconies, often supported by long poles and trusses.

Clarendon Heights, taking its name from the boulevard below it, dates to the 1930s. The houses are mainly Mediterranean style villas with stuccoed walls and tile roofs; most have arched picture windows to take in the sweeping panorama of the city below. At 196 Twin Peaks Boulevard is a cottage by Bernard Maybeck, another of his more modest efforts. Further west is Sutro Forest, where Adolph Sutro himself supplied seedlings for children to plant on the barren, windswept hillside. A large, Disneyesque castle, built by the descendants of Sutro in the 1920s, has been converted into a radio station. Above it towers a television broadcasting tower which seems like something dropped by creatures from another planet.

On the northern slope, below Sutro Forest, is a wondrous, hidden enclave, reached by way of Woodland Avenue at Parnassus. Edgewood Avenue, above Woodland, is paved with bricks and planted along both sides with flowering plum trees, which in Spring create a bower of blossoms. The handsome, rustic houses, most of which are in the brown-shingle style of the Craftsman era, are the work of distinguished architects such as Louis Mullgardt (226 Edgewood).

One can only imagine what the Spanish and Mexican settlers would have thought to see houses and apartments climbing up the steep slopes of Twin Peaks, or the constant stream of cars and tour buses circling the Breasts of the Indian Maiden, and disgorging hundreds of tourists who snap pictures of each other huddling in the cold, or buy souvenir sweatshirts to ward off the chilly wind and fog from the ocean. The original name of Twin Peaks suggested at least some small degree of reverence, if not for any particular Indian Maiden then at least for the female form. It is hard to feel any reverence today for the gently rounded hills that seem to have been snared by the roadway winding around them and tamed into submission.

Perhaps Jose Jesus Noe once rode his horse up to the top, where he might have looked down with great satisfaction at the vast land grant he had claimed from the Mexican government: to the west, a wide expanse of sand dunes stretching toward the ocean; to the east, the creeks running down past the Mission to Laguna Dolores, and halfway up the slope the fine adobe house he had built where Alvarado School stands today. He could hardly have pictured the view the tourists see, but perhaps he too shivered in the wind from the sea.

THE TOWN GOD SPANKED

1906 - 1940

RECOVERING FROM DISASTER

If God, they say, spanked the town for being over frisky,
Why did he burn the churches down and save Hotaling's whiskey?

ANYONE EVEN SLIGHTLY informed about San Francisco history knows that at 5:13 a.m. on April 18, 1906, citizens of the gayest, most pleasure-loving city in the world were jolted from their beds by the strongest earthquake ever measured in North America. (A stronger one occurred in 1811 in Missouri, changing the course of the Mississippi River, but no one was there to measure it.) The shaking, which lasted little more than a minute, seemed an eternity to those who lived through it. The 1989 Loma Prieta earthquake, much briefer and not nearly as strong, was sufficient to make us all understand what it feels like when our world threatens to disintegrate around us.

Facing Page: By the second day of the 1906 fire, buildings on Market Street were burning, as helpless firemen struggled to find water for the empty hoses. The interior of the Spreckels building is ablaze, with glowing fires visible in the lower windows, and clouds of smoke billowing from the upper floors. The frame and exterior of the building survived, but the interior was gutted, and had to be rebuilt. Today, with the bulbous dome removed and a sleek Art Deco sheathing, the building is hard to recognize as the same one. (Author's collection)

A few days after the quake, on O'Farrell Street at the corner of Grant, the wreckage has been scooped to the side, to allow wagons to get through. An unidentified but well-dressed man stands on the corner, perhaps where he once had a shop. Even after an earthquake and fire, one did not go downtown without a coat, tie, and hat. (Author's collection)

In 1906, when those fortunate enough not to have been hit by breaking glass or falling masonry were able to gather their wits, they were confronted by a world which would never again seem quite secure. Stunned, they spoke in whispers as they looked through rising dust at buildings minus chimneys, windows and cornices, at once-sturdy houses and hotels twisted and sunken in a grotesque parody of order, and at flimsier structures which had completely disintegrated into piles of rubble and broken timbers.

The story of the 1906 earthquake and fire has been recounted thousands of times by those who survived the disaster. Written accounts by survivors, as well as by later historians, would fill the shelves of a small library. One well-known history, published in 1959 and reprinted many times, *The Earth Shook, The Sky Burned*, by the late William Bronson, gives an hour-by-hour, block-by-block account of the holocaust, with hundreds of pictures.

The superb 1989 book *Denial of Disaster*, by city historian Gladys Hansen and former Fire Chief Emmet Condon, offers evidence that city officials denied the extent of the earthquake's destruction, and either ignored or deliberately concealed thousands of fatalities.

Their account reminds us that San Francisco is still a city built primarily of wood, that areas of highly unstable ground were rebuilt after 1906 without sufficient seismic reinforcement, and that the potential for disaster is still great. The book's astounding photographs make its points doubly convincing.

Since we are concerned here with the construction, not the destruction of San Francisco, we refer readers to these two books, plus many others, now out of print but available at libraries or used bookstores, which provide the reader with ample understanding of the three terrible days in 1906 when San Francisco suffered the most dreadful devastation ever inflicted on an American city.

One effect of the disaster was that more than 200,000 San Franciscans were left homeless. To meet the initial crisis the U.S. Army provided thousands of tents; then some 5,600 redwood and fir huts were built. Clustered in eleven refugee camps, these little houses, many of them measuring only 10 x 14 feet, rented for $2 per month. Bath houses, toilets and laundries were communal. After one year the houses were given to the tenants, to be moved to the new owners' chosen sites. The earthquake cottages were scattered all over town.

The fire jumped to the west side of Van Ness Avenue between Pine and Clay Streets. This view, looking northeast at Franklin and Clay, shows the Stetson house (far right) at Clay and Van Ness. J.B. Stetson refused to evacuate, and stubbornly fought the fire, thus saving the houses behind his, including the Zellerbach house, with two decorative spires. (Author's collection)

Some were converted to tool sheds or garages facing alleys. Others were given more spacious additions and were converted, with shingled siding, into cozy cottages; some owners combined three or four of the little huts to make a single house for their families. A recent survey found some 45 of these cottages still serving as comfortable housing. Enthusiasts have formed a Society for the Preservation of San Francisco's Refugee Shacks. Two of the shacks have been preserved by the Presidio Museum, and can be seen, in their original condition, just behind the museum building.

An interesting variant of emergency housing was a small village of abandoned trolley cars, located in the avenues out by Ocean Beach. This little settlement, known as "Carville," continued to thrive for many years after 1906. The trolleys, set amid beds of geranium and iceplant, had a picturesque, albeit raffish charm. The famous California sculptor Arthur Putnam and his wife were two of the more distinguished householders of Carville. Putnam's patron, Alma de Bretteville Spreckels, who had been born nearby on a farm in the sand dunes and now (after 1913) lived in the grandest house in San Francisco, was a regular caller on the sculptor in his trolley-car beach house.

Among the countless contributions made to San Francisco following the 1906 tragedy was one from the beloved American actress, Maude Adams. A notice in the New York newspapers announced that the entire proceeds from her coming performance of "L'Aiglon" would be forwarded to the San Francisco Relief Fund. But this was only the beginning of what Miss Adams did for the city she loved.

In June 1907 she took her entire company to San Francisco, where they reserved a temporary theater for a full month. At every matinee and at every evening performance, she played to packed houses in the roles for which she was most beloved, "Peter Pan," "L'Aiglon," and "Quality Street." She held one moonlight performance of "L'Aiglon" at the Greek Theater in Berkeley. The San Francisco theater was huge and made of tin, she recalled, and it rattled whenever the wind blew.

"For those courageous people," she once said, "there was no past; there was a long, long future and there was no fear. What had happened once could happen again, but every day, like fishermen putting out to sea, each man embarked on his own little raft, confident of floating home. Not only the people—the houses, the trees and the streets themselves—everything seemed eager to take up its part and go on again. It was uncanny, that feeling of everything beginning."

By 1907 most of those insurance companies who met their commitments (only five are said to have paid one hundred cents on the dollar, while many others reneged completely) had paid off enough money to create a real building boom, attracting scores of workmen from every part of the United States. The city rose from its ashes with almost alarming speed. A very visible result was the hundreds of bay-windowed flats and apartment houses which still cover the slopes of Nob, Telegraph and Russian Hills, as well as those blocks of the Mission District extending from 5th to 20th Street, where the fire was stopped. Practically a rubber stamp of one another, they are a familiar part of the San Francisco landscape.

Generally referred to today as "Edwardian," these buildings loosely followed the Roman Revival Style popular in the city just before 1906. Completely of frame construction, their first floors are generally given a veneer of yellow or Roman brick. The finer examples have a columned entrance porch, sometimes with marble steps and paneling, and perhaps leaded, beveled glass in the front door and side panels. Above the first floor are rows of curved bay windows whose large glass panes are also curvilinear, especially at corners. The heavy roof lines are turned out with modillions and cornices, and any stray door or window handsomely ornamented with pilasters and consoles, in the approved Roman Revival style.

Within are apartments, many of which survive virtually unaltered today. Unlike many later apartments, these often contain a full dining room with a glass-doored china cabinet and a high plate rail. Pocket doors separate the dining room from the small parlor, which often held a folding "Murphy Bed" concealed behind a wide door, making furniture placement difficult. The gas-burning grate, of mouse-hole size, usually boasts a large, columned mantelpiece with built-in mirror above. The bathroom features a large clawfoot tub and an imposing oval pedestal sink; the toilet, with its overhead tank, is in a separate cubicle. In the kitchen are built-in cabinets, one of which is a "cooler" with a screened opening to the outside to let the chilly sea air keep foods fresh. In the middle of all these rooms is a small windowless foyer, sometimes called a "deciding room" because it has so many doors.

Thanks to the low cost of labor, these apartments often featured a profusion of woodwork, paneling, wainscoting, picture molding, and gracefully coved ceilings. The effect suggests oxymorons: "compact grandeur," "lavish economy," "practical extravagance." In 1907 San Franciscans considered these apartments to be the ultimate in sophisticated city living. In the Victorian era, a middle-class family, often with several children and assorted relatives, had lived in a house or a full flat, usually with at least one servant, while single people lived with relatives or in residence hotels. In post-1906 San Francisco families were likely to be smaller and servantless. In exchange for a loss of privacy the apartment dweller got the convenience of gas and electricity—perhaps even a telephone—and automatic hot water (no more cold-water flats). Later generations have found these comfortable apartments an integral part of "the San Francisco experience."

BARRIERS BURNED

by Charles K. Field

It ain't such a terrible long time ago
That Mrs. Van Bergen and me
Though livin' near by to each other, y'know,
Was strangers for all ye could see.
For she'd a grand house and horses to drive,
And a wee rented cottage was mine,
But now we need rations to keep us alive
An' we're standin' together in line.
An' Mrs. Van Bergen she greets me these days
With a smile an' a nod of the head;
"Ah, Mrs. McGuinness, how are you?" she says
"An' how do you like Government bread?"

She fetches a bag made of crockydile skin
An' I've got a sack when we meet,
But the same kind of coffee and crackers goes in,
An' it's all of it cooked in the street.
Sure Mrs. Van Bergen is takin' it fine,
Ye'd think she was used to the food;
We're gettin' acquainted, a-standin' in line,
An it's doin' the both of us good.
An' Mr. Van Bergen and Michael, my man
(They've always been friendly, the men)
They're gettin' together and layin' a plan
For buildin' the city again!

St. Luke's Episcopal Church, at the southeast corner of Van Ness and Clay Streets, shows major earthquake damage on the second day of the fire. The handsome rectory and the residence of David Cohn, to the right of the church were soon to be dynamited. The smoke in the background is from the burning of houses on Nob Hill. (Courtesy California Historical Society)

ALONG VAN NESS AVENUE — On the third day of the 1906 holocaust the exhausted fire crews and the U.S. Army hoped to stop the fire at Van Ness Avenue. All along the east side of the street, backfires were set in the hope of leaving nothing to feed the flames advancing down the western slopes of Nob Hill. When this failed, the fire-fighters used dynamite. Virtually all of the mansions along the east side of Van Ness were obliterated. In places the incredible heat of the flames ignited houses on the west side, and five blocks burnt between Sutter and Clay Streets, where the fire spread west as far as Gough Street.

After the fire many of the surviving houses on Van Ness were converted to commercial use until the downtown section could be rebuilt. As a result Van Ness Avenue became a secondary commercial street, as one by one the surviving dwellings were torn down to make way for apartment houses, parking lots and automobile showrooms. In 1915 the Packard company commissioned Bernard Maybeck to design a magnificent showroom for their fine motorcars. It still stands on the northwest corner of Van Ness and Ellis, a classical temple equal to any of the banks. Its pale peach-colored marble columns have been painted over, but the lustrous black piers and the splendid frieze remain. Not to be outdone, the Cadillac agency erected an elaborate Spanish-Moorish showroom across the street; these two buildings were the only car showrooms that could be described as a gift to the street.

East of Van Ness, at Larkin and McAllister Streets, the City Hall which had taken 29 years to build and had cost, thanks to graft and corruption, something like $7 million, crumbled in the earthquake, its columns shattering on the pavement to reveal to all the shoddy construction. Vital city records were lost in the fire that followed.

The new City Hall, built between 1913 and 1916, is San Francisco's greatest ornament. Occupying two blocks bounded by Van Ness, McAllister, Polk and Grove Streets, it faces the Civic Center Plaza to the east, but has an imposing entrance on Van Ness as well. Built in the French Renaissance style, its walls are of California granite rather than the traditional limestone, which would not stand up well in salt air.

Although its estimated cost of $3.5 million seemed excessive in that day, the citizens were willing to foot the bill as a matter of civic pride. President Taft, on a visit to San Francisco, declared it to be "The City that

363

San Francisco's magnificent City Hall, widely regarded as the most beautiful public building in America, is shown here in its pristine glory in the early 1920s, with its original graceful fountain and reflecting pool, lost in the building of a vast underground garage. A complete renovation, necessitated by the 1989 Loma Prieta earthquake and finished in 1999, included a lavish application of gold leaf to the dome and lantern, at a reported cost of $450,000. It was money well spent. (Courtesy San Francisco Public Library)

The architects of City Hall, John Bakewell, Jr., and Arthur Brown, Jr., with the French designer Jean Louis Bourgeois and an unidentified fourth man, pose before a scale model of the west rotunda wall. (Courtesy of the papers of Arthur Brown, Jr.)

Knows How," and San Franciscans firmly intended to live up to the accolade.

Rising from street level to a height of 308 feet, higher than the Capitol Building in Washington, the dome of copper, ornamented with heavy gold leaf, was said to be patterned after the dome of Les Invalides in Paris. Figures in the pediments at the front and back of the building were the work of Jules Crenier, while the medallions and other interior decorations were done by a French sculptor named Evan, who was so unpopular with some of the workmen that tools and bits of masonry occasionally fell in his path from the dome above. The handsome French paneling of the mayor's office and the press room was the work of Laroulandie, a young Frenchman who soon after lost his life in the battle of the Argonne.

Thanks principally to the genius of architect Arthur Brown, Jr., the proportions and ornamentation of this building present a beauty seldom if ever surpassed, even by the original European masters of the French Renaissance. John Bakewell, Jr., the supervising architect, dealt with the temperamental work crew and found solutions to the practical problems which constantly arose, allowing the inspired dream of the design to become a reality.

Philip Johnson, one of America's leading contemporary architects, was once asked if he could name an American building which he would like to claim as his own work; his instant reply was "The San Francisco City Hall." We can perhaps be thankful that the Beaux Arts disciplines of proper scale and use of ornamentation, having been thrown out the window by the post-World War II practitioners, are again being revived.

True to the unity demanded by apostles of the Beaux Arts school, the Civic Center, fronting the City Hall's eastern façade, was surrounded by buildings designed in a compatible spirit, even though each of the encircling structures was designed by a different architect. No displays of non-conformist egotism here! Admirers of the Civic Center are often heard to remark, "Thank God the earthquake came in 1906 instead of 1956!"

The huge Civic Auditorium, begun in 1913, was hurried to completion in time for the 1915 Fair by John Galen Howard, architect of the University of California at Berkeley. To the east was the new Public Library, begun in 1916. Its architect, George Kelham, included a grand staircase, in keeping with the splendid one in City Hall. Modern architects deplored it as an extravagant waste of space; no such sin was to be committed in the new library built at Larkin and Fulton Streets, completed in 1996, and designed by architects James Freed and Cathy Simon. The new library has two styles: a "classical" façade, with metal tubes representing columns, fronts the Civic Center Plaza, intending to match the other buildings in the set. The façades facing Grove and Hyde Streets are in the stripped-down "modern" style, perhaps on the theory that no one would be able to see both styles at the same time. Anyone standing at the corner of the Civic Auditorium, at Grove and Larkin Streets, is reminded of the old cliche applied to late Victorian buildings, which had "Queen Anne fronts and Mary Anne behinds."

In the 1930s Arthur Brown designed a Federal Building for Washington, D.C., and he seems to have reproduced the same structure for the Federal Building on the San Francisco Civic Center. With its rusticated lower floor and handsome lanterns, it does justice to the other structures around the plaza. The State Building, on the north side of the plaza, is in the compatible Italian Renaissance Style. Badly damaged in the 1989 earthquake—a reminder that the site was originally marshy ground—it has recently been renovated and reopened.

After a long, drawn-out battle in which some politicians argued that it was undemocratic to spend city funds on an opera house, the War Memorial Opera House was completed in 1931, thanks to substantial private donations. Arthur Brown designed the Opera House and the neighboring Veterans' Auditorium in the French Renaissance style, clearly displaying the architect's mastery of understated elegance. Linking the two buildings is a small park with a fine grillwork fence, patterned after one in the Place Stanislaus in Nancy.

Brown deliberately omitted a grand staircase in the Opera House because he felt that patrons would only use it as a showcase for their jewels and costly gowns. Yet the splendid lobby makes an elegant setting for just such a display on opening night, an event which attracts hundreds of ticketless people who stand outside to see the opera-goers make their entrances. On this and other gala occasions the buildings of the Civic Center are magnificently lighted, as if to show that San Francisco still is the city that knows how.

COMMERCIAL BUILDINGS — For the seventh time, San Francisco arose from its ashes, this time a city beautiful in its new maturity, certainly a more conventional American city outwardly. In the business section and along Market street many of the gutted steel-framed structures, towering over the ashes and rubble of their neighbors, were rebuilt more or less exactly as they had been. Until the advent of recent high-rise structures, one could easily visualize Market Street as it had looked before 1906; it was outwardly very much the same.

Pissis & Moore's Parrott Building, housing the Emporium, got back its splendidly domed interior, while across the street the Flood Building came to look as though it had never been gutted by fire. The same was true of Albert Pissis's beautiful Hibernia Bank, Willis Polk's Merchants' Exchange, Daniel Burnham's Mills Building on Montgomery, and Bliss & Faville's St. Francis Hotel on Union Square. The Examiner and the Chronicle buildings were restored in somewhat altered form, and Claus Spreckels's Call building, the tallest in the city, continued to raise its curious knobby dome, with 36 round windows, above Market and Third Streets. The Palace Hotel was deemed beyond saving, but stubbornly resisted the demolition crews as long as possible; its two-foot-thick brick walls refused to fall over, and had to be dismantled piece by piece at a cost of $100,000.

The Reid Brothers' Fairmont Hotel on Nob Hill, which had been almost ready to open when disaster struck, received new interiors and structural reinforcement; this was an important early assignment for architect Julia Morgan, recently graduated from the Ecole des Beaux Arts in Paris. The extravagant mansions which had crowned Nob Hill had burned like the cheapest tenements, and were soon replaced by luxurious apartment houses and hotels. Nob Hill would hold its fame as an elegant faubourg , but only the red sandstone walls and the bronze fence of the Flood mansion remain to remind one of another day.

South of Market Street, the fading glories of Rincon Hill had all disappeared on the first day of the conflagration, and the area, until the coming of the Bay Bridge, was given over to light industry, warehouses, and cheap hotels. Old St. Patrick's Church survived, but lost what had been America's largest Irish parish when residents of the area moved out to the Mission District.

Chinatown, formerly housed in brick commercial buildings dating back to the 1850s, was leveled, and city fathers hatched a plan to move all the Chinese to Hunter's Point. Fortunately a completely new Chinatown grew up on the old site before the plan could be carried out, the only change being to rename Dupont Street as Grant Avenue. One unique new structure was the Chinese Telephone Exchange, a jewel-like pagoda of red lacquer and gold leaf, which today houses a bank.

Buckets of tears may have flowed over "the City that was," but few mourned the loss of the Barbary Coast when all the crimp joints, brothels and dance halls along Pacific Street between Kearny and Montgomery burnt in 1906. The street was quickly rebuilt, and kept its roistering reputation even through Prohibition. In the 1930s the block was renamed the "International Settlement," which tried

Old Chinatown, with its rich, colorful history, was totally obliterated in the 1906 disaster. The Chinese telephone exchange, built in 1912 on Washington Street near Grant, was a major architectural contribution to the rebuilding of the city. Inside, rows of telephone operators like Harriet Ng (right) had to memorize 2,300 Chinese names, many very similar, and to speak five different dialects in order to connect callers to their parties within seconds. (Courtesy San Francisco Public Library)

with some success to keep up the spirit of its predecessor's notoriety as a tourist attraction: it was off limits to servicemen throughout the war, and pretended to be naughty at least until the 1950s.

Across Broadway and up the lower slopes of Telegraph Hill the Italian and Spanish habitations and shops were rebuilt in a pattern similar to that of former times. The old family style restaurants in this quarter came back, and with them came the Bohemian crowd as well as other patrons who appreciated a great six-course dinner with wine for 75 cents.

In 1906, through superhuman effort, the U.S. Navy and a group of young San Francisco volunteers were able to rescue the massive Montgomery Block, where Duncan Nicol had dispensed his world-famous Pisco Punch. At Poppa Coppa's restaurant in the basement the Bohemian crowd gathered, on the night after the fire had finally been extinguished, to raise their glasses in salute to a great new San Francisco. They could not

have imagined that their beloved "Monkey Block" would be torn down 53 years later to be replaced by a parking lot, now the site of the Transamerica Pyramid.

JACKSON SQUARE — San Francisco is richer for having one historic district of around three blocks, which escaped the 1906 devastation and the developers as well. Known today as Jackson Square, this district is centered around Jackson Street and extends to the north side of Washington and the south side of Pacific. Montgomery and Sansome Streets are the western and eastern boundaries. Thanks to the efforts of Percy Stidger, manager of the old Montgomery Block, and tenants of the Block, this area was rescued from the flames of 1906. Spared were the pioneer brick structures fronting Washington and Jackson Streets, including Jim Flood's old Auction Lunch Saloon on Washington, and one of the fancy boarding houses run by Mammy Pleasant in the 1850s. For years the notorious Barbary

The Geary Theater, originally called the New Columbia Theater (the old Columbia on Powell Street was burnt in 1906), was an early attempt to replace one of the 23 theaters destroyed in the earthquake and fire. William Faville and Walter Bliss were the architects. Built in 1910 of brick and stone on a steel frame, with remarkable ceramic decorations on the façade, the theater has served for decades as a showcase for the greatest stars of the theater world: Sarah Bernhardt, Fanny Brice, Helen Hayes, Isadora Duncan, Ruth St. Denis, Clark Gable, Lionel and Ethel Barrymore, Chauncey Olcott, BIllie Burke, Mrs. Patrick Campbell, Ellen Terry, Maude Adams, Ina Claire, Frederic March, Basil Rathbone, Edward G. Robinson and many others.

Beginning in 1912, movies were occasionally shown in the theater, although legitimate stage productions were always the mainstay.

In 1966, the American Conservatory Theater, a company founded in Pittsburgh by the brilliant director William Ball, was persuaded to settle in San Francisco, with the Geary Theater as its main venue. Many San Franciscans will never forget the first season, beginning in January 1967, when A.C.T. presented sixteen plays in the Geary and Marines Memorial Theaters, including Edward Albee's *Tiny Alice*, Moliere's *Tartuffe*, and Arthur Miller's *Death of a Salesman*. Extraordinary actors left audiences cheering. Peter Donat, Michael Learned, Jay Doyle, Rene Auberjonois, Richard Dysart, Will Geer, Paul Shenar, Harry Frazier, Ruth Kobart, DeAnn Mears, Ken Ruta, Angela Paton, William Paterson, and Ray Reinhardt, among others, made this season the beginning of a theatrical Renaissance in the city, the effects of which are still with us. (Courtesy San Francisco Public Library and A.C.T.)

In the 1989 Loma Prieta Earthquake, the Geary's interior was badly damaged when heavy steel lighting frames fell from the ceiling onto the front nine rows of seats. Fortunately it happened in the late afternoon, when the seats were empty. Six years later, after Herculean fund-raising efforts, the theater was re-opened after a complete renovation, with a dazzling new lobby, comfortable seats, and a complete restoration of the beautiful ceiling. (Courtesy American Conservatory Theater)

Coast on Pacific Street kept developers away, even after World War II, when the Barbary Coast faded into memory. As a result, this little area, built over the land-fills of the 1850s, might be compared to a fly in amber.

Built in the decade between 1854 and 1864, the buildings in Jackson Square show a natural cohesiveness. They somehow survived the earthquake of 1868, which put an end to brick construction in most of San Francisco; all these structures are of brick, with here and there a fling at granite rustication on the lower floors. Most are in the Italianate style, or what was then known as the "English Roman Style." The windows and doors are extremely tall and narrow, and are usually crowned with pediments. The Hotaling Building, at 451 Jackson, has pediments and quoins of cast iron applied over the brick walls, a common feature of commercial structures in those days. Some people remember the cast-iron pilasters and trim on buildings in the old produce district, which was demolished to make room for the Golden Gateway project; now the Hotaling Building is the only example left in San Francisco.

The Yeon Building, at 423 Jackson, is of particular interest, for during the rehabilitation of the area, John Yeon, a leading American architect from Portland, Oregon, purchased what was left of the old French

Consulate, tore it down, and then re-used the materials to create a duplicate of the original structure.

While most of the buildings in the complex were handsomely restored, one exception was the fine Pioche-Bayorque Building at the southeast corner of Jackson and Montgomery. In the 1960s it was given a sleazy "modern" exterior when it became a famous but short-lived Playboy Club. We can only wonder whether the Playboy Bunnies realized they were in the midst of history while they were making it.

The same is true of the building housing Doro's Restaurant and its next door neighbor, which once housed the historic Black Cat Bar and Restaurant, birthplace of the gay rights movement in San Francisco. These two structures, facing Montgomery Street, are part of an antique row which for many years contained the wonderfully restored law offices of the late attorney Melvin Belli, and the Golden Era Building, later a furniture showroom. North on Montgomery Street, at the northeast corner of Jackson, is the old Lucas Turner Bank, whose director in pre-Civil War days was William Tecumseh Sherman, better remembered for his siege of Atlanta and his march across Georgia. Even without its third story, lost in 1906, this building is a shining example of preservation for contemporary use.

The leaders of this restoration project were Ted Griffith, who ran a decorator's supply house, and interior designer Clarence Slade, who together established the Jackson Square Neighborhood Association. Their knowledge and foresight saved the district from greedy developers, who wanted the land for still more blank-faced highrises. The district is now faced with the California U.R.M. Ordinance, which requires all unreinforced masonry buildings to be made earthquake proof—whatever that means, in view of the fact that some of the greatest losses in the 1989 Loma Prieta quake were those marvels of engineering, the freeways. Several owners of Jackson Square properties were reluctant to accept the historic district designation; will they now insist on demolishing their buildings rather than take on the expensive seismic upgrading required by the state? If these beautiful buildings are lost, San Francisco will also have lost the last visual reminders of the time when the waterfront was pushed from Montgomery Street to Sansome.

Directly across Montgomery Street from this historic row is the beautiful Banco Populare Italiano Operaia Fugazi, built in 1909 for banker John F. Fugazi. Its original architect was Charles Paff, who planned it to be a five-story structure, but it ended up with only two stories and an ornamental cupola at its southern tip. The cupola was later removed when the structure was given a third floor and an addition at the rear.

The Fugazi bank was later taken over by A. P. Gianinni's Bank of Italy, which later became the Bank of America. The gleaming white ceramic exterior adds to the jewel-like appearance of the building, which is San Francisco Landmark #52.

Long the financial center of the west, San Francisco boasts many handsome—and some not so handsome—banking establishments. Most beautiful is the Bank of California at 400 California Street. Designed in 1909 by the firm of Bliss & Faville, it is a granite pavilion with fluted columns surrounding an immense single chamber some four stories high. In 1967 the firm of Anshen & Allen designed the adjoining high-rise building flanking the west side of the Bank of California. The new tower has fluted walls in honor of the columns of its jewel-like neighbor; the designers were praised for their sensitivity. We leave it up to the observer to decide whether the praise is warranted.

The Wells Fargo Bank building, on its original historic site at California and Montgomery, once boasted a four-story façade of cast iron, replete with caryatids and all the other lavish ornaments typical of the 1870s. When the structure was completely rebuilt in the 1960s, this façade was dismantled and stored at the Maritime Museum; it may again some day see the light of day. In honor of its glorious past, Wells Fargo has installed an excellent California history museum, open to the public, inside the bank. And the top-floor bank officers' club features a huge blow-up of Muybridge's famous panoramic photographs of San Francisco in the 1870s, making a dramatic contrast with the actual view now seen through the glass walls opposite.

At One Sansome Street, Albert Pissis' classically inspired Anglo Bank, built in 1910, later had its banking room extended into the high-rise structure adjoining on the north. Then in the 1970s the high-rise was completely renovated by Pereira & Associates, and the Parthenon-like little bank building at its side was converted into an atrium. Its splendid coffered ceiling was removed and replaced by a glass skylight. Passersby are often startled to see, inside the conservative bank façade, the brilliantly sunlit interior.

Willis Polk's Crocker Bank for decades connected one of San Francisco's most prominent names with the financial district's most prestigious address at One Montgomery Street. There is no longer a Crocker Bank (it was absorbed by Wells Fargo in the 1980s), but the little vampires created by sculptor Arthur Putnam still ornament its bronze window trim. In 1983, through an odd, Faustian compromise with the city planning department, the bank building was decapitated, leaving only the white marble and bronze lobby, so extravagant that it seems intended to make the lowly depositor wonder whether he is good enough to keep his money in such a place. In return the city allowed construction of the 37-story Crocker Center (now called Telesis Tower) designed by Skidmore, Owings & Merrill with their usual egg-crate façade. The adjoining Galleria, supposedly a contemporary version of the famous Galleria in Milan, has a vast arched glass top, offering the ultimate challenge to window cleaners.

No observer bent on taking in the most glorious buildings in the city should overlook the Merchants' Exchange, at the southeast corner of California and Montgomery Streets. Built in 1902 on the design of Danial Burnham and Willis Polk, it was one of the tallest buildings in San Francisco, standing out in post-fire photos as a gutted pile above the ruined financial district. Julia Morgan designed a handsome new interior after 1906, and the building was splendidly restored in the 1960s. In the bank at the end of the lobby visitors may enjoy the superb maritime murals by William Coulter, a leading artist of his time. The paintings had been plastered over for decades.

THE PANAMA PACIFIC EXPOSITION

SEVERAL EXCELLENT BOOKS describe the Panama Pacific Exposition of 1915 in far more detail than is possible here. Most easily available is *San Francisco Invites the World*, by Donna Ewald and Peter Clute, published in 1991. Certainly, though, mention should be made of the grand opening parade, which included virtually every able-bodied man, woman and child in San Francisco. With bands playing and huge banners flying, they marched up Van Ness Avenue to Fort Mason, then turned westward to the gates of the Exposition. The nominal purpose of the Exposition was to hail the opening of the Panama Canal, which would vastly improve trade with the East Coast and Europe. But the fair was also a celebration of San Francisco's almost total recovery from the 1906 Earthquake and Fire, and this in a span of only nine years.

More than $5 million was needed as an initial cash outlay for the fair, and San Franciscans from every walk of life gave unstintingly. In today's currency the amount might equal at least $500 million.

Architects from all over the world designed exhibits for various countries. San Francisco, of course, drew mainly from its own talent pool: Willis Polk, Arthur Brown and John Bakewell, Louis Mullgardt, Walter Bliss and William Faville, Julia Morgan, the first woman to graduate from the Ecole des Beaux Arts, and Bernard Maybeck, whose perishable Palace of Fine Arts was so beautiful no one could tear it down when the rest of the buildings were demolished. The crumbling structure stood until 1962, when it was carefully replicated, at a cost of $7 million, in reinforced concrete.

Eastern architects who were leaders of the Beaux Arts school also contributed important designs to the 1915 Fair: McKim, Mead and White, Thomas Hastings and Henry Bacon. Perhaps because all these architects had undergone the disciplines of the Beaux Arts movement, the Exposition evoked a spirit of inventiveness within the scope of the classical medium, and thus achieved a feeling of architectural unity throughout. Jules Guerin's color scheme of terra cotta and cerulean blue helped to create the dreamy mood of harmony and balance. The fountains, lighted at night, the sweeping lagoons, the flower-filled courts offering sweeping vistas of the sparkling bay, the glittering Tower of Jewels, remain among the most treasured memories of those who are still around to talk about the fair. Even the magnificent Golden Gate International Exposition on Treasure Island in 1939-40 could not match the splendor of the 1915 Fair, according to observers who attended both.

It seems sadly ironic that the city's two greatest expositions should have taken place when the rest of the world was at war, and when America's involvement was imminent. A jubilant San Francisco turned out in April 1919 to welcome home two California regiments, both of which had fought in the battle of the Argonne. Evergreen arches, reviewing stands and giant banners decorated Market Street. When the 363RD and 347TH Regiments began their orderly march, the welcoming throngs, no longer containable, pressed forward to embrace the returning heroes. No further march was possible.

Above: The 1915 Panama Pacific International Exhibition was San Francisco's way to show the world the city had recovered from the worst urban disaster in the history of America. Indeed, the world had never seen such splendor. Maybeck's Palace of Fine Arts shown here in a 1915 lithograph, was just one of dozens of astonishing buildings at the fair, and was the only survivor when the rest were demolished. The original lath and plaster structure, badly deteriorated, was duplicated in reinforced concrete in the 1960s, because San Franciscans simply refused to part with it; they approved a $5 million bond issue for its restoration. (Courtesy Gustav Trolle Bonde)

The enormous glass dome of the Palace of Horticulture looms above a row of modest shingle style houses along Lombard Street. (Courtesy California Historical Society)

Two original lithographs from the 1915 Fair show the Festival Hall (above) and the Court of Abundance and Tower, designed by Louis Mullgardt, one of the city's leading architects. (Courtesy Gustav Trolle Bonde)

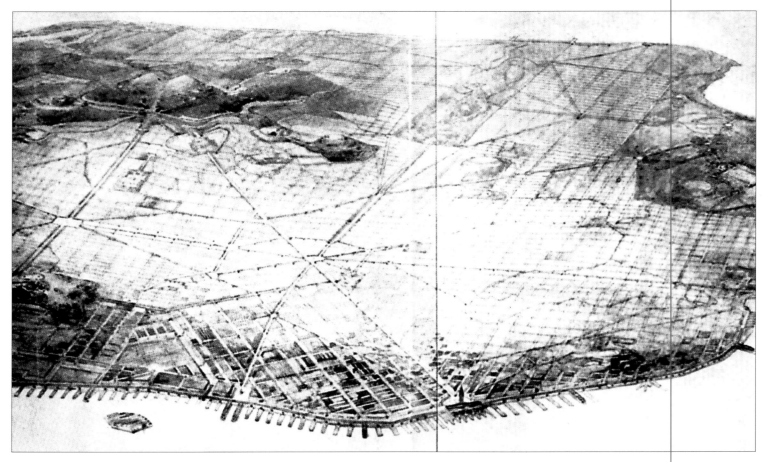

Chicago architect Daniel Burnham, commissioned by the Committee for the Improvement and Adornment of San Francisco, developed a plan in 1905 called "San Francisco Beautiful," featuring a grand boulevard encircling the entire city, and a spacious civic center at Market and Oak Streets, with streets radiating outward like spokes from a wheel. The Ferry Building at the foot of Market Street, the basin below Fort Mason, and the Presidio are main features of the waterfront. (From the facsimile edition of the Burnham Plan, published by Urban Books, 1971)

THE BURNHAM PLAN

THIS IS THE STORY of a city that might have been—a fantastic scheme never fully realized. Its creators might have learned from history that, in democratic societies with no all-powerful ruler such as a Caesar or a Napoleon, there is no force powerful enough to level entire cities and rebuild them in accordance with one grand, unified plan. This has held true for centuries, even when events seemed to offer ideal circumstances. In 17TH century England, royal prerogatives seemed above debate. And in 1666 the greater part of London was levelled by a great holocaust. In the aftermath of the fire, King Charles II called in Christopher Wren to create a grand scheme for London to wipe out the narrow, foul-smelling streets which had been the city's medieval legacy. Wren, one of the greatest architects in British history, obliged with a scheme which included grand promenades and elegant parks. Was his plan followed? No. The merchants and landowners went to court over their property rights, and King Charles's wishes were never realized. In just this way, history repeated itself in San Francisco.

One of the key players in this grand scheme was James D. Phelan, a public-minded and wealthy San Franciscan who served as mayor of San Francisco from 1899 to 1903, but after serving two terms chose not to run for re-election. Rather, he directed his efforts toward the improvement and beautification of his city. Impressed by the monumental architecture he had seen in the cities of Europe, he organized the Committee for the Improvement and Adornment of San Francisco, comprised of 26 public-spirited San Franciscans. J.W. Byrne, president of the Pacific Union Club, and

William Davis, president of the San Francisco Art Association, assisted Phelan in selecting the committee.

The committee, after considering many brilliant Americans to design a master plan for the city, ultimately selected Daniel Burnham, one of Chicago's leading architects and a major contributor to the great neo-classical Chicago Exposition of 1894. Burnham also was one of America's most active advocates of "The City Beautiful" movement, which called for a more ordered and monumental architecture for American cities. "Make no little plans," was Burnham's admonition as he gravely accepted the challenge of "A San Francisco Beautiful."

Willis Polk, who at one time had worked in Burnham's office, designed a redwood shingled studio on Twin Peaks to serve as Burnham's living quarters on his many trips to San Francisco to supervise the work. These quarters, referred to as "the shack," commanded a grand view of the city. The shack also housed an office for his full-time staff, headed by Edward H. Bennett.

Unsurprisingly, Willis Polk served on Bennett's staff, as did a number of San Francisco's finest architects. John Galen Howard, a Beaux Arts graduate commissioned by Phoebe Apperson Hearst to create a plan for the University of California campus, was one of the leading contributors to the plan. Berkeley is still fortunate in possessing much of Howard's most significant work.

John Bakewell, Jr., and Arthur Brown, Jr., who would one day design San Francisco's magnificent City Hall, were then only recent graduates of the Ecole des Beaux Arts, but they, too, made significant contributions to the Burnham Plan. These men, along with Howard, were creating a regional school to train local architects in the principles of Beaux Arts design. (Of course, the stylistic concepts of the Burnham Plan were strongly Beaux Arts or classical in design.)

The Burnham Plan designers took the "no little plans" motto to heart, and, with mixed results, went about envisioning a completely new city. The Burnham Plan's design for a civic center has been realized to some extent, though not as fully as might have been hoped. The Opera House and Veterans' Building, which added their beauty to the Civic Center in the 1930s, owe their size and proportions to Willis Polk's plans; Arthur Brown merely dressed them up with his own inimically suave detailing. For years, the magnificent Renaissance dome of the City Hall set the tone for that part of San Francisco's skyline, until the upended ice trays decreed by the Federal and State governments intruded into the area. Other high-rise buildings, most notably the checkerboard California Automobile Association building on Van Ness, have been allowed

Daniel Burnham

to dwarf City Hall until now its dome is hard to find amid the boring rectangles around it.

In their grand scheme, this group addressed problems which still confront city planners and freeway engineers today. The automobile was not yet a cause for great concern, but the agony of gridlock today certainly would have been relieved if their plan for a grand boulevard to encircle the entire city had been followed. The Bayshore Highway was one aspect of the plan which was executed, but such concourses only dump more traffic into the city; one-way streets do little to alleviate the problem once the cars arrive. Another of the plan's recommendations was to carry the Panhandle of Golden Gate Park all the way to Market Street. The Burnham Plan would have created beautifully landscaped parkways on either side of this central strip.

One of the major blessings of the 1989 Loma Prieta earthquake was the damage it did to the Central Freeway, leading to the Civic Center, and the Embarcadero Freeway, which for thirty years had blocked off the Ferry Building from Market Street. Both freeways have been demolished. The improvement to the Embarcadero is absolutely dazzling. San Franciscans had grown used to the heavy, oppressive

375

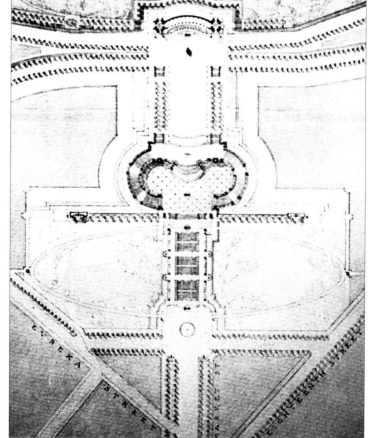

Top and Left: The Burnham plan brought Market Street out to a great circular park at the foot of Twin Peaks, approximately today's Castro Street.

Facing Page: Telegraph Hill was to become a true focal point, a Ziggurat topped by a huge monument and surrounded by noble structures, all in the Beaux Arts style. (From the facsimile edition of *The Burnham Plan*, published by Urban Books, 1971)

presence casting its shadow and its grinding noise on the foot of Market Street, shutting off the view of the Ferry Building's handsome façade and the gallant clock-tower which had survived the 1906 earthquake only to be blotted out by an engineering monstrosity. The removal of the freeway is like an enormous weight lifted from our shoulders, leaving us buoyant and optimistic; we feel drawn to the waterfront, to the sparkling waters of the bay and the fine views of the Bay Bridge. Even the hideous Vaillancourt Fountain, which unfortunately survived the 1989 quake, recedes to the edge of the view and becomes less important.

The demolition of the Central Freeway has made a comparable difference. The observer standing on Fulton Street at Alamo Square can again see in superb perspective the noble west façade of City Hall and the elegant park between the Opera House and the Veteran's Building. One can only wonder how, in the 1960s, the engineers of the State Highway Department managed to perpetrate such a brutal crime on the city. And one recalls the remark of a Pacific Heights dowager when she learned of the original construction of the freeway: "I'm not sure I care to be five minutes closer to Los Angeles."

Park Presidio Boulevard and the circular turnaround at the top of Telegraph Hill owe their existence to the Burnham Plan, but the ziggurat scheme to completely encircle Telegraph Hill with a spiral approach was never developed, nor were the other complex street designs. The schemes for parks, balustraded stairs and belvederes to cover those spaces too steep to utilize otherwise, remain only a part of an abandoned dream, which would have made San Francisco America's most architecturally beautiful city.

Ironically, Burnham's project was completed in April of 1906. Three thousand copies of it, along with the models and schematics, were delivered to City Hall on the very eve of the earthquake. It is said that a grand exhibit was being prepared in the rotunda of the old City Hall. Following the dawn of April 18TH, however, the people of San Francisco would be too preoccupied with other matters to consider the purely visionary schemes for a new San Francisco. In the frantic scramble to rebuild the city, property owners stubbornly clung to their 25-by-100-foot lots laid out along the gridiron streets. A few copies of the Burnham Plan survived the 1906 debacle, but they have only become sad reminders of a city that might have been.

ARCHITECTURE IN THE NEW SUBURBIA

UNLESS THE CITY is leveled again as it was in 1906, there will never again be the sort of residential expansion needed to house a population which more than doubled its pre-1906 count. Surrounded by water on three sides, the city could only expand first westward, then southward to the county limits. Between 1906 and the post-WWII boom years more than fifty new neighborhoods mushroomed up to fill what had once been thought of as far-flung county limits.

In the early 1950s the Governor of California, campaigning for re-election, was photographed standing triumphant on a freeway overpass, showing the voters his progressive, expansionist confidence. Sacramento celebrated the fact that every fifteen minutes a new permanent arrival was helping to make this the most populous state in the nation. Today Sacramento thinks differently, and many government leaders in the nine Bay Area counties are asking for building moratoria. Meantime the cost of building has escalated to the point that the dream of every Californian owning his own home has become just that—a dream. The large tracts of single-family homes built in San Francisco earlier in the century now seem to be historically remote.

Two very different schools of architecture were popular in San Francisco in the early years of the 20TH century: the rustic, unpretentious Craftsman style, and the more sophisticated Beaux Arts style, based on accurate period revivals. Although the two styles represented completely different approaches to architecture, in the hands of the best Bay Area architects, Willis Polk, Ernest Coxhead, Arthur Brown, Bernard Maybeck and Julia Morgan, the two styles were often skillfully combined. In the hands of building contractors who insisted on being their own designers, the results were far less successful.

The Craftsman style, which grew out of William Morris's Esthetic Movement in England in the 1870s, was the only decorative style created with consideration for the income of the more modest homebuilder. Its hallmarks were simplicity, sturdiness, honesty. At its best it produced a cosy, intimate, warm, homey effect. At its worst it was dark, heavy, oppressive, gloomy. The style was, if not proletarian, at least anti-elitist. John Ruskin, an avid supporter of the Esthetic Movement, wrote that the classically-inspired Palladian house "made sybarites of its occupants and slaves of its retainers."

In contrast, supporters of the Beaux Arts school thought, as Edith Wharton put it, that the influences of good taste would "trickle down from the more affluent to the middle classes." In 1902, Mrs. Wharton, a successful novelist and chum of Henry James, collaborated with a Boston architect with the very Boston-sounding name of Ogden Codman, in a book entitled *The Decoration of Houses*. Here they clearly defined the Beaux Arts approach to architecture: "Architecture does not address itself to the moral senses but to the eye. . . Qualities such as boldness, honesty, cleanliness, and purity may be desirable in humans, but make strange analogies to apply to architecture. . . . Proportion is the good breeding of architecture. It is that seemingly intangible essence which gives repose and distinction to a room or to an entire house."

The Beaux Arts school was as eclectic in its use of historic traditions as was the architecture of the Victorian Age, but paid strict attention to the tried-and-true laws of scale, proportion, and the judicious use of ornament, rules which apparently were lost on the Victorians as the 19TH century progressed.

LIFE IN THE SUBURBS — In the thirty years after the the automobile came into general use and before the birth of television, the living patterns of middle class San Francisco suburbanites differed little from those followed by the rest of America's middle classes. Most families had one car, so father took the trolley to work, leaving the family jalopy with mother, who acted as family chauffeur and errand runner. She did her shopping at the corner store, or drove to a commercial street in her neighborhood: Clement, Irving, Outer Geary, or Chestnut Street, for example. Children usually walked to school.

In the evenings the family sat together, actually looking at the radio (or at each other) as they listened to their favorite dramas, comedy hours, or musical shows. On Friday or Saturday night the family would take in a movie at a neighborhood theater. On special occasions the family might go to one of the great cinema palaces downtown, like the magnificent Fox Theater at Market and 10th (demolished 1963).

During the Depression, movie theaters and sports events did enormous business, for people needed to escape the grim realities of the times. Crowds of 40,000 or more attended high-school football games at Kezar Stadium (demolished in 1990, and rebuilt in an elegant but modest form). The San Francisco Seals were a true home baseball team, enjoying the fanatical loyalty of thousands of fans when they played at Seals Stadium at 16TH and Bryant Streets (demolished in 1959).

To bring in more patrons, the movies offered two feature films, a newsreel, a travelog, and a cartoon, with free chinaware, bingo, or "Bank Nite" on Thursdays. Between features at the big downtown houses there was always a full hour of vaudeville, with prancing chorus girls, dog and pony acts, magicians or comedy skits, some of which dated to the days of the old Orpheum circuit, back in the 1880s.

THE FABULOUS FOX THEATRE — No recollection of a vanished San Francisco would be complete without a reminder of the glories of the fabulous Fox Theatre (note the properly elegant spelling of "theatre," used from its inception). Many San Franciscans joined a city-wide campaign in the 1960s to "Save the Fox." It was suggested that the huge auditorium, seating 4,500, might be converted to a symphony hall. But the city fathers disregarded the will of the people, and one of America's grandest temples of escapism fell, like so many of its peers, to the wrecking ball.

No San Franciscan who grew up in the 1930s or 40s will ever forget the marvels of this most magnificent link in the Fox Theatre chain. There were Fox Theatres in St. Louis, Detroit, and Brooklyn when the last sweep of optimism which halted with the Crash of 1929 produced this colossal monument to escapist entertainment. For sheer grandeur it topped even New York's famous Roxie Theater, which until then was the grandest movie palace of them all.

The elaborate Market Street façade, with its vertical baroque sign proclaiming FOX, was only a hint of what was to be seen within. One crossed a tessellated marble sidewalk to a gilt-bronze ticket cage with beveled, etched glass, a little like an overgrown sedan chair. A long row of gilt-bronze doors, inset with more etched glass, led to that gilded cave of wonders which was the lobby. Crossing this immense room on the thickly padded Aubusson-style carpet felt like walking on mashed potatoes. One bought popcorn, raisinets and licorice vines at a magnificent refreshment stand staffed by smartly uniformed attendants. The style might be described as Spanish-French rococo at its most ornate, reminiscent of grand cathedrals and palaces, with gold leaf gleaming from the ceilings and stalactites suspended from it. Between the vast panels of rich brocade, gold rococo decorations slithered up the walls.

At the far end of this vast chamber was a grand, carpeted stair whose curvilinear newel posts burst out in hydra-like candelabra. The walls were filled with gilt-framed paintings, and in niches stood enormous vases of Sevres porcelain, said to have come from the palace of the lately deposed Tsar of Russia. The ladies' rest room boasted elaborate French boiserie, reputed to have come from a boudoir of the Tsarina. Elaborate toilet sets were laid out on dressing tables for patrons to use. Here, and in the men's room as well, everything that wasn't gold was marble.

At the head of the grand staircase was a small Wurlitzer organ, where young Joaquin Garay, a popular local tenor, would sometimes give concerts. From this huge landing, long upper galleries circled the room, with gilt chairs and sofas where one might sink after admiring the works of art.

If the lobby was a breath-taking experience, the interior of the theater was even more eye-popping. Easing into one of the tapestried seats, one was afforded a view of what seemed to be acres of gold leaf, relieved along the sidewalls with baroque boxes suspended between gilded piers and decorated with swags in cloth of gold. As in an old-world opera house, there were two receding tiers of galleries reaching to a ceiling studded with domes, decorated with candy-box ladies and gentlemen dressed in the style of Watteau and Fragonard.

The centerpiece of all this splendor was the mighty Wurlitzer organ, originally installed to accompany the movies during that brief period before the advent of talking pictures. The ranks of pipes on this organ could make the entire building and everything in it vibrate, including the customers. The mighty, crouching beast of an instrument, when not playing for the movie itself, was used to accompany the orchestra of Rube Wolff, while the lines of fabulously costumed chorus girls kicked up their heels in precise rows. Dazzling lighting effects were thrown on the golden proscenium to accompany selections like Wagner's "Ride of the Valkyries" or The "1812 Overture."

In the 1940s, many thousands of American serviceman took their pals or their dates to this palace of entertainment for a last splurge before shipping out to the war in the Pacific. By the 1950s, as television kept former moviegoers at home, the enormous theater gradually became a white elephant. The Fox fell into the hands of the receiver, Herbert and Mortimer Fleishacker's Anglo Bank. The art works were placed on the auction block, upon which the bank was sued by Mrs. Fox, who claimed them as her own. (I have always wondered what became of the little marble statue of a newsboy wearing a cap, which was my personal favorite.) Then, after a bitter campaign by the "Save the Fox" faction, came the inevitable wrecking ball. Mortimer Fleishacker's response to the outcry was, "Why doesn't the public put their money where their mouth is?" To this day, San Franciscans who pass the

A
Gala
Event
in
San Francisco's
Theatrical
History

Stars
Fireworks
Parades
and
Civic
Celebration

FOX THEATRE

The Fox Theatre, which opened on June 28, 1929 (above), was one of the largest and most ornate movie palaces in the entire country. When it closed in 1959 with a "Farewell to the Fox" presentation (left), thousands wept. The city could have bought the building for conversion into a Symphony Hall, but chose to reject the proposal. The Fox was demolished, to be replaced by the most dismal highrise building on Market Street. (Courtesy San Francisco Public Library)

The interior of the Fox Theatre seemed to indulge every possible fantasy in decoration. The lobby and staircase (left) were gilded and polished and decorated to the ultimate degree. The interior (above) seated 4,500 people in a room so lavish as to make the movie viewer feel like a prince of the realm. (Courtesy San Francisco Public Library)

In the early years of the 20th Century building styles changed radically from the ornate Victorian to simpler Edwardian and then, like these, to Craftsman style, Shingle style, and later the Picturesque style, which enabled the homeowner to choose between the Swiss chalet, the English Tudor, the French chateau, the Spanish casa, or even the Gingerbread House as a model for his domicile. (Courtesy James Scott)

drab Fox Plaza building tell visitors that this was the site of the Fabulous Fox. After the building was demolished, some of the fixtures, including the etched glass doors and the sedan-chair box office, were incorporated into a small theater on Pacific Street near Montgomery, appropriately named the Little Fox. Alas, this too has joined the list of things past.

On Sundays after church the roads were lined with family cars headed for the still open countryside along El Camino Real, or to the ferry slips at the end of Van Ness Avenue and at the foot of Market Street, where they waited in line to catch a ferry to Marin County. A trip like this was an all-day event, likely to involve a blowout or a puncture; every car was equipped with a tire pump and a kit for patching inner tubes.

For festive Saturday nights the big hotels all offered tea dancing and dinner dancing in their ballrooms. When radio was still a novelty, some hotels, like the Palace and the St. Francis, offered dance music sent by "wireless" from New York or Detroit. During the Depression years there wasn't a single major hotel that wasn't operating in the red. Then, in 1936, architect Timothy Pflueger was commissioned to convert the Jackling penthouse at the Mark Hopkins Hotel into a cocktail lounge. The Top of the Mark was successful enough to pull the hotel out of the red. The Sir Francis Drake, the Fairmont, and the St. Francis soon followed suit with view rooms of their own.

After the 1906 Fire, the Tait brothers, who had run the St. Dunstan restaurant at Van Ness and Sutter, moved south to O'Farrell Street, calling the new place Tait-Zinkands. There was a large ground-floor dining room, and smaller apartments on the second floor, each furnished with a couch, for more "intimate dining." On the third floor was the Peacock Room, for dancing. During Prohibition guests brought their own bottles and drank their booze from teacups. To avoid police harassment—or perhaps the escalating cost of payoffs—Tait's removed to a large shingled house at Ocean Beach, south of Golden Gate Park. The former owners of this immense house had played host to a sect which practiced respect for all religions. As a result, the place had a Moslem chapel, Buddhist and Shinto temples, and other rooms dedicated to various religious beliefs. When the building was converted to a restaurant, the chapels provided wonderfully exotic settings for dining and dancing. The smart set, in their Stutz Bearcats or Packards, could drive out to Tait's in a few minutes to partake of the racy atmosphere. Tait's closed after the repeal of Prohibition, and in 1940 the deserted old building burnt to the ground.

From 1905 to 1920, variations on the Craftsman style became dominant in "The Avenues," roughly from First to Nineteenth Avenues on both sides of Golden Gate Park. The look was rustic, sturdy, informal, rather plain compared to the extravagantly decorated Victorian styles, but not entirely without ornament, as these houses show. Garages under the picture windows gradually became standard features as the automobile came to be thought of as essential to family life. (Courtesy James Scott)

Shorty Roberts', another beach resort further south, managed to survive Repeal, while nearby gin-mills like Topsy's Roost and the old Canary Cottage did not. Further inland, at the corner of today's 19th Avenue and Sloat Boulevard, was another Prohibition resort known as the Trocadero, housed in a fine old Victorian house. Created as a mecca for the horse-racing crowd, it had once served as a hideout for political boss Abe Ruef, before his forced retirement to San Quentin in 1908. Legend has it that one of the doors still carries bullet holes dating to Ruef's sudden departure from the place. In 1932 the house and the surrounding acreage, with its magnificent stand of eucalyptus trees, was donated to the city by Mrs. Sigmund Stern, in memory of her husband. Today, on Sunday afternoons in summer, thousands of San Franciscans gather to hear free concerts in the glade below the old Trocadero.

THE RICHMOND DISTRICT — In these days when affordable housing begins at a figure over $300,000, it is hard to believe that, beginning around 1910, houses in the Richmond District sold for $4,000 to $6,000. For that price you got a house with a 25-foot frontage, two stories above a full basement, which had room in front for the family motorcar. After all, it was Henry Ford's invention of the affordable automobile that made life in the suburbs possible. Who today can imagine a suburban house without a garage? By 1912 people had even begun building garages into the basements of their Victorian houses in the Western Addition.

Although the huge developments of entire districts did not take place until the early 1900s, those streets in the Haight Ashbury bordering the Panhandle number scores of large houses and flats in the Queen Anne and early Craftsman style which clearly proclaim their construction to belong to the late 1890s. On 6th Avenue, north of California Street, is a row of six houses in the half-timbered Medieval style which partakes of both the Queen Anne and the transitional Craftsman periods. These houses, designed by John Pelton, were but a small subdivision, predecessors of the vast Richmond District development. Pre-dating the automobile, they are without garages.

In suburbs with 50-foot frontages, such as Ingleside Terrace, Westwood Park, St. Francis Wood and Forest Hill, the garages could be placed in a back corner of the lot, with a 10-foot-wide strip for a driveway. But a 25-foot frontage required the garage to be underneath the house. San Francisco is unique among American cities for the miles of two-story houses built above garages. From First Avenue to 42nd Avenue, spreading south from the Presidio to Fulton Street on the north border of Golden Gate Park, the Richmond District is made up of such houses.

Behind the one-car garage on the ground floor were usually a servant's room and lavatory, a laundry room, a rumpus or game room where clothes were hung to dry on rainy days, a storage room, and a scary little chamber where a large, dirty coal-burning furnace crouched. The outside front stairs, veneered with terrazzo, led to the glass-paneled front door, beyond which was a vestibule leading to a stairhall of near manorial proportion. At the front, the living room boasted a large "picture window" looking out at a similar house across the street, garage below, picture window above. Gregarious Americans like their living rooms to face the street, to keep an eye on the comings and going of neighbors, unlike Europeans, who usually place the living room at the rear, overlooking a garden or court. Since the Richmond District had neither the space nor a suitable climate for front porches, the picture windows provided the view of the street.

The Richmond District was developed primarily in the era of the rustic, cozy Craftsman style. Ceilings were made to seem lower by the use of imitation beams. The large fireplace, usually of clinker brick (a brick that has been fired into tortured clusters), was flanked at either side by a waist-high bookcase. French doors with beveled glass panes brought light to the windowless hallway. Across the wide stair-hall, glass doors led to a dining room with built-in glass-doored buffet, more ceiling beams, and high, dark-stained wainscoting topped by a plate rail for displaying heirloom crockery. In the center was a heavy "diving bell" chandelier with a stained-glass shade.

Often between the dining room and large kitchen was a breakfast nook, which could double as a serving pantry. At the window end was a built-in table flanked by quaint, wooden-winged benches, usually with hinged seats for storing back issues of National Geographic or The Delineator. The kitchen was strictly utilitarian, since no guest would ever dream of setting foot in it, and even the *pater familias* rarely saw it.

On the stair landing was an art-glass window, usually pink and green, opening into a light-well between houses, while upstairs were three or four large bedrooms and a white-tiled family bath. At the rear might be a large, glassed in sun porch, a marvelous feature on cold, foggy summer days, and often the lightest, most comfortable place in the house.

JORDAN PARK — Jordan Park is a special surprise to be encountered among the narrow-fronted houses of the Richmond District. Its streets are wider and its lots are larger than those of its neighbors, and its handsome, spacious houses suggest a more formal era, when San Francisco ladies wore their furs, hats, and gloves, even on the shortest errands. Jordan Park, a level area of eight city blocks, bounded by California, Arguello, Euclid and Parker streets, offers no spectacular view, nor even a public park to justify its name. It is a pleasant neighborhood for the families of professional men, most of them physicians, thanks to the proximity of Children's Hospital on California. Several families living here are of two or three generations' descent from the original occupants of the park.

Maps from the 1870s show Laurel Hill Cemetery extending as far as Arguello Boulevard (then called First Avenue). The land on which Jordan Park stands was once part of a "silent city of the dead." By 1900 it had become Old Pioneer Park, and eight years later came the covenants which established its boundaries and its intent to become an exclusive enclave, free of any commercial development. The Park gets its name from attorney William Jordan, whose spacious grounds at 51 Commonwealth are now shared with an Armenian church. Henry Hilbush was the developer.

LONE MOUNTAIN AND THE UNIVERSITY OF SAN FRANCISCO —Four blocks south of Jordan Park, crowning the slopes of former Lone Mountain Cemetery, is the Jesuit stronghold comprising the University of San Francisco, Lone Mountain College, and the magnificent Church of St. Ignatius, named for the founder of the Jesuit order. This is the fifth successive church built by the Jesuits since their arrival in San Francisco in 1849. The first Jesuit school and church were established in 1855 by the Italian missionary, Father John Nobli, on the Market Street site later occupied by the Emporium. Within four years, a little wooden structure on the property was expanded to become the College of St. Ignatius. Meanwhile, Father Nobli helped to establish the College of Santa Clara, at Mission Santa Clara. Yet another attempt to establish a school in the buildings adjoining Mission Dolores was finally abandoned in 1856.

In 1880 a magnificent new St. Ignatius College, occupying the block bounded by Hayes, Franklin, Grove and Van Ness, on the site of today's Davies Symphony Hall, replaced the Market Street establishment. This complex was destroyed in the 1906 conflagration, and temporary quarters were found at the corner of Shrader and Hayes Streets while a new location was sought. John H. Pope, a civil engineer, proposed the concept of the present St. Ignatius Church, at the crest of Fulton Street.

William Jordan's Mediterranean style house on Commonwealth Avenue in Jordan Park shows the spacious effect achievable on a lot wider than 25 feet. Jordan Park residents in their large brown-shingle or stuccoed houses may hear ghosts wailing at night, a legacy from the graveyard that once occupied the site. (Courtesy James Heig)

The fifth St. Ignatius Church, designed by architect Charles J. Devlin, and dedicated on August 2, 1914, has been described as "Jesuit Baroque" in style. But Devlin drew his inspiration from more severe classical English and French sources, rather than from the curvaceous baroque historically attributed to Jesuit patronage. The semi-circular sanctuary follows the pattern of the original Christian basilicas of ancient Rome. The building's superb acoustics (very probably achieved without the aid of an acoustical engineer) make it ideal for musical performances. Graceful towers, more than 300 feet high, flank the columned and pedimented façade whose walls are of buff-colored brick set off by architectural details in cream and yellow terra cotta. The magnificent domes, the coffered ceilings, and the handsome campanile make this church a glorious architectural achievement. In recent years the exterior of the church has been lighted at night, making a brilliant addition to the skyline as seen from four directions.

The Jesuit University of San Francisco, which surrounds the church today, is a mixture of architectural styles ranging from Spanish Revival to postmodern, showing what happens when an institution expands haphazardly over the course of seventy years without benefit of an architectural plan. The most recent additions to the campus, on the south side of Fulton, are an insult to the beautiful St. Ignatius Church across the street.

Directly behind the University, along Turk Street, is Lone Mountain College for Women, built in 1932, after the last of the cemeteries had been cleared from the slopes of Lone Mountain. The architect, H.A. Minton, designed for this magnificent site a cluster of buildings with two side wings embracing a central bell-tower. The style was described as Spanish Gothic; one is unavoidably reminded of movie-theater architecture of the 1920s. Many contemporary architects would regard this style as a joke, a misguided, Disneyesque throwback to a style that never existed to begin with. True, Julia Morgan would have done it much better. And yet, stepping inside the buildings, the visitor is struck by the solidity, the superb quality of the details and finish, the solid oak doors with Gothic panels and bronze hardware, the rather clumsy but beautifully made light fixtures. In the right wing, the Rossi Library, donated by the family of then-Mayor Angelo Rossi, is a truly marvelous achievement, a complete design, including all fixtures, furniture, and leaded-glass windows, displaying a quality of workmanship that would be impossible today.

St. Ignatius Church, on a hilltop location at Fulton and Parker Streets, and visible from many parts of the city, is illuminated at night, adding a powerful presence to the city skyline. The church, completed in 1914, replaced the former St. Ignatius at Van Ness and Hayes Streets, destroyed in 1906. The architect, Charles Devlin, using classical English, French, and Renaissance models as his guide, built the church of pale brown brick, with columns, towers and other decorative elements sheathed in ceramic tile. Often used as a concert hall, the church has superb acoustics; the experience of listening to music in the magnificent interior space is truly breathtaking. (Courtesy San Francisco Public Library)

The San Francisco College for Women, built on Lone Mountain in 1932, is now a part of the University of San Francisco. The architect, H.A. Minton, said it was in the Spanish Gothic style; it was built to meet high standards of quality in construction. The college could accommodate 500 young women, plus faculty and sisters of the Sacred Heart order. With elegant curving drives up from Turk Street, and a splendid staircase leading down from the heights, its design is vaguely reminiscent of movie palace architecture of the 1920s. (Courtesy James Heig)

The entrance to Lone Mountain College is a sweeping drive, curving up from Turk Street. In the center, spilling down the southern slope of the steep hill, is a monumental stairway, built in the form of a chalice, which might be called San Francisco's version of Rome's Spanish Steps. The stairs, landings, benches, urns, curved balustrades, and flower beds give a sense of generosity and fine extravagance to the whole site, which many San Franciscans have never visited.

Lone Mountain College for Women, run by the Carmelite Order for almost 50 years, was absorbed by the University of San Francisco in 1978, and is now a part of that co-educational institution.

WEST OF TWIN PEAKS — No doubt it was in anticipation of the Twin Peaks Tunnel, completed in 1918 by City Engineer Michael M. O'Shaughnessy, that work began on the suburban developments west of Twin Peaks. Ingleside Terrace was begun in 1911 by the Urban Development Company, headed by Joseph Leonard. The first houses in this tract were bungalows in the Craftsman style, but in the 1920s, when California "went Spanish," the style changed to pastel and white stucco houses with red tile roofs. As a result this tract and nearby Westwood Park are a mixture: a Craftsman bungalow with a picture window peering out from a low-gabled porch with squat columns and baskets of hanging ferns may stand next to an ornately stuccoed Mediterranean villa with arcaded porch and a bonnet of red roofing tile over its picture window.

The most elaborate houses of Ingleside Terrace line the east side of Junipero Serra Boulevard, where the side streets are set off by imposing entrance gates. Tudor mansions stand next to Spanish villas and French chateaux, all faced to view the blue Pacific. Behind this row are blocks of fairly substantial houses, but further east the size diminishes to one-story bungalows that are very modest indeed.

Urbano Drive in Ingleside follows the exact oval of the old Ingleside race track which Claus Spreckels and other racing buffs built there in 1883. For years after houses had replaced the stables, myriads of horse flies plagued the residents every autumn. The 26-foot sundial off Entrada Court, which residents believed to be the world's largest (and perhaps it is), served neighborhood children as a terrifying slide.

ST. FRANCIS WOOD AND FOREST HILL — Just as Ingleside Terrace and Westwood Park began as architectural expressions of the Craftsman school, St. Francis Wood was a product of the Beaux Arts school. This is admirably illustrated in the grand St. Francis Boulevard, which was planned by William Law Olmsted, Jr., son of the great planner of New York's Central Park, and John Galen Howard, a Beaux Arts graduate who established the School of Architecture at the University of California in Berkeley. Howard had also co-ordinated the plans for San Francisco's new Civic Center, and had designed many of the Hearst buildings on the Berkeley campus. St. Francis Boulevard, with its grand sweep of plantings, pergolas and splashing fountains, embodies the Beaux Arts spirit every bit as much as does the Civic Center. These two grand schemes are today the only surviving realization of the Beaux Arts ideal in San Francisco.

Mason McDuffie, head of the firm that developed St. Francis Wood in 1912, probably intended to make the park-like setting a suitable foil for the mansions of California millionaires. Certainly the tract had its share of large houses. But any dream of grandeur its developers entertained came to a sudden halt with the crash of 1929. Thereafter, lot frontages were reduced to forty and fifty feet, and the new houses, most of which were attractive versions of Spanish, Tudor, French, or American Colonial styles, were usually of more modest size. A strong neighborhood association controlled architectural design, as well as enforcing racial covenants which were not abolished until the 1950s. The Egyptian Consul, Mr. Toulba, was challenged in the 1930s by people who thought his family might ruin the neighborhood.

Louis Mullgardt, best known for his elaborate Mediterranean villas, and Henry Gutterson, who designed a number of quaint, rustic cottages in the English Tudor and Georgian styles, were among the leading architects of St. Francis Wood. Masten & Hurd built more eclectic Colonial, Tudor and Georgian houses. All these architects helped in the early planning of the development. (See pages 264-267)

Actually it was a conformity of scale, coupled with lush landscaping, much of which came from the 1915 Panama Pacific Exposition in the Marina, which gave St. Francis Wood a distinctive, unified look. Residents chose the locale for its remote, almost wilderness quality. Only a few blocks in the upper reaches of the tract offered any view of the Pacific. Except for the eucalyptus trees, St. Francis Wood might have been a nice suburban development dropped down anyplace in the Midwestern or Eastern suburbs. As a consequence, it has never been regarded as particularly a monument to San Francisco regionalism.

In these houses, careful attention to correct period detail would have won hearty approval from the staunchest Beaux Arts advocate, but there was also a note of restraint in most of them that made them modern in appearance and function. They were not slavish

Park Merced, a huge post-World War II complex built near Lake Merced by the Metropolitan Life Insurance Company, mixed high-rise apartment buildings with rows of townhouses ranged along wide boulevards and grassy circular parks. It was among the first projects of its kind in the world, completed in 1951. This picture shows the architects' rendering superimposed on an actual aerial photograph, with eleven high-rise buildings; only five of the towers were actually built. Chief architects were Angus McSweeney, L. Schultz, and Thomsen and Wilson. The complex housed thousands of people who settled in San Francisco after the war—veterans and their families, people who had come to work in San Francisco during the War years and wanted to stay —and more than a few long-time residents of the city who wanted to try a new way of living in a planned community. Visitors from abroad came to inspect the complex, and took the ideas home with them, resulting in similar developments, particularly in Scandinavia and Germany. (Courtesy San Francisco Public Library)

copies of the historic periods they represented. One can only wonder how strong was the role which myth-making Hollywood played in the popularization of such period houses. The Hollywood influence certainly existed; in the hills above Hollywood Boulevard are suburbs remarkably similar to St. Francis Wood, a little more tamed and manicured, a little "cuter" in the pastel Southern California light.

All of the San Francisco developments used Spanish street names, a reflection of the romantic notions people held about life in early California. Earlier, many streets such as Noe, Sanchez, Guerrero, Valencia and De Haro were named for actual settlers in the city. Then the list of Spanish explorers and missionaries was dredged up: Portola, Junipero Serra, Cambon, Palou, and Balboa, to name a few. Next came the almost countless names from the Spanish calendar of saints: San Pablo, Santa Paula, Santa Ynez, San Benito. But who, or what, were Lunado, Moncado, and Teresita? Developers looking for more Spanish street names must have been driven to the Madrid telephone book. The ridiculous extreme of this tendency was reached in the 1960s in Marin County, when developers near Novato called their tract "San Marin," thereby conferring sainthood on a rebellious Miwok Indian.

Forest Hill, like St. Francis Wood to the south, began in 1911 with formal Beaux Arts concepts. A grand stairway leads up the side of a steep hill to no particular destination, and here and there are scattered a dried-up fountain or two and a couple of colossal urns. The graceful, curving streets follow the contours of heavily wooded hills. Bernard Maybeck's rustic houses, like those in the Berkeley hills, seem at home in this setting. (see page 268) Indeed, a fine neighborhood clubhouse and two hillside dwellings were his work. But most of the houses are in the American Colonial, Spanish, and French styles. Off the grand stairway leading nowhere is a particularly charming little mansarded French house which, in its setting of feathery trees, looks like a dream of Hubert Robert or Fragonard.

SEA CLIFF — The beautiful district of Sea Cliff, laid out in 1912 in the outer Richmond District by planner Mark Daniels and developer Harry B. Allen, is almost entirely a collection of Beaux Arts period houses following sinuously curved streets. Unlike the other suburbs, Sea Cliff affords marvelous panoramic views of the the Golden Gate and the Marin headlands. Below it is Baker Beach, named for Colonel Edward Baker, who died a hero's death in the Civil War. The land on which Sea Cliff stands once belonged to him.

Although there are French manors and a number of half-timbered Tudor houses, the predominant style of Sea Cliff is Mediterranean. Many of these houses were designed by Appleton and Wolfard, who also designed several of the finer houses in the Marina. Willis Polk designed three handsome houses at 9, 25, AND 45 Scenic Way. At 850 Del Mar is a rare contemporary house by Wurster, Bernardi & Emmons.

Those readers old enough to recall Carlton B. Morse's Sunday evening radio saga, "One Man's Family," (1932 to 1945) will recall that the Barbour family lived in Sea Cliff. Listeners recall the mournful sound of the foghorns on the bay as Clifford, Paul, Hazel, Jack or Claudia Barbour, caught in the sloughs of despond, would announce to the family that he or she was going out for a walk, and Father Barbour would invariably say, "Yes, yes, Fanny. Yes, yes." Their voices were so distinctive that one can hear their exact intonation today, fifty years later. Mr. Morse, in his nineties, said that people still sometimes called him to report excitedly that they had just bought the house where the Barbour family lived in Sea Cliff; he felt obliged to tell them that the house was purely fictional, no matter what their real estate agent might have told them.

West of Sea Cliff is the Lincoln Park Public Golf Course; near its 17TH hole rises the stately California Palace of the Legion of Honor, a museum of European (originally French) art built as a memorial to the California boys killed in World War I, and patterned closely after the Palace of the Legion of Honor in Paris. Alma de Bretteville Spreckels, who persuaded her husband Adolph Spreckels to build the museum and give it to the city, received the medal of the French Legion of Honor for her work during the war. Commanding one of the most spectacular view sites in all California, the main floor of the museum ironically has no windows. Architect George Applegarth, one of San Francisco's distinguished graduates of the Ecole des Beaux Arts, also designed the Clift Hotel, as well as many other commercial and residential buildings in the city, during his long career. After the Loma Prieta earthquake of 1989, the museum was closed for three years for a complete renovation, expansion and seismic upgrade. Fortunately the beauty of the original building remains intact, despite the startling eruption in the courtyard of a small imitation of the glass pyramid at the Louvre in Paris. Inside the museum is an architectural gem: the Florence Gould theatre, an oval auditorium of admirable proportions, marvelous acoustics, and very refined French decorations.

THE MARINA DISTRICT — North and west of the Cow Hollow area are the blocks of sandcastle-like houses of the Marina, built on the filled lands created

The California Palace of the Legion of Honor, in Lincoln Park, contains America's finest collection of works by Auguste Rodin; the museum and the sculpture were gifts to the people of San Francisco from Alma and Adolph Spreckels. The architect, George Applegarth, studied at the Ecole des Beaux Arts in Paris. The museum is shown here nearing the end of construction in 1924. (Courtesy San Francisco Public Library)

by the 1915 Panama-Pacific Exposition. In earlier times there had been two amusement parks, Seaside Gardens and Herman's Harbor View, for frivolous young San Franciscans. Both stood in the area just east of the present Palace of Fine Arts and the St. Francis Yacht Club. On Sundays brass bands would board special cable cars which ran out Union Street to Steiner. From there a little steam train carried passengers to Harbor View, where the band played in a pavilion for dancing and families with children strolled and picnicked in the park. The resort offered cracked crab, steam beer and hot saltwater baths at Herman's bath house. The marshy land was also home to a boatyard.

At Gashouse Cove, a brick gashouse, once the property of the San Francisco Power and Light Company, still stands on Buchanan Street, just behind the Marina Safeway. For many years the gashouse, with its handsome round corner rooms at the front and a great cavernous hall behind, served as a splendid antiques shop, with a beautiful garden shop adjacent, selling only white-blooming plants. Today it is a real estate office.

After the 1915 Exposition had been dismantled, the Marina was planned to be an area of villas built on large lots on curving streets. In fact it was laid out in the usual grid pattern with a few variations, and build-

ing lots had the typical 25-foot frontages. Some prosperous members of the city's Italian colony were among the first buyers. They built commodious Mediterranean style houses with large picture windows fronting Marina Boulevard, with incomparable views of the bay. Passersby on Marina Boulevard also had incomparable views of the families within, especially of their heroically scaled lamps with ruffled shades placed exactly in the center of each picture window. One house with five large windows offered the same number of lamps. Such displays are recalled as happy reflections of San Francisco's exuberant soul, may it live forever!

A row of striking Mediterranean houses sprang up along the little park and lagoon surrounding Bernard Maybeck's romantic Palace of Fine arts. (See page 372) Created for the 1915 Exposition, the palace was spared by the wreckers. It was just too beautiful to destroy. Built to resemble a romantic ruin, it actually became one as its lath-and-plaster decorations slowly softened and crumbled in the fog and salt air. For years the Army used its crumbling rear galleries as a storehouse for military equipment. Then in the 1950s Walter Johnson donated some $2 million and spearheaded a local campaign to reconstruct the Palace in concrete, as a city landmark. The voters of San Francisco, to their

The Sunset District's houses, with four or five compact rooms built over a garage, a tiny landscaped lawn in front, and a back yard big enough for children to play, were a refuge for the burgeoning population in San Francisco before and after World War II. The houses were affordable, comfortable, and fairly easy to maintain because they were small. Starting in the 1930s, generations of San Franciscans grew up here, went to school and married in the district. The houses now bring a handsome price, especially as the Asian population spreads westward from former cramped quarters downtown. (Courtesy James Heig)

everlasting credit, passed a bond issue for $5 million to complete the reconstruction of a building whose sole purpose was as an object of beauty. Today the restored structure has found its uses: a theater fills the south portion of the gallery, while the world-famous Exploratorium, a science museum for children, occupies the north end. The rotunda, as always, is simply there to look at, and it amply repays the voters for their generosity.

THE SUNSET DISTRICT — It is only fitting that our story of the building of San Francisco should end by wandering off into the Sunset. For it was in the Sunset District that the last of San Francisco's major developers made their stand: the Gellert brothers, Ray Galli,

Chris McKeon, the Stoneson brothers, and last but certainly not least, the Brothers Doelger, Henry and Frank. Beginning in a modest way in the 1920s, these developers were caught up in the tide of building created in the 1930s, when the Federal government, in order to stimulate the dying housing industry, created FHA loans. Here was a potential building boom just waiting to happen, as thousands of San Franciscans, both newlyweds and retiring couples, found the answer to their hopes and dreams in this easy financing scheme.

In the years between 1934 and 1942, Sunset District houses mushroomed so fast that entire blocks would reach the completion stage within a single day. One section, between 27TH and 39TH Avenues, Quintara and Kirkham Streets, was known as "Doelger City" for the dynamic duo who had suddenly become the biggest home builders in the USA. Row after row of stuccoed boxes went up, built cheek-by-jowl, each with a tiny patch of lawn in front and a picture window over a garage door. The two-bedroom houses are still known in the trade as "junior fours," meaning a living room, kitchen, two bedrooms and a bath. Instead of a dining room there is a niche or small alcove, appropriately called a "dinette." Meals might occasionally be served here, but families no longer dined; they grabbed their meals off the food bar in the kitchen. The picture window in the "front room" looks out across the thinly landscaped street to another row of identical houses. A false roof in front and an elaborate stucco façade slapped onto an otherwise plain wooden box designates the style. Some false roofs are tiled to match the fancy white Spanish façades of the "true Mission style." The contrast between the decorated fronts and the plain wooden rear elevations echoes the Victorian predecessors with "Queen Anne fronts and Mary Ann behinds."

Banks, of course, are happy to finance houses which are modestly enough priced for an easy turnover should a tenant default on the mortgage. Esthetics do not normally enter into questions of finance. Henry Rousseau, one of a prestigious family of San Francisco developers, once attended a meeting of the American Institute of Architects. When somebody asked him point blank what he was doing in this gathering of credentialed experts, he announced that not only did he have a degree in architecture, but that his developments had contributed more to Bay Area housing than had the work of all the members of the AIA put together.

The houses of the Sunset District have often been been ridiculed by architectural purists, or by residents of stately houses in Pacific Heights. Such attitudes are of no importance to the district's inhabitants, who are quite content in their snug little bungalows with meticulously trimmed shrubbery in front. Young couples with double incomes feel lucky to be able to buy a house in the Sunset at today's prices—upward of $400,000. While the houses, viewed as a part of the cityscape, may not constitute a true architectural style, they have begun to look positively delightful in comparison to the rows of boxes built on the hillsides further south, in the 1950s and 60s.

Today the houses have marched across the former truck gardens and sand dunes, past the Sunset, through Daly City, into Colma, Pacifica, South San Francisco, and on down the peninsula. Where will it end? One can travel today from San Francisco to Morgan Hill without ever really being out of town.

EPILOGUE: SAN FRANCISCO AT THE MILLENNIUM

The only permanent thing in the world is change, as a great philosopher once said. San Francisco amply illustrated that idea in the latter half of the 20th century. We note here only a few of the changes, especially those that have had a strong impact on the lives of people living here.

The biggest change has been in the downtown skyline. Fifty years ago Coit Tower was the defining feature; now it has been overshadowed by the big brown Bank of America and the Transamerica Pyramid. The high-rise buildings erected downtown since 1960 — mainly in the so-called International or Post-Modern styles, are too numerous to be included here. In any case, there is very little to be said about most of them, since they have no tops, no bottoms, no sides, no significant decorative details; to talk of proportion or scale or balance in 40 stories of repeated identical modules would be absurd. Perhaps in fifty years some architectural historian may find it possible to describe such buildings in glowing terms, but today their charm eludes us. Meanwhile, Timothy Pfleuger's great Art Deco buildings, the Pacific Telephone Building at 140 New Montgomery and the Medical Building at 450 Sutter, are dwarfed by the huge structures around them.

Residential architecture in the post-war period has been largely confined to areas cleared by redevelopment, in the Western Addition, the old produce district, and South of Market. The old residential hotels south of Market Street — many of them flophouses — have given way to huge new complexes full of small, efficient apartments, suitable for the hectic lifestyle of the modern age, or the controversial live-work units, supposedly built for artists, and typically consisting of a large light room with a kitchen and bath by the front door, and a balcony or loft for sleeping.

The Western Addition redevelopment disaster had at least one beneficial effect: it spurred preservationists to organize. In the 1950s and early 1960s, the restoration of old houses was haphazard, engaged in by individuals. Most of these were gay men, who had the resources, the taste, and the courage to buy run-down houses in dangerous neighborhoods and spend years restoring them, often to better-than-new condition. In Noe Valley, Eureka Valley, and all over the Western Addition, these restored houses attracted admiration, and the trend spread to the straight community. Preservation groups such as the Victorian Alliance, San Francisco Heritage, and the Alamo Square and Duboce Triangle Neighborhood Associations, among others, began to acquire clout with the Planning Commission. A Landmarks Board was formed. Hundreds of buildings were designated as city landmarks, and were afforded at least some protection against demolition. The rehabilitation of abused but fundamentally sound properties became known as "gentrification," generally used as a pejorative term. But gentrification has saved hundreds of irreplaceable structures, at no cost to the taxpayer, in contrast to redevelopment, which wasted untold millions of public funds.

The 1989 Loma Prieta earthquake, despite its tragic consequences, brought about major changes for the better in the city: the destruction of the ugly Embarcadero freeway, and the creation of a fine pedestrian walkway along the waterfront, with palm trees and the beautifully restored old streetcars, collected from cities all over the world, running along beside it. The F-Line, running from Market and Castro to Fisherman's Wharf along the Embarcadero, is a delight to tourists and residents alike, a rare example of an amenity that is aesthetically pleasing, historically interesting, and useful, all at the same time.

The new baseball stadium, unfortunately named PacBell Park, is another rarity: a modern building that is both handsome and functional, and that is entirely harmonious with its near neighbors and with the city as a whole. The architects, Hellmuth, Obata & Kassabaum, have designed a major structure so attractive that people go there to enjoy the building as well as the game.

The Museum of Modern Art, designed by Mario Botta, is the most prominent building in the Yerba Buena Center area. Its huge cylindrical skylight, sliced on the bias, was originally supposed to have a circle of trees around its top perimeter; fortunately wiser heads prevailed. The building's chief attraction is the superb brickwork of its exterior. For once it is the bricklayers rather than the architect who made a statement.

Older residents can remember the time, fifty years ago, when the streets and sidewalks of the city were bare of trees. In harsh midsummer sunlight the cityscape could be oppressively, blindingly white. Today, thanks mainly to the Friends of the Urban Forest, there are an estimated 195,000 street trees in the city, with more being planted every year. Green foliage has transformed some streets into veritable bowers, with branches meeting overhead. And San Franciscans no longer need be content with seagulls and pigeons; the trees have attracted many species of birds, including migratory ones such as mourning doves, mocking birds and robins, once a rare sight in the city.

By far the most significant change within the city limits is the conversion of the Presidio from a military base into a National Park — the only urban National Park in America. But one important string was attached: within a few years, the park must pay for its own repair and upkeep. That is no small task, considering the hundreds of historic buildings on the site, which contains some of the best military architecture of the 19TH and early 20TH centuries. Letterman Hospital and its surrounding acreage will become a film studio. Worthy non-profit organizations will find quarters in some of the fine old brick buildings. The Presidio Museum, already well established, will continue to display important memorabilia. The former Officer's Club is already showing art exhibitions. Some buildings are used for student housing. Recitals and concerts resound in the chapel.

One important part of the Presidio plan is to establish an international center to further the world's environmental protection and make it compatible with economic growth. Students and scholars would share their research, to formulate a truly global defense of the world's air, water and energy sources, wildlife, rain forests, mountain ranges, prairies, and the ocean. What a splendid and worthy project for the new millennium. And what a fitting use for a historic site, where the Spanish soldiers built their humble quarters more than two centuries ago, dreaming of defending the Golden Gate with their fine bronze cannons, which are still there. Let us hope the planners heed Daniel Burnham's enjoinder to members of the City Beautiful movement: "Make no little plans, for they do not stir men's blood."

SOURCES

—Alexander, James B., Sonoma Valley Legacy. Sonoma Valley Historical Society, 1986

—Atherton, Gertrude, A Daughter of the Vine. Dodd, Mead & Co., New York, 1923

—Baer, Kurt, Architecture of the California Missions. University of California Press, 1958

—Baird, Joseph, Time's Wondrous Changes, California Historical Society, San Francisco, 1962

—Bancroft, Hubert H., Bancroft's Works: History of California, San Francisco, 1890

—Becker, Robert, Designs on the Land. Book Club of California, San Francisco, 1969

—Beebe, Lucius, The Golden Era. Howell North, Berkeley, CA, 1957

—Beechey, Capt. Frederick, Narrative of a Voyage of Discovery to the Pacific and Bering Straits, 1825-1828. London, 1831

—Biggs, Donald. Conquer and Colonize. Presidio Press, San Rafael, CA, 1977

—Blaisdell, Marilyn, San Francisciana: Photographs of Sutro Baths.

—Blake, Anson, "A San Francisco Boyhood," California Historical Society Quarterly, Vol. 37, Sept. 1959.

—Brechin, Gray, Imperial San Francisco. U.C. Press, Berkeley, CA, 1999

—Brown, Charles, Memoirs. manuscript, Bancroft Library, University of California, Berkeley

—California Missions, Lane Publications, Menlo Park, 1978

—Colton, Walter, Three Years in California. A.S. Barnes, New York, 1850

—Davis, William Heath, Seventy-Five Years in California. San Francisco, 1889

—Dickson, Samuel, San Francisco is Your Home. Stanford University Press, 1947

—Dobie, Charles C., San Francisco, A Pageant. Appleton-Century, New York, 1934

—Eldridge, Zoeth S., The Beginnings of San Francisco, 2 vols, San Francisco, 1912

—Elwood, Catherine Crary, Manuscript, 1962. Santa Clara County Library

—Engelhardt, Father Zephyrin, O.F.M., San Francisco or Mission Dolores. Franciscan Press, Chicago, 1924

—Engenhoff, Elizabeth, "Fabricus." Supplement to California Journal of Mines, April 1952

—Fink, Augusta, Adobes in the Sun. Chronicle Books, San Francisco, 1972

—Genthe, Arnold, San Francisco Chinatown. Moffat, Yard & Co., 1925

—Gullard, Pamela, and Lund, Nancy, History of Palo Alto: The Early Years. Scottwall Associates, San Francisco, 1989

—Hannaford, Donald, and Edwards, Revel, Spanish Colonial or Adobe Architecture of California. Architectural Book Publishing Co., Stamford, CT, 1990

—Hansen, Gladys, San Francisco Almanac.

—Hansen, Gladys, & Condon, Emmet, Denial of Disaster. Cameron & Co., San Francisco, 1989

—Heintz, William, The Mayors of San Francisco.

—Hendry, G.W., and Bowman, J.N., "Spanish and Mexican Adobes of the Nine San Francisco Bay Area Counties." manuscript, Bancroft Library, University of California, Berkeley.

—Holdredge, Helen, Firebell Lillie, Meredith Press, New York, 1967

—Hoover, Rensch, Rensch & Abeloe, rev. Kyle, Historic Spots in California, Stanford University Press, 1990

—Jacobson, Pauline, City of theGolden Fifties. U.C. Press, Berkeley, CA 1941

—Kip, William I., Memoirs. Archives of Grace Cathedral, San Francisco

—Kirker, Harold., California's Architectural Frontier. Huntington Library, San Marino CA, 1960

—Kostura, William, Russian Hill, The Summit. Aerie Publications, San Francisco, 1997

—Lewis, Oscar, and Hall, Caroll D., Bonanza Inn. New York, Alfred Knopf, 1939

—Lewis, Oscar, The Big Four. New York, Alfred Knopf, 1938

—Lewis, Oscar, Mission to Metropolis. Howell North, Berkeley, CA, 1966

—Lewis, Oscar, Silver Kings. University of Nevada Press, Reno, 1986

—Lockwood, Charles, Suddenly San Francisco. San Francisco Examiner Books, 1978

—Longstreth, Richard, On the Edge of the World. MIT Press, Cambridge, MA, 1983

—Marryat, Frank, Mountains and Molehills, Clio Publications, Santa Rosa, CA, 1977

—McAllister, Ward, Society as I Found It. Cassell & Co., New York, 1890

—McKee, Alice Hooper, "Childhood Memories of Rincon Hill," December 1935 program for the San Francisco Garden Club.

—Myrick, David, San Francisco's Telegraph Hill. Howell North Books, Berkeley, 1972

—Neville, Amelia Ransom, The Fantastic City. Houghton Mifflin Co., New York, 1932

—O'Brien, Robert, This is San Francisco. Whittlesly House, New York 1948

—Official Papers of the Settlement of Yerba Buena, 1842. Hall of Records, San Francisco City Hall

—Olmsted, Nancy, Vanished Waters. Mission Creek Conservancy, San Francisco, 1986

—Pecora, Joseph, "History of the Phelps House." Published in the newsletter of the Alamo Square Neighborhood Association.

—Phillips, Catherine Coffin, Portsmouth Plaza, The Cradle of San Francisco. Privately printed by John Henry Nash, San Francisco, 1932

—Polk, Willis, Series in the San Francisco Newsletter, 1899.

—Purdy, Helen Throop, San Francisco As It Was, As It Is, And Where to Find It, Paul Elder, San Francisco, 1912

—Richards, Rand, Historic San Francisco. Heritage House, San Francisco, 1991

—Robbins, Phyllis, Maude Adams: A Biography. Putnam, New York, 1956

—San Francisco Call, February 17, 1907.

—San Francisco Chronicle, December 30, 1906, & August 8, 1934, page 28.

—San Francisco Examiner, Mar. 2, 1870, Dec. 25, 1878, Oct. 2, 1887, Dec. 13, 1892, June 8, 1978, page 27.

—Shumate, Dr. Albert, The California of George Gordon. Arthur Clark Co., Glendale, CA, 1976

—Shumate, Dr. Albert, Rincon Hill and South Park. Windgate Press, Sausalito, CA, 1988

—Soule, Frank, et al, Annals of San Francisco. D. Appleton, San Francisco, 1855

—Taylor, Bayard, El Dorado. New York, 1884

—Thomes, William H., On Land and Sea. Laird & Lee, Chicago, 1892.

—Vail, Wesley D., San Francisco Victorians. Wabash Press, Sebastopol, CA, 1978

—Vancouver, George, A Voyage of Discovery. London, 1801

—"Vignettes of Early San Francisco Homes and Gardens," published by the San Francisco Garden Club, 1935.

INDEX